D1397789

BUSINESS-TO-BUSINESS INTERNET MARKETING

Third Edition

Praise for *Business-to-Business Internet Marketing, Third Edition*

"If you are going to read only one book about Internet marketing this year, read this one....For those who are not familiar with the science of direct marketing, Silverstein provides an opening chapter that is one of the best overviews of direct marketing that I've seen....Silverstein argues that the basics have not changed from classic direct marketing to Internet direct marketing. What has changed is how those basics are applied to the Internet. And this is why 'Business-to-Business Internet Marketing' should be at the top of your "must read" list....Can you tell I like this book? I've already bought five copies to give to associates and it's at the top of my list of recommended business books. Apply Silverstein's principles and you'll be on your way to Internet sales success."
　　Mike Bayer, CompuServe

"This is by far the best book on Internet marketing yet. Barry Silverstein...knows what he is talking about. This book is filled with case studies of B2B success, and practical rules for how to profit on the Web. A must for anyone thinking of B2B Web commerce.
　　Database Marketing Institute

"This 'crash course' in business-to-business marketing is an excellent introduction for the newcomer and a worthwhile refresher for the veteran....Silverstein presents dozens of techniques that can be applied to major strategies, each invaluable in building business profitability. Silverstein backs up his points with excellent real-world examples and a variety of case studies."
　　Amazon.com Reviews

"...step-by-step, battle-proven advice on how to use the Internet to sell to business....Silverstein shows how to use Web sites and e-mail to clean up mailing lists and generate highly targeted lists of potential customers. Most importantly, he lays out the costs of such projects, their estimated responses and their return on investment (ROI), proving conclusively that the skillful use of the Internet is a real cost-saver when it comes to focusing on solid prospects....By the end of the book, you're convinced that the Internet really will revolutionize business-to-business marketing."
　　Arthur Andersen's Knowledgespace.com

BUSINESS-TO-BUSINESS INTERNET MARKETING

(handwritten: √259)

Third Edition

Seven Proven Strategies for Increasing Profits Through Internet Direct Marketing

Barry Silverstein

MAXIMUM PRESS
605 Silverthorn Road
Gulf Breeze, FL 32561
(850) 934-0819
www.maxpress.com

WITHDRAWN FROM
J. EUGENE SMITH LIBRARY
J. EUGENE SMITH LIBRARY STATE UNIVERSITY
EASTERN CONN. STATE UNIVERSITY CT 06226
WILLIMANTIC, CT 06226-2295

Other Titles of Interest From Maximum Press

Marketing on the Internet, Fifth Edition: Zimmerman, 1-885068-49-2

Marketing With E-Mail, Second Edition: Kinnard, 1-885068-51-4

101 Ways to Promote Your Web Site, Second Edition: Sweeney, 1-885068-45-X

Internet Marketing for Less Than $500/Year: Yudkin, 1-885068-52-2

Internet Marketing for Your Tourism Business: Sweeney, 1-885068-47-6

Internet Marketing for Information Technology Companies: Silverstein, 1-885068-46-8

Exploring IBM Technology, Products, & Services, Third Edition: edited by Hoskins, 1-885068-44-1

Building Intranets With Lotus Notes and Domino 5.0: Krantz, 1-885068-41-7

Exploring IBM Personal Computers, Eleventh Edition: Hoskins, Wilson, 1-885068-39-5

Exploring IBM RS/6000 Computers, Tenth Edition: Hoskins, Davies, 1-885068-42-5

Exploring IBM AS/400 Computers, Tenth Edition: Hoskins, Dimmick, 1-885068-43-3

Exploring IBM S/390 Computers, Sixth Edition: Hoskins, Coleman, 1-885068-28-X

For more information, visit our Web site at
www.maxpress.com
or e-mail us at *moreinfo@maxpress.com*

Publisher: Jim Hoskins

Manager of Finance/Administration: Donna Tryon

Production Manager: ReNae Grant

Cover Design: Lauren Smith Designs

Compositor: PageCrafters Inc.

Copyeditor: Debbie Miller

Proofreader: Kim Stefansson

Indexer: Susan Olason

Printer: P.A. Hutchison

This publication is designed to provide accurate and authoritative information in regard to the subject matter covered. It is sold with the understanding that the publisher is not engaged in rendering professional services. If legal, accounting, medical, psychological, or any other expert assistance is required, the services of a competent professional person should be sought. ADAPTED FROM A DECLARATION OF PRINCIPLES OF A JOINT COMMITTEE OF THE AMERICAN BAR ASSOCIATION AND PUBLISHERS.

Copyright 2001 by Barry Silverstein.

All rights reserved. Published simultaneously in Canada.

Reproduction or translation of any part of this work beyond that permitted by Section 107 or 108 of the 1976 United States Copyright Act without the permission of the copyright owner is unlawful. Requests for permission or further information should be addressed to the Permissions Department, Maximum Press.

Recognizing the importance of preserving what has been written, it is a policy of Maximum Press to have books of enduring value published in the United States printed on acid-free paper, and we exert our best efforts to that end.

Library of Congress Cataloging-in-Publication Data

Silverstein, Barry, 1948-
Business-to-business Internet marketing : seven proven strategies for
increasing profits through Internet direct marketing / Barry
Silverstein.— 3rd ed.
p. cm.
Includes bibliographical references and index.
ISBN 1-885068-50-6
1. Internet marketing. 2. Industrial marketing. I. Title.
HF5415.1265 .S535 2000b
658.8'4—dc21
00-011106

To Peter W. Evans:
With gratitude for your friendship and partnership

Acknowledgments

I could not have written this Third Edition without having unlimited access to the greatest source of information in the world: the Internet. I am grateful to the Internet marketers who display their work on the Web for all to see, and to the Internet reporters and commentators who freely share their knowledge through their e-mail newsletters and Web sites.

I also want to thank the clients and employees of Directech | eMerge, my associates in advertising, direct marketing and Internet marketing, my publisher Jim Hoskins, and especially Sharon, Debra, and Maxine for their patience and support.

Barry Silverstein

Disclaimer

The purchase of computer software or hardware is an important and costly business decision. Although the author and publisher of this book have made reasonable efforts to ensure the accuracy and timeliness of the information contained herein, the author and publisher assume no liability with respect to loss or damage caused or alleged to be caused by reliance on any information contained herein and disclaim any and all warranties, expressed or implied, as to the accuracy or reliability of said information.

This book is not intended to replace the manufacturer's product documentation or personnel in determining the specifications and capabilities of the products mentioned in this book. The manufacturer's product documentation should always be consulted, as the specifications and capabilities of computer hardware and software products are subject to frequent modification. The reader is solely responsible for the choice of computer hardware and software. All configurations and applications of computer hardware and software should be reviewed with the manufacturer's representatives prior to choosing or using any computer hardware and software.

Trademarks

The words contained in this text that are believed to be trademarked, service marked, or otherwise to hold proprietary rights have been designated as such by use of initial capitalization. No attempt has been made to designate as trademarked or service marked any personal computer words or terms in which proprietary rights might exist. Inclusion, exclusion, or definition of a word or term is not intended to affect, or to express judgement upon, the validity of legal status of any proprietary right that may be claimed for a specific word or term.

Foreword

Today, more than ever before, managing business information means managing an organization's most important resource. In the course of a single day, a company exchanges enormous amounts of critical information with outside business partners and processes equally huge amounts created by internal business applications. These information flows are the lifeblood of today's global economy.

Thanks to the Internet and its associated technologies, the twenty-first century will transform the economics of global commerce. Analysts estimate that by the year 2003, approximately $1.5 trillion worth of goods and services in the United States will be exchanged between companies using Internet transactions, with average annual growth between now and then of 55%—about 10 times faster than the growth of the U.S. GDP. There are forecasts that an additional $1.0 trillion will be exchanged electronically outside the U.S. in 2003, bringing the total global market forecast for the underlying value of electronic transactions three years from now to a staggering $2.5 trillion.

With Y2K remediation issues now behind them, businesses all over the world are focusing investment and attention on becoming wired to electronic trading communities in order to reap huge economic benefits from competing at "Internet speed." The start of sweeping social revolutions seldom coincides with important changes in the calendar, but in the case of Internet commerce, the fireworks celebrating the start of the twenty-first century also sounded the start of a new era in business— the Information Age. In the Information Age, computers and networks will dramatically change the way business is conducted around the world, and the pace of change will be nothing short of breathtaking.

Indeed, the Information Age has begun and it will reshape global commerce as profoundly as have electricity, telephones, railroads, and airplanes. Just as the labor-intensive Agrarian Age yielded to the capital-intensive Industrial Age in much of the civilized world, the knowledge-intensive Information Age is the next inevitable social order. It is a new chapter in global macroeconomics where knowledge replaces labor and capital as the primary form of incremental productive capacity.

Labor and capital historically have been the main ingredients in the solution to the persistent commercial problem of balancing supply and demand. Overtime and inventory are the two most common manifestations of labor and capital being applied to correct an imbalance between supply and demand. These costly ways of meeting customer requirements are driven by information deficits in the supply chain created by slow, manual, sequential business processes developed for the physically networked world of the Industrial Age. The supply chain of the Twentieth Century was knowledge-challenged. But with the advancement of the Internet and its associated technologies, the twenty-first century will transform the economics of global commerce by getting the right information to the right place at the right time, every time!

Adding intelligence to the supply chain requires the combination of a state-of-the-art technology, a business process understanding to build and manage trading communities, and a global reach. The New World of business-to-business Internet commerce is much different from the past. In the Old World, e-commerce was about eliminating paperwork by automating purchase orders of high-volume direct materials with pre-selected suppliers over proprietary networks. In the New World, e-commerce is much more spontaneous and the appetite for real-time information about product and service markets over public networks is almost insatiable. This change is nothing short of profound and we must make equally profound changes in our businesses to capitalize on this revolution.

If companies want to compete at "Internet speed" in this new age, they must demand state-of-the-art business-to-business e-commerce solutions. With a burgeoning global presence, the need to communicate in multiple data formats and protocol types is mandatory. The days of "brochureware" for casual observation on a Web site are gone.

One of the biggest issues facing business-to-business electronic commerce today is the integration of disparate back office applications with Web servers and the routing of inter-company messages over various public and private networks. Companies that do not have powerful message brokering and data transformation engines will not be able to maintain a competitive edge.

Automating the procurement process has been a dream of most sourcing general managers for many years. Thanks to the Internet, this dream can today be a reality, with the potential to shave 10-15% of the costs out of procuring goods and services. Companies typically spend weeks at a time negotiating special terms with their preferred suppliers and then never implement procedures to ensure their employees adhere to the contracts. A thing called "maverick purchasing" is quite common in most businesses—where employees purchase from non-preferred suppliers or purchase from preferred suppliers at list price rather than the contract price.

With the right technology, software, and services, companies can build powerful marketplace exchanges that are integrated with front office and back offices systems for truly interactive real-time exchanges of information and transactions. Never before have trading partners had such a great opportunity to communicate with one another in real time about product development, configuration, availability, pricing, shipment, delivery, payment, and support. Annoying "voice mail jail" will rapidly become a thing of the past as buyers and suppliers communicate over the Web with dynamically updated information from mission-critical computer systems.

It is truly a new business world that is unfolding before our very eyes. The companies that cannot adapt to the New World and the new speed of business will find themselves the dinosaurs of the new millenium. This is nowhere more true than in marketing. The manner in which we market in the Information Age now speaks volumes about the technological savvy of the provider. You can't run. You can't hide. Be assured that in this New World, to not communicate is, indeed, to communicate. This Third edition of *Business-to-Business Internet Marketing* gives you the tools you need to communicate the right message and become a successful e-marketer. You control your destiny: adapt—or face extinction.

Harvey Seegers
President and CEO
GE Global eXchange Services

Table of Contents

Chapter 3:
Generating and Qualifying
Leads with Your Web Site   106

Chapter 6:
Using Internet Events for Marketing   188

Chapter 7:
Executing e-Fulfillment   225

Chapter 8:
Building Customer Relationships   263

Chapter 9:
Using Business Communities and Exchanges   298

Chapter 10:
Developing Internet Partnerships   334

Chapter 11:
Selling on the Internet   365

Chapter 12:
Integrating Online and Offline Marketing   **401**

About This Book

Web sites can be navigated at will and, in a sense, this book can be, too. You can read it sequentially, or move around from chapter to chapter.

Chapter 1 provides a necessary foundation for the business-to-business (b-to-b) direct marketing principles discussed in the rest of the book. This "crash course" is both an introduction for novices and a refresher course for experienced direct marketers.

Chapter 2 talks about "the Age of the e" in order to demonstrate the impact the Internet has on business in general and, specifically, on business-to-business. It suggests that a new response model called "intersponding" will emerge as a result of the Internet's vast influence.

Chapters 3 through 11 cover the seven proven Internet marketing strategies that are the core of this book. All of the strategies have been updated with new examples and many more site references. Unlike the two previous editions, this Third Edition includes screen captures of Web pages to illustrate some of the examples. These screen captures are the copyrighted property of the Web site owners.

Chapters 3, 4, and 5 cover the first strategy, generating and qualifying leads. Chapter 3 addresses how to use your Web site to generate and qualify leads. Chapters 4 and 5 look at the same strategy, but they demonstrate how to use online advertising and e-mail, respectively.

Chapter 6 discusses the rapidly growing b-to-b Internet marketing strategy of using Internet events, and Chapter 7 explains how to execute e-fulfillment.

Certainly one of the most significant areas of Internet marketing is building customer relationships, and this is the topic of Chapter 8.

Chapter 9 covers the use of business communities and exchanges, and Chapter 10 addresses the use of Internet partnerships. These two areas were new to the Second Edition, and they have been significantly revised in the Third Edition.

Chapter 11 is logically, the last of the seven strategies: selling on the Internet. This is ultimately what every b-to-b Internet marketer would like to achieve.

Finally, Chapter 12 has been updated to address the increasing integration of online and offline marketing. It offers specific examples for integrating the two, as well as an Internet marketing action plan and internal marketing department staffing suggestions.

The book concludes with a comprehensive resource section divided into two parts, designed specifically for the business-to-business Internet marketer.

Appendix A provides a complete list of every Web site referenced in this book, in order of appearance. It also contains a specially selected compilation, by category, of Web sites that should be of particular interest to the b-to-b marketer. In addition, you will find a selected list of books of relevance to b-to-b marketers.

Appendix B is a glossary of direct marketing and Internet marketing terms.

Also included is information about how you can be a resource on business-to-business Internet marketing.

Your "Members Only" Web Site

The Internet marketing world changes most every day. That is why there is a companion Web site associated with this book. On this site, you will find the latest Internet marketing news, book updates, expanded information, and other business-to-business Internet marketing resources. However, you have to be a member of the "Business-to-Business Insider's Club" to gain access to this site.

When you purchased this book, you automatically became a member (in fact, this is the only way to join). To access the companion Web site, go to the Maximum Press Web site located at *www.maxpress.com* and follow the links to the "Business-to-Business Internet Marketing" companion Web site. When you try to enter the companion Web site, you will be prompted for a User ID and Password. Type the following:

- For User ID: *bus2bus3e*

- For Password: *canyon*

You will then be granted full access to the "Members Only" area. After you arrive, bookmark the page in your browser and you will never have to enter the User ID and Password again. Visit the site often and enjoy the Internet marketing news and information with our compliments—and thanks for buying the book. We ask that you not share the "User ID" and "Password" for this site with anyone else.

Introduction

The original edition of *Business-to-Business Internet Marketing* filled a need in the marketplace. At the time of its publication, it was the first book to show how to apply proven business-to-business (b-to-b) direct marketing principles to the Internet.

The book's popularity, along with the continuous and dramatic change that is occurring in Internet marketing, demanded a Second Edition, published about one year ago. The Second Edition of *Business-to-Business Internet Marketing* sold more copies in six months than the original edition sold during its lifetime.

The Second Edition substantially revised the original edition's five proven strategies, and added two new strategies, for a total of seven. For this Third Edition, I wondered whether the set of seven strategies would need to be expanded. What I found in my research is that these strategies are still valid and comprehensive. In fact, they have now become established and are widely practiced by b-to-b marketers. (I like to think the Second Edition had a little something to do with this!)

Rather than artificially expand the number of strategies, I therefore chose to re-evaluate all of them. This led to the realization that the first strategy, Generating and Qualifying Leads, was so fundamentally important that it deserved more attention than it received in the first two editions. As a result, that strategy is now sub-divided into three chapters, so that it can be discussed in the context of Web sites, online advertising, and e-mail.

The remaining six strategies have also been significantly updated and expanded. Readers will find many more examples and site references. For the first time, readers will see screen captures of select Web pages to illustrate each of the strategies.

I retained Chapter 1, the "crash course," because I have received numerous comments about its value as a b-to-b direct marketing primer. Chapter 2 has been renamed *The Age of the "e."* That ubiquitous "e" seems to be finding its way into every facet of marketing, business, and life. The chapter itself has been completely revised to include current statistics and new thoughts on the impact of the Internet on business and marketing.

The final chapter recognizes that the business world is now moving to a truly integrated model of online and offline marketing. The chapter includes specific examples illustrating how to integrate electronic and traditional direct marketing media, along with an action plan and staffing considerations.

Those are the details about the book's new content, but what about the book's *purpose?* That purpose remains very much the same as for the original and second editions: to educate b-to-b marketers about the awesome power of Internet marketing. More than that, the real purpose of this book is to explain that b-to-b Internet marketing is no longer an isolated practice by a few visionary companies; *it is now becoming mainstream marketing.*

How did we get to this point of marketing dominance by the Internet? It turns out that b-to-b marketers were the real drivers behind this phenomenon. It was b-to-b marketers, not consumer marketers, who *first* understood the Internet's value as a viable medium for awareness, lead generation, and now, direct selling. It was b-to-b marketers who understood so well the potential of the Internet as both a marketing tool and a sales channel. It was b-to-b marketers who recognized that the Internet was the electronic embodiment of the interactivity and responsiveness that direct marketers had been touting all along. Only when America Online made its foray into cyberspace did the Internet begin to reach mass media potential and gain wide consumer acceptance.

Today it is "B2B"(business-to-business) that has captured the excitement of the investment community, becoming the fastest growing, most lucrative, and most promising segment of the new Internet economy. The reality is that *everything* is moving to the Internet. We are witnessing a technological and economic shift of unprecedented proportion. Worldwide consumer usage of the Internet is skyrocketing. Businesses large and small are moving their entire IT infrastructures to the Internet. New Internet-based businesses are forming at a dizzying rate. A new-world economy dependent on digital cash, digital signatures, and a wireless Internet is on the way. We are living in The Age of the e.

B-to-b direct marketing is being swept up in this electronic maelstrom. Direct mail and telemarketing are being challenged. Direct mail will not disappear; instead, this medium will become a legacy system that will feed the Internet instead of dominating marketing as it did in the past. E-mail communications will rise dramatically, as will reliance on the Web. Direct mail and other traditional direct marketing media will become supporting players as the Internet dominates the marketing world and the world at large.

Take heart: Everything that works in direct marketing transfers almost point by point to the Internet. As you will see in this book, all of the core b-to-b marketing strategies—lead generation and qualification, event marketing, fulfillment, customer marketing, building community, partnerships, selling—all of these apply, and they *can be enhanced* with Internet marketing.

The underlying principles are the same; the marketing methodology is the same. What is radically different is the electronic nature of marketing. The Internet is not so much a new direct marketing channel, but rather a new way of doing business. Internet marketing is a form of direct marketing that goes so far beyond what could be accomplished before that it is almost beyond comparison. Now b-to-b marketers can actually close the loop and *complete the marketing and sales cycle* at one time, in one place, online.

Internet marketing will be the best avenue for b-to-b companies to effectively compete in The Age of the e. This is the most fundamental change our marketing world has ever seen. So jump on board...this promises to be one heck of a ride.

1

Business-to-Business Direct
Marketing—A Crash Course

This "crash course" in business-to-business direct marketing has been a popular feature of the first two editions of the book, so I have retained it in this Third Edition. Readers have found the first chapter valuable because it provides a tutorial on the principles and practices of direct marketing, which "directly" relates to Internet marketing. The chapter covers all the basics, from audience and offer to creative and media formats. If you are a seasoned direct marketer, you can skip this chapter or use parts of it selectively as a refresher. If you are relatively new to direct marketing, this chapter is essential material.

As you will see, Internet marketing is interactive, responsive marketing—marketing that engages an individual, encourages interaction, and elicits a response, as does direct marketing. What is new about Internet marketing is the electronic medium itself and the way the Internet applies to the process of direct marketing

Direct marketing has been interactive, responsive marketing since its beginnings. It started as print advertising in colonial America, with newspaper classifieds. As national magazines emerged in the 1890s, direct marketing was used to sell off the page, but it was mail that drove direct marketing to new heights. Mail promised to deliver on direct marketing's dream—capturing the spirit of personalized communication in one-to-one correspondence. Since then, direct marketing has expanded into telephone, television, radio—and today and tomorrow, the Internet. The key word here is "direct."

As a true indication of the Internet's widespread influence on direct marketing, the Direct Marketing Association continues to aggressively pursue Internet initiatives that are changing the fundamental shape of this influential organization. Soon, the new definition for direct marketing, if the terminology remains, may be all marketing that is interactive. While direct marketing and interactive marketing co-exist as distinct and separate forms of marketing, the lines continue to blur. My basic premise is that Internet marketing has its roots planted in direct marketing. Read on to see how.

Basic Principles

Imagine what it was like to sell a product at the turn of the twentieth century. You probably had little if any formalized manufacturing, distribution, or marketing methods, and if you wanted to reach the prospective buyer of your product directly, you had to go door-to-door, or perhaps use the only national advertising medium available at the time: magazines.

Yet as early as the 1890s, marketers of products for business were using *direct marketing* actively and, in some cases, brilliantly. They faced the kinds of problems you face today: how to reach the right audience with a compelling message about a product, how to make that product seem irresistible and necessary, how to get the prospective buyer to *inquire* and to *buy*.

A print ad from 1910 is a stunning example of no-risk mail order in its earliest implementation. The ad's headline reads Underwoods Only $3 Down. The beginning copy reads

> Genuine Underwood Rebuilt in our own factory just like new for ONLY $3 down—NOT ONE CENT MORE *until you have tried the machine 10 full days at our expense. Balance on easy monthly payments.*

and the offer copy at the close of the ad reads

Yes, you can have your money back if you want it. After you have examined the typewriter carefully, used it to write letters, if you decide for any reason whatever that you do not care for it, you may return it to us at our expense and every penny you have paid will be cheerfully and promptly refunded.

The language may be a bit archaic, but you get the point. This is a free trial offer targeted to businesses—promoting the latest technology of the day, the typewriter.

This is a remarkable offer for the early 1900s. Think of the shipping complexities and the monetary risk accepted by the advertiser to put a very heavy typewriter into the hands of the prospect. It is the equivalent of sending a top-of-the-line personal computer on a no-risk, approval basis to a prospect today, yet this marketer pulled out the stops to sell typewriters direct to the business consumer—with an irresistible offer that every direct marketer can learn from.

I have two primary reasons for sharing this early form of business-to-business direct marketing with you.

1. The techniques we use today in direct marketing are tried and true, tested methods. They were utilized in the early 1900s and they worked. They are utilized today and they work. This should give you a sense of perspective, in that direct marketing is grounded in basic, fundamental, universal principles, and practices with lasting relevance. As Goethe said, "Everything has been thought of before. The problem is to think of it again."

2. Do not be afraid to reach for the stars and take a direct marketing risk now and then. Consider the Underwood typewriter ad. You could undoubtedly claim it was a huge risk for the marketer. On the other hand, the offer was so irresistible and had so little risk associated with it from the prospect's perspective that anyone who was even considering the purchase of a typewriter had to be compelled to take advantage of the irresistible ten-day, no-obligation free trial. Getting that heavy piece of machinery into a serious prospect's hands—someone who put a little bit of money down, who was willing to accept the shipment, and who may never have been able to travel to a

store to buy it, was a brilliant and aggressive direct marketing strategy. After all, once the prospect had it in hand, imagine how difficult it would have been to return it!

Now let us fast-forward to the more recent past.

We are in the mid-1970s. America is falling in love with technology—space, cars, electronics, we cannot get enough of it. The boom years of the computer are yet to come, but the electricity is in the air. A guy named Joe Sugarman reads America's interests and finds a technology niche: consumer electronics. Sugarman is a self-taught direct marketer, the ultimate direct marketing Renaissance man. He learns to do it all, finding and acquiring the products, formulating the marketing and media strategies, writing and designing his own ads.

He looks at direct marketing through different colored glasses (which now, by the way, are "BluBlockers." After some tough times, Joe re-engineered his business and decided to market BluBlocker sunglasses direct to the American public through television infomercials. Once again, Joe pioneered the use of direct marketing, only with a different product). Instead of using the traditional direct marketing media that one could assume would work for his product line, Sugarman suspects there is a higher demographic target for what he is marketing, the well-heeled business person. So, he does something that is a breakthrough: He places his direct response ads in the pages of *The Wall Street Journal*. It has never been done before—using the respected business daily to sell products direct to the business consumer.

Everything about the direct response ads is different...

- They have unusual, catchy headlines and subheads, such as

THERMOMETER BREAKTHROUGH

A new computer can take your temperature in seconds and tell you when to drink coffee.

LASER BEAM DIGITAL WATCH

Never press another button, day or night, with America's first digital watch that glows in the dark.

- The ads use very long copy, three columns of it set small and justified, to look like editorial matter.

- Subheads are used to break the copy into segments and lead the reader through the text.

- Often, the copy is narrative in nature, sometimes in the first person. The copy is almost painfully loaded with technical detail about the product that is being promoted, yet it bombards the reader with product benefits and arcane uses for the product that no one would even think of.

- The ads feature black-and-white product photography (also unusual in the 1970s for *The Wall Street Journal*) that often shows the insides of the products so that readers get a sense of the technology behind them.

- The ads pitch expensive, sometimes eclectic products—many of which we might define today as "impulse buys."

- Every product comes with an ironclad 30-day money back guarantee. It is almost eerie how much the language sounds like that Underwood ad from 1910:

  If you are not absolutely satisfied with the JS&A Digital, then return it within one month for a prompt and courteous refund.

- There is no coupon. There is no big 800 number. Rather, at the end of every ad, there is a simple call to action—the reader is urged to order today via credit card. This is followed by a large logo, JS&A NATIONAL SALES GROUP, an address, and below the logo, the words CALL TOLL-FREE with an 800 number. The logo and even the address of the company are a mark of sheer genius. The company name is actually Joe and, in the early days, just his secretary. The address, "One JS&A Plaza," is a nondescript industrial building—but with a unique, very important sounding address that Joe managed to get the local post office to approve.

At its time, this advertising was a singular breakthrough. The *Wall Street Journal* had previously not been used this way, or to this extent, as a direct marketing medium. In fact, no direct marketer has since used it as aggressively.

Sugarman later took the model for advertising in *The Journal* and migrated it to another medium that was ideally targeted to the business executive: frequent flier magazines. Here, too, the ads were breaking new ground.

Sugarman established a wildly successful multimillion-dollar consumer electronics business using only direct response print advertising in media targeted to business executives. He also provided the technology world with a business model that spawned numerous other lookalike direct marketing companies, which, in part, helped send JS&A into decline. Among them were Cincinnati Microwave, a successful direct marketer of in-car radar detectors; DAK, a direct marketer of consumer electronics; and The Sharper Image, a mail order marketer and retailer of high-tech electronics and other upscale consumer items. The Sharper Image remains as an icon of high-tech gadgetry today, still publishing a lavish catalog and selling products through national stores, typically located in malls, and over the Internet.

I know all this about Joe Sugarman because I was privileged enough to attend an exclusive retreat with him more than 20 years ago. You see, Joe did not miss a trick. He turned his mail order success into an opportunity to share his knowledge with other direct marketers. He put together a weeklong program, which he offered at his Wisconsin estate. He told his story and provided his students with an intimate perspective on his trials and tribulations. He pretty much tore down everything I thought I knew about direct marketing and made me view it through the marketing equivalent of BluBlockers. What I remember most of all is his philosophy of how he did it: Joe Sugarman learned all the rules of direct marketing—and then he broke them.

Markets, Markets Everywhere

Now we will turn to the specifics of business-to-business direct marketing. First, we need to define our markets so that we have some common ground for comparing and contrasting media, offers, and creative approaches.

The broad market for direct marketing can be divided into two "worlds"—the consumer world and the business (or business-to-business) world, defined as follows:

- The *consumer world* is composed of every suspect, prospect, or customer who considers the purchase of a product for himself, herself, or another consumer. The purchase is a "personal" buying decision.

- The *business-to-business world* is comprised of individuals who, although they are still consumers, take on the *additional* responsibility of evaluating and purchasing products for a business they own or for a business that employs them. I like to think of the prospect in this world as "a consumer with an in-box."

- A third, "in-between" world exists: the *"SOHO" world*. This is the Small Office, Home Office market. Typically it is composed of owners of very small businesses, sometimes run out of a household. In this world, the consumer/business owner really has both personal and business responsibility, all the time. This is a rapidly growing world that should not be overlooked, because prospects are ready and willing to buy business products directly.

It is important to define these worlds because they have different direct marketing "rules." These rules have a very real impact on how you, as a business-to-business direct marketer, reach, and communicate with that world.

For example, reaching the consumer world is often done through mass media, such as television, and national magazines. On the direct mail and telemarketing side, it is most often done based on demographic criteria—whether the consumer lives in an apartment or a single-family home, whether or not the consumer is married, what the household income of the consumer is, and so on.

Reaching the business world with direct marketing, however, is very different. Typical media include print advertising in general business publications or the trade press, telemarketing, and direct mail. Television is viable only for the largest direct marketers. Radio during "drive time" is growing as a direct marketing medium to reach businesses.

Direct mail is still the leading business-to-business direct marketing medium, but the Internet is catching up. With direct mail, you are directing your message to someone at a business address, so many factors enter into proper targeting. Such "business demographics" as size of the company, type of business, the individual's functional area of responsibility, the person's job title and purchasing authority, and other criteria are selected to hone in on the appropriate prospect.

The larger the business, the more likely it becomes that many individuals are involved in a business decision. So, reaching *multiple levels* in an organization may be necessary, and there are "subworlds" within each business, based on the kind of product you are selling and the most appropriate audience for it. As for the "in-between" world of the in-home or very small business, that world is becoming more and more attractive to direct marketers. As a result, an increasing number of lists targeting these smaller businesses are becoming available.

We have defined the basic worlds in which your prospects and customers live. Now we need a brief definition of how these individuals should be classified into categories for direct marketing purposes.

To move from the general to the specific, your entire potential audience is generally known as your *universe*. The first and typically largest part of the universe is *suspects*—people whom you "suspect" might be interested in your product or service. The next category, *prospects*, is that group of individuals within the suspects who are *most likely* to be in a position to consider purchasing your product or service. In the most general sense, you want to be able to identify *unqualified* versus *qualified* prospects by some criteria that you establish. Most companies engaged in ongoing prospect qualification further classify prospects by some type of ranking structure. An example of this would be Very Hot/Hot/Warm/Cold, or A/B/C/D.

The criteria used to determine the rank of a prospect are typically based on whether the prospect has a budget and his or her likelihood to purchase within a certain time period. This information is most often added to prospect records via input from the sales force in the field, because they have the most direct knowledge. Increasingly, however, direct marketing programs ask these questions on reply cards, Web response forms, or through telemarketing scripts so that prospects can be *pre-qualified* for the sales force.

After the prospect category comes the *customer* category. It is obvious what a customer is, but some companies make the mistake of not sub-classifying customers as well as prospects. For example, a customer who purchases many products and services from you over an extended period of time should be classified as a "frequent buyer"—someone who is more important than an occasional or one-time buyer. A customer who purchased from you in the past but has not purchased in some time would be better off classified as a "former" or "dormant" customer for future marketing purposes. The former customer is, in a very real sense, a qualified prospect with a twist—someone who used to do business with you but no longer does, or has not done so for some time.

Some companies do not pay a lot of attention to former customers, but they should. It makes good marketing sense to segregate these customers on a database for special treatment. It is worth the investment to find out why they have not purchased for some time, and what the company can do about it to recapture the customer. Because the cost of acquiring a customer is so much higher than the cost of keeping a customer, former customers can bring value back to a company if they can be recaptured at a lower cost.

Until now, we have been addressing prospects and customers from the perspective of the end user. For many business-to-business marketers, there is a whole other class of prospects and customers: channel partners. Channel partners are typically companies who play a role in the marketing or sales of the originating company's products. Examples of channel partners include:

- Companies with products or services that *complement* the originating company's products or services. In the computer industry, hardware manufacturers often partner with software publishers to provide the end user with an integrated solution.

- Distributors of the originating company's product, who may be companies or independent representatives who have their own set of prospects and customers.

- Resellers of the originating company's product, who take the product, sometimes add something to it, such as services and support, and resell it. In the computer industry, these are often known as Value-Added Resellers (VARs).

- *Retailers*, who resell the product in stores, via traditional mail order, or over the Internet.

These channel audiences present the business-to-business marketer with a level of complexity that affects marketing in general and direct marketing in particular. It is often valuable to establish entirely separate but coordinated marketing programs that address the individual needs of channel partners. Special care should be taken to develop programs that, to the extent possible, avoid channel conflict.

What Are You *Really* Selling?

The last set of definitions will help define the market in which *you* live. In marketing, your world can be defined by a number of criteria (actually, they are the same basic criteria we used to define the business world).

You can first define what you sell as a product (a tangible), a service (an intangible), or a combination of both. You can more specifically define your market by the type of product or service you sell. Most often, this relates to a way of defining business types called Standard Industrial Classifications (SICs). There are hundreds of SIC codes, each of which represents a business type. Your product or service fits into one of them.

After you know your own SIC, you also know your *competitors'* SIC. That can be very useful. SIC codes can open up a world of competitive research and list information to the direct marketer.

So far this is pretty basic stuff. Now think about this: Can you define what you are *really* selling? How would you describe it? Would you say it is computer software—or would you say it is a computer software spreadsheet or database product? Would you say it is an electronic component, a chemical, or a motor? Or is it a business service?

Well, these are all trick questions. The truth is, you are not selling any of these things. Because in direct marketing, your product is really defined by the prospect. Whatever it is you think you are selling does not really matter. What matters is the perception of the prospect of what you are selling. The prospect says "I don't care about your product—*what's in it for me?*"

This is why the most successful business-to-business direct marketers position their products differently based on the specific audiences they are most interested in reaching. Furthermore, these successful direct marketers engage in promoting *benefits and advantages* before they promote product *features*. In the information technology business, this is often called *solution selling*. After the prospect is convinced of the product's benefits ("What's in it for me?"), he or she is more likely to want to know about its specific "hard-core" features.

An attendee at one of my seminars told me a little story that turned out to be a very good way to dramatize the difference between a product's features and benefits. Let me preface the story by mentioning that it was told to me by a woman, because the story is somewhat sexist and I wish to take no responsibility for your reaction to it!

It is the story of FAB, the laundry detergent. FAB was designed to incorporate an important Feature, Advantage, and Benefit. The difference between them was as telling as the cleaning power of the detergent itself:

- The *feature*: FAB has blue crystals.

- The *advantage*: FAB makes clothes bright and makes them smell good.

- The *benefit*: Your husband will love you.

In the context of America in the 1950s, when FAB was at its height of popularity, the advertising world was portraying just this kind of message. After all, it mirrored of the way contemporary society was pictured in the advertising media of the time: the husband went off to work, and the wife stayed home doing the laundry and running the household. So, FAB was not really a laundry detergent at all—it was an ingredient for a successful marriage!

Behind the FAB example is an important lesson for all of us. The product has a name and a brand. Advertising experts will tell you that the brand image itself is important, that the brand itself will convey a message about the product. That is true, but for direct marketing purposes, we will deal with something more tangible—the product's features, advantages, and benefits.

A product's *features* are physical attributes, the nuts-and-bolts of a product. They describe only the characteristics and qualities of the product. They do nothing, in and of themselves, to turn the product into something that is desirable to purchase.

A product's *advantages*, however, go one step further. Advantages speak to the product in use. What does the product really do? How does it work? What results does it achieve for the user? Advantages begin to position the product in the mind of the prospect or customer as something that may or may not be desirable for purchase.

Finally, a product's *benefits* focus on what the product does for the prospect or customer. How will the product make life better, easier, richer for the product's user? Why should the prospect or customer consider this product over another and, ultimately, purchase it?

Learning a Lesson from Consumer Marketers

Direct marketers understand that basically, people are people when it comes to universal needs, desires, likes and dislikes. In his classic book *Successful Direct Marketing Methods*[1], Bob Stone includes a list of "basic human wants"—things that humans like (making money, saving time, achieving comfort, etc.) and do not like (criticism, pain, loss of money, etc.).

These same basic human needs translate well into the business-to-business world. Humans in the business world like to be acknowledged for their hard work. They do not like to be singled out when something goes wrong in their job. They like to make money. They do not want to be fired. Review Stone's entire list—you will find it applies to business-to-business direct marketing.

In fact, we can apply the lessons of consumer direct marketing to business-to-business direct marketing in other ways. Virtually every direct marketing concept in existence has been passed down, adapted, and reused. (Remember the old Underwood ad!) Free trials, money-back guarantees, and product demonstrations came out of that ancient marketing world and are now accepted direct marketing practices. It pays to keep your eyes open for direct marketing trends all around you. You can be sure if you see something repeated in direct marketing that *it is working*.

A great way to keep on top of trends in direct mail marketing is to keep a "swipe file." Set up a few file drawers to house direct mail samples that you like or do not like. Start saving the mail you get at home and at the office. If you really want to get organized about it, segment the mail into consumer and business-to-business, or by product, or by objective, or by size, or go completely off the deep end and cross-reference them. (I did this once and gave up after about a month.)

The point is, if you save the stuff, you can review it every now and then to get ideas, see what is working, and develop a sensitivity to what you like and what you do not like. The medium itself is the best training ground.

You will notice that the most effective direct marketing snares you first with all the benefits of the product and, after having done that, backs up the benefits with point-by-point features. Even when you find a list of the features, you will notice that they often relate directly to product benefits and that they just as often are in "you" language: "You can save time ...." or "You will save money ....". This *personalizes* the product message by bringing the prospective buyer into the picture as often as possible.

Take a good long look at the print advertising and catalogs produced by successful mail order marketers of any products, but especially business-to-business products. Review the product copy, read and reread the guarantees. Analyze the ordering terms and conditions.

Notice how these marketers handle shipping, returns, credit cards, and telephone ordering. When it comes to selling directly, leading mail order companies in the consumer market, such as L.L. Bean and Lands' End, are studies in how to do it right. Many of these types of marketers have successfully transferred their skills to the business-to-business market.

Lands' End, for example, has a Corporate Sales catalog that leverages their consumer brand and makes it attractive to business buyers. The Corporate Sales catalog features luggage, sport shirts, sweaters, towels, hats, gift certificates, and more—all "Lands' End quality" but customizable with a company's logo and identity. The catalog caters to the business buyer, yet has the same top-quality look and feel as the consumer catalog—outstanding photography, benefit copy that is easy to read, product codes and prices that are easy to find, and a few testimonials from happy business customers thrown in. There's an 800 number on every spread with the words "Just Ask" above it.

Business-to-business mail order marketers are just as adept at direct marketing—take a look at any number of catalogs targeting businesses for proof.

The Special Requirements of Business-to-Business Direct Marketing

Earlier, we discussed the fact that your product or service is really defined by the *perceptions and needs* of a specific audience. What about the nature of your product in relation to your potential audience? Do the qualities of your product or service make it very specialized? (This is a common characteristic of technology products.) Generally, this means that your product or service:

- May be usable only by an audience with special expertise or previously acquired knowledge, or may require training to be used,

- Is focused on a particular kind of "vertical" or specialized solution, and therefore probably has a much smaller universe of people interested in it or already using it,

- Is probably more expensive than the "average" product, and,

- Is likely to involve more than one individual in evaluating or purchasing it, resulting in a longer sales cycle.

These are the kinds of product issues that affect your entire direct marketing program—because they drive whom you must reach, the offer you need to make, the content and structure of your message (the "creative"), and the way you implement part or all of the direct marketing program.

That's why business-to-business direct marketing tends to be a *highly focused, highly targeted* process. List selection becomes an absolutely critical component, because you must research and acquire just the right type of list, with appropriate selection criteria, to increase your chances of success in reaching your best target audiences.

Developing an offer is equally important. In lead generation, the offer must appeal very specifically to the type of audience you are targeting. Typically, the higher the price of your product, the more you need to *pre-qualify* the prospect and make that person "work harder" for your offer. In order generation, on the other hand, it is essential to entice the prospect to evaluate your product or service instead of or in addition to another product or service, and to make it attractive to purchase that product immediately. All the details must be included so that the prospect can make a purchase immediately.

Finally, when you execute the creative, the approach must be *appropriate* to the audience. If, for example, your product is targeted to scientists, you probably already know that these individuals are interested in facts, figures, experiments, and supportable claims. Well-documented non-promotional material is likely to work better for this technical audience than "glitzy" advertising approaches with little in the way of detail.

Why Audiences Are Getting Smaller

More and more, it is becoming likely that you will not be able to use "universal messages" for everyone. Most business-to-business marketers eventually realize that they are playing in a segmented, specialized, and sometimes very fragmented marketing world. This means that your product or service may have uniquely different appeals to different audiences. To boost response beyond the merely acceptable level, you have to acknowledge those differences and target to them.

It may not be good enough to combine marketing messages in a direct mail lead generation campaign for a product that can serve the purposes of two audiences. Take "life scientists" and "environmental scientists," for example. Both audiences are made up of scientists, but they each have different interests. Your product may look the same to you, but it could very well look different to these two specialized audiences. By splitting apart the messages targeted to each of these two scientific audiences, you can:

- Target life scientists and environmental scientists separately,

- Make an offer that directly appeals to each group of scientists, and

- Use very specific product benefits targeted to each group of scientists—messages that are appropriate for the very different applications each group would have for your product.

Yes, your direct marketing costs will be higher. By segmenting the audience and segmenting the messages, you have created two versions of something, but with mail, it is relatively easy to keep almost everything the same and change only the copy by printing an original and one or more versions on the same print run. In this example you would break the final mail file into two segments and mail the appropriate version to each of the segments.

Despite the increased cost, this kind of "micro-segmentation" will pay off in the long run. A direct mail piece that recognizes the individual needs of the target audience and speaks to those needs almost always pulls better than a piece that is more generalized. If you do not believe it, then test it yourself.

Program Strategies

The objective of this section is to provide you with a strategic framework for building effective business-to-business direct marketing programs—regardless of the products or services you are promoting. First, we will address some of the primary challenges you face in business-to-business direct marketing.

Piercing Business Screens

How do you break through? Getting through the business screen is becoming more and more difficult. With direct mail, you will have to get your piece through the mailroom (in larger companies), then through a potential administrative screener, and finally, to the top of the "read me" pile in the recipient's in-box.

Business-to-business direct mail tests generally support the use of first class mail as a first step in breaking through to the business prospect. First class mail travels faster and must be delivered "in a timely manner," according to U.S. Postal Service requirements. Standard mail (formerly known as third class, or bulk rate mail) has a lower priority, even though it travels at about half the price of first class. Just as important, first class mail tends to be delivered more frequently *within* larger businesses.

Delivery studies conducted by the Postal Service in cooperation with the Direct Marketing Association (DMA) indicate that first class mail is delivered more often, and faster, than standard mail. If you can afford it, go first class—or at the very least test it against standard mail to see the impact on deliverability and results.

Another good reason to use first class mail is the fact that it will often be forwarded or, if need be, returned to the sender if the address is bad. (In the industry, this is called a "nixie.") It is important to keep an eye on the nixie rate if you are using first class mail. An unusually high nixie rate means that the quality of the list(s) you are using is suspect.

Will a "live stamp" achieve better mail delivery? Yes and no. It probably would not make much difference to a corporate mailroom, but it could help getting the piece by an administrative assistant. Stamps attract the attention of the recipient because they are in the minority in business mail. Most mail has an indicia (a printed area in the upper right hand corner with permit information) or is metered.

What kinds of mailings break through? That depends. An envelope package with no promotional copy (called a "teaser") and an uppercase and lowercase address has the potential for breaking through to a senior management audience. Invitational formats and dimensional packages also seem to break through to this level. Self-mailing pieces and catalogs work well for mid-management, technical professionals, and below.

On the telemarketing side, voice mail makes it almost impossible to break through to managers, unless the telemarketer gets lucky.

Finding the Right Audience

Identifying the right audience in the first place is no easy task. Later, we will talk about the numerous business list sources that are available for use. As previously mentioned, segmenting a list into identifiable audiences and targeting those individuals with carefully constructed offers and audience-appropriate copy and graphics will generally pay off in higher response.

Executing Cost-Effective Direct Marketing Campaigns

Telemarketing and direct mail are not inexpensive. An average outbound telemarketing call to a prospect (when you finally get the prospect on the phone) can typically cost from $7 to $15. A typical direct mail piece, based on its complexity, quantity, and postage, can typically cost $1 to $5 or more.

Despite these seemingly high costs, both media compare very favorably to a single cold call made by a salesperson, which can cost upward of $350 per visit, when all costs are considered. Nevertheless, executing cost-effective direct marketing campaigns is a challenge that requires careful management and control.

Leveraging Other Marketing Efforts

For direct marketing programs to have the highest impact, they cannot work in a vacuum. It is important to tie direct marketing to other media and get the most out of media synergy and integration—whether it is public relations, advertising, or event marketing.

Meeting Sales Goals

The majority of business-to-business direct marketing is lead generation. The direct marketing is designed to generate and often qualify leads for a sales organization. Business-to-business direct marketers often have a huge responsibility to feed good leads to sales offices and channel partners, sometimes on a worldwide basis. They need to ensure that their efforts are working—so they need programs to be constantly monitored and sales managers to assist with feedback from the field.

Establishing Objectives

You can start to meet all of these challenges by first establishing some basic direct marketing objectives. Anchor your program by answering the following three questions:

1. *Which businesses* do you wish to penetrate?

2. *Which individuals* in those businesses are you trying to reach?

3. *What actions* do you want those individuals to take?

Be sure to answer these basic questions for each and every direct marketing effort. Then use the following sample statements to set both your *general* and *specific* direct marketing objectives for every program.

Your general objectives should be stated this way—

"My objective is to generate qualified leads."

"My objective is to generate orders."

"My objective is to upgrade customers."

"My objective is to get past customers to buy again."

Your specific objectives should be stated this way—

"My objective is to generate a 3 percent response rate, with 30 percent of the responses generated defined as qualified leads."

"My objective is to generate 25 orders, each with an average value of $25,000."

"My objective is to get 20 percent of the customer base to upgrade their purchase."

"My objective is to reactivate 50 customers within three months."

The Marketing Pyramid

With your general and specific objectives in mind, you can now formulate your direct marketing program strategy. To help you do this, we use the *marketing pyramid*. The marketing pyramid is a flexible tool that you can use to help set program strategies. We will use it here to break an audience into specific, defined segments. This particular marketing pyramid (Figure 1.1) represents a total "audience universe," combining customers, prospects, and suspects.

As you recall, "suspects" are individuals whom you suspect may be interested in your product. "Unqualified prospects" have expressed an interest; "qualified" prospects have passed through your qualification screen. "Past customers" did business with you previously, but are now dormant; "customers" do business with you now.

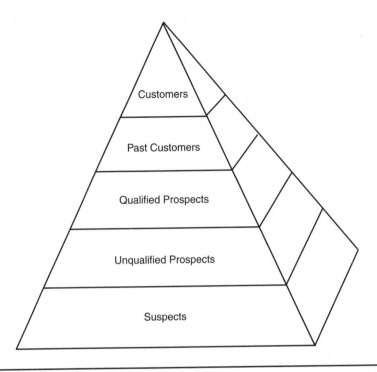

Figure 1.1. The marketing pyramid.

Notice that the pyramid is broadest at its base and gets smaller as it reaches the top. Each segment of the pyramid gets smaller as you progress upward. The size of each segment, though, is *opposite* to its importance. In other words, "suspects" is the least important segment, and "customers" is the most important segment. As you look at this pyramid, think in terms of your own company's prospects or customers. Imagine what the make-up of each segment might be.

Now think about how you might *interpret the pyramid* if it consisted of prospects only. Perhaps your bottom segment would be "unqualified prospects." Your next segment progressing upward might be "prospects with a long-term interest," and the very top of the pyramid might be "hot prospects ready to close."

You can also interpret the pyramid in terms of your customer base. The bottom of the pyramid could be, for example, one-time buyers, and the very top of the pyramid could be customers who buy numerous products from you with great frequency.

Putting the Marketing Pyramid to Use

Following is another marketing pyramid (Figure 1.2), but this time it is representative of a hypothetical software company's customer base. Take a moment to read the description of each lettered segment accompanying the pyramid.

Software Company's Customer Base

A: Purchasers of a site license of the customized version of the software product, running on a minicomputer, using four to six applications. These purchasers have also signed a service and support agreement.

B: Purchasers of a single copy of the customized version of the software product, running on a minicomputer, using up to three applications. No service and support agreement.

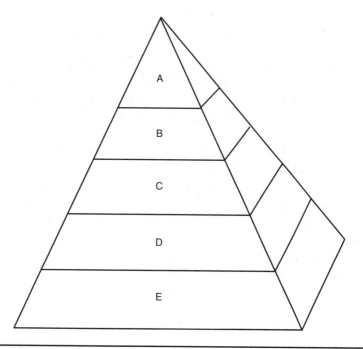

Figure 1.2. Marketing pyramid.

C: Purchasers of a single copy of the noncustomized version of the software product, running on a minicomputer, using only one application. No service and support agreement.

D: Purchasers of multiple copies of the PC version of the basic product.

E: Purchasers of a single copy of the PC version of the basic product.

What do you notice about this pyramid? Going in reverse order, as you progress up the pyramid from E to A, the segments get smaller. More important, *they increase in terms of their value* to the software company.

By the time you get to the top of the pyramid, see what happens to the customer relationship? The relationship the company has with the customer in segment A has *intensified* significantly and become worth much more to the company. As you would expect, the individual customer at the top of the pyramid is of higher value than the customer at the very bottom of the pyramid, not only in terms of products and services purchased, but also in loyalty and longevity.

Now please try an exercise so you can see how the marketing pyramid applies to your own needs. Figure 1.3 shows the same marketing pyramid we just reviewed, only this time, the segment descriptions accompanying the pyramid are blank. Make a copy of the blank pyramid and fill in your own segment descriptions on the lines, using what you know about your own company's customer base. Use any definable criteria you wish that applies to customers—products purchased, amount of purchase, recency of purchase, frequency of purchase, and so on, but use as many definable criteria as possible in each segment so that you are really describing the relationship the customer has with your company. Build the pyramid so that, from bottom to top, the relationship intensifies. You should end up with your most valued customers at the top of the pyramid. (If you prefer, you can do this exercise with prospects instead of customers.) Please complete this exercise now.

Your Segment Descriptions

A: _____

_____

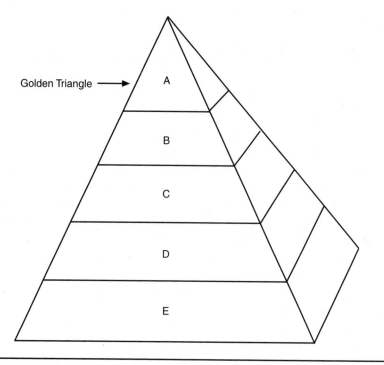

Figure 1.3. The Golden Triangle.

B: _____

_____

C: _____

_____

D: _____

_____

E: _____

_____

Take a good look at your marketing pyramid and reread each segment description. Now get a highlighter—any kind will do—and highlight segment "A" in the pyramid itself. That is right, just color in the little triangle at the top of the pyramid. That little triangle is your *Golden Triangle*. It represents a gold mine for your company, because it is the very top of your customer base.

In many organizations, the Golden Triangle is equal to about 20 percent of the total customer base. This follows the "80/20 Rule," or Pareto's Principle, which states that 20 percent of your customer base is of greater value than the other 80 percent. In some companies, 20 percent of the customer base also causes 80 percent of the problems!

The percentages themselves are not as important as the concept of disproportionate segment value. The 80/20 Rule works for most companies in relative terms. That means that a much smaller portion of your customer base tends to be of greater value than the rest of the customer base. Segmenting your customers using the marketing pyramid makes that fact apparent.

Now ask yourself this: Does your company do anything *differently* with those more valuable customers in the Golden Triangle? Do you communicate more frequently with them, for example, do you have a special newsletter for them, or do you give them preferential treatment, such as a frequent buyer program? In other words, is your company mining the gold? You might be surprised to learn that many companies do not treat their very best customers in a different way at all. Maybe your company is one of them.

Another Use for the Marketing Pyramid

Here is another interesting fact to consider about your marketing pyramid. If you can segment your customer base or your prospect base, you can also *prioritize* the audience by segments. The marketing pyramid forces you to think hierarchically—D will have a higher priority than E, C will have a higher priority than D, and so on. After you prioritize your audience segments, you can build an entirely segmented direct marketing program. You can actually base the intensity of your direct marketing activity on the priority of the segment.

For example, the software company used to illustrate the pyramid concept may want to structure a customer communications program that calls for two newsletters with a special editorial slant on PCs sent to segments D and E on an annual basis. However, the company would be wise to invest in a special newsletter that focuses on minicomputers and send it four times a year to segments A, B, and C. Also, the company may want to include a personalized letter only to the customers in segment A with each issue of that newsletter. Maybe the company can offer something special to segment A in that letter. After all, segment A is the *Golden Triangle*. This is direct marketing at its best—building a program that takes strategic advantage of audience segmentation.

Now that you have experimented with the marketing pyramid, use it again and again as your own "secret tool" to segment audiences and develop more effective program strategies that address those segments. Based on your own segmentation scheme, you could vary your direct marketing program in intensity to fit with the levels of the pyramid. The marketing pyramid provides you with an easy way to help you think programmatically—and keep your program strategies on track.

One last point: Remember the first marketing pyramid—the one with the combination of suspects, prospects, and customers? If you turn it upside down and slice off its top, it turns into something else (Figure 1.4). This is more than merely an upside down marketing pyramid. Now it is a *marketing funnel*. Here is the way it works....

You throw suspects in the top...

...shake them down until they become prospects...

...develop a qualification process to push them down the funnel...

...get those top prospects ready for being contacted by your sales force...

...and presto...

...that is when customers drop out at the bottom!

Audience and Media

Formulas exist in direct marketing to establish basic principles. When a formula is used repeatedly, you can be reasonably confident that it works—over and over again. One of those often-used formulas is the

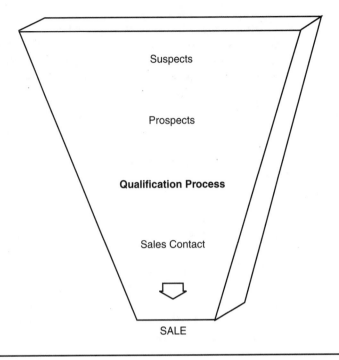

Figure 1.4. The marketing funnel.

40/40/20 Formula (Figure 1.5). This formula expresses the relative impact of audience, offer, and creative on the success of a direct marketing program. It suggests that audience and offer are of equal importance and the creative is of lesser importance.

The percentages themselves are a subject of debate among some direct marketers. Personally, I think audience is more important than offer, because if you are not targeting the right audience, nothing else matters, and although offer is undoubtedly second only to audience, in my experience, I have found that the format or creative approach are often the swing factors. Increasingly, the creative plays the role of attracting the attention of the audience and getting the direct marketing noticed in the first place, so although the offer itself is crucial, it may never get noticed if the creative does not do its job well.

We will address offer and creative in the next two sections, but with the assumption that audience is still Number One, we will examine the audience factor first.

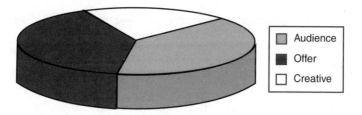

Figure 1.5. The 40/40/20 Formula.

The Consumer with an In-Box

The recipient of your direct marketing is a "consumer" like any other. The big difference is that this person is a consumer in a business setting—with different responsibilities in his or her *"business life."*

In consumer direct marketing, we first look at *demographics*—attributes such as a consumer's gender, age, income, and where the consumer lives. Business attributes are different. The demographics of business include, the:

- Individual's functional area/job title,

- Individual's purchasing authority/influence,

- Individual's department and department size, and

- Company size and type.

Three Key Audience Strategies

There are three important audience strategies you should consider when you design direct marketing programs:

1. Micro-Segmentation

Business-to-business direct marketers have discovered that there is no such thing as a single audience for their products or services. Rather, there are numerous audience segments—each of which has separate and distinct needs.

Micro-segmentation is the process of breaking an audience into finely defined segments and then targeting those segments with appropriate offers and messages. As demonstrated earlier with the marketing pyramid, an audience can be subdivided into distinct segments, using value-based criteria to distinguish one segment from another. Then direct marketing activity can be keyed to each of those individual segments.

2. Cross-Functional Direct Marketing

In the context of the typical business organization, buying decisions, especially for products over a few thousand dollars, are today made by groups of individuals. As a result, direct marketers increasingly need to extend the reach of their programs to different functional areas within an organization, and perhaps even different levels within a functional area.

There are multiple buyers and influencers in any organization who play a role in the buying decision. You may know with reasonable certainty who your primary target is, but secondary targets can be just as important to reach. You may have to reach business buyers and influencers in three basic management areas:

- General management—CEO, COO, president, general manager

- Financial management—CFO, controller, purchasing manager

- Functional management—Marketing, sales, IT, HR

Audience situations can be far more complex than that, however. For example, if you market information technology products, you may also have to reach technology buyers and influencers:

- Senior management—CIO, VP

- Mid-level management—Director, manager

- Technical management/end user—Engineer, programmer, software developer

One of the primary objectives in reaching multiple levels is to create widespread awareness for your product or service. Ideally, your direct marketing promotion will spur "cross-talk" among various employees. In fact, you can design direct mail to actually *create* that cross-talk. Here are two examples of how to accomplish this:

- Mail to one manager and include an additional piece in the envelope. Ask the recipient to pass along the additional piece to another colleague who might be interested.

- Send a mailing package to two or more managers in the same company and reference each of them in the letter copy, or include their names in a "CC" notation at the bottom of the letter.

3. Relationship Direct Marketing

Individuals in a business are not always ready to buy products or services when you are ready to sell them. Factors you cannot control, such as the company's budgeting process, the need for additional approvals, or purchasing procedures, may have a direct impact on plans to purchase. There may be a casual interest in the product, but not an immediate need.

The smart business-to-business direct marketer compensates for this uncertainty by making sure to be in front of prospects *periodically*— with a program of regular, ongoing communications (often called a continuity program). This is important for a number of reasons:

- It provides numerous opportunities for the prospect to respond at different times—when the prospect is ready to do so. There is evidence that, if a prospect is interested in a product but does not need it immediately, he or she will retain the mailing piece for future reference. It is not unusual for a direct marketer to receive a reply card from a campaign mailed to prospects or customers months or sometimes even years earlier.

- It builds awareness so that the prospect may already have the product or service in mind when a purchase decision is reached.

- It encourages pass-along by the prospect to other levels within a prospect's functional area, and to functional areas other than the prospect's area.

- It provides opportunities to reach new individuals who may take over the prospect's job—not insignificant, given the high turnover in many business positions today.

- It offers yet another marketing opportunity should the prospect move on to another company where he or she may be in a position to influence a purchase.

Audience Strategy and Mailing Lists

Audience strategy drives the process of evaluating and selecting mailing lists. As you may know, there are three basic kinds of lists:

1. *Your House List.* The house list is typically made up of customer and prospect names collected via a variety of methods: input from the sales force, trade shows, leads from various media, and so on.

   The house list should be segmented into customers and prospects, with further segmentation of each based on criteria available on the list. Ideally, the customer list will be further broken down using value-based criteria, such as RFM data (Recency, Frequency, and Monetary value). Prospect lists should be subclassified into segments based on their likelihood to purchase: A, B, C, D, or Hot, Warm, Cold.

   House lists can be a company's best-performing lists—*if* they are properly structured and segmented, and scrupulously maintained.

2. *Response Lists.* These are lists with names of individuals who have demonstrated a propensity to respond. Typical response lists include subscriber, buyer, and member lists.

3. *Compiled Lists.* These lists are compiled from a variety of sources, including telephone directories.

Conventional list wisdom used to rank response lists above compiled lists in terms of being most effective in generating response. Although this is still true in most cases, the business-to-business list world now has available some interesting hybrid lists that combine the best qualities of response and compiled lists. These lists often include additional data, usually acquired via telemarketing surveys, which make them more valuable to marketers.

Tens of thousands of business-to-business mailing lists, telephone number lists, and now e-mail lists are available. You should carefully evaluate all types of lists with target audience segmentation criteria in mind. You begin the process by surveying all available lists and narrowing down the choices based on selectable criteria available on each list. Some lists are quickly eliminated because they do not have adequate criteria. After you make your selections, you order the lists and generally perform "merge/purge" data processing to eliminate the duplicates.

For the most part, lists are rented for use, not sold. You rent the names on the list for one-time usage. In some cases, you may want to obtain the names for multiple or unlimited usage, which can be negotiated. If a name responds, you own it. Otherwise, you cannot reuse the name without paying for it again. (List owners and managers seed rental lists with decoy names. It is both illegal and unethical to make unauthorized use of rental lists.) Typical business-to-business response lists rent for $175 to $250 per thousand names. There are additional charges of $5 to $10 per thousand names for selection criteria and keycoding.

The list review and acquisition process is not for the inexperienced or queasy. The business of lists can be bewildering. Because the ultimate success or failure of a direct mail campaign rests largely on the list sources, you may want to work with direct marketing agencies or others qualified in list segmentation and selection.

Using SICs to Select Lists

One of the most common means for selecting lists is using SIC codes. SIC stands for Standard Industrial Classification, a government-originated system that is a standard method of identifying business/industry types. The old SIC system, usually composed of four identifying numbers, has been enhanced by such vendors as Dun & Bradstreet to include six or even eight numbers. This permits much finer targeting for business-to-business direct marketers than ever before—and it makes available up to *15,000* different SICs.

By overlaying SICs with geographic data from MSAs (Metropolitan Statistical Areas) or SCFs (Postal Sectional Center Facilities), direct marketers can precisely target the type of company they want in the specific geographic location they want.

The big news on the horizon is that SICs are expected to be replaced by a new coding structure called NAICS (the North American Industry Classification System) in several years. NAICS will provide the business-to-business direct marketer with far greater detail in categories that are more relevant than SICs.

To some extent, adoption will be voluntary. Both systems are expected to coexist through the year 2000. With the United States, Canada, and Mexico cooperating on the implementation of NAICS, it is likely to become the new standard for business classification and will therefore be of great importance to direct marketers in the next century. Keep your eye on this development—the implications are enormous.

Limit Your Risk by List Testing

Testing is one of direct marketing's great differentiators. Although you can test many other things—media usage, offers, creative approaches, even types of postage—list testing is generally an experienced direct marketer's first priority.

Basically, list testing means selecting a test quantity from several different lists, coding each list for tracking purposes, and evaluating the results with the intent of reusing some lists, adding new lists, and potentially eliminating some lists. Again, this is something you should not "fool around" with—a direct marketing agency or experienced list broker can be a valuable ally when it comes to list testing.

Direct Marketing Media

Following are brief discussions of the basic media available to the business-to-business direct marketer.

Direct Mail

This consists of self-mailers, letter packages, collateral, postcard decks, and catalogs.

Self-Mailers

These include anything not mailed in an enclosure: postcards, flyers, multi-panels with tear-off reply cards, brochures, and "all-in-one" formats. Self-mailers are often used to generate leads and seminar attendance, and less often for order generation. They can also be used as the first part of a two-step approach (step 1: generate lead; step 2: fulfill lead).

Packages

These are still the most common form of direct mail, typically consisting of a letter, reply card/form, reply envelope, enclosure(s), and outside envelope. Lead generation packages tend to be "lighter," order generation packages "heavier" on information. Packages could also be dimensional to carry videotapes, sample products, demo disks, and so on, and they can be used as the first or second part of a two-step approach (see Self-Mailers). Packages vary greatly in size, contents, and creative approach.

Catalogs

These are multi-page, multi-product pieces that typically include all ordering information in one place. In the technology marketplace, catalogs are very common for selling software, some computer hardware, electronic components, accessories/supplies, and so on.

Telephone

The phone can be used in two primary ways: outbound and inbound. Inbound use can be further divided into 800 (advertiser-paid) and 900 (caller-paid) numbers. Inbound phone services are primarily used for taking leads and orders. "Natural" speech is preferable to scripting, but scripting is essential for message control. To develop leads you must get all basic information, including the source code, and qualify the prospects as much as possible. In taking orders you must get all credit card information, bill to/ship to addresses, and phone number. You should also get the source of the order and should be prepared to give out ordering information. Providing an order verification number is a good idea.

Outbound telephone communication can be used in a variety of ways, including taking surveys, qualifying leads, prompting customer or hot prospect orders, verifying names/addresses, and so on. Scripting and experienced telemarketers are essential.

Print Advertising

This category includes ads, Free Standing Inserts (FSIs), and blow-in/bind-in reply cards, which may provide coupons, 800 numbers, Web site addresses, and reader service numbers. It is magazine/journal advertising with a *direct response* objective and can be used for both lead generation and order generation. Print advertising is typically not as efficient as direct mail for quality lead generation because it is primarily an awareness medium, so it is more often used for low-dollar-item (under $200) order generation. Distinguishing features are long copy, heavy on benefits, an order coupon or accompanying bind-in reply, and an 800-telephone number.

Electronic or Interactive

Media used here include CDs and disks, fax/interactive fax, and the Internet: e-mail, newsgroups, user groups, and the World Wide Web. This, of course, is the focus of the book, so we won't go into any detail here.

Broadcast

This category includes radio, TV, video, and satellite/cable TV. Television has not traditionally been effective for business-to-business direct marketing because it is primarily an awareness medium, although targeted satellite and cable television may present better opportunities in the future. Radio is sometimes used to generate leads or orders. Video plays a role in direct marketing, primarily as fulfillment.

Other Media

Other media used for direct marketing include events (seminars, trade shows) and overnight deliveries.

Media Integration

In an ideal world, offers and creative messaging will be designed to "cross over" various media, and the media will be intelligently combined and integrated to give the direct marketer the most bang for the buck. You should consider utilizing more than one medium in an integrated fashion for several reasons:

- *A single medium is no longer adequate to break through to the typical business-to-business audience.* Today's business-to-business audiences are more sophisticated, busier than ever, and overwhelmed with promotional communications. As a result, if your offer and message are reinforced across several appropriate media, and effectively used in combination, you have a better chance of breaking through the clutter.

- *Integrating direct mail and telemarketing offers you a potent "one-two punch."* Utilizing direct mail and outbound telemarketing in particular has proven effective in numerous combinations, including the following:

  - **Call–Mail–Call:** Call first to prequalify or verify an important list of names. Follow with a primary direct mail piece. Follow up to a portion of the list with telemarketing.

  - **Mail–Mail–Call:** Mail a primary direct mail piece to a list. Follow up with another mailing a few weeks later. Follow up with a call to respondents and to select nonrespondents.

  - **Call–Mail–Call:** Call an important list to announce a mailing. Follow with a primary direct mail piece. Follow up with a call to respondents and select nonrespondents.

Telemarketing is also one of the most effective media for handling inbound responses.

- *Audience, offer, and creative strategies can be cost-effectively leveraged across numerous media.* If your core direct marketing strategies are sound, you can leverage your work across media. Do it effectively and you can spread your costs, achieve impact for your brand, and gain offer and message consistency throughout a campaign.

Later in this book, we will explore in depth how to integrate the Internet with other direct marketing media.

Offer Development

Second only to audience in importance is the offer. There are really two parts to the direct marketing offer...the underlying offer and the direct marketing or promotional offer.

The Underlying Offer

The underlying offer is composed of your company, your products, your services, and (more important) your target audience's perception of these things. It may be obvious, but the underlying offer can have a definite impact on the effectiveness of the promotional offer and therefore on results. For example, if a company or product has little or no awareness, the direct marketing will have to work extremely hard to do its job. Similarly, if the perception of the company is positive or negative, this can affect direct marketing results in a good or bad way.

The underlying offer is also a key differentiator in influencing the ultimate buying decision. Products or services and the companies behind them must have credibility with the prospective purchaser. Many years ago, there used to be a saying in the computer business: "You cannot get fired for buying IBM." The rationale was that, if something went wrong, the purchaser could at least say he or she had bought the product from the world's largest computer company. IBM undoubtedly leveraged that very powerful and credible position in the marketplace—even if their products were not always superior to others.

Today, that mentality in business is far more subtle—but it still exists. In business-to-business marketing, the purchaser is looking for reasons *not* to buy. After all, the wrong purchasing decision can potentially jeopardize an individual's performance or credibility on the job. That is why it is very important to build a case in your direct marketing that helps to remove any doubt about your company and your product or service. You must be able to assure prospects that they take no risk when they consider purchasing from you.

One powerful way to build credibility is to let others do it for you. A commonly used technique that works repeatedly in this regard is the testimonial or case study. Companies always seem to achieve better than average results when they have good, solid success stories with names of customers who can be referenced. Another way to build credibility is to use statements, white papers, benchmark reports, or mentions of industry awards from objective analysts, journalists, publications, or industry experts.

The Direct Marketing or Promotional Offer

The promotional offer is what you, the advertiser, are willing to give to the target audience to elicit a response. The promotional offer is critically important in business-to-business direct marketing today, because it helps to differentiate your product or service from everyone else's. The reality is that your direct marketing heavily competes not just with other direct marketing, but with other advertising and promotional media for products and services which may be the same or similar to yours. It often takes a compelling offer for your product or service to stand out from this crowded field.

Strong promotional offers embody differentiation and call positive attention to your product or service. Offers that work the best have high-perceived value to the prospect. That means there is something irresistible about the offer—something that motivates the prospect to take action—either to inquire, or to make an immediate buying decision.

Remember the 40/40/20 Formula? If you agree that offer is second only to audience in importance, you need to find ways to develop high-value offers that relate to the target audience—and elicit a high-quality response.

Basic Rules for Offer Development

- *Your offer should be directly related to your direct marketing objective.* The promotional offer changes based on two basic direct marketing objectives: lead generation and order generation. In *lead generation*, the offer should be something of high-perceived value so that the prospect will want to respond and provide qualifying information to get the offer. If you want to generate qualified leads, offer something of specific value to the target audience that they really want to "buy" from you with "marketing currency"—the answers to questions you ask. The offer should be audience-appropriate (a technical white paper is likely to be an appropriate offer for software developers, whereas a management book is probably a more appropriate offer for business executives). However, be careful. The offer should be related to your product or service, not something so general as a free T-shirt or a contest with valuable prizes, or you will get a lot of false positives, from people who just want your offer but are not good prospective buyers.

  Evidence of how your product or service performs in real situations with named customers tends to have high-perceived value as an offer. Testimonials from users in the form of case histories, before and after comparisons, or problem/solution success stories are desirable, especially if they demonstrate your product's superiority in the marketplace. Success stories will be stronger if you can get permission to reference specific customers and use their photos, quotes, and so on. An alternative is to use stories in which you disguise the identity of the customers, but these are not nearly as effective.

  Special reports, research studies, industry reports, market analyses, and white papers can be strong offers if they are positioned as objective, or better yet, if they are authored by outside objective consultants or industry experts. This type of offer tends to position the marketer as a leader in its field, willing to share information and educate the target audience.

A **comparative analysis** that provides a point-by-point comparison of your product or service, versus the competition, can be powerful if you are attacking a market leader. Ideally, such an analysis would include a cost-justification component that allows prospects to objectively determine for themselves that your product is the better value. This type of offer works well in a fill-in-the-blanks worksheet format, or as an interactive exercise on a disk, CD, or Web site. If you use this approach, be sure you can validate your claims.

Seminars or special events involve a specialized set of logistical and promotional requirements, but they do have a proven ability to attract qualified prospects. Event offers may include free seminars (typically half-day events with a top-notch agenda, guest speaker, and giveaway at the end), teleforums (a seminar held via telephone, often with a number of customers or guest speakers present), demo days (often tied in with a trade show), and virtual seminars (Web-based seminars; these will be discussed in detail later in the book).

In *order generation*, the offer must be compelling enough to turn a prospect into a customer or encourage another order from an existing customer. Order generation offers may include free trials (typically 30 days in length), price incentives, product add-ons, gifts, or other items to motivate purchase. These offers should also include all terms and conditions of purchase. A satisfaction or money-back guarantee has become almost a standard and necessary part of order generation. To succeed at generating orders, you must offer something that adds real value to the product. A deadline on the offer provides a strong incentive for the prospect to take action *now*.

- *Often, you already have lead-generating offers available to you without even knowing it.* For example, analyst or industry white papers, special reports, and benchmark studies are high-value offers. In fact, any information that is perceived to be objective is valuable. Analytical tools, such as checklists, electronic worksheets, and ROI analyses are valuable, and information packaged in an interesting way—

downloadable from the Web, on CD, on video, on an audio-tape—may be desirable, as long as the quality of the information is high.

Keep track of all the information available in your organization. Use the Internet to research other information that might be appropriate for use as a promotional offer. Build an "offer arsenal" of possible promotional offers that you have available for use over time.

You can sometimes take a "generic" offer and slant it to a specific target audience to make it seem to have higher value. For example, a white paper that might apply to all industries can easily be targeted to a specific audience simply by writing an industry-specific "wrapper" around it.

- *The value of the offer should increase based on the anticipated difficulty you will have in generating a response.* For example, if you are targeting a very high-level audience, a report authored by a well-known consulting group is preferable to a company-authored report. If you are trying to recapture a dormant customer's business, a limited-time, customer-only discount or package deal is probably desirable. You may find the offer idea chart shown in Figure 1.6 useful in developing your own direct marketing offers.

Offer Description Makes a Difference

Do not underestimate the power of the written word when it comes to successful offers. It is just as important to describe the promotional offer in benefit terms as it is to describe the product or service itself. The offer must sound like something the prospect "can't live without"—within reason, of course.

If the promotional offer is a special report, tantalize the prospect with what he or she will learn by reading it. If the offer is a free trial, build up the benefits of the product and highlight the risk-free nature of the offer. Promote the offer with strong, active words that make someone want to pick up the phone and ask for it right away. Use deadlines if appropriate, and always make the call to action prominent.

If You Want to Generate...	You Should Consider These Offers...
An unqualified lead	Free information without qualification questions
A qualified lead	Any of these with qualification questions required: free information, free gift, premium item, seminar, demo, sample, free trial, analysis, free book, newsletter subscription, etc. Offer could be front-end, back-end, or both (time limit recommended).
A new order	Gift upon purchase, discount, additional product, add-on service, multiple product discount, complementary product, extended warranty, satisfaction or money-back guarantee, easy payment terms, free shipping, buyer club, etc.
A repeat order	Same as for a new order, but more emphasis on continuing customer relationship; cross-selling, frequent buyer, etc.
An order from a former customer	Major incentive, such as deep discount, sweepstakes/contest, etc.

Figure 1.6. Offer idea chart.

Offers That *Don't* Work

Some business-to-business direct marketers simply do not spend enough time on developing an effective offer. Here are a few examples of offers that are doomed to fail.

The "If I Build It They Will Come" Offer

This is the most common offer—and it is really a non-offer. The business-to-business marketer assumes that the prospect knows all about the company and the product or service being promoted, and therefore makes a nebulous offer, something like "Send for free information." This offer does nothing to distinguish a product, nor does it work hard enough to attract prospects. It is a throwaway offer—and that is what most qualified prospects will do...throw it away.

The "Hey Isn't This Cool" Offer

This offer is just too cool for words—you know, a T-shirt, a baseball cap, a trendy mouse pad, a beach ball, whatever. The problem is, most of the time this kind of offer generates false positives—people who would love to have the gimmick, but have no real interest in the underlying offer (your product). This kind of promotional offer will typically generate a high response, but unless you carefully pre-select your audience and ask numerous qualifying questions, you will be spending a lot of money sending gifts to people who will never buy your product.

The "You Need a Law Degree to Figure It Out" Offer

This is the kind of offer that has so many strings attached, or is so complicated or convoluted, that the prospect is basically left scratching his head. If you are trying to generate an order, of course you have certain terms and conditions you need to convey, but if your primary objective is generating a lead, you should make it easy, easy, easy to take advantage of your offer.

Creative Execution

The 20 percent in the 40/40/20 Formula is the creative execution. It may be last in impact, but the creative is certainly first in impression. Increasingly, it is the creative product—the copy and graphics—that distinguishes a piece of direct mail or a direct response ad and makes it stand out from the crowd.

Formatting has reached a new level of sophistication. In direct mail, there is an ever-widening array of formats. Most of them continue to be variations on the basic self-mailer, envelope package, or catalog, but there seems to be an increasing use of odd-size pieces—oversized postcards, square mailers and packages, tubes and boxes—in an effort to penetrate the screen. Gimmickry such as pop-ups, sound chips, gift items, and posters is now used more often in business-to-business marketing in an attempt to heighten response.

Direct mail creative execution itself has become just as sophisticated, if not more so. There was a time when advertising was the "prettier" medium, but not any more. Full-color photography and illustration are commonplace, and excellent design is no longer foreign to business-to-business direct mail. Desktop publishing and stock artwork have contributed to the refinement of direct mail's look and feel.

To some extent, the impact of television and now the Internet have contributed to the creative product. Copy used to drive direct marketing execution, but this is no longer the case. Now the best direct marketing is a carefully coordinated combination of both copy and graphics—sometimes it is hard to tell where one ends and the other begins.

What distinguishes great direct marketing creative execution? Regardless of the medium used, you will find that effective business-to-business direct marketing creative work (copy and graphics) has a number of distinguishing characteristics:

- *Great creative is audience-appropriate.* The most effective direct marketing creative appeals to a specific target audience and is delivered through media to which that target audience responds. The copy and graphics are not developed, designed, and written for the marketer but rather for the prospect to whom the promotion is directed. This aspect of the creative work differentiates direct marketing from general advertising. Direct marketing creative tends to be less about the company and the product and more about what the company and product can do for the prospect. This creative spin could be a tough pill to swallow for some "corporate types" who are so protective of their corporate image that they forget they are addressing prospects. *Great direct marketing creative is really a very careful combination of conveying the appropriate corporate message in a way that is very appealing to the target audience* (not always an easy task).

- *Great creative keeps the focus on benefits.* In direct marketing, benefits (what the product does for the prospect or customer) are always stressed over features (what the product does). Look at the following examples of copy written about a software product that works with Windows 95: copy with a focus on features, "Windows 95-compatible, with integrated GUI"; copy with a focus on benefits, "Works seamlessly with Windows 95 so you can just load it and go, fast and easy. And everything's point and click, so it's a snap to learn and use."

Notice the difference? The first example simply details the features; the second example describes those features in such a way that the prospect can answer the question, "What's in it for me?" Although it is often a good idea to include both features and benefits, benefits should always take priority.

- *Great creative includes just enough detail.* It is important to convey some detail about a product or service without overwhelming the prospect—especially in lead generation. Too much detail and there would not be anything left for the prospect to ask for. Too little detail and the prospect would not have a good sense of the product—and might not inquire at all.

  In order generation, the opposite is true. When you are using direct marketing to sell direct, you need to provide *all* the detail necessary so that the prospect or customer can place an order.

- *Great creative includes a prominent call to action.* A direct response piece may have a handsome appearance, but its ultimate responsibility is to elicit a response. That means that the call to action must be easy to find. Good direct marketing makes the call to action prominent, sometimes repeating it. What action you want prospects or customers to take and how they should respond should be very clear.

  The most common call to action is still a physical reply form of some sort, typically a reply form or a business reply card that can be mailed or faxed. Offering multiple response paths tends to increase overall response. In terms of lead priority, phoned in responses tend to be the hottest leads, then faxed in responses, and then mailed in responses.

  However, the Internet is changing that dynamic. Web response paths, and to a lesser extent e-mail response paths, are surging in popularity, both with marketers and respondents. Industry experience suggests that the Web response path is second only to inbound telephone in generating quality leads.

Creative Work That Breaks Through

With direct mail and print advertising in particular, it has become more and more difficult to break through to the prospect. One reason is because of promotional clutter. Promotional clutter is at an all-time high. Now virtually every medium is being used to convey promotional messages, and all direct marketers pay a price in terms of diminishing response. Some of the typical promotional media a business manager has to face each day are shown in Figure 1.7.

With this kind of environment, creative execution that has the ability to break through is important. Direct marketing creative work must:

- **Have Impact.** The direct marketing should arrive in a "package" that is appropriate for the prospect or customer. Direct response advertising needs to stand out from the competition in a trade journal or newspaper to attract a reader's attention. Direct mail should be appropriate to the target audience: Mailing packages tend to work better with senior managers in larger organizations; self-mailers are fine for mid-level managers and below in larger organizations, and even for senior managers in small businesses.

- **Be Readable.** Regardless of the medium, the direct marketing should be readable. Short sentences and paragraphs are preferable. Copy should be crisp and clearly written. In general, type

Advertising: Newspaper
Advertising: Magazine
Direct Mail—External
Internal Mail/Memos
Telephone/Voice Mail
E-mail—External and Internal
World Wide Web
Fax Transmissions
Overnight Deliveries

Figure 1.7. Typical media impacting a business manager each day.

should be easy enough to read for an aging U.S. population; current demographics make it likely that part of most business-to-business audiences are in the over-40 age bracket.

- **Be Inviting.** Good direct marketing makes you feel as if you are being invited to take advantage of a great opportunity, often at no obligation or risk. The tone of the promotion should be non-threatening, friendly, and invitational.

- **Be Intriguing.** Creating a sense of excitement, or doing something unusual, is often necessary to break through promotional clutter. You can accomplish this by considering the use of high-impact graphics or photography, unique formats in direct mail such as dimensionals, and animated graphics in electronic media.

- **Be Compelling.** Do not forget that the ultimate objective of your direct marketing is to *get a response*. Everything about the direct marketing creative should work to that end, no matter what. Look at the direct marketing as a "greased chute": Imagine that every element of a mailing package, or every word of an ad or telemarketing script, is designed to push the prospect down a chute. The more compelling the creative, the more you have greased the chute—so the prospect moves faster and faster towards responding.

How to Write Winning Direct Marketing Copy

In the old days of direct marketing, copy was king. The copywriters called the shots; in fact, they often started in the business as salesmen and later translated their face-to-face selling arguments into lengthy direct response ad copy. Graphics were not nearly as important in these early days.

That has changed considerably with today's highly visual approach to advertising and promotion. In an era when technology has driven desktop publishing to new heights, photographic imagery and relatively sophisticated artwork have become common in most promotional media, and direct marketing has followed suit. Full color is almost a prerequisite, although direct marketers sometimes attempt to break through by using black and white as a contrasting differentiator.

There is no question that "look and feel" now plays a key role in the creative product. Whatever the graphic approach, however, the underlying importance of the core creative concept is the message itself—expressed in a *copy platform* that sets forth the selling argument and the basic content of the direct marketing. Without that, the direct marketing is little more than pretty pictures. In that context, here are seven tips to help you write winning direct marketing copy.

1. **Me, Not We.** Characteristic of winning direct marketing copy is the "me-to-you" correspondence style of writing. Great copy is really a conversation or dialogue between the writer and the reader. It engages the prospect in a copy web net of sorts—by weaving a story that ends in a strong, convincing reason to respond.

2. **You, You, You.** Perhaps the most important word in direct marketing is "You"—something the reader just cannot get enough of. Using "you" tells a prospect that it is him or her you care about—and forces you to focus on the prospect's real needs and desires.

3. **Write Like You Talk.** Excellent direct marketing copy has a certain informality to it. The copy is conversational, friendly, and easy to read—almost as if the writer is conversing with the reader. (Do not mistake this tip for poor writing—sloppy copy does not reflect well on the marketer!)

4. **Make the Complex Simple and Make the Simple Complex.** Your direct marketing may need to promote a product that is complex and involved or, alternatively, a product that is quite simple. A wonderful trick of direct marketing copy pros is to make complex products seem simple and simple products seem complex—merely by adjusting the copy. The former helps overcome product objections; the latter "romances" even the simplest of products—making both seem all the more desirable.

5. **Benefits Come First.** If you have a good grasp of the prospect's "pain," then you can turn it into a marketing gain—by showing how your product or service is of benefit in meeting the prospect's needs or solving the prospect's problem.

6. **Over—and Over—and Over Again.** Repetition is important in direct marketing copy because people tend to *scan* rather than read entire documents. Repeat important benefits, highlighting them with graphic techniques such as bullets, bold type, underlining, and color.

7. **Strong Open, Strong Close.** You have a few seconds to capture a reader's attention, so the opening salvo should be strong—whether it is teaser copy on an envelope, the first sentence of a letter, the headline of an ad, the start of a Web page, or the beginning of a telemarketing call. Just as important, the "close" must include a strong call to action to motivate the prospect to respond now.

Adjusting the Creative Execution to Different Media

Direct marketing creative execution should embody all of the qualities we have been talking about, but the creative output must be adjusted for different media.

Direct Mail

In direct mail, the creative execution must fit within a specific format. With a self-mailing format, the cover of the piece tends to contain the most compelling headline and graphic. The mailing panel is equally important, however, because it carries the recipient's name and address; it is therefore a good idea to put offer-related "teaser" copy on this portion of the self-mailer. Inside the self-mailer, copy and graphics typically must work around folds, flowing logically from panel to panel. It is a good idea to have boxed-in lists of bulleted benefits and, if appropriate, graphics with call-outs illustrating product benefits. Self-mailers often have tear-off reply cards, which should be both prominent and easy to complete and fax or mail.

A mailing package offers more creative flexibility than a self-mailer in that it has more elements: typically, an outside envelope or other carrier, a letter, a brochure or other kind of insert, and a reply device—a reply card, or a reply form with a reply envelope. Each of these elements is written and designed separately, but they must function together as a coordinated unit. Well-constructed mailing packages contain elements that effectively reinforce one another.

The catalog format offers the most creative flexibility because it has the most real estate. Here, each page is a separate element, sometimes functioning as part of a section and then as part of the whole. Effective catalog pages tend to be a well-organized, integrated combination of descriptive copy and supporting graphics. All ordering information must be clearly spelled out. The call to action should be prominent on each page, and the order form should be a focal point of the catalog.

Telephone

Creative execution for telemarketing is restricted to copywriting, but it is no less important. In fact, too many business-to-business direct marketers do not spend enough time carefully crafting outbound telemarketing scripts.

A telemarketing script should be written conversationally, but it should be a basic guide, never to be read verbatim by the telemarketer. Good telemarketers learn to deliver scripted copy in their own style so that it sounds natural and friendly. The telemarketer must be able to engage the listener immediately, so strong opening copy that gets right to the key benefit is advisable. Telemarketing copy must be short, yet packed with benefits. It should help guide the listener and encourage action.

Print Advertising

Print advertising has many of the qualities of direct mail creative execution, but the available space tends to be a challenge. Typically, a print ad is a full page or less in a trade journal or newspaper. The ad competes with numerous other ads in the same medium, as well as with the editorial content of the publication. Ad placement can be an important factor in the ad's overall effectiveness. In trade journals, bind-in reply cards can increase responsiveness, largely because the ads are easier to find when leafing through the magazine. The interrelationship between copy and graphics is of prime importance in print advertising. The ad must grab a reader's attention so that he or she stops turning the page, then engage the reader, and finally lead to a response.

Broadcast

Television is not yet a viable medium for business-to-business direct marketing. Direct response television typically targets consumers with longer commercials or infomercials on shopper channels or at nonpeak broadcast times. Television shows targeted to business are used primarily as vehicles for awareness advertising.

Radio, on the other hand, is used with increasing frequency as a direct response medium. Radio is very targetable in local markets, and costs are reasonable when compared to other media. "Drive time" on news stations in particular is known to be a good business-to-business buy. Copy for radio is akin to a print ad with no visual image—it must create a visual image or use compelling benefits to attract attention. Radio copy should make a strong informational offer, using a telephone number or Web site address repeated several times as the response path.

Electronic/Interactive Media

Electronic or interactive media presents the business-to-business direct marketer with the most exciting creative potential. There are three basic media, each with its own creative considerations: CD-ROMs, e-mail, and the World Wide Web. E-mail and the Web are Internet-based media. The CD-ROM medium offers opportunities to execute full-fledged multimedia promotions with scripted copy, music, and full-motion video. From a direct marketing perspective, CD-ROMs should incorporate plenty of interactivity and, if appropriate, facilitate response. CDs are also increasingly being used to "connect" to the Internet; for example, an electronic catalog can be housed on a CD and, through a link to a Web address, can be automatically updated. This technique gives the CD-ROM a longer shelf life and draws a prospect or customer to the marketer's Web site for additional information.

E-mail is currently a text-only medium, although "graphic e-mail" is on the horizon. The creative aspects of e-mail will be addressed later in this book.

The Web is certainly the interactive area receiving the most attention from direct marketers. Creatively, the Web combines the qualities of several direct marketing media, with some of its own unique ones. It is similar to direct mail in that it can accommodate integrated copy and graphics. Like broadcast and CD-ROM, the Web also facilitates the use of sound and multimedia, but the Web is unique in its construction and its instant interactivity—both of which require special creative considerations. You will find more about that later on as well.

Implementation and Analysis

All of the material in this chapter until now has provided the building blocks you need to develop sound strategies and execute effective business-to-business direct marketing programs. As a direct marketing practitioner, you soon realize that implementation is very much an ongoing, never-ending cycle of setting strategy, planning programs, executing projects, measuring and analyzing results, and starting all over again in an effort to do even better. Now you will see how you can continually improve and refine your direct marketing programs.

How to Build Your Marketing Database

Perhaps the area with the most "payback potential" is your house list—or what should be your marketing database. The house list usually starts as a simple name and address file of customers to which various prospect lists may be added over time. If the house list is intelligently segmented and scrupulously maintained, it can become the basis for a true marketing database—a list that is *enhanced with marketing intelligence* about each of the individuals on it.

Unfortunately, too many businesses fail to recognize the value of their house list and, as a result, it falls into general disrepair. In the business world, there could be any number of significant reasons for this:

- *The list has the wrong contacts.* For companies selling to larger businesses, the in-house "customer list" may actually be comprised of purchasing managers—the people who issue the purchase orders, not the *real* buyers, influencers, or decision-makers. That is because the list was originally built from "bill to" records—accounting data that is typically easier to get and more up-to-date than end-user information. You should be collecting the "ship to" contacts for direct marketing purposes. Your marketing and sales departments should work collaboratively to populate the in-house database with the names, titles, and addresses (which may be different from the corporate purchasing addresses) of the "real" end-user customers.

- *The list is actually many different lists.* The larger the company, the more likely it is that no centralized database of customers and prospects even exists; rather, a number of in-house lists are really spread across numerous company business groups, divisions, or subsidiaries—often worldwide. Even worse, these unique lists contain duplications and inconsistent data fields, and may even be maintained with different database programs. Sometimes, company politics perpetuates separate list sources. If this sounds like your organization, you should work toward centralizing the marketing database while allowing each separate organization its own usage rights.

- *The list is embarrassingly out of date.* The data turnover on a business list is frightening. Imagine how often employees come and go, or change titles, mail stops, and phone numbers, in larger organizations. Many companies simply cannot keep up with basic database maintenance. You should maintain origin dates of all records and check to make sure "old" data (which could be as little as six months old) is reviewed and updated. Communicate with customers and key prospects periodically and ask them to help you keep your list updated, and think twice before you try to handle list maintenance inside. You may be better off investing the money in outsourcing the data entry to protect the integrity of your valuable marketing resource.

- *The list cannot be segmented.* If you market your products or services to different audiences, you should collect the data necessary to identify and segment those audiences. A marketing database is not much of a database if it does not include meaningful criteria (such as job title, size of company, and SIC) that can be used to break the customer or prospect database into smaller segments and then can be targeted with appropriate messages. The marketing database should be designed to accommodate segmentation criteria, including customer value data (such as RFM, or Recency, Frequency, and Monetary value). Then you should accumulate, maintain, and utilize this data for marketing to customers and prospects.

- *The list is not being used often enough.* If the house list isn't being used as part of a regular, ongoing direct marketing program, the list is not performing to its maximum potential. Without regular use, the list is not being continuously cleaned and maintained, and vital data is not being added in selectable fields, and that means a valuable resource is being wasted.

Strategies for Better Databases

- *Profile customers first and use the customer profile to build a target prospect profile.* In direct marketing it is a known fact that, in many ways, your best prospects tend to mirror your best customers. That is why it often pays to profile your customers by using the data in your marketing database to analyze your customers' characteristics. Once you know what your customers "look like," you can then apply that profile to building a profile of target prospects.

- *Use outside sources to continually build your database.* View your marketing database as a "living" thing that needs to grow. You can use a variety of outside sources to build your list, starting with the most obvious source—current customer information provided by your sales and account service organizations. Then concentrate on the prospect portion of the database (keeping it separate from customers). Continually add to and "scrub" the prospect database by adding prospect lists from sales reps, trade show and seminar attendees, advertising and PR inquiries, direct marketing respondents, and so on. Always code each prospect so that you know the source.

- *Segment and prioritize the database.* Segment your database into meaningful audiences so that you can prioritize those audiences for direct marketing purposes. If possible, break customers into identifiable segments that represent their importance to your organization. Break prospects into "hot/warm/cold" categories based on purchasing criteria you establish.

- *Use the database as the core of your direct marketing programs.* After you have built and segmented your database, use it! The database should become the core of every direct marketing program—the central repository of marketing intelligence—the marketing resource that helps you identify your best customers and prospects.

Questions to Ask About *Outside* Databases/Lists

Because outside lists play such a crucial role in successful direct marketing, it is important to know what to ask about them. Use the following as a checklist of questions to ask when evaluating outside lists for usage in direct marketing programs.

- Does the list have—

  - accurate titles?

  - full addresses, including mail stops if available, suite numbers, ZIP codes?

  - phone numbers and fax numbers with area codes, if available?

  - e-mail addresses, if available?

- From which sources was the list built?

- How often is it updated?

- Will the list provider assure the accuracy of the list or guarantee deliverability?

- Are test quantities (generally a minimum of 5,000 records) available?

- How often is the list used, and by what kinds of marketers?

- What are the conditions of usage? (One time, unlimited, etc.)

- Are there any restrictions?

- Are tapes, disks, or labels available?

- Is keycoding available and at what cost?

- Which selects are available and at what cost?

- How long does it take to get the list?

- For e-mail lists, are the addresses all verified as "opt-in?"

- For multiple list databases, is duplicate elimination available and at what cost?

Why Direct Mail Still Works

There is growing concern among business-to-business direct marketers that direct mail is losing its effectiveness. Typical lead generation response rates tend to be in the 1½ percent to 4 percent range, and typical order generation response rates are usually below 1½ percent. Depending on the price point of your product or service, the audience you are targeting, and the quantity you are mailing, these response rates may not be enough to justify the investment.

That is why testing is critically important. Although there are upfront costs for creative and production, the unit cost of direct mail falls fairly dramatically as the quantity increases. It may be cost-effective to test direct mail in increments of 5,000 pieces to determine the impact of lists, offers, creative, format, or even timing and type of postage on direct mail response. A 5,000-piece quantity will yield statistically valid test results, although some direct marketers test with even smaller quantities.

A basic rule of thumb is to test one thing at a time so that you know which variable is affecting response. The goal is to build a "control"— a mailing that continues to be successful—and then test against the control until you beat it consistently and establish a new control. This is the scientific aspect of direct mail and is often neglected by the inexperienced business-to-business direct marketer, who does little if any testing on a regular basis.

Despite industry concerns, direct mail continues to rate near the top in terms of most effective media utilized by business-to-business direct marketers. This continues to be true even with the increasing usage of telemarketing, and the remarkably rapid growth of Internet marketing. Why?

Direct mail compares very favorably to other media costs. You can reach a prospect at a total cost that typically ranges from $1 to $5, versus $7 to $15 or more for an outbound telephone contact. Direct mail compares very favorably to direct selling—it typically costs at least $350 to make a single sales call to a single prospect. For marketers of complex, high-end products, it is not uncommon for the prospect to require multiple personal visits before a sale is made, so the cost of selling is more like three to five times the cost of a single sales call. Direct mail helps reduce that cost by pre-qualifying a prospect so that the salesperson can potentially reduce unproductive selling time.

Direct mail continues to be the medium with the most precision. Direct mail provides the following advantages. You can:

- **Segment** an audience by certain selection criteria,

- **Target** that audience very precisely with a specific offer and specific message,

- **Control** the communication—who gets it and when,

- **Test** variables to determine their impact on response,

- **Measure** and track the response by list source and by type of responder, and

- **Analyze** the results and compare them to previous mailings to improve ongoing direct mail efforts.

Nonetheless, e-mail is making very rapid gains in b-to-b, and might someday supplant direct mail as the preferred b-to-b direct marketing medium.

How Long Does Direct Mail Take?

Time frames vary based on the complexity of the mail program, the quantity produced, and the production methods used, but Figure 1.8 is a typical implementation time table.

The Ins and Outs of Postal Service Requirements

Any time you use direct mail, you need to be aware of the requirements established by the U.S. Postal Service—and there are many. It is suggested that you check with the U.S. Postal Service *(www.usps.gov)* regularly or consult a mail house for updated information regarding postal requirements. Here are just a few of the basics.

First Class Mail

First class mail is letter, flat, or postcard-size mail that travels at the established first class rate. Postcards are defined as a single piece with a minimum thickness requirement no larger than 4¼ inches high by 6 inches wide. Letter mail must be a maximum of 6¼ inches high by 11½ inches wide and 1 ounce or less to mail at the first class rate. If it is larger, then it is a "flat" and there will be a per piece surcharge. If it is over 1 ounce, additional postage rates will apply based on the number of ounces. If the piece does not fit into a height/width grid provided free of charge by the Postal Service, it is a size that cannot be automated and will therefore not only cost more but likely travel slower than mail that can be automated.

Task	Time
Plan, set objectives, identify market	1–2 weeks
Analyze/select lists, develop offer, define format	1–2 weeks
Execute creative work, order/receive lists	2 weeks
Order materials, execute list processing	2–3 weeks
Print production, mailing services	2–3 weeks
Total	8–12 weeks

Figure 1.8. Typical direct mail time table.

Standard Mail

Standard mail, formerly "third class" or "bulk rate" mail, has similar size requirements for letter and flat mail, but different rates apply.

Automation

A reclassification that began in July 1996 has continued to impact mailers ever since—mostly in a positive way. The U.S. Postal Service basically "pays" mailers for keeping their address files up to date, using 9-digit ZIP codes, presorting, and barcoding their mail. The more of the burden you take upon yourself, the cheaper it is to mail.

The Postal Service will provide assistance with address updating free of charge in some cases, but the smartest long-term strategy with any mailing list that you control and use on a regular basis is to care for it. The list should be continuously cleaned, updated, and formatted to take full advantage of the postal requirements. If it is feasible, the list should be appended with 9-digit ZIP codes and barcoding information. It should also be run against the NCOA (National Change of Address) file maintained by the Postal Service and implemented by approved mailhouses nationally.

When using outside lists, you should weigh the increased cost of data processing services related to NCOA, 9-digit ZIPs, and barcoding against the cost of mailing at the un-discounted postal rates. Whether you save money or not is often based on mailing quantities and the condition of the lists you use.

The newest advance in postal technology brings together postage and the Internet. In April 1998, the U.S. Postal Service tested and licensed computer-generated postage that can be purchased online and then printed directly onto envelopes. And in early 1999, the Postal Service also tested its own brand of Internet innovation: "PostOffice Online" (www.postofficeonline.com). This new program, targeted to small businesses, features the ability to generate shipping labels, pay for postage on packages, and arrange for package pick-up, all online. In addition, PostOffice Online allows a mailpiece to be created online, sent electronically to a USPS-approved printer, and mailed directly to a mailing list, all via the Internet.

Implementing Media Integration

Today, experienced business-to-business direct marketers utilize a combination of media to maximize the power of direct marketing and achieve superior results. The accompanying table (Figure 1.9) depicts a direct marketing media integration plan.

Explanation of the Media Integration Plan

1. Direct mail and print advertising are utilized to generate leads.

2. *Response* comes in via reply mail, inbound phone calls to an 800 number, faxes of the reply device, e-mail inquiries, or through a Web response form at a special URL, or Web address.

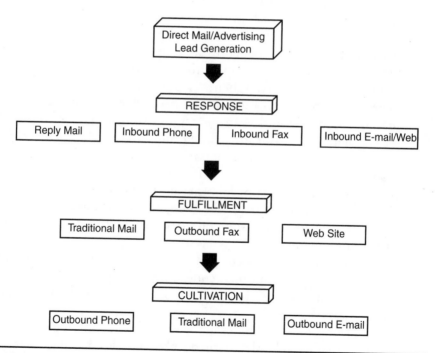

Figure 1.9. Media integration chart.

3. *Fulfillment* takes place using traditional direct mail or outbound fax, or the respondent can be fulfilled instantly by receiving information and/or the offer at the Web site.

4. The respondent's name, address, phone number, e-mail address, and answers to qualifying questions are collected at the response stage and used to initiate a *cultivation* process, which uses outbound telemarketing, traditional mail, and outbound e-mail to periodically contact and requalify the prospect.

How to Make Lead Programs Accountable

Tracking response and analyzing results is ultimately what makes business-to-business direct marketing accountable. In a sense, order generation programs are easier to analyze than lead generation programs—they either generate sales or they do not.

Tracking begins with the most basic of techniques: coding. All list sources should be coded by assigning a "source code"—a unique identifier of letters or numbers for each list source—so that you can track response by list. Whenever possible, the list code should appear on a direct mail reply form or card. Based on the production method used, the code can be printed somewhere on the reply device, generated onto it, or printed onto a label that is affixed to the reply device or to the mailing panel as a peel-off label. A majority of respondents tend to use peel-off labels, but it is always a good idea to include a line of copy instructing them to do so. Telemarketers should be trained to ask for the code, and Web response forms should have an area in which the code can be entered or selected from a drop-down menu.

A tracking code can contain other identifying data. For example, you could include additional codes that track geographical area, company size, industry, job title, and so on if you select your lists utilizing such criteria.

Some in-house databases may use unique identifying codes for each record, either a randomly assigned alphanumeric code or a "match code" based on pieces of data from name and address, assembled in a unique way. These kinds of codes will tell you who responded from a house file, but you would have to relate the respondent's record back to the original database to gather tracking data for a particular mailing.

Lead generation programs can be difficult to track. You inevitably receive responses that are not identifiable (sometimes called "white mail"). Furthermore, even though you may have a handle on the exact number of leads and the quality of leads generated, tracking them through to the sale often requires the cooperation of a telesales, direct sales, or channel partner organization.

This is essential, because what appears to be a successful lead generation effort may not be. Generating a high quantity of inquiries, for example, may look good, but if those leads are largely of low quality, then the program was probably a failure. Only by sending those inquiries through a lead screening process, and then sending the resulting qualified leads through a prospect qualification process, can you ascertain whether or not the lead program was truly successful.

That kind of analysis means that the direct marketer needs information that often goes beyond the responsibility of direct marketing alone—into the area of sales conversion. Assuring *total trackability* from point of inquiry through conversion to sale is a goal every direct marketer should strive for. This means you will need at least two things:

1. A closed loop system. Ideally, you will have a "closed loop system" that gives you the ability to track a prospect from the point of inquiry, through the various stages of prospect qualification, through the contacts made by the sales organization, and ultimately to the point of sale. Your marketing database can be the central repository of contact information in the process, but you must establish a full-circle system that provides checkpoints and mechanisms so you can effectively track progress each step of the way.

2. *Full cooperation from the sales organization.* Not even the best closed-loop system will work without the full cooperation of your sales organization and channel partners. Most tracking systems break down when the lead leaves the marketing area. Sales organizations are neither motivated nor compensated to

keep marketing updated on leads followed up on or the progress of prospects. It is therefore important for senior marketing and sales management to *work together* so everyone in the organization understands the importance of conversion to sale information in analyzing the effectiveness of direct marketing.

This concludes the Business-to-Business Direct Marketing "Crash Course." Entire books have been written on the subject, so only the highlights were covered here, but the content is essential background as you move forward into the world of business-to-business Internet direct marketing.

As you will see in subsequent chapters of this book, much of what is "hot" about the Internet involves interactivity, online response and fulfillment, and database-driven customization. These concepts will sound familiar to you, because they all come from the world of direct marketing.

Useful Tools

The accompanying checklists and worksheets (Figures 1.10 to 1.14) are self-explanatory. They will be helpful in constructing and measuring any direct marketing program.

Notes

1. Bob Stone, *Successful Direct Marketing Methods*, 6th Edition, 1996, NTC Business Books, Lincolnwood, IL.

Audience Checklist

Purpose of this checklist: to facilitate the audience list selection process.
Specifically describe your target audience here:

_____

_____

_____

_____

_____

_____

_____

	YES	NO
House list will be used	❏	❏
Customers will be suppressed	❏	❏
Competitors will be suppressed	❏	❏
Outside lists will be used	❏	❏

Criteria to be considered for selecting lists, if available:

Company

	YES	NO
Company size (sales or number of employees)	❏	❏
Company type (SIC or other industry select)	❏	❏
Geographic location	❏	❏
Headquarters vs. branch offices	❏	❏

Other specific company criteria (list):

	YES	NO
_____	❏	❏
_____	❏	❏
_____	❏	❏

Individual

	YES	NO
Job title	❏	❏
Functional area	❏	❏
Purchasing authority for product/service being promoted	❏	❏
Budget available for purchase	❏	❏
Purchase timeframe	❏	❏

Other specific individual criteria (list):

	YES	NO
_____	❏	❏
_____	❏	❏

Figure 1.10. Audience checklist.

Offer Checklist

Purpose of this checklist: to help determine potential appropriate offers.

Indicate whether or not you have any of the following available, or can acquire any of the following, to be used as direct marketing offers

	YES	NO
Information of high perceived value	❏	❏

Describe: _____

_____

Analysis or analytical tool	❏	❏

Describe: _____

_____

Product demonstration	❏	❏

Describe: _____

_____

Free product trial	❏	❏

Describe: _____

_____

Seminar	❏	❏

Describe: _____

_____

Premium incentive (gift or promotional item)	❏	❏

Describe: _____

_____

Purchase incentive (incentive offer to buy product)	❏	❏

Describe: _____

_____

Other possible offer(s):

_____

_____

_____

_____

Figure 1.11.   Offer checklist.

Copy Worksheet

Purpose of this worksheet: to help identify key points in developing direct marketing copy.

1. Briefly describe your product or service.

   _____

   _____

   _____

2. List up to 5 key benefits of your product or service.

   (Benefits indicate what value the prospect derives from using your product or what problems the product solves.)

   1. _____

   2. _____

   3. _____

   4. _____

   5. _____

3. List any unique benefits that distinguish your product or service from its competition.

   1. _____

   2. _____

   3. _____

4. List any differentiating benefits the prospect will derive from doing business with your company (service, technical support, training, etc.).

   1. _____

   2. _____

   3. _____

Figure 1.12. Copy worksheet.

Program Measurement Worksheet

Purpose of this worksheet: to help you measure program results.

How to use this worksheet: Fill in all information for a specific program to measure leads generated, cost per lead, and conversion to sales. Transfer response information from the Response Summary Worksheet. If you have made projections, compare them with actual program results and calculate the variance.

Program name: _____   Date: _____

Period covered from: _____   to: _____

	Projected	Actual	Variance
Program cost	_____	_____	_____
Number of contacts made or pieces mailed	_____	_____	_____
Cost per individual contact or piece	_____	_____	_____
Number of responses received	_____	_____	_____
Cost per response	_____	_____	_____
Percentage of response (response rate)	_____	_____	_____
Number of hot leads	_____	_____	_____
Hot lead percentage of total responses	_____	_____	_____
Number of warm leads	_____	_____	_____
Warm lead percentage of total responses	_____	_____	_____
Number of cool leads	_____	_____	_____
Cool lead percentage of total responses	_____	_____	_____
Number of leads converted to sales	_____	_____	_____
Percentage of conversion (conversion rate)	_____	_____	_____
Revenue generated from converted leads	_____	_____	_____
ROI (revenue marketing cost=X:$1.00)	_____	_____	_____

Figure 1.13. Program measurement worksheet.

Response Summary Worksheet

Purpose of this worksheet: to summarize direct mail response on a daily, weekly, monthly, quarterly, or annual basis.

Program name: _____   Date: _____

Program mail date: _____

Period covered from: _____   to: _____

Number of contacts made or pieces mailed   _____

Number of responses received   _____

Percentage of response (response rate)   _____

Number of hot leads   _____

Hot lead percentage of total responses   _____

Number of warm leads   _____

Warm lead percentage of total responses   _____

Number of cool leads   _____

Cool lead percentage of total responses   _____

Number of leads converted to sales   _____

Percentage of conversion (conversion rate)   _____

Figure 1.14.   Response summary worksheet.

2

The Age of the "e"

The "e" is everywhere. It has overtaken the English language and found its way into our everyday conversation. Companies are renaming themselves to include the "e." Ways of doing business are today not in favor if they are not e-enabled. E-marketing is just one component of the massive rush to e-business.

It is clear that the issue is not that the Internet has fundamentally changed business, and marketing, forever. Now the issue is, how will businesses and marketing organizations re-engineer themselves to survive and thrive in the new Age of the "e."

In this chapter and throughout the book, you will see statistics regarding Internet usage, e-business and business-to-business e-commerce that are changing so quickly they will be out of date by the time you read this sentence. In fact, there are now Web sites, such as *www.statmarket.com*, which track Internet statistics daily. Some of these statistics are staggering. For example, various sources have reported that the Web housed over 6 million sites by mid-2000, with over 250,000 sites being added *monthly*. A January 2000 survey conducted by Inktomi (*www.inktomi.com*) and the NEC Research Institute indicated that there are at least 1 billion unique Web pages in existence. More than 86 percent of them are in English.

IDC (*www.idc.com*), a leading IT research firm, said one-third of the U.S. households had an Internet connection, and half of them made a purchase online by the end of 1999. On the business side, IDC said that U.S. corporate spending on Internet-related technology reached $85 billion by the end of 1999, and would grow to $282 billion by the year 2003, a 50 percent compound annual growth rate. IDC predicted that some industries' Internet spending would grow even faster from 1998 to 2003; for example, transportation is expected to invest in Internet technology at a compound annual growth rate of over 70 percent.

Results of a study conducted by the University of Texas and released by Cisco Systems in June 1999 indicated that the Internet generated over $300 billion in the United States in 1998 and was responsible for 1.2 million jobs. According to the study, the Internet economy ranks with industries such as telecommunications ($270 billion) and automobiles ($350 billion) and is now one of the top 20 economies in the world.

A mid-2000 study by market research firm eTForecasts (*www.etforecasts.com*) indicated that Internet usage would increase by 100 million by the end of 2000, for a total of some 375 million users worldwide. Research by ACNielsen (*www.acnielsen.com*) in 2000 indicated that 64 percent of Americans age 12 or older used the Internet in 1999, and 31 percent of these users were online every day.

A study released in May 2000 by Jupiter Communications (*www.jup.com*) predicted the commercial e-mail market would reach $7.3 billion by 2005, and consumers would feel the effect, as e-mail volume would increase forty times. A June 2000 report by Jupiter forecasts $6 trillion in online trade in the U.S. b-to-b market by 2005. From 2000 to 2005, b-to-b online industrial commerce will increase by twenty times, says Jupiter.

Forrester Research (*www.forrester.com*) and The Yankee Group (*www.yankeegroup.com*) both predict b-to-b e-commerce will reach $2.7 trillion in 2004. The Gartner Group (*www.gartnergroup.com*) predicts a b-to-b e-market that could grow to over $7 trillion in 2004.

Even Internet domain names have become big business. In January 1999, for example, it was reported that a domain name sold for $10 million. Check out GreatDomains (*www.greatdomains.com*) and see for yourself how this marketplace is unfolding.

There is no hesitation today to embrace the Internet as the definitive way to re-engineer network infrastructures and extend the enterprise. Even entirely new businesses, "dot coms," are being built around it.

The Internet is dramatically re-shaping traditional businesses as well. America Online's blockbuster merger deal with Time Warner is just one example. The anti-trust case against Microsoft by the U.S. Government is another. While it was focused on Microsoft's competitive practices, the case was largely concerned with the company's tactic of embedding the Microsoft Explorer Web browser into its Windows operating system.

This chapter considers the Internet's pervasive influence on business and marketing. It is a preamble to the core of the book—seven specific strategies that show you how to use the Internet to improve business-to-business marketing and increase profits.

The New Paradigm

Before we head off into an exploration of marketing in cyberspace, I would like to put the subject of technology-driven marketing into historical perspective from my own vantage point. In 1974, I became employee number 51 at a small company called Epsilon Data Management. Epsilon was in the business of helping fund-raising and membership organizations communicate with their constituents—past, current, and future donors or members.

Epsilon's real business, though, was database marketing. The four Epsilon founders had helped pioneer the use of computer technology to take massive lists of donors' names and addresses and "smarten" them with data. Each donor record was constructed with variable-length fields so that a lot of data could be stored and tracked. Because each donor could also be given a unique identification number, the data could drive fund-raising programs that recognized the individual donor's unique characteristics.

Epsilon was one of the leaders in a technique called "variable upgrading." When each donor received a computer-generated letter, the suggested donation amount could be varied, based on the donor's previous contribution. A majority of donors would in fact upgrade their gifts to the new suggested amount. Even in mailings of several hundred thousand letters, the technique could be applied. I remember watching the line printers chunking out the letters on continuous form paper.

I was amazed as the letter-quality line printers were directed by the computers (mainframes back then) to spit out very respectable correspondence without hesitation. Each letter had a different name and address, and each letter and accompanying personalized reply slip had a different suggested gift amount inserted into the letter text. Signatures were preprinted or postprinted on the paper stock in blue ink, perfectly positioned with the computer-generated text, to simulate hand signing. It all looked very believable, and it was responsible for raising millions of dollars.

I was witnessing a paradigm shift, of course, although I did not realize it at the time. The 1970s were the early days of computer personalization driven by database marketing, now a common and accepted practice.

In those days, it took mainframes in climate-controlled, glass-enclosed, raised-floor computer rooms to make all of this marketing magic happen. Today, you could run a sophisticated database program that does much the same thing, only better, right from your desktop.

The reason for this reminiscing? To demonstrate that, over 25 years ago, something quite profound happened to marketing. Computer technology changed it forever.

We can state without reservation that the impact of the Internet on marketing today is no less profound, and once again, database marketing is playing a key role in the evolution of marketing, driving the Internet to be the ultimate one-to-one relationship-building marketing tool.

Computer technology has stretched across physical boundaries, and we have created a virtual world no less real than our physical one via networked communications. The Internet has caused networking, telecommunications, hardware, and software companies to completely reengineer themselves. Practically all other businesses are following suit by reorienting their business operations and information systems for the electronic future. Organizations are feverishly building intranets (internal Internet-based networks) and extranets ("private use" external Webs), depending more and more on the Internet for entire networking infrastructures.

As a testament to this fundamental change and the influence the Internet is having even in the Information Technology media, *Communications Week*, long a major computer industry publication, was renamed *Internet Week* (*www.internetwk.com*) in late 1997. The media revolution continues as others follow suit. In May 2000, *PC Computing* changed its name to *Smart Business* and *PC Week* became *eWeek*. *Business 2.0*, focusing on the Internet economy, became one of the most successful magazine launches ever, and now there are more publications (both in print and in electronic versions) covering the Internet and the Web than in any other publishing category.

The World is Very Wired

Today the Internet is already a mature medium, despite its newcomer status. It is certainly the technology area with the most significant and explosive growth ever. From late 1998 through early 2000, the Internet's economic impact on the U.S. economy was clearly proven just by the amount of venture capital invested in Internet companies, and by the number of successful Internet company IPOs launched. By early 1999, Internet IPOs had dominated the stock market, creating another round of young billionaires, not unlike the software boom decades earlier. By late 1999, it was the "dot coms" that moved "offline," dominating the airwaves, feverishly snapping up television time, and grabbing national magazine and newspaper space to launch their fledgling brands.

The Internet is very serious business, and it is an unavoidable fact of business life. A 1999 study by Forrester Research said that 98 percent of large businesses (more than 1,000 employees) and 45 percent of small businesses (less than 100 employees) will do business online by 2002. The Internet is fast becoming the marketing medium of the present (and the future) as it stakes its claim to marketing dominance.

Arguably, the most fertile ground for business-to-business media opportunities today is the Internet. The number of unique visits major Web sites receive on a daily basis is astounding. It can be in the tens or hundreds of thousands. And this is not just the sites you would expect to get that kind of traffic; there are some unknowns, too. Ever hear of Blue Mountain Arts *(www.bluemountain.com)*? According to leading Internet measurement service Media Metrix (*www.mediametrix.com*) this site, which offers free e-mail greeting cards, received over 12,000,000 unique visitors during a single month in late 1998. That is over 20 percent of the total online audience at the time. E-mail newsletters are proliferating as well. Some of the major Information Technology newsletters report circulations approaching one million readers.

There has never been a time in the business-to-business world when a mass medium has held such potential. Consider the national publications that span the general business market. Circulations in the hundreds of thousands are considered large. Now consider the top trade publications serving your particular industry. Circulations in the tens of thousands are significant. The Internet has the potential to dwarf those kinds of numbers fairly easily. The Internet is more accessible to more people globally than any other medium except television. Web sites and e-mail newsletters are for the most part free.

The Internet has, quite logically, hit the business-to-business marketing world with a vengeance. Even so, early marketing on the Internet was not always elegant. In fact, we have seen every form of marketing experimentation and, at times, excess.

E-mail

E-mail began, innocently enough, as a convenient electronic means of communication between one person and another over a local area network. It was largely restricted to, and intended for, internal use.

It was really such companies as America Online (*www.aol.com*), CompuServe (*www.csi.com*), and Prodigy (*www.prodigy.com*) that popularized the notion of e-mail communication outside the boundaries of corporate networks. Seasoned Internet users may have learned how to send and receive e-mail, but consumers and general business users needed both Internet access and e-mail software to take advantage of electronic communications. They got it through the private online service providers.

America Online (AOL), for example, recognized the true mass-market opportunity early on, even though CompuServe and Prodigy got there first. AOL used aggressive marketing tactics to saturate the market. I would be surprised if any reader of this book has not received a diskette from America Online at one time or another, either through direct mail or as a result of buying a "bagged" magazine with a disk enclosed. It was America Online that first told millions of young and old alike "You've got mail,"a phrase so ingrained in popular culture that it became the name of a Tom Hanks movie.

America Online, CompuServe, Prodigy, and a few other early online service providers put their own marketing front ends on the Internet to give it shape and make it palatable for "the rest of us." While setting the agenda, the online services were unabashedly self-serving and restrictive, and as such, had to scramble and reinvent themselves when the popularity of the Web in particular usurped them.

In late 1999, Prodigy and SBC, the nation's largest local telephone company, announced they would combine their Internet operations, with SBC taking 43 percent ownership of Prodigy. This deal would immediately turn Prodigy, a once-failing ISP, into a powerhouse with more than 2 million customers. But more importantly, Prodigy would now have broadband access to the 100 million people served by SBC.

AOL has managed to survive and succeed, despite market pressures. After going through a public relations battering over inadequately supporting the service requirements of its burgeoning user base, AOL recovered and is still going strong. By 2000, AOL had over twenty million subscribers and reached a new level of prominence with two blockbuster acquisitions, CompuServe and Netscape. In acquiring its rival, CompuServe, AOL obtained a primarily business membership base of two million subscribers. Under AOL's ownership, CompuServe has been maintained as a separate brand, announcing a major update to its software called "CompuServe 2000." It remains unclear, however, whether CompuServe will continue to be run separately.

The acquisition of Netscape was even more strategically important. In the battle for browser dominance with Microsoft, Netscape may have been losing ground, but adding AOL to the equation could certainly make things interesting. In combination with the anti-trust suit against Microsoft, and the fact that Sun Microsystems (creator of Java and Jini) has now aligned with Netscape, the Internet browser wars take on a whole new meaning.

But the biggest deal was yet to come. On January 10, 2000, AOL announced the unthinkable: a plan to merge with Time Warner. Incredibly, the smaller but more highly valued AOL would own about 55 percent of the new company in a stock deal that would be valued at $350 billion, the largest to date in U.S. history.

Regulatory issues notwithstanding, the business and economic significance of such a combination cannot be minimized. If ever there was a question about the Internet's dominant influence, it was resoundingly answered with the AOL—Time Warner deal. Industry and financial analysts alike immediately recognized the implication: that the world of e-commerce and media would change forever. At its most basic level, it brings together the online prowess of AOL with the deep content and broadband access of Time Warner. But it means far more than that if you look at all of the properties each company holds, as well as the far-reaching influence such a mega-corporation will have. This one merger is as telling of the future as any.

The deal dwarfed the 1999 merger of EarthLink and Mindspring, an effort to play catch up to AOL's rising star. Together, these ISPs would serve over three million users. Growth across consumer and business-focused ISPs has been brisk, even as the traditional telecommunications and cable firms enter the ISP space.

With the mass acceptance of external e-mail, this "private" one-to-one communication quickly became another promotional channel for business-to-business marketers. It wasn't long before unsolicited e-mailings ("spamming") were commonplace.

The heat is very much on those who do not respect an individual's privacy on the Internet. For example, the Direct Marketing Association (*www.the-dma.org*) launched an electronic media privacy program in 1998, encouraging organizations that use the Internet for direct marketing to post a privacy policy prominently on their Web sites. In March 1998, the Federal Trade Commission initiated random inspections of over 1,400 Web sites to determine if such policies were generally in place.

It is this kind of environment, coupled with the Internet's explosive growth, that led to the posting of a whole section about privacy on the Federal Trade Commissions Web site (*www.ftc.gov*). It also led in 2000 to the creation of a Web site sponsored by the Justice Department and the FBI for businesses and consumers to report suspected Internet frauds (*www.ifccfbi.gov*).

Newsgroups

These havens for information sharing are part of the "Usenet," an Internet-related network of e-mail boxes and newsgroups. Newsgroups were designed to be informal discussion groups, yet some marketers have unwisely tried to invade them with commercial messages. With the generally negative response from newsgroup users, most marketers have backed off and are more cautious about promotional activities surrounding newsgroups. Some newsgroups will allow promotional messages, but marketers are advised to carefully follow each newsgroup's specific rules.

The World Wide Web

Likened to the Wild West in its infancy, the Web as a quickly maturing adolescent was still a place with a lot of electronic marketing flotsam and jetsam. But now the Web is beyond that in terms of business usage. Industry estimates put the number of Web pages created each day at close to *two million*. In the early days, marketers glutted the Web with "brochureware"—nothing more than corporate collateral posted on Web sites. Although this is still often the case, business-to-business marketing use of the Web is proliferating as inferior marketers begin to weed themselves out. The tantalizing promise of the Web—electronic commerce—has now emerged as a significant factor for business marketers.

Why All the Marketing Excitement About the Internet?

The Internet is Boundless

According to *CyberAtlas* (*www.cyberatlas.internet.com*), there were almost 111,000,000 Internet users in the U.S. by the end of 1999. Japan ranked second in the world with some 31 million users, according to InfoCom Research. InfoCom anticipated over 100 million users in Japan by early 2004. The Computer Industry Almanac projected 490 million people worldwide would have Internet access by the year 2002. According to the 1999 annual Internet study by Nielsen Media Research and CommerceNet (*www.commerce.net*), 55 million people in North America have used the Internet at least once to shop online. In 1994, Internet users numbered only around one million.

The economic impact is staggering. The Direct Marketing Association's annual "Economic Impact" study of direct and Internet marketing, conducted by The WEFA Group, showed the Internet to be the fastest growing direct marketing medium. In business-to-business marketing alone, Internet sales grew at a compound annual growth rate of 195 percent from 1994—1999. That growth rate will be nearly 50 percent annually from 1999 to 2004. Business-to-business direct sales over the Internet will reach over $53 billion by 2004, up from some $7 billion in 1999.

Imagine the impact on business-to-business marketing if, with this kind of future, marketers begin to significantly shift their promotional dollars from traditional media to Internet-related advertising and marketing activities. Surely, that is inevitable.

Projections for the growth of business opportunities on the Internet are enough to make marketers swoon. Television has long been accepted as the world's greatest marketing medium for reach. At some point in the not-too-distant future, the Internet could quite possibly overtake television or converge with it.

Actually, convergence is already here. WebTV (*www.webtv.com*), now owned by Microsoft (*www.microsoft.com*), provides easy television access to the Web via a low cost set-top "terminal." Other entries in this emerging market take a different approach. WorldGate Communications (*www.wgate.com*) feeds Web pages directly through a cable system's set-top boxes.

The legitimate question of whether or not the consumer will *want* to view the Web in this fashion remains, but the Internet/TV technologies and services mentioned here and others now in development will continue to blur the lines between television and the Internet. The consumer convergence market may not directly affect the business-to-business marketer, but next on the horizon for businesses is convergence in a different form. Now every type of portable communications device, from laptop to organizer to cell phone to pager, will move into the Internet realm as wireless communications technology advances.

On the service side, major telecommunications and cable companies have already entered the ISP market. Communications giants are lining up to compete in the massive Internet and wireless Internet market. AT&T and cable leader TCI merged in 1998. Worldcom owns UUNET, the world's largest business ISP. Cable television network USA Networks agreed to merge with Internet portal Lycos in late 1998, but the deal was called off in 1999. The Internet access alternatives available to businesses and consumers are proliferating, as are the ways access can be provided. You can now obtain Internet access over both telephone and cable connections. Someday it may be bundled with your electric service. The end result will be the same: the commoditizing of the Internet.

One of the biggest concerns has been the bandwidth associated with delivering Internet service. As more people sign up for Internet access and actively use the Internet to conduct business, networked portions of the Internet can become choked with traffic. The demand for bandwidth rises exponentially, but even the bandwidth problem is on the way to being alleviated. Massive technological improvements are being made to the Internet infrastructure by leading networking companies.

Innovations are coming from all sides. In the greater Boston area, for example, Continental Cablevision, a cable television company, was purchased by telecommunications giant US WEST and renamed MediaOne (*www.mediaone.com*). More than the name changed—the company now offers "broadband" to select Boston area communities. Broadband is basically Internet access over cable—and it is feeding hungry Internet users with electronic information at blazingly fast speeds.

Broadband is one significant advance, but it is not the only way that consumers and businesses are getting high-speed Internet feeds. Tele-communications and cable companies alike are introducing DSL into markets with the hope that it will be the killer Internet access application. That is because DSL can share phone lines, using modems that are 50 times faster than conventional modems.

DSL and other technologies mean the time is soon at hand when Internet access will be a utility. People will not even need to think about turning it on and off, because it will be more like the telephone, cable television, and electricity.

But DSL is only the beginning. The year 2000 saw a new surge: the movement towards a wireless Internet. Cisco Systems, the leading manufacturer of networking devices, was an early leader. In December 1999, the company announced its plans to offer Internet connections up to ten times faster than DSL via low-frequency microwave transmission. In 2000, hand-held computing devices and cell phones began incorporating wireless Internet access.

Another movement in late 1999 probably helped fuel Internet growth even more dramatically, as free Internet access became a popular phenomenon in the U.S. By November 1999, for example, free access provider NetZero (*www.netzero.com*) had acquired more than two million users. Alta Vista (*www.altavista.com*), the search engine that re-invented itself as a portal offering free access, acquired 800,000 users in its first three months of service. Other free access providers followed suit in the United States and worldwide. Of course, users agree to view plenty of advertising in exchange for free Internet access. With companies such as Gateway and Compaq bundling in Internet access with their hardware, and creative telcos using free or reduced-cost access as a new business hook, the entire world of the ISP was turned upside down. The free access concept even penetrated the DSL market by early 2000.

The Internet Makes Global Marketing a Reality

The Internet continues to grow as rapidly worldwide as it has in the United States. Europe and Asia are already seeing extraordinary increases in Internet usage. The Internet therefore has already become the first truly cost-effective, widespread global marketing medium. With the Internet's roots in worldwide networking and its technology enabled via simple telephone line or television cable access, any marketer theoretically could reach any online consumer anywhere in the world at any time. Information can be transmitted via e-mail or over the Web and received instantly, without regard to time zones or geographic location. No technical skills are necessary to receive it.

Very little on the Internet is currently regulated in terms of international markets. As such, the Internet represents a kind of worldwide electronic free trade zone. Nations are just now trying to determine what regulations and taxes, if any, should be imposed. The World Trade Organization in 1998 reached agreement among its 132 member countries to not impose customs duties on electronic commerce transmissions.

Also in 1998, the U.S. and Japanese governments agreed to keep electronic commerce essentially free from regulation and cooperate at an international level to remove barriers to electronic commerce. A nonprofit organization was established by the U.S. government to take over the technical management of the Internet Domain Name System (DNS). The Digital Millennium Copyright Act was passed to ratify and implement the World Intellectual Property Organization (WIPO) Copyright Treaty and the WIPO Performances and Phonograms Treaty, protecting copyrighted material online.

As for the Internet's continuing worldwide reach, international acceptance is growing rapidly. Although the Internet is still predominantly an English language medium and the largest area of Internet activity is in the United States, European mirror sites of U.S. multinational companies are springing up. Worldwide organizations now acknowledge a Web site is a business mandatory. Multiple-language versions and country-specific editions of Web sites are becoming more common.

This growth promises to continue as global e-commerce becomes a reality. The introduction of the "Euro" as most of Europe's consolidated currency will help fuel the Internet economy. With the acceptance of digital certificates, which will both verify a sender's identity and make sure the recipient is authorized, digital "cash" transactions could become common the world over.

The Internet Reaches People with Intellect, Power, and Money

Despite the ubiquitous nature of the Internet, early Internet users were somewhat elite—educated, influential, and upscale. In the case of businesses, this often means key decision makers.

The core audience of the Internet is still there, even as the Internet becomes more of a reflection of the U.S. and global population. It is likely that these affluent individuals will still be primary users of e-commerce and thus continue to form the core of the Internet's true buying public. The Internet is home to these desirable and discerning consumers and business people. They are predominantly individuals who may watch television only occasionally but are avid Internet surfers and in many cases Internet buyers. And by the way, the Internet has shaken its early reputation as a predominantly male haven. The earlier referenced 1999 Internet study by Commerce.net says 46 percent of Internet users in North America are women.

As the Internet marches into consumer homes via low-cost access from ISPs under severe competition, the bar will drop even further, changing the demographics and making it more a reflection of society. Yet business-to-business marketers will still be able to find and target the upscale, influential buyers they are looking for—those who started the stampede in the first place.

The Internet Offers Increased Business Penetration

As a business tool, the Internet is unprecedented in its penetration of the business community. As previously mentioned, the Internet's historic roots are implanted in science and business, and business-to-business usage has continued to lead the growth of the Internet. With the emphasis on intranets and extranets, business-to-business usage is virtually exploding, even as consumers "sign on" at a dizzying rate. The Internet will continue to be an accepted place, potentially the preferred place, for businesses to do business and for marketers to reach business people. In fact, the opportunities for segmentation and targeting proliferate dramatically with the Internet's growth.

One of the very real differentiators of the Internet's power is that it has a remarkable *leveling effect* on business. It can make a very small company look larger than it is. That means even a tiny company can compete, at least electronically, with organizations many times its size. That company can now extend its marketing efforts through the Internet to any part of the globe and take advantage of the same Internet channel used by industry giants. Internet technology is inexpensive, widely available, and can be completely outsourced. A company does not have to make a major investment to get on the Net and use it as a powerful means of marketing.

An encouraging statistic is that Internet business penetration is finally reaching down into the small business market. A study of small business Web presence, commissioned by Prodigy Biz, the third largest small business Web hosting company in the U.S., was conducted by International Communications Research in late 1999. The study reported that one-third of businesses with less than 100 employees had a Web presence in 1999, up from 19 percent the previous year. 90 percent of respondents felt they would benefit from the Internet, with the top three anticipated benefits being promoting to prospects, e-commerce, and better customer service.

Even if a company does not aggressively use the Internet to market itself, that organization can benefit greatly from using the Internet as a competitive research and business learning tool. This is one of the sometimes hidden benefits of the Internet. It is nothing short of amazing how much information companies post about themselves on their Web sites. Sometimes you have to wonder if they are so enamored with the technology that they will put even the most sensitive company documents out there for anyone to see. This is a gold mine for all of us who consider some form of marketing as our livelihoods. What used to take weeks of work now takes minutes, because competitive research can be accomplished with a few clicks of the mouse. The value of this aspect of the Internet extends far beyond marketing alone. With the amount of information resident on the Web, virtually any research in any discipline can be conducted online and at no cost for the information itself.

On the downside, however, the Internet is certainly seductive. A number of studies have suggested that unrestricted employee Internet usage can seriously reduce company productivity. As a result, an entire business centered on "site blocking" has developed, as software companies pitch products that cut down on unauthorized Web visits.

Another hidden benefit of the Internet for marketers is the way in which it improves overall business efficiency. Beyond marketing, using the Internet to do business is both efficient and competitively wise. My company, Directech | eMerge (*www.directechemerge.com*) is a direct marketing agency whose business efficiency has dramatically increased because of the Internet. Of course, we routinely use e-mail to communicate with clients and prospects. We also present conceptual creative work over our own secure "WorkWeb." Some of our clients prefer to view work this way, and as a result, it has replaced paper layouts. This way of doing business is particularly advantageous when we need to present creative work to a local client contact in Massachusetts along with contacts on the West Coast or in Europe who need to review the work simultaneously. In fact, it helps the local client enormously.

At other times, we have posted direct mail work on a client's intranet or extranet so its sales force, distributors, or resellers could see the work prior to distribution to customers and prospects. Not only does this facilitate communications, it also eliminates the cost of printing an overage of the mailing and sending it to these internal audiences.

One of the fastest growing applications in this area is Internet conferencing. Through such technologies as Internet telephony and audiovisual streaming, communicating in real time over the Web is becoming commonplace, dramatically increasing business efficiency as cybermeetings replace face-to-face meetings.

The Internet Provides a Unique Form of Communications Intimacy

If marketing is about building relationships, then Internet marketing is about building lasting relationships. With the medium's maturation and the increasing integration of database marketing practices, targeting and one-to-one marketing on the Internet will be the norm, and that means marketers will be able to address the individualized needs of constituents.

In Chapter 1, I talked at length about *targeting,* a fundamental principle of effective business-to-business direct marketing. Targeting on the Internet, as you will see in subsequent chapters, is not only feasible, it can be just as efficient as direct mail in reaching particular audiences. There are as many specialized Web sites as there are specialized trade publications—primarily because virtually every specialized publication has established a sister Web site. That means you can be as selective with Web-based media as you can with print-based media.

The same is true of lead generation and order generation programs. You can select the most appropriate Web sites for banner ad placement and reach a targeted audience, as you would with traditional print media. Outbound unsolicited e-mail certainly does not have the acceptance of traditional direct mail, but the use of e-mail is another option that should be considered, if cautiously. Legitimate opt-in lists of individuals who are willing to receive promotional e-mail are increasingly available for rental. Customers and prospects whom are receptive to promotional e-mail could form the basis for an e-mail list that is potentially one of your best-performing lists. E-mail lists will continue to come onto the market, and the selection criteria will continue to improve as promotional e-mail gains acceptance. E-mail newsletters are enormously popular because they put valuable information into subscribers e-mail-boxes, usually free of charge. E-mail is one-to-one correspondence, quite like traditional direct mail. Today at least, e-mail is private, personal, and read more attentively than any other medium.

The World Wide Web is truly an intimate and personal "playspace" for adults. Used effectively, the Web can deliver personalized content to each and every visitor, or even automatically to a visitor's computer desktop via push technologies. As a result, a marketer can initiate a one-to-one relationship via e-mail and the Web with a prospect, customer, or business partner. The marketer can also learn from that relationship via database marketing and grow the relationship over time.

The Internet Changes the Economics of Marketing

The stunning cost implications of electronic marketing in part fuel the Internet's unprecedented growth. The Internet is not only cost-effective, it is downright cheap in comparison to other media. The Yankee Group (*www.yankeegroup.com*) estimates that Internet direct marketing is 60 to 65 percent cheaper than traditional direct mail marketing.[5]

A marketer can build and host a Web site and reach a worldwide audience at a cost that is far less than the cost of one national television commercial. Electronic communication has a whole different cost structure from traditional print, direct mail, telemarketing, or television media. There are no media placement costs associated with launching a corporate Web site or employing e-mail as a marketing medium. You may have to rent e-mail addresses, but you do not have to engage printers or mailhouses, or pay postage, when you disseminate e-mail. There are no hotel, travel, or on-site materials costs for virtual seminars and events. There are no printing and mailing costs for electronic fulfillment. Even order-taking is cheaper with the Internet, especially if electronic catalogs are used to replace traditional paper catalogs.

The Internet Establishes a Brand New Sales Channel

The Internet completely transforms the selling process for marketers. Even early successful electronic commerce users have found that they can dramatically reduce the cost of sale via the Internet. The story of Amazon.com (*www.amazon.com*), a company that defied the standard practice of opening retail store locations and instead chose to sell books exclusively on the Internet, is legendary.

Amazon.com became one of the most successful Internet business launches ever and forged the way for other hard goods marketers (including many competitors) to stake their claim on the electronic frontier. (More about Amazon.com later.) With the advent of secure online ordering, electronic commerce will undoubtedly reach its full potential as more marketers use the Internet to sell their goods and services.

A review of both specialized and general media sources suggested that 1997 was the year the Internet found its legs as a tool for selling. Although electronic commerce was still in its infancy, 1997 saw the Internet's first $1 billion in advertising revenue, according to Reuters, up from $267 million in 1996. As proof positive of the future, consumer goods giants took to the Internet in 1997, not just by establishing top-shelf Web sites, but by aggressively integrating Internet advertising and electronic commerce initiatives into their promotional marketing strategies. In 1998, consumer giant Procter and Gamble organized an unusual Internet marketing summit to elicit ideas for future initiatives.

In 1998 and 1999, e-commerce really hit its stride. There was greatly increased activity on the consumer side, but the majority of Internet-based sales have still been generated by businesses selling to businesses. The successes of the past few years have been nothing short of mind-boggling.

Dell Computer (*www.dell.com*) is testament to that. By the end of 1997, it was widely reported that Dell logged $4 million a day from online sales. By 2000, Dell had reportedly achieved ten times that number: *$40 million a day* from e-commerce alone. According to the company, online sales accounted for 25 percent of Dell's business by early 1999, and by 2000, half of Dell's revenues were from online sales. To fuel that growth, Dell launched a second e-commerce site (*www.gigabuys.com*) in March 1999. The site began by offering some 30,000 computer-related products beyond the Dell product line for corporate customers.

Dell was not the only company achieving such spectacular business-to-business success. Networking giant Cisco Systems (*www.cisco.com*), had already established an industry-leading e-commerce benchmark by the end of 1997, averaging $9 million per day of online sales. That translated into 40 percent of the company's total annual revenue being generated via the Web even in those "early days" of e-commerce. Cisco's numbers by the first quarter of 1999 reached $21 million a day. Intel (*www.intel.com*) reportedly pulled in $2.5 billion of online income in the first quarter of 1999.

Intranets and Extranets

Business-to-business companies are not just driving electronic commerce. They quickly went beyond Internet marketing usage alone, creating intranets and extranets, perhaps two of the most-used words in the trade press in their current reporting of the Internet.

Both intranets and extranets are now becoming populated with marketing initiatives. Technically an Internet-enabled internal network intended primarily for employee usage, an intranet is a media channel in and of itself—a very targeted one, in fact. Imagine if a Fortune 500 company were to allow advertising on its intranet—so that its employees would receive promotional messages from select providers of products and services. What if that same company was to actively promote its own products and services, and those of its divisions, to the employee base? This kind of intra-company advertising can easily occur over an intranet—and it is already in use.

Through an intranet, large companies can market themselves very effectively and provide highly valued service to a very targeted audience—their employees. Now companies are building enterprise information portals (EIPs), a kind of super-intranet through which employees and other insiders can easily access all of the company's information resources from anywhere.

An extranet is really a private label Web site, offering access to a select group of customers, prospects, partners, or suppliers outside the sponsoring organization's network. It is the extranet, and all its variations, that companies started using in earnest in 1997 to help solidify existing business relationships and form new ones.

These extranets have proliferated rapidly and now take on numerous forms. Some extranets service only customers; others are targeted specifically to business partners. Some are designed as private consortiums where members share resources and do business with each other. Still other extranets provide private-access seminars, courses, and conferences, either free or paid, to prospects, customers, partners, or students. The extranet is both a useful marketing channel itself and, like an intranet, a place to potentially reach targeted audiences.

This, too, is an aspect of the Internet that is not quite the same as any other medium. You can create intranets, extranets, Web sites, Web communities, and newsgroups—tangible places where business can be conducted, marketing information can be exchanged, and dialogue can occur—and then you can use these newly created media vehicles to place promotional advertising that takes further advantage of Internet marketing.

Even at the beginning of the Internet marketing curve, there was a remarkable richness to the medium. Now there is no turning back. There can be little doubt that the Internet is having a permanent impact and a lasting effect, not just on marketing, but on the manner in which businesses conduct business.

The Transformation of Direct Marketing

Please bear with me as I review direct marketing history. I think you will see the relevance. In Chapter 1, you learned that direct marketing actually started in the late 1800s in the United States. This is when marketers began to create and place direct response advertising in some of the country's leading national magazines. These magazines were the only medium available to reach large portions of the population with advertising messages. Many of those early ads used direct marketing techniques, such as cutout coupons and money-back guarantees that you would recognize today. Even more remarkable, numerous ads promoted products for direct sale to the American consumer.

I collect these old ads. (In fact, I have collected many of them via purchases on eBay, an online auction site. More about auction sites later!) They line the walls at my direct marketing agency to remind employees that ours is a business with deep roots. One ad, which I referenced in Chapter 1, stands out as an example of early America's invincible spirit. The ad, as you may recall, promotes an Underwood typewriter. The advertiser offers to ship it to the reader *on approval*—without obligation! Imagine what it took to send a heavy typewriter across the United States in the early 1900s. Imagine the faith the manufacturer must have had in the consumer.

That was just the beginning of direct marketing's rising popularity. With the advent of direct mail, the direct marketing business went through its own paradigm shift. Cut-out coupons that appeared in early direct marketing advertising did not go away—they still exist in newspaper circulars and in some print advertising—but the new format for the coupon became the business reply card and order form in direct mail. Generating leads and orders quickly became the staple of consumer and business-to-business direct marketers alike.

Database marketing was another direct marketing breakthrough of historic proportions, yet a small technological innovation that truly changed the direct marketing business forever was something far simpler, and it is this innovation that opened the door for personal direct marketing interactivity: *the toll-free 800 telephone number.*

The 800 number has been in existence since 1967, yet it has been so thoroughly embraced by the world in recent years that the supply of 800 numbers has already been exhausted. In 1996, 888 numbers were introduced and in 1998, 877 numbers had to be added to supplement 800 numbers.

The impact of the 800 number on direct marketing cannot be underestimated. Remember my reference to Joe Sugarman in Chapter 1? Well it was Joe who first used the toll-free number as a direct marketing order vehicle in those ads in *The Wall Street Journal.* He created a whole new form of "we pay for the call" marketing, launched new businesses such as 1-800-FLOWERS, and changed the dynamics of the inquiry and order process forever. The toll-free number functionally reverses telephone charges so that the caller does not pay, but it does something more important than that: the toll-free number *extends a marketer's reach.* It removes a physical, costly barrier to eliciting a response from a prospect or customer. Now, the individual can make a quick, easy call to any location without paying for it, and if the telemarketer is so staffed, that person can call on any day and at any time.

Think about what the 800 number really does. It means that a marketer can effectively open up the entire North American market and serve customers from anywhere, still maintaining the brand and product awareness so important to the marketer. In many cases, a marketer can even select a toll-free number that supports and enhances the brand. (Some examples: 1-800-CALL-ATT, 1-800-THE-CARD [American Express], 1-800-MATTRES [Dial-a-Mattress].)

The 800 number is now universally recognized and accepted by all marketers, but it revolutionized mail order marketing. Mail order marketers learned that by offering an 800 number, two things happened.

1. Their number of orders via the 800 number out-pulled other response paths.

2. In addition, the *total* number of orders from all sources generally increased as well. In other words, adding the 800 number had a residual effect: *It increased the overall volume of orders coming in from all response paths.*

This is a principle that applies well to business-to-business direct marketing. *By offering multiple response paths, you tend to increase overall response.* That is because individuals tend to respond, well, individually, and by offering them many response options, you respect each individual's desired way of responding. Some people are comfortable picking up the phone; others prefer responding via mail or fax. Still others would much rather respond over the Internet.

Let us return to that 800 number. You would be hard pressed to find any serious mail order marketer who does not offer an 800 number. Of course, you still may chuckle when you see and hear them repeated over and over again on those silly television commercials, but they work—or you would not see them repeatedly used. Mail order success with the 800 number led to general business success. Now the 800 number has reached mass acceptance.

The 800 number has become so commonplace in business communications that any business interested in getting responses considers using one. There is a toll-free telephone book and a toll-free number to call for toll-free directory assistance. Toll-free numbers are in use by local plumbers and electricians. You can even get your own personal toll-free number, so friends and family can reverse the charges on you!

With mass acceptance comes the "put it everywhere" syndrome. It was not long before you began to see 800 numbers appearing frequently in print ads and television commercials. You even began to see them as customer service enhancements on consumer goods products—cereal boxes, potato chips, detergents, and the like.

In effect, the 800 number has now become not only an accepted part of marketing, but an accepted part of life, part of the fabric of America, a commodity that is no longer just a marketing gimmick, but rather a necessary business tool.

The Internet Address Is the New 800 Number

Have you noticed that there is something new at the bottom of magazine ads and at the end of television commercials? It is not an 800 number anymore, it is the URL (Uniform Resource Locator) of a Web site. Look for the "www" on ads and on TV. It is everywhere, the way the 800 number used to be. The Web address seems to be gaining rapid acceptance as the new 800 number—at least in the minds of advertisers and their advertising agencies, and that is just one basic reason why the Internet will transform direct marketing. It is a transformation that is destined to reach far beyond what the 800 number had to offer.

Suppose Internet usage continues to grow at its current rate. That means the Internet will be the medium with the most extensive reach—perhaps even topping television. As indicated earlier, widespread acceptance and dropping access prices will dramatically accelerate this growth.

What will this growth mean to business-to-business direct marketers? The use of direct marketing itself continues to grow in its own right. As mentioned earlier, a Direct Marketing Association study says that direct marketing is expected to outpace total U.S. growth through 2002, growing at a rate of almost 7 percent annually.

This same report projects that interactive marketing will grow by *54 percent* annually through 2002, and that electronic commerce will grow by nearly *61 percent* annually. These statistics are supported by similar projections from numerous respected research firms. You will find many of them referenced elsewhere in this book. All of the forecasts point to the same conclusion: It will not be long before the Internet will be the undisputed king of the media world.

What we have, then, is an interesting phenomenon. From a marketing perspective, use of the Internet is growing at such a rate that it will soon overshadow and surpass traditional media.

This suggests an intriguing scenario on the near horizon that business-to-business marketers must take into consideration:

> *If the Internet takes over the lead, and other media flatten out, then other media will be subordinate to the Internet and, therefore, they will primarily be used to support the Internet.*

The Internet Is the Future of Business-to-Business Marketing

I believe that, even now, we have reached a point of intersection between usage of the Internet and usage of traditional direct marketing media (Figure 2.1). At this intersection point, the Internet and other media cross. After the intersection point, the Internet trajectory continues upward and traditional media begin to flatten out. As the next few years progress, usage of the Internet goes up steeply, so the gap widens.

In business-to-business marketing, the Internet incline is likely to be much steeper than in consumer marketing. Earlier adoption of Internet marketing by business marketers is the primary driver of this phenomenon. With the Internet playing such a key role generally in businesses, the use of Internet marketing should accelerate even more rapidly In the next few years, you will likely see a very different marketing world emerging.

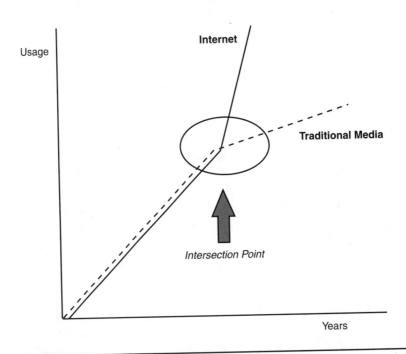

Figure 2.1. The Internet and traditional direct marketing media are now at an intersection. Over the next few years, the Internet trajectory continues upward, while traditional media begin to flatten out.

Every fact in this book supports the inevitability of the Internet. All the conditions are right. It appears from every perspective that the planets are aligned for the Internet to ascend, unchallenged, into marketing dominance.

My own "direct" experience has convinced me that the Internet is as much a true direct marketing medium as it is a new, exciting channel that will enhance all forms of marketing communications and facilitate response.

I think the Internet will surely dominate—but it will not completely replace other media. I cannot see direct mail dying off, any more than other forms of direct marketing and advertising have disappeared. Direct mail will continue to have its rightful place, as advertising has had before it, but direct mail will know its place, and it will not be at the top of the list any longer.

Moving into the Future Means Transitioning Now

As traditional media become subordinate to the Internet, business-to-business marketers will face a new media world—one that has different kinds of challenges. With the upward spiral of the Internet trajectory, you will need to adjust your marketing and media strategies. What this really means is that you will need to redefine your use of direct marketing in the context of the Internet and ready yourself for a future that looks very different from the past.

You can begin by taking advantage of the intersecting point where the Internet and traditional media cross now. You can continue to use advertising, mail, phone, and other traditional media. You would be wise, however, to increasingly enhance them by adding Internet response paths, offering Internet fulfillment, using e-mail for follow-ups, driving individuals to your Web site, and inviting prospects and customers to virtual events that occur on the Internet.

> *Now is the time to take a new look at what you are doing and build a transitional marketing strategy that will combine the best of traditional media usage with the emerging world of Internet media usage.*

At the end of the book, you will find a complete blueprint to help you implement this transitional strategy. For now, here is an overview of the basic steps you will need to take:

1. *Assess your Internet marketing readiness.* Now is the time to evaluate your organization's Internet marketing capabilities. Will you be ready to transition to largely Internet-based marketing in a year? What about in two years? Evaluate your company's current use of Internet technology, and your current use of Internet marketing.

   - Do you already take inquiries over the Web? Are you doing electronic fulfillment? Are these things in your future plans?

   - Is your Web site capable of order entry, processing, and tracking?

   - Do you have a marketing database that can be integrated with the Internet? Have you started to use database-driven Internet marketing?

   - Is your organization planning investments to make all of this happen?

2. *Begin the move to Internet direct marketing.* Do not let the assessment process deter you. The fact is that most of the business-to-business marketing world is at the beginning of the Internet trajectory, just as you are. The important thing is to understand your current state of readiness and recognize where you are today—and where you will need to be soon. Start the move to Internet direct marketing now. Capitalize on the Internet trajectory by integrating the Internet with your use of traditional media and conventional direct marketing. (You will see how in the next chapter of this book.)

3. *Prepare your management for the Internet-dominated future.* The Internet has already captured top-of-mind awareness among senior management at many companies. Make sure your company is one of them. Help your management prepare for the electronic future by sharing Internet direct marketing information from authoritative sources. You will find some of them in the Appendices.

4. *Develop an Internet marketing action plan.* If you are in a position to do so, participate on or chair a committee in your organization that is charged with developing an implementation plan for using the Internet as a strategic marketing tool. You may find that there is an even larger issue—using the Internet as a strategic business tool. If management is already on that course, so much the better. Then Internet marketing and electronic commerce can be positioned as a logical subset of your organization's Internet business plan.

The Escalation of Global Internet Marketing

As a marketing medium, the Internet is well on its way to becoming the easiest, most cost-effective route to global marketing. There has never been a single medium that, even at its inception, offered this promise. The Internet is very much a medium that already has the infrastructure necessary to serve international markets from the United States, and to encourage businesses from outside the United States to market their products and services here. Now how does all of this impact business-to-business marketing?

If your company markets products or services to businesses and it has any kind of substantial sales revenue, chances are there already is an international marketing component to your business. Many U.S. companies have already established a strong foothold beyond the boundaries of the U.S. Taking full advantage of the global economy is nothing new for them.

What *is* new, however, is the global marketing impact of the Internet. The Internet truly flattens the world. Even if the business-to-business marketer wants to make use of e-mail alone, global marketing becomes an inexpensive reality. With an e-mail address in hand, a marketer can reach anyone, anywhere. E-mail is delivered in most cases to an individual's personal computer private mailbox. It is almost guaranteed to be read. Sending e-mail from the United States to Hong Kong is no more expensive than sending it from one town in Massachusetts to another. The Internet simply does not recognize physical distance. What could be more attractive for a global marketer?

The primary place for business to be done on the Internet is, of course, the World Wide Web. There are currently some one million Web sites and over 2 billion unique public pages on the Web and the growth is not letting up. All those URLs start with *http://www...,* representing the World Wide Web, although in many browsers, it isn't even necessary to input www. anymore. Most of us simply call it the Web, but we should not overlook the significance of those first two Ws.

Surf the Web and you quickly realize that you can happen upon non-U.S. sites very easily. (They are typically identified by a country abbreviation at the end of the UL, such as *.uk* for the United Kingdom.) It is just as easy to get to a site in any state as it is to get to a site in any country of the world. It is no less complicated to get to a U.S. site from outside this country. It is all quite transparent and instantaneous.

It is not difficult to understand why this phenomenon occurs. You can search, find, and link to any Web site in the world, by entering its URL. Your computer does not care where the host computer is—and at this stage of the Internet's life, *you pay no premium or penalty for accessing a site on the other side of the globe.* Probably all you do is make a local phone call and, magically, you are connected.

That is one extremely compelling reason why global Internet marketing—and the electronic commerce associated with it—is predicted to escalate so dramatically in the next several years. Today, nothing flattens the world, or brings it closer at a lower price, than the Internet. Business-to-business marketers with global goals are now establishing mirror sites and multiple language versions of their Web sites; Internet translation tools are available that make this easy to do. It is only a matter of time until these same marketers use their Web sites to accept and fulfill orders online from customers worldwide.

In fact, they do not even have to learn how to process the orders. Today, there is a whole class of Web sites that "insulate" the marketer from the entire order-taking and fulfillment process. These "electronic malls" or Web communities are really Web storefronts, established by an electronic commerce "reseller" who "rents" space to marketers on a multi-advertiser Web site. Some malls are set up so that the marketer still handles inquiries and orders. Others overlay an order-processing front end onto the site so that the marketer becomes one of many who take advantage of a system already in place—at a cost that may be far lower than doing it in-house.

There are, of course, both advantages and disadvantages to such an approach. On the positive side, the marketer gets someone else to do all the promotional, technical, and operational work. On the negative side, the marketer shares resources and customers with others on the site and therefore relies on the site owners' capabilities to bring in and support the business. You also have to be wary of advertising costs, which can mount up quickly. Nonetheless, it is a fascinating business model—one that can potentially launch a marketer's worldwide business effort quickly and cost-effectively.

For some marketers with a large international component to their businesses, the Internet is nothing short of a marketing miracle. Imagine the small importer or exporter, for example. With the Internet, this business owner can communicate 24 hours a day, 7 days a week, with points worldwide via inexpensive e-mail. The savings on international phone calls, faxes, delivery services, and travel can be astonishing.

Approach Global Marketing with Caution

Despite all the apparent benefits of global Internet marketing, it should be pointed out that marketers cannot take other countries and their populations for granted. The European countries are a good example. Europeans live on a single continent, have open borders, trade freely, and are currently engaged in moving to a unified European currency, yet each country retains its very distinct personality and, in the case of marketing, individuals in each country may react differently to promotions.

Some countries are more advanced than others in adopting the Internet, and some people are more receptive to its use. While English-speaking countries generally appear to be the fastest adopters, other countries are fast becoming huge Internet markets.

In 2000, 37 percent of Canadian households were online, with 17 percent of them shopping online, according to Forrester Research. Forrester predicts that, by 2004, 45 percent of Canadian households will be shopping online, representing total online revenues of nearly $18 billion Canadian dollars.

Europe in general is catching up to the U.S. in Internet growth. The European Internet population will reach over 100 million by the year 2003—35 percent of the total adult population—according to a July 1999 report by Morgan Stanley Dean Witter. In June 2000, Jupiter Communications predicted that online advertising in Europe would reach $1.5 billion in 2001 and grow to about $4 billion by 2004.

Asia is a growing market, although there are obviously significant language issues in developing Internet content. Online commerce in Japan will increase from 1998's $1.65 billion to $8.26 billion in 2001, a 500 percent increase, according to a 1999 study. Jupiter Communications says online advertising alone will grow to $2.6 billion by 2004.

Additional issues may occur that could create barriers to Internet-related marketing activities. For example, Europeans generally are less likely to share personal profile information. In fact, some countries have regulations restricting the use of such information. E-commerce may also be less desirable to Europeans because of individual country currencies, individual country taxes, shipping products across borders, and other issues. As a result, you cannot assume that an Internet marketing program that works successfully in the United States will automatically succeed globally.

The Internet generally makes global marketing less complicated, but marketers with a sizable stake outside the United States should take advantage of the medium's ability to version messages for different prospects based on where they reside—respecting their individuality and catering to it. With that in mind, the Internet clearly has the potential to escalate global marketing in a way no medium before it has done—providing business marketers with a potential for worldwide business they could previously only dream about.

The New Response Model: "Intersponding"

We have been talking about how the Internet will transform direct marketing and drive the globalization of marketing. Now it is time to address the most intriguing aspect of Internet direct marketing: *how the Internet will fundamentally change the way people interact with marketers and respond to them.*

The Nature of the Internet

It is important to put the Internet in the context of other direct marketing media to discover whether or not it "looks and feels" the same—so we know how suspects, prospects, and customers will react to it.

What Is Its Content?

Internet content is diverse. Like print advertising and direct mail, the content of the Internet is largely based on the written word. As with printed media, the Web portion of the Internet can and does rely on graphic images to support marketing messages.

What Is Its Form?

Unlike print and direct mail, the Web enables moving graphics and sound to be conveyed to the suspect, prospect, or customer. In that respect, it is more like radio or television, and like the telephone, the Web can enable one-to-one, interactive communication with e-mail or, as technology progresses, even with voice. Yet, unlike any direct response medium, the Web can present the suspect, prospect, or customer with a *virtually unlimited amount* of marketing information in multimedia format.

What Is Its Delivery Format?

Print advertising is delivered through magazines and newspapers. Direct mail is delivered via the U.S. Postal Service or another delivery service. Radio and television are delivered via airwaves through passive listener or viewer devices. Telemarketing is delivered over telephone lines. Only the Internet (at least until computers truly converge with televisions) is delivered directly via a computer. This is the most intriguing part of Internet direct marketing—and one of the primary differentiating factors that sets this medium apart from any other.

Finally, unlike any other medium, the computer delivers Internet-based Web content in an entirely new form: *nonlinear information.* All other media are linear: They have a beginning, middle, and end. Direct response print advertising has a headline at the beginning, body copy in the middle, and a call to action at the end. A direct mail package is typically organized in a very logical, linear fashion: The outside envelope is first, followed by the letter, brochures and any inserts, and the reply device with a call to action, and each individual element of the package is linear, with a beginning, middle, and end.

Each element in a good direct mail package reinforces the offer and call to action, so even if two different people read the package elements in a different order, all of the elements relate and ultimately lead to the call to action. This is true, by the way, of other direct mail formats as well, such as self-mailing pieces and catalogs. Direct mail is logical, linear, and integrated. Even telemarketing calls and direct response television commercials are logical and linear, with a beginning, middle, and end, but then we come to the Web.

The Web Defies Logic

Admittedly, many Web sites are logically designed to lead you through from beginning to end, yet the Web site is faced with a technical limitation that is paradoxically its most unique strength. Web sites need to be *nonlinear* so that each visitor can have immediate access to the majority of the information on a site. This is essential because the Web site visitor sees one "page" at a time on the computer screen, yet the Web site has many pages which must be served up to the visitor. How does the visitor find out what is on those pages?

The functional way most Web sites deliver this nonlinear information is through a home page. On that home page, the visitor typically will see almost every area or section of the site's contents at the same time. It is more like a book's table of contents than anything else is, but not quite, because the sections on the home page are nonlinear and modular. You could flip through the sections of a book and move from page to page, but most readers still tackle a book from beginning to end.

The Web site, on the other hand, invites nonlinear reading. The home page encourages movement and flexibility, even though each section has its own purpose and its own content. It is a very different look and feel.

Actually, the difference is startling. With every other direct response medium, the direct marketer makes a concerted effort to *progressively disclose information* to the suspect, prospect or customer in a logical, sequential pattern.

With the Web, however, the visitor is exposed to everything simultaneously. He or she has the ability to see it all, at least on the surface, at one time, from this giant control panel called the home page, and here is the important point:

> *The visitor is no longer directed by the marketer—instead, the visitor does the directing.*

You could make a case that a direct mail catalog provides the same flexibility. In some respects, it does. The reader can thumb through the pages of a catalog randomly, and its contents page is kind of like a Web site's home page. However, when the visitor to a Web site browses pages, he or she is exposed to far more "eye candy" and interactivity than with a printed catalog. A Web site is not physically bound, as a catalog is, so the nonlinear nature is more evident—a benefit as well as a feature.

With a Web site, the visitor has a new level of control over the manner in which information is delivered. He or she can randomly move around the Web site, starting anywhere, going anywhere, finishing anywhere or not finishing at all. In fact, a visitor can leave a page or an entire site very quickly, go to other pages at numerous other sites, and return just as quickly.

Web pages become almost separately interconnected elements, functioning as tiny bits of marketing information in a much greater scheme of things, sometimes melding from one marketer's site to another. This presents a challenge for Internet marketers—to keep visitors on your site and to remind those visitors of exactly where they are: on *your* site.

It also means that there is a whole new dynamic in Internet marketing. With the power in the hands of the prospect or customer, the marketer needs to be mindful of that individual's wants, needs, likes, and dislikes. Instead of randomly receiving promotional messages from you, as might be the case with direct mail or advertising, the Internet prospect or customer expects you to *either ask permission to communicate or to know when to make a contact.*

The Internet promotes one-to-one communications intimacy and encourages a correspondence relationship between the marketer and the end user—the kind of relationship that demands something of one another. This is conceptually different from traditional marketing, and marketers need to deal with the implication.

With the Web, it is almost as if the visitor is a bumblebee, moving from flower to flower, creating his or her own unique formula for consuming marketing information—a formula designed to meet his or her uniquely individual needs. It is truly randomized, because things just do not happen when you expect them to, and a visitor may want to interact with you at any time during the process.

Intersponding: A New Response Model

In fact, I believe the Internet creates an entirely new response model, which we can call "intersponding"—a new kind of *interactive, instant, interspersed* pattern of responding. To see what this means from a marketing perspective, let us go back to that Web site visitor. There he or she is, navigating through a Web site, uniquely and freely. Perhaps no two visitors move through a Web site in exactly the same way.

The visitor goes from place to place, consuming bits and pieces of information as the need arises, sometimes at random, sometimes in logical order. Because Web browser software makes it so easy to go from page to page with "back" and "forward" buttons, the pattern may be quite complex. That is a good reason for your Web site to provide navigation elements that remain on pages appearing after the home page, so that the visitor can continue to move with total freedom from section to section, yet recall the section for reference. It is just as easy for the visitor to print an occasional page when the need arises.

The Web makes it easy to select and copy text and graphics from other Web sites—and even to obtain the HTML (Hyper Text Markup Language) source code for each Web page with a simple click of the mouse. This is unheard of, and unthinkable, in any other medium! It provides a level of insider access to a Web site visitor (who could just as easily be your competitor as your customer). It puts the power of not just easy information access, but easy information duplication, in the hands of the individual.

In sum, the Web offers a single unique individual a very unique, personal way of interacting with information on your Web site or through one-to-one e-mail communication. In a very real sense, the information this person receives is being individualized, because the visitor is requesting and receiving it in just the way he or she wants it to be delivered.

The level of individualized information will intensify even further as databases are used to enhance Web sites. With database marketing, the marketer will be able to capture information about how the visitor is using the Web site and use that information to structure and refine the information flow to the visitor. When the visitor returns to the Web site, the Web site will "know" the individual's likes and dislikes and feed personalized information to him or her by creating Web pages on the fly that include uniquely personalized content.

This is already a built-in aspect of a growing number of sites on the Web, which allow you to individualize or personalize pages by providing profile data. The data is analyzed by a database engine. Web pages are then created just for you. You can "pick them up" at the Web site, or have them "pushed" to your computer in some cases. Try it yourself. Go to *www.individual.com* and create an individualized news page, just the way you want it. Or visit any of the larger commercial sites or portals and find the "My Page" feature for a completely personalized experience on each site.

Now, what about the *responding* part of "intersponding?" Well, this is truly interesting: If a Web site is set up correctly, the visitor can instantly respond at any time along the way—whether it seems logical or not to respond at that point. Some Web sites embed e-mail response areas so that visitors can click an underlined address, type in an inquiry or response, and send it immediately. Many Web sites go beyond that, however, by using interactive forms. These forms collect basic information about the visitor—name, address, phone number, and so on—and sometimes ask qualifying questions of the visitor. Well-constructed Web sites prominently show a link to this form on the home page and provide multiple links to the form throughout the site. Even better, the visitor is offered something special (good direct marketing!) for completing and sending the form. It can be sent with a simple click of the mouse. We will talk more about these Web response forms later.

*But wait, there's something wrong....*So far, all of this does not sound very different from the traditional way of responding, does it? The Web site has a form that a visitor fills out and sends—the same as with a direct mail reply form or order form, the same as with a call to an 800 number. What is the big deal? Remember this is not responding, this is intersponding. There is another facet of intersponding that makes it completely unique.

> *Not only can the visitor interactively respond via the Internet, he or she can also instantly be fulfilled via the Internet.*

After the visitor sends the Web response form, he or she can *instantly* and *automatically*:

> Receive an answer that verifies the visitor's instructions or acknowledges an order,

> Receive a more detailed acknowledgment of ordering information via return e-mail,

> Unlock or receive documents or special Web pages, personalized to the specific needs of the visitor,

Download a demonstration, trial, or full version of a software product onto the visitor's computer for immediate use,

Gain access to a private event or virtual seminar that offers the visitor a free interactive learning experience, and

Be acknowledged as a *returning* visitor or customer, and therefore be given special treatment. For example, the visitor's name, address, and previous ordering information can be stored by the marketer and recalled for use by the visitor when a new order is placed.

Each of these potential responses is an "intersponse"—an interactive, instant fulfillment of the visitor's inquiry—an immediate payback for the visitor's time and trouble.

Intersponding feeds the need for so many things on the part of the prospect or customer:

- Instant gratification

- Total and immediate responsiveness

- One-to-one communication

- Personal correspondence

- The ease and convenience of an automated response

Intersponding *completely changes the relationship* the prospect or customer has with the computer, the Internet, and the marketer. Even though the prospect or customer is sitting in front of a machine and typing on a keyboard, the response he or she receives is warm, personal, and intimate—because it is intended just for him or her and it is delivered instantly, a direct response to an immediate need. Properly executed, it is the ultimate in fulfillment—what everyone expects when they think of personalized customer service and responsiveness. Ironically, it is what good old-fashioned commerce used to be.

In the American past, there was a time when you could visit a friendly neighborhood store and the proprietor recognized your face and knew your name. He or she knew your family, too, and also knew what you liked to buy, how much you needed, and when you would probably be back. In short, the proprietor had a relationship with you.

The proprietor was not just a store clerk, but a person. He or she chatted with you about the weather, ordered products for you, held them for you when they came in, and sent you on your way with a smile when you were done shopping.

For the most part, we have relegated these kinds of personal business relationships to the past. We have few experiences in our consumer or business lives that replicate them. It is sad, but people just do not seem to know whom they are doing business with anymore.

Maybe that is one more reason for the Internet's popularity. The Internet can, in a business relationship sense, be that proprietor. It may be sobering to think that individuals need to go to a computer to get the same kind of personalized attention they received from a real live store clerk years ago, but the reality is that businesses cannot always provide that kind of face-to-face contact anymore. Customers are all over the world, retail establishments are depersonalized and automated, and the cost of maintaining intense personalized relationships is high.

With the Internet, maybe that will not be a problem anymore. With the Internet, maybe intersponding can be the new response model that will make marketing personal once again.

Seven Proven Internet Marketing Strategies

In the following chapters, we will explore in detail seven proven Internet marketing strategies you can put to work to dramatically improve your business-to-business marketing efforts and increase profits:

1. *Generating and qualifying leads with the Internet.* Lead generation and qualification is the heart of most business-to-business marketing programs. Learn how lead practices apply to the Internet, how the Internet can be integrated with direct mail and telemarketing, and how to use e-mail, Web response forms, Web sites, and Web advertising to enhance your lead generation and qualification efforts.

2. *Using Internet events to promote products and services.* The Internet offers business-to-business marketers a remarkably

cost-effective alternative to live conferences, seminars, and similar promotional events. In addition, the Internet can be used to promote and enhance traditional marketing events. See how you can create Net events that bring qualified prospects to you.

3. *Executing e-fulfillment.* You can use the Internet to qualify prospects and instantly fulfill their requests for information via "pull" and "push" technologies. Find out how to create instant e-fulfillment programs.

4. *Building customer relationships with the Internet.* Discover the power of the Internet in developing one-to-one relationships with customers and providing customers with superior service around the clock. Learn how to develop a customer-driven extranet.

5. *Using or establishing business communities and exchanges.* See how successful business-to-business marketers take the concept of the Web community and apply it to their own marketing programs. Learn how to participate in business communities and maybe even build one of your own.

6. *Using the Internet to create and manage partner programs.* Find out how the Internet brings new meaning to partnering. Discover the power of affiliate marketing programs, partner links, and partner service sites.

7. *Selling over the Internet.* Learn how business-to-business marketers are successfully launching electronic stores on the Internet, securely selling everything from books to industrial products—and generating millions of dollars a day.

Each of these seven strategies is grounded in the fundamental principles of direct marketing. They are timeless concepts that you should recognize, because they have been taken straight out of a direct marketing playbook. Internet marketing may require a new set of practices and a new way of thinking, but it is, at its heart, good, solid direct marketing. Read on and see for yourself.

Notes

1. Nielsen Media Research and CommerceNet, *Study on Internet Commerce, www.commerce.net*, April 1999.

2. International Data Corporation, *IDC Predictions '99: The "Real" Internet Emerges, www.IDC.com*, copyright 1998, International Data Corporation.

3. The Direct Marketing Association, *Economic Impact: U.S. Direct Marketing Today,* Direct Marketing Association, Inc., New York, 1998.

4. U.S. Department of Commerce, *The Emerging Digital Economy*, April 1998. (*www.ecommerce.gov*)

5. Melissa Bane, Senior Analyst, The Yankee Group, "Is Successful Web Marketing a Myth? *Sales and Marketing Series: Web Marketing—Myth and Reality,* a presentation of the Massachusetts Software Council, Natick, Massachusetts, February 6, 1998.

6. International Data Corporation, *The Western European Forecast for Internet Usage and Commerce, www.IDC.com*, copyright 1997, International Data Corporation.

7. DSA Analytics, *The Internet User and Online Commerce in Japan, 1999,* from the CyberBusiness Series, as reported in News from the Direct Marketing Association, March 1999.

3

Generating and Qualifying Leads with Your Web Site

The lead generation and qualification process is common to virtually every business-to-business marketer, large and small, regardless of industry or target audience. Most marketers know they could be doing it better, and many have now learned that the Internet can significantly improve the process.

This chapter is the first of three that discuss lead generation and qualification in the context of the Age of the "e." The basic steps remain the same, but you will learn how using the Internet will necessitate change. This chapter explains Internet-enhanced lead generation and qualification techniques specific to your Web site. In the next two chapters, we will cover the use of online advertising and e-mail.

Leads and More Leads

Before we discuss using your Web site for lead generation, we should look at the ways in which leads are generated using traditional direct marketing media, starting with direct mail.

Over the past few years, direct mail response rates in general have been declining. Several factors probably contribute to this, including the proliferation of advertising mail, the media conflict caused by general advertising and telemarketing, and now, the real shift of consumer interest and advertisers' attention to the Internet. There is increasing competition in virtually every product category. Individuals in business are overwhelmed, as are consumers, with hundreds of promotional messages each day.

Typical direct mail lead generation raw response rates are between 1 and 2 percent. When a traditional lead generation mailing response rate exceeds 3 percent, it is often a time for celebration. Order generation response rates generally fall below 1 percent because generating an order with direct mail is a tougher challenge than generating a lead.

Response rates can be enhanced by using follow-ups to original mailings. A follow-up is generally a simple letter or a "double postcard"—a postcard mailing that includes a tear-off business reply card that can be returned by the prospect. Such a mailing can be mailed to the same list as the original mailing, using the same offer, at a very low incremental cost. Typically, a follow-up mailing lifts the response rate by one-half of the response rate to the original mailing. If the original mailing achieved a 2 percent response, the follow-up is likely to achieve an additional 1 percent response.

Is a 2 percent response rate really good enough today to justify continued promotional investments in traditional direct mail? Are there proven strategies to lift response rates—and more important, to generate a *higher percentage of qualified leads*? How can you get your share of the other 98 percent of the audience who, for whatever the reason, did not respond?

One answer could be *leveraging your direct marketing across several complementary media*. Yes, direct mail is still the proven lead generation medium that can be most effectively and precisely targeted, tested, controlled, and measured, but when it is enhanced with other media, direct mail becomes even more effective and efficient in getting the job done.

Enhancing Direct Mail With Telemarketing

Some business-to-business direct marketers have achieved significant success boosting response rates by adding *telemarketing* to the media mix. Industry experience suggests that telemarketing seems to have the most positive impact on direct mail when it is used to follow up with both respondents and non-respondents. Here are two examples:

1. If an individual responds to a mailing or an ad, or attends an event, a call from a telemarketer can often further qualify that person's interest. This individual can then be prioritized and placed in the appropriate response or lead category.

2. If an individual receives a direct mailing and does *not* respond, a follow-up call from a telemarketer may prompt a response. In fact, there is some evidence that aggressive telemarketing which is conducted right after a direct mail campaign can increase overall response, even if the target audience has not yet responded.

Telemarketing does have some drawbacks, however, when applied to lead generation in the business-to-business market:

1. Telemarketing is significantly more expensive than direct mail on a per-contact basis. A high-quality direct mail contact in a quantity of 10,000 may cost in the $2.50 to $5.00 range, but a telemarketing contact could cost from $7.00 to $15.00 each for a few thousand calls.

2. Telemarketing costs do not typically decline on a unit cost basis with increasing quantities because telephone line charges and personnel costs remain stable. Direct mail costs almost always decrease on a unit cost basis as mail quantities increase.

3. More and more, business-to-business telemarketing is being screened out by voice mail or assistants answering the prospect's phone, especially in the case of management. The result is that it can take five to seven phone calls to connect with a "live" target prospect—if at all.

Obviously, this means you need to carefully control the use of telemarketing as it relates to the lead generation process.

Quantity or Quality?

We have established that direct mail, when enhanced by telemarketing, may produce higher response rates than direct mail alone, but the incremental cost could be significant. In a moment, we will see if the same holds true with Internet-enhanced direct mail lead generation. First, however, there is an issue we need to address: the *quantity* of responses versus the *quality* of responses.

Earlier, we talked about the challenge of falling direct mail response rates. A knee-jerk reaction to this problem may be to increase mailing quantities. At first glance, it seems like a logical strategy. If response rates are declining, you simply mail more, right? In many cases, this is exactly what you *should not* do.

As you probably know, the economics of direct mail marketing are such that the more you mail, the less each mailing unit costs. For example, you might be able to mail 50,000 self-mailing pieces at a cost of $1.50 each. That same mailing piece, however, may cost you $3.00 each at a quantity of 20,000. This simple fact of direct marketing life may lead to the mistaken belief that mailing more equals more response. That may be true, but here is the question you need to ask yourself: Is a higher response rate what you *really* want?

If you are marketing higher-priced products to businesses, this may not be what you want. Suppose you are marketing a product at a price point of $5,000. Businesses with 25 or less employees may not be a good market for your product. Chances are a business owner or manager of that smaller size company would not purchase a product at that price unless it were absolutely essential. To limit your risk, you would probably not want to mail to these smaller businesses, so you would use mailing lists that provide selectivity on the basis of business size.

Suppose your sales channel has found that the product is very appealing to a particular individual within a business, such as the person in charge of marketing, and your channel partners have also told you that certain vertical industries seem to be more interested in the product than others. You would want to make sure that the lists you use offer additional selectivity to accommodate these audience characteristics: You would select on the basis of names and titles of Marketing Directors or Managers, if they are available, and SICs (Standard Industrial Classification codes) to get at the right industries.

Using list selection criteria is a basic direct marketing technique to winnow down the universe and ensure that you are selecting the right audience with pinpoint accuracy. Business-to-business direct marketers recognize this process as *targeting:* fine-tuning your audience selection criteria so you can be sure you are making the right offer to the right people. The obvious result is that *your total mailing quantity will decrease,* not increase, and typically, your total number of responses will decrease as well.

If you have ever worked for or with any marketing or sales professional who is used to general advertising and trade shows as primary methods of promotion, you know this is not an easy concept to convey. After all, you are reducing your number of marketing impressions, so your potential to generate total response would logically go down. In addition, each marketing impression will now cost significantly more than if you had done a broader campaign. However, that marketing or sales professional needs to learn to look under the surface for the truth— with your help of course. You are going to show him or her that reducing the *quantity* actually results in increasing the *quality* of the leads generated. Targeting works because it is based on the basic concept that it is better to generate a higher percentage of quality of leads than to generate a high number of responses of lesser quality.

Why Is Lead Quality So Important?

In many cases, mailing a lower quantity at a higher unit cost will beat mailing a higher quantity at a lower unit cost, maybe not in overall response, but in *quality* of response. And most b-to-b marketers recognize that it is better to have a higher percentage of qualified responses from a smaller pool of leads than a lower percentage of qualified responses from a larger pool of leads.

When direct mail is highly targeted, it can be highly efficient. With the advent of the Internet, there is a whole new opportunity for direct marketers to not only increase this efficiency, but actually escalate the Return on Investment (ROI) of lead generation programs.

Business-to-business direct marketing is the *opposite* of advertising, or general media marketing. Direct marketing uses a rifle rather than a shotgun. In some cases, as with lower priced products with broad appeal that are sold directly, it may be worthwhile to increase mail quantities rather than reduce them. Generally, however, the highest return and lowest risk comes from mailing narrow and smart—targeting a more finely defined audience that is more likely to be interested in your product in the first place.

How to Apply Targeted Lead Generation to the Internet

What if you could apply the same targeted direct marketing strategy to the Internet? Imagine if you could target interactive media just as you target direct mail, and imagine if the incremental cost of Internet direct marketing were so low that you could improve the results of your lead generation campaign at almost no risk. It is possible—with the mail-enhancing power of the Internet.

First, by introducing the Internet as an electronic response path in your mailing piece (pointing the prospect to either an e-mail address or, better yet, a specific Web URL) you can potentially increase overall response to your mail campaign. Then, if you enhance your direct mail with carefully targeted Web advertising or opt-in e-mail, you can increase the overall response rate. Finally, if you create a special Web response form (WRF) to capture responses and ask respondents to answer a number of qualifying questions, you can significantly increase the number of qualified leads. The bottom line is that you enhance your direct mail lead generation by leveraging the Internet. You acquire more qualified leads from your direct marketing lead generation campaign at a very low incremental cost. Let us use a hypothetical marketing situation to demonstrate the real impact of the Internet on traditional direct mail lead generation. Later in this chapter, we will get into more detail about each of the program components mentioned below.

Using the Internet Enhances Direct Mail Response

First, here is a direct mail lead generation program utilizing only traditional media: Joan Marketer at AnyNet, Inc. (a fictional company) is about to mail a high-quality first class mailing to 20,000 Networking Managers in medium to large-size companies. Her goal is to generate *qualified leads* for an Internet networking product solution, "TraffiKop," with an average sale price of $15,000.

Joan has executed these kinds of mailings previously, so she knows the approximate cost as well as the anticipated results. She will have a direct marketing agency rent a number of mailing lists, eliminate the duplicates and build a mail file, create a high-quality, four-color self-mailing piece, and mail it. Joan plans to offer a free Analyst's Report about TraffiKop. She will use a business reply card, fax-back, and 800 number response paths in the mailing piece. In Figure 3.1, you see what Joan's projected ROI looks like, based on her previous experience with direct mail promotions.

Now we will *enhance* that same direct mail lead generation program with Internet direct marketing. Joan does the same mailing for the same amount of money, but she enhances the direct mail with Internet direct marketing as follows:

1. Joan uses a Web banner ad on AnyNet's Web site home page to reinforce the direct mail promotion.

2. Joan runs that same banner ad as a test banner ad campaign for one month on one Web site targeted to network managers.

3. Joan incorporates a special Web URL into the mailing piece as one of the response paths.

4. The URL leads to a mailing-specific Web response form posted on AnyNet's corporate Web site.

Quantity mailed	20,000 pieces
Total mailing cost	$60,000
Unit cost	$3.00
2.5% response	500 responses
Cost per response	$120.00
Qualified lead rate of 20%	100 qualified leads
Potential sales at $15,000 average sale	$1,500,000
Sales close rate of 10%	10 sales
Projected sales at 10% close rate	$150,000
Projected ROI	2.5 : 1

Figure 3.1. Direct mail comparison chart.

5. Joan asks prospects to include their e-mail addresses on the direct mail reply card or on the Web response form. She asks if AnyNet can use the prospect's e-mail address for future communications. She collects the e-mail addresses of respondents who provided them for a follow-up campaign.

Let us look at each of these steps individually in overview form. Later in this chapter, you will find specific detail about each of these program elements so you can see how to create and place Web banner ads, design a Web response form, and conduct an e-mail campaign.

Step 1: *Create a Web banner ad.* Joan has a Web banner ad created to coordinate with the direct mail. Cost: $2,500. She invites her Webmaster to lunch and gets him to agree to place it on the AnyNet home page. The banner is linked to a special Web response form (see Step 4).

Step 2: *Place the Web banner ad.* Joan also places the banner ad for one month on a Web site targeted to networking managers. The Web site guarantees that the banner ad will appear 100,000 times in that month. The banner is linked to a special Web response form. Cost for the research and 100,000 impressions (1 month): $9,000. Total cost for the banner ad campaign: $11,500.

Step 3: *Incorporate a special URL into the mailing piece.* Joan adds a Web response path to her mailing piece; she includes a special URL along with the phone and fax numbers, and the tear-off business reply card.

Step 4: *Develop a Web response form.* Joan has a special Web response form created to post on her Web site. The form has the same look and feel as the mailing piece and reiterates the major copy points. The Web response form asks the visiting prospect to answer several qualifying questions. When these questions are answered, the prospect will be able to instantly access and read the offer, the Analyst's Report, online.

The Web response form has a link to AnyNet's home page at the end of the form. Versions of the form are created to accommodate the two different banner ads (one on the AnyNet site, and one on the commercial site targeted to networking managers) so response can be measured separately. Cost to create the Web response form: $2,000 (not including response processing or reporting).

Step 5: *Collect the e-mail addresses for a follow-up campaign.* On the Web response form, prospects are asked to provide AnyNet with permission to communicate with them via e-mail. Those who answer "Yes" and include their e-mail addresses are added to an e-mailing list. These respondents receive an e-mail acknowledgment to their response. They also receive a follow-up e-mailing two weeks later that makes a special limited time offer if they purchase "TraffiKop." Cost for the e-mailing: Joan purchases an e-mail software distribution product for a few hundred dollars and decides to handle this part of the campaign in-house.

What is the Payback?

Let us see how this Internet activity affects Joan's direct mail program— in particular, the ROI. Figure 3.2 "Program A" is a repeat of the previous information—the direct mail lead generation program using only traditional media. Figure 3.3 "Program B" is new—the direct mail program enhanced with Internet direct marketing.

Analysis of Programs A and B

This example is fictional, but the statistics used in the two accompanying charts are based on real-world experiences. Here is an analysis of programs A and B.

1. The mailing quantities are the same in both A and B. The *qualified lead rate* (the percentage of leads considered to be of high quality based on purchase time frame and budget criteria set by AnyNet) is the same in both A and B, as is the *sales close rate* (the percentage of qualified leads which are ultimately converted to sales) and the average sale of $15,000. With all

Quantity mailed	20,000 pieces
Total mailing cost	$60,000
Unit cost	$3.00
2.5% response	500 responses
Cost per response	$120.00
Qualified lead rate of 20%	100 qualified leads
Potential sales at $15,000 average sale	$1,500,000
Sales close rate of 10%	10 sales
Projected sales at 10% close rate	$150,000
Projected ROI	2.5 : 1

Figure 3.2.   Program A: Traditional direct mail lead generation.

Quantity mailed	20,000 pieces
Total mailing cost	$60,000
Additional cost of Internet activities (Banner ad, ad placement, WebResponse Form)	$13,500
Total campaign cost	$73,500
2.8% response (Response *enhanced* with the use of a Web URL in the mailing piece)	560 responses
Additional response 1. AnyNet home page banner ad 2. Banner ad on commercial Web site (100,000 impressions @1.0% click-through rate=1,000, with 25% of the click-throughs completing the form)	100 responses 250 responses
Total responses	910 responses
Cost per response	$80.77
Qualified lead rate of 20%	182 qualified leads
Potential sales at $15,000 average sale	$2,730,000
Sales close rate of 10%	18 sales
Projected sales at 10% close rate	$270,000
Projected ROI	3.7 : 1

Figure 3.3.   Program B: Internet-enhanced direct mail lead generation.

the direct mail statistics held constant, we can segregate the impact of Internet direct marketing.

2. The cost of program B is $73,500 vs. $60,000 for program A. That is $13,500, or 22½ percent, higher than program A.

3. The number of responses is higher in program B than in program A. That is because Internet direct marketing increased the overall number of responses from 500 to 910—almost double the responses from mail alone.

4. Notice that cost per response drops from $120 for program A to $80.77 for program B.

5. The dramatic increase in responses resulted in an equally dramatic increase in qualified leads from program B, even though the original mailing quantity was maintained. This led to a corresponding increase in the number of sales and in total sales revenue.

   Some direct marketing experts believe that a Web response form respondent could actually be a higher quality prospect than someone who responds via mail or fax. That is because this individual took the time to go to the URL and fill out a form on the Web, which takes some effort. If this is true, then using the Internet as a response path could potentially increase the number of qualified leads even more than this example indicates. However, we have used the same qualified lead rate for both programs A and B.

6. We did *not* include the e-mail follow-up campaign in program B, because then we would have to include the cost of a direct mail follow-up campaign in program A to keep things even. The e-mail follow-up campaign could potentially add even more revenue at a very low incremental cost.

IMPACT OF THE INTERNET ON DIRECT MAIL LEAD GENERATION

With an additional $13,500, or a 22½ percent increase in the total budget, Joan improved the ROI of the lead generation program from 2.5:1 to 3.7:1, by enhancing traditional direct mail with the Internet!

In this program, the Internet was not used in a vacuum. It was added to the existing direct mail campaign. As with direct mail, the Internet should be used in a very targeted fashion. In this example, media for the Web banner advertising campaign was researched and carefully chosen. The Web response form was designed specifically to qualify respondents. E-mail was not broadcast widely to individuals who did not want it, but rather targeted to prospects who already demonstrated an interest in the product *and* gave permission to communicate with them via email.

When you use the Internet in the same careful, precise and efficient way in which you use direct mail or telemarketing, it becomes *Internet direct marketing.*

> *Internet direct marketing can be targeted, tested,*
> *controlled, and measured—just like direct mail marketing.*

Because of the current economics of Internet usage, Internet direct marketing can be even more cost-effective than traditional direct mail lead generation. After all, there are no materials or postage costs.

There is an added bonus to Internet direct marketing: There is nothing to physically produce, so your production timeline is compressed. Instead of waiting to print and mail something, you can get on the Internet very fast, and you can make modifications to programs just as fast. That means you can see the results of your efforts quickly as well.

Although the Internet can be proven to enhance the traditional media used in your lead generation programs, it is probably premature to assume that the Internet can replace direct mail or telemarketing entirely. For one thing, the Internet is not yet a precision medium for targeting. It has not reached the level of maturity of direct mail in terms of your ability to hone a prospect list by using key criteria to select exactly the right individuals for a mailing program.

In addition, access to individual names and titles via the Internet is problematic. As you will see in the next chapter on e-mail, prospecting via the Internet presents a whole set of unique challenges to the business-to-business marketer.

You must also consider the fact that Internet lead generation and qualification is still relatively new as a marketing practice. Some target audiences may be comfortable with it; others may not. The acceptance of the Internet as a means of self-qualification will vary from prospect to prospect. Nevertheless, augmenting traditional lead generation media with the Internet is something you should be doing.

The Internet Can Improve Your Entire Lead Management Process

Think about how to incorporate the Internet into your own lead qualification process. Remember the marketing pyramid in Chapter 1? By turning the marketing pyramid upside down, we got a "Marketing Funnel," representing the various stages of the lead qualification process. We talked about how a lead moves down the funnel from "cool" to "warm" to "hot"—until it turns into a sale.

Ask yourself how the Internet can play a role in *facilitating* that process:

- How can you use the Internet to generate leads in the first place?

- How can the Internet support and enhance your use of traditional direct marketing media?

- How can you incorporate the Internet into your existing lead qualification process so that it helps to produce a larger number of qualified leads and, ultimately, a higher lead close rate?

- How can you move toward true electronic lead capture and qualification over the Internet—integrating that information with your marketing database?

- How can the Internet enhance the relationships you have with marketing and channel partners—so that they, too, benefit from your lead generation activities?

- How can the Internet help you strengthen the relationship between your marketing and sales organizations—so you receive the feedback you need to know how well your lead generation and qualification programs are working?

- How can the Internet become a feedback mechanism for prospects—so you can continuously requalify them and know where they stand in the qualification process?

- How can you apply Internet technology to automate your sales lead management system—so it becomes a flexible, responsive system, accessible across your enterprise and to select parties outside your enterprise?—so you can increase response, qualified leads, and profits.

A First Step: Web Response Forms

The Web Response Form (WRF) is the electronic equivalent of a direct mail reply card and, as such, represents a fundamental change in the way people may prefer to respond. A WRF can be part of a "landing page" or "jump page"—a termination point of a specialized URL designed to funnel response from traditional or interactive direct marketing media. Unlike the passive e-mail address, the WRF is active. In fact, it is *interactive*. And Internet marketers are using it with great success. See Figure 3.4 for an example of a Web Response Form.

Here is how it works. You place a direct response ad, you send out a piece of direct mail, you place a banner ad or e-mail newsletter ad, or you send out an e-mail. In the call to action, you may include traditional response paths, such as an address or fax number, and an 800 or 888 toll-free phone number to take inquiries or orders. But you add as a response path a special Web URL, set up as a *unique identifier* for the specific campaign, if possible.

The special Web URL can "hang off" of your existing Web site. Simply create a URL address, such as *www**[your Web site name].com/* [promotional identifying word]. The downside is that some individuals may go to the corporate Web address anyway, dropping the extension. These kinds of special URLs therefore work best when they are direct links from within an e-mail. You should expect a percentage of total leads generated by a campaign using a special URL to go to your corporate Web site rather than the special address, so it is generally a good idea to mention the campaign on the home page and then drive prospects to the same WRF off of the home page. In order to track the respondent back to a particular list or other coded criteria, you should assign an access code, generate it onto the mailing piece in a prominent place, and then ask the respondent to enter that code on the WRF.

Better yet, you can apply for a *completely unique* URL that relates specifically to the product promotion—although there is an additional cost associated with it. Completely unique URLs associated with a high value offer may be beneficial because they lead the prospect *away* from a general Web site's home page. That is important if you are truly trying

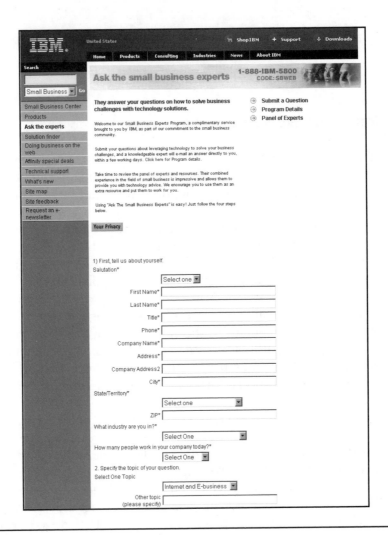

Figure 3.4. IBM Ask the small business experts.

to track the lead back to a specific campaign, rather than have it go to a general Web page where you cannot track it.

Why? For the same reason you include a reply card in direct mail and say "Respond today for this free offer by returning the reply card" instead of saying "Contact us for more information." In direct marketing, you need to facilitate response by telling the respondent specifically what to do and where to go. Making a specific offer instead of offering general information is a proven response generator. Asking for a specific response to that offer facilitates and potentially increases response.

Directing a prospect to a corporate Web site in a lead generation campaign opens up a multitude of options that could actually be a barrier to response. When prospects go to a Web site's home page instead of a Web response form, they may not be able to easily find the response path. That is because many home pages are busy and filled with links, and most Web marketers do not give a lot of thought to including a WRF that stands out from all the home page clutter.

There is another nasty side effect to not using a WRF. Business-to-business prospects are becoming far more accustomed to the Web as a means of learning about companies and their products. That means they may go to a company's general Web site when they see an ad or receive a piece of direct mail—even if a special URL is included in the promotion. Prospects visit the general Web site, look around, find the information they want, and then leave. As a result, the campaign generates responses, maybe even good leads, but they cannot be attributed to that specific campaign. The campaign "leaks leads," because the marketer never captures any identifying information about the prospects. When the marketer analyzes the campaign, it may look as if it did not do so well, when leads were actually coming in—but through a response path that *was not being measured* as part of the campaign.

That is why it is essential to tie a compelling and unique offer to your WRF—preferably something a prospect can receive *only* by going to that specific WRF. If the offer is unique, prospects will be more likely to go to a special place to get it. A common mistake is making a direct marketing offer that is already on your Web site. If anyone can gain access to the offer through your corporate Web site, and it is not necessary to provide identifying and qualifying information to read it, you may get a visitor—but you will not get a lead.

Obviously, if you do a lot of direct mail promotions, and you do not find it feasible to use different URLs for your WRFs, you could use your home page as the destination. But then, it is important to have a prominent area on your home page that highlights promotions so respondents can get there quickly. This should link to a promotions page that briefly describes each promotion and shows a graphic so the respondent can relate it back to the direct mail piece received. As mentioned earlier, if you wish to track the response by list or other key criteria, you will need to generate a tracking code on the mail piece and ask the respondent to fill in that code on the WRF.

Web Response Forms Tighten the Process

The WRF is designed to tighten the lead generation and qualification process. When the respondent goes to your special URL, he or she finds the WRF—a page or a series of pages, along with an interactive form, reinforcing that individual's interest immediately. The WRF potentially turns that preliminary interest into *an action*. A WRF can also capture valuable marketing information about the respondent and ask qualifying questions.

WRFs can be especially effective as the termination point of Web banner advertising. The Web banner ad can be linked directly to the WRF. The prospect clicks on the ad and is routed instantly to the WRF. In this case, since the banner ad is just a teaser, the WRF can be a Web response area, perhaps even a Web "mini-site." The purpose of the Web response area is to share information so that the prospect can make a more informed inquiry and possibly even a purchase.

A Web response area can be thought of as "electronic fulfillment" (more about this later). Electronic fulfillment is something that is fast becoming a standard in the Age of the "e." As the cost of printed materials goes up, electronic fulfillment becomes more attractive.

There may be a time when all that is needed in a direct mail lead generation campaign is a cost-effective postcard that alerts a prospect to an informational offer that can be obtained by visiting a special URL. There, the prospect arrives at a Web response area and finds complete information about the offer and the product being promoted. The prospect can then "pay" for the offer with "marketing currency" by typing in his or her contact information and answering some qualifying questions. The prospect sends the form, the marketer gets the lead, and the prospect instantly receives the offer online via electronic fulfillment. Very tidy.

The Basics of Constructing Web Response Forms

Web response areas and WRFs can be constructed in a number of ways, but here are some of the basic things to include:

- A headline at the top of the WRF welcomes or thanks the respondent for visiting. The headline acknowledges the fact that the respondent came to this special page to get or do something. The headline should tie in directly with the promotion itself in terms of graphic look and feel and copy.

The WRF reinforces the promotion and summarizes the offer. It is a good idea to use some of the same copy from the original promotion to integrate and leverage the messaging.

If necessary, one or more pages provide product information.

Instructional copy tells the respondent *what he or she will receive* if the WRF is completed and sent. The offer can be handled in a variety of ways:

– Instant fulfillment: The respondent sends the form and instantly receives the desired information in return.

– Unlock and download: The respondent sends the form and receives instructions for how to unlock and download a document or software, typically a trial or demonstration version of the product.

– Private access: The respondent sends the form and receives an acknowledgment, either instantly or via return e-mail, that includes a special URL and/or password which allows access to a separate private Web area or virtual event (more about virtual events in Chapter 4).

– Traditional fulfillment: The respondent sends the form and receives the information requested via fax or traditional mail, or receives an item ordered via traditional mail or delivery service.

• The form itself allows the respondent to interactively fill in basic data: name, title, company name, address, city, state, zip code, phone number, fax number, and e-mail address. The form should also ask several qualifying questions, including whether or not the prospect grants permission to use e-mail for correspondence. Some marketers make certain questions required (i.e., the form cannot be sent unless the required fields are completed).

– It is generally a good idea to offer a link to the corporate Web site only at the *end* of the WRF, or on the acknowledgment page the respondent receives once the WRF is sent. This funnels the respondent's actions and does not let him or her "escape" from the WRF but gives the person the ability to learn more by visiting the corporate Web site after responding.

The WRF is an excellent way to capture responses electronically. Including a Web URL typically helps increase overall response to a direct marketing campaign. If the target audience is composed of technical professionals or individuals who frequent the Web, they may in fact prefer the Web response path to more traditional response methods. Individuals who "live" on their networks and use the Web extensively for research and information are far more likely to respond over the Web than they are to return a reply card or make a phone call.

Finally, there is growing evidence that individuals who respond via WRFs are highly qualified prospects. I was involved in one print advertising campaign in which a special Web URL was used in addition to the traditional mail, fax, and phone response paths. A tear-out business reply card accompanied the ad. The advertising ran in national trade publications targeted to IT professionals.

Twenty percent of the total responses came in via the Web. Of those responses, over 50 percent were considered high-quality leads. This is two to three times greater than the norm for qualified leads generated by traditional print advertising or direct mail lead generation.

There is some logic to this if you consider the fact that a Web respondent has to "work harder" to respond. Finding the URL may be easy, but typing in all the requested information and answering questions on a computer screen takes some time and effort. There is no easy way around this. WRFs can be simplified by using drop-down menus for multiple choices (to indicate your state, for example) or radio buttons and check boxes, but individuals still need to type certain basic contact information, which can be tedious. Doing so suggests that the prospect wants to obtain the offer or get more information and is willing to do a little bit of work to get it. In today's high-pressure, compressed-time business environment, that is an important indication of a prospect's interest.

Despite the WRF's advantages as a response mechanism, it is not entirely foolproof. Even if you use a special URL, potential prospects could go to your regular Web site instead. That is why, if you are doing a promotion that features a special URL, you might want to mention that promotion *and* have a link to a version of the WRF on your Web site home page for prospects who show up there instead of coming to the special URL.

Another potential problem is the interactive form itself. Be sure it is constructed properly (most forms use CGI or JavaScript) and that you test it with several different computers and browsers. It is also a good idea to try it out on several different people to see if the form is easy to understand and easy to use. You need to assure that the respondent can easily send the WRF—and that you receive the information you need.

Using Your Web Site for Lead Generation and Qualification

Is the money being invested in your Web site offering you a true return on your marketing investment?

To obtain a marketing ROI from your Web site, you need to be able to prove to yourself and to your management that it is achieving *measurable results*. This means your Web site must be structured to capture and qualify leads, and potentially to accept online orders from prospects and customers.

Many books are available that cover how to build and improve Web sites. Such books go into the necessary detail you will need to execute a Web site project. Our focus here is not on the design and technical elements of building Web sites but instead, on how to use your Web site in the context of direct marketing—to *generate and qualify leads, get response,* and *achieve measurable results*.

Not All Web Sites Are Response Oriented

The fact is that the majority of sites on the Web today may be marketing sites, but not as many as you might think are *direct* marketing sites. You can prove this to yourself by visiting your favorite sites, or by going to any of the Web's "best" sites as reported by various trade publications and Web sources.

From a direct marketing perspective, a lot may be lacking in even those business-to-business Web sites considered to be "the best." In many cases, they may be nothing more than brochureware.

Seize the Opportunity to Set Your Web Site Apart

For a Web site to be used as a lead generation and qualification tool, it must follow the basic principles of good direct marketing.

Begin with the design of your Web site and its home page. Earlier in this book, you read about the nonlinear nature of the Web. You saw how a site visitor could jump from place to place, freely, and randomly. This is true, but it is also true that a Web site can be designed to *highlight or emphasize certain areas* so that the visitor is drawn to them. The design of a page can assist the visitor in locating offers and finding a Web response form.

One possible way to influence the visitor's navigational path is to make the most prominent part of your home page a special offer, highlighted by an animated graphic. If it stands out from the rest of the page and leads to a Web response form, the offer could potentially draw a majority of visitors to that area. Another way is to feature a promotional area that makes the same offer to visitors as a current direct mail or direct response-advertising campaign. Leveraging the direct marketing offer could potentially enhance response.

The Web provides the distinct marketing advantage of speed. An offer could easily be posted on a Web site in time to coordinate with any direct marketing campaign—before the campaign even appears in print. If the offer is prominently featured on the home page, perhaps through an on-site banner ad that ties in creatively with the direct mail or advertising, you would gain from the power of integrated media.

Good direct marketing copywriting can also improve the effectiveness of a Web site. Direct marketing copy tends to be written in a friendly, me-to-you style with a heavy emphasis on benefits. It uses short sentences and an informal structure that makes it easier to read and follow. It makes liberal use of "graphic signals" and eye rests, such as indented paragraphs and bulleted lists.

As you explore Web sites, read the words carefully and evaluate the structure and quality of the writing. Notice how tedious it is reading lengthy copy on a computer screen? A good site will take that into account by keeping sentences and paragraphs short; using frequent subheads in bold or in color; breaking copy into sections; using bulleted lists, tables, and indents; and bolding or italicizing appropriate words and phrases.

Incorporate Direct Marketing Techniques into Your Web Site

Here are a few ways you can use direct marketing to improve the efficiency of your Web site in generating and qualifying leads.

1. *Make it easy for a prospect to locate and gain access to a Web response area.* Many Web sites either bury the response area or do not even have one. A prominent response area on a Web site, even a simple Web response form, will encourage prospects to identify and potentially qualify themselves. Reinforcing that response area throughout the Web site by providing links across many of your site's pages will remind prospects of the offer and give them multiple opportunities to respond.

2. *Create a promotional area with special offers.* Turn your response area into a promotional area, featuring special offers, which change from time to time. Tie these offers in with direct marketing campaigns by leveraging the copy and graphics used in other media and "Web-izing" the creative for use on your site.

3. *Place an "on-site" banner ad.* A banner ad is a promotional technique most often used as advertising on other Web sites to draw people to your Web site, but you can also create and place a self-promotional banner ad on your *own* site—to draw attention to a response area on your site. The banner ad could reinforce a campaign in other media or promote a free offer independently and could link to an on-site Web Response Form.

4. *Offer a free subscription to an e-mail newsletter on your site.* As mentioned before, an e-mail newsletter is really an electronic continuity program that gives you the ability to communicate periodically with prospects and customers. You can offer

an e-mail newsletter to prospects who provide you with contact information and answer questions on a Web subscriber form. Then build a list of subscribers and send them an e-mail newsletter regularly. Use the e-mail newsletter to convey valuable information, as well as to make offers and further qualify prospects.

5. *Drive traffic to your Web site via traditional media.* After you invest in a Web site, be sure to capitalize on its existence. Promote the Web site aggressively, especially if it has informational or educational value. Include your Web site address in all promotions and on business cards. Drive traffic to your Web site using other media. For example, business-to-business marketers are achieving significant success generating Web site traffic by simply mailing an oversized postcard promoting the site to prospects and customers. If you have a special offer of any kind, make that offer on your Web site and promote it in order to drive individuals to the site.

Characteristics of Effective Marketing Web Sites

Use the following as a checklist to determine if your own Web site includes some of the more common characteristics of effective marketing sites.

Compelling, Well-Designed Home Page

An effective marketing Web site starts with a well-designed home page. The home page is not unlike the cover of a magazine. It should be interesting, attractive, and intriguing to your target audience. Key content areas should be highlighted so that visitors can find what they need quickly and easily. The home page itself serves as a gateway into the entire site. From a marketing perspective, it should embody the personality of your company and immediately convey a distinct message. It is generally a good idea for the home page to have a look and feel that complements your corporate or promotional identity.

Here's something to consider in page design. In May 2000, a research study conducted by Stanford University and The Poynter Institute tracked eye movements of individuals reading an online news site. The most interesting finding was that the majority of readers were attracted to the article text FIRST, not the graphics or photographs. During the entire reading sessions, 92 percent of article text was looked at, compared with 64 percent of photographs and 22 percent of graphics. Banner ads, however, did better than expected, with a 45 percent showing.

While you don't want to over-react to such a study, especially since the sample was small, the researchers concluded that a Web site's "first chance to engage the reader is through text." You can find the study at *http://www.poynter.org/eyetrack2000/index.htm*

Timely Updating

The Web is a dynamic medium that demands freshness. Some marketers take advantage of this by prominently posting the date each day on their Web sites. Others include daily updates to give the impression of immediacy. Although daily updating may be too ambitious a goal for some, you should at least set a periodic update schedule, perhaps monthly, and adhere to it.

Consider establishing a prominent "What's New" area so you can localize the information that needs frequent updating. Change this area on a periodic basis. Review the remainder of your site at least quarterly for possible updating. Consider refreshing the look of the home page at least every year.

One clever technique for keeping your home page "fresh" is to employ rotating images or copy that changes within the page. You can set up your home page so that it actually has several different versions, or specified areas, which continuously change as visitors hit the page. In this way, each hit generates a page with a different image, providing the impression of a new page with every visit.

Intuitive Navigational Flow

The nonlinear nature of the Web requires a navigational system that is structured to offer visitors maximum flexibility and freedom to move around. Most navigational systems use several "buttons," icons, or images, accompanied with words or phrases, to identify major areas of a Web site. Often these buttons run across the top or down the left side of the home page, sometimes in frames that remain visible on subsequent pages. Once inside a particular section, additional navigational buttons or text links may be necessary to help the visitor move from page to page.

Continuously improving Web technology is making navigational systems more useful. It is becoming increasingly common for the navigation buttons to "respond" or appear highlighted when visitors roll over them with the mouse. Some buttons or icons "respond" when clicked on by moving or changing color, or even producing a sound (although that generally requires a plug-in). These techniques bring enhanced CD game-like interactivity to the Web and help visitors feel like they are making something happen when they roll around the site or click on their mouse.

The increasing use of "dynamic HTML," JavaScript, and Java applets will make navigational systems even better, as long as a visitor's browser supports these technologies. With dynamic HTML, for example, visitors can see subtopics in drop-down menus when they roll over navigational buttons on the home page. This is especially useful for sites with a lot of depth beneath the home page.

Regardless of the technologies employed, the key point is to make navigating a Web site easy, intuitive, and "idiot-proof." As more people become Web-adept, they will move through Web sites and pages skillfully and quickly. Web sites with well-founded navigational structures will assure that visitors have a good experience—and stay awhile.

High-Value Information Content

An effective marketing Web site offers visitors reasons for spending time at the site *and* coming back. Snappy graphics and technological tricks attract attention, but they soon lose their impact if there is no substance to the site. Most Web experts agree that "content is king." Good sites go beyond simply providing product details—they also include product benefits and, more than that, offer high-value information that visitors can use, *whether or not they purchase the product*. The rationale for this is simple: If prospects or customers learn something from a Web site, they will come back for more. Many times, they will also "pledge allegiance" to the site's sponsor by considering that company's product for purchase when the need arises. You lose nothing by posting high-value information that relates to your products or services on your Web site—by doing so, you help to position your company as a knowledgeable leader in your field and gain the respect and potential buying interest of visitors to your site.

Fast Response Time

Do not underestimate the "hang time" problem with the Internet. The Web has not so jokingly been referred to in the industry as the "World Wide Wait" because the continuous growth of Internet traffic, combined with increasingly sophisticated technology, can sometimes make getting onto the Web—and navigating Web sites—a painfully slow experience. You can do a lot on your end to help ease the problem by designing your Web site for the fastest response time so that pages load quickly. In general, that means containing graphic images to small files, being careful of full page background graphics, and assuring that any advanced technologies, such as integrated databases, multimedia, Internet telephony, or live chat, are supported by adequate Web servers.

Response Orientation

A good lead generation and qualification Web site should provide prospects and customers with opportunities to interact and respond. Response paths should stand out and be clearly defined on the home page and referenced throughout the site. Offers should be prominent and lead directly to qualifying Web response forms. Downloads should be easy to execute. Customer service areas should include e-mail links, online forms, and, if possible, 24-hour auto-responders.

Games and contests can help to draw attention to response areas, but they can also generate a large number of unqualified responses—so use them with caution. Make your Web site active, not passive. Make calls to action prominent, and make it easy for visitors to find response areas by instructing them where to go and what to do.

Respect for Privacy

This is listed as a characteristic for effective Web sites because it is becoming increasingly important as the Internet grows more influential as a business-to-business medium. It is recommended that you post a privacy policy on your Web site. You can create your own privacy policy simply by "filling in the blanks" of a free form provided by the Direct Marketing Association at *www.the-dma.org*. The form leads you through a series of questions to help you determine what to tell your site visitors about the way in which the information they provide will be protected and used.

The Internet privacy issue looms as states, the Federal government, and other countries scrutinize cyberspace. It is far too easy to abuse someone's right to privacy electronically, and good b-to-b marketing use of the Web should include ethical practices. Post a privacy policy on your Web site, refuse to use unsolicited e-mail unless you are certain it is acceptable to the recipient, and protect the privacy of any e-mail marketing lists you have in your possession.

How Do You Get Repeat Visitors to Your Web Site?

If a prospect visits your Web site and *does not* complete and send a Web response form, you do not necessarily lose the lead, as long as you design your Web site for repeat visits, to encourage the prospect to check in periodically.

The most successful Web sites enjoy heavy repeat traffic because there is something new for the prospect to experience each time he or she visits. The most common way to achieve this on a Web site is through a "What's New" or "News" area, which is updated as frequently as possible, but even these areas are passive and will not by themselves turn visitors into leads.

The key is to find ways to encourage a dialogue and build a relationship with visitors so that your site will be tops on their list of bookmarks. A frequent browser today could be a buyer tomorrow. Here are a few technology-driven techniques you can use to engage visitors and turn a Web site monologue into a dialogue.

Automated E-mail Response

It is easy to build in a "mail to" e-mail link so that visitors can instantly inquire about your products or services, but it is just as important to respond promptly if not instantly. There are a variety of auto-responder or autobot tools available that can respond automatically to such requests. On good electronic commerce sites, for example, your order can be instantly acknowledged as soon as you place it. An e-mail message is sent to your mailbox verifying your order and providing you with an order number and shipping information. This is also a good way to prevent fraud, because if the recipient did not place the order, he or she can immediately inform the sender of the e-mail.

Cookies

Cookies are not quite as controversial as unsolicited e-mail, but they do cause some concern in the Web community. Cookies are basically little files that your computer stores when you pay a visit to a particular Web site. A cookie allows the Web site to identify your computer when you return to the site. Although your Web browser can be set to alert you to the use of cookies and "turn them off," most users are not even aware they can do this.

On the positive side, a cookie can be very useful in identifying a returning visitor so that the Web site can provide customized Web pages on the fly, if the appropriate database technology is in place. The ultimate value is that a visitor can have a very personalized experience and see pages intended just for him or her. This is a strong motivation for the visitor to return to that particular Web site. E-commerce Web sites routinely use cookies to identify returning customers and help facilitate the ordering process.

Some online advertising resources are using advanced technology which goes beyond the basic cookie. This technology can not only identify the user's address, but also the country, and organization of the user. This information is then used to deliver advertising targeted to the user.

While personalization and customization on the Internet is increasingly common and even desirable, this kind of information intimacy could spook some users if they are not prepared for it. It is a good idea to mention, somewhere on your site, that you use cookies or other such tools for relationship marketing to benefit the visitor and to encourage the visitor to inform you if that is objectionable. We will talk more about customization in later chapters.

Databases, Interactivity, and Multimedia

Java, Sun's Web programming language, is a platform for building interactivity that is not simply cute, but very useful. There are a wide variety of interactive tools that can really benefit visitors to the extent that they will come back and use them repeatedly. For example, using JavaScript, you can build an automatic calculator into a worksheet so a visitor can do a personalized ROI analysis online. You can offer a survey form that, when completed and sent, triggers exactly the right personalized information to be delivered to the visitor. You can build a database of products or solutions and let visitors select their own criteria to locate just the right ones. Since Java is built in to current versions of Web browsers, the Web visitor can automatically take advantage of these enhancements.

Internet database and communication technology has advanced to the extent that entire books are being written about it. Suffice it to say here that such technologies are revolutionizing marketing on the Internet. Tools are now available that permit mass customization of e-mail and Web pages, offering completely personalized communications to unlimited numbers of users. Online query tools and search engines are so powerful that requests for information can be pinpointed with remarkable precision. Internet interactivity has advanced to the point at which chat sessions are now commonplace and online events, discussed in the next chapter, can include real-time audio, and video.

You can provide visitors with a wide variety of multimedia experiences—and the technologies to do so are getting better every day. To hear sound and view extended-time graphic motion or video, visitors will often need to download special software or use a "plug-in" browser accessory, but Web technology is advancing so rapidly that multimedia tools that do not require plug-ins are already on the market. Even video conferencing can be accomplished online with inexpensive digital cameras and the appropriate software. Multimedia opens up all sorts of possibilities for attracting repeat visitors, especially if you combine it with interactivity and personalization.

Creating "Mini-sites"

A "mini-site" is a smaller, self-contained Web site that can stand on its own or be part of a larger Web site. Mini-sites are an effective way to launch a promotion, highlight a product, or drive response to a special offer. Because they are set up as discrete Web areas, they can be used to generate and qualify leads for specific campaigns. Here are two examples.

Mini-site Helps Launch a New Product

An IT company wanted to launch a new software product to a target audience of technical professionals and senior executives. A high-impact direct mail package was created. It included a personalized letter, a die-cut color brochure, and a personalized reply form, mailed in an unusually-sized outer envelope. The offer: an interactive tour of the software product. To encourage response, the offer was enhanced with a free downloadable white paper, plus a special discount on the product if purchased. The prospect was instructed to visit a special URL of a mini-site created especially for the product promotion.

Upon visiting the mini-site, the prospect was asked to provide a code from the mailing piece for tracking purposes, in addition to name, title, and basic contact information. Then the prospect could gain access to the mini-site, which included the product tour, along with benefits targeted to each specific audience who received the mailing. Also included was a special offer section. After the direct mail promotion was complete, the mini-site was attached to the corporate Web site as a special area featuring the new product.

Mini-site Promotes Special Offers

A leading telecommunications company wanted to make several specific service offers to small businesses in a particular region. The offers were to be promoted via television, print, radio, direct mail and Internet advertising. A mini-site was created to promote and consolidate the special offers, and its URL was used in all of the advertising. Prospects who visited the mini-site saw graphics from the television commercials and print ads, reinforcing the campaign. They could go to the specific offer that interested them from the home page of the mini-site. Once in the individual offer area, a prospect was asked to select his or her state so the state-specific offer Web pages could be served up to that individual. While prospects may have been responding to one of the service offers, they could see the other offers on the mini-site. This meant the company had the opportunity to cross-sell other services.

The mini-site was also accessible through the company's corporate Web site via an on-site banner that promoted the special offers.

How Do You Measure the Direct Marketing Effectiveness of Your Web Site?

In the early days of the Internet, counting Web site hits may have been acceptable. But today, direct marketers realize that hits are irrelevant to overall result measurement. The gross number of hits a Web page gets simply represents the physical interactions performed by one or several individuals. Hits do not tell you anything about the level or quality of response, or the leads generated or qualified.

There are a variety of Web analysis tools and service providers at both the low end and high end that now go beyond counting hits. You can use these tools and services to track and analyze the visitor's *interactions* with your Web pages—sometimes right down to how long someone stays on a certain page or even a certain item on the page. This kind of information can be very useful in improving your Web site and making general judgments about marketing efforts. There are second generation tools and services that improve analysis considerably. Now you can learn even more about the way a visitor interacts with your Web pages.

For example, WebTrends *(www.webtrends.com)* offers numerous products that provide enterprise management, analysis and reporting for e-business and Internet-based systems. Some of WebTrends' products perform data mining of Web traffic information, so companies can integrate real-time and historical visitor data with other corporate and marketing databases. NetGenesis *(www.netgen.com)* offers NetAnalysis, a behavioral analysis solution that allows companies to investigate Web site visitor behavior, site content, search engine keywords, and click-throughs. In May 2000, NetGenesis published the "E-Metrics Report," the first comprehensive study focused on business metrics for the new economy. The report defines and standardizes new Web metrics such as the personalization index and the freshness factor. This report is available free at *www.netgen.com/emetrics/*

From a direct marketing perspective, nothing beats obtaining hard, quantifiable data about and from visitors—and determining if those visitors are qualified prospects. That is what you get when you collect leads through Web response forms, asking questions so that you can qualify and prioritize your leads into prospect groups. Then you have the data you need to analyze true *responder* activity, not just visitor activity. That is the true measurement of a Web site's success, and this is not unlike the everyday demand for marketing accountability put on the traditional direct marketer.

Employing Web Site Links to Generate Leads

One of the unusual technological aspects of the Web is the ability visitors have to seamlessly link from not just one page to another within a single Web site, but from one Web site to another just as easily. As a result, a visitor to your site can instantly visit any other site with a quick click of the mouse, if you provide a live link. Similarly, a visitor on any other site can visit your site if there is a link to your site present on that other site. That is why employing Web site links is a whole separate uniquely Web way of generating response and, potentially, leads. There are both free and paid links available to Web direct marketers, and each kind of link has its trade-offs.

Free Links via Search Engines and Directories

After you have built a Web site, you want it to be found easily by customers, prospects, investors, prospective employees, journalists, and other audiences. One of the most popular ways people find Web sites is via Internet searches. However, people rarely go beyond the first few pages of results, so you need to get your Web site to appear in the top 20 search results to be noticed.

The most common search tool is the search engine. Search engines use programs or intelligent agents, called "bots," to actually search the Internet for pages, which they index using specific parameters as they read the content. The agent will read the information on every page of your site and then follow the links.

If you have a Web site, you are already listed somewhere. One way to find out where is to use free tools available on the Internet to find your listings. One such tool, TRACKbot, available at *www.position-it.com*, is a free real time search engine tracking service that tracks your Web site pages within the top 100 positions with seven top search engines.

To register with search engines, you simply submit your URL on their submission form. Even if your URL is not registered with search engines, they will eventually find you since these bots are continually roaming the Internet looking for new sites to index. The bots will periodically visit your site looking for changes and updates.

Any time you make significant legitimate changes to your site, you should resubmit your site to the search engines. Search engines normally visit on a regular schedule. However, these search engines are growing smarter every day. Some monitor how often the site is updated and adjust their "revisit" schedule accordingly.

Unlike search engines, *directories* will not find your site if you do not tell them about it. Directories do not use bots or other intelligent agents to scour the Internet for new pages.

In order to be listed in a directory you need to submit or register your site information and URL address. This is best accomplished by visiting all the directories in which you want to be listed and filling out the required form.

Submitting to the search engines and directories is a very time consuming but extremely important task. Take your time, do your research, know the ranking strategy employed and prepare your submission for optimal results. See Appendix A for some of the leading search engines. For more information on getting listed on search engines and other helpful techniques, check out *www.promotingyoursite.com*.

Other Sources of Free Links

Another avenue for free links is an informational Web site. Not all informational sites accept free links, but some do. Some informational sites represent a number of sources, such as magazines or newspapers. Others are Internet-based directories or "yellow pages." Still others are special interest, affinity groups or "Web communities" established as loose affiliations of a number of organizations. The best way to find these sites is to do some searching of your own using keywords that may lead to business interests similar to yours.

You can also look for free links on Web sites that share similar or complementary characteristics to yours. An example might be a company that markets to the same kind of audience you do, but does not sell a competitive product or service. Such sites may already have free links to other sites, but if they do not, it does not hurt to inquire. Simply contact the Webmaster and ask if the site will accept a link. Be aware, however, that the site will almost always want a reciprocal link—which means you will have to provide a link to that site from your Web site.

That may sound harmless, but there are some risks involved. For one thing, you want to be sure to provide links only to legitimate, "clean" sites to which you would feel comfortable sending visitors. (It is probably wise to have some general disclaimer copy on your site so that you do not become liable for another site's content.)

A bigger issue, from a marketing point of view, may be whether or not you want external links to appear on your site. By providing an external link, you provide a "side door" for a prospect to easily exit your site—and perhaps not come back. Some Web experts believe that external links only serve to encourage the fickleness of a Web site visitor and that such links should be used sparingly.

Paid Links

An increasing number of Web site owners are trying to build traffic and create credibility for their sites—as well as generate income. A paid link is one way to do that, and they are common on the Web. Basically, the Web site owner offers a link to your Web site for a fee, usually based on a set period of time, although it could also be based on the number of "impressions." (More about that in the chapter on Web advertising.)

You pay the fee and the Web site owner posts your link. For an additional fee, you may be able to get a more detailed listing or description of your Web site; for an even higher fee, you may be able to purchase advertising space on the Web site. Some or all of this could be available at special promotional pricing, or even free for a limited time, so that the Web site owner can build up the site with lots of links.

A Future Consideration for Your Web Site

As the Internet shrinks the world, it is useful to keep in mind that the world speaks more than English. While English predominates across the Web, a b-to-b company who markets internationally needs to consider the implications of creating its Web site in different languages. According to Jupiter Communications (*www.jup.com*), within a few years, two-thirds of the world's online audience will be non-English speaking. Forrester Research (*www.forrester.com*) supports this with its own prediction that 50 percent of all online sales will be sold outside the U.S. by 2004. Forrester says moving towards multilingual Web sites will be an inevitable necessity.

Don't overlook this trend if you anticipate doing serious business in non-English speaking countries. A June 2000 survey of over 150,000 European Internet users across 15 countries by Pro Active indicated that 65 percent of the respondents prefer sites in their own language. In fact, it seems that Europeans prefer online companies that use their own country's suffix as opposed to ".com."

At some point, if you have any interest at all in broadening your business beyond the U.S., you will likely need to build mirror sites which accommodate both the languages and cultural differences of other nations. Already, leading global b-to-b marketers are recognizing this important need. Take a look at the FedEx Web site (*www.fedex.com*) (Figure 3.5) to see how a truly global company solves the problem. FedEx customizes its Web site for every country in which it delivers packages. Each country page is written in the appropriate language, carries appropriate photography of people native to that country, and lists the delivery and rate information specific to that country.

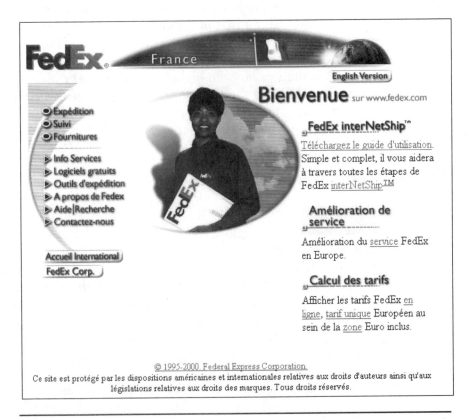

Figure 3.5.   FedEx Web site for France is in the country's native language and includes country-specific rates and services.

The Best B-to-B Web Sites

You could probably make the assumption that the best b-to-b Web sites are also the b-to-b Web sites making the best use of Internet marketing. Of course, it depends on the criteria used to select the best sites. In a July 2000 issue of *Business 2.0* magazine, the "most usable" b-to-b sites were listed. The source, WebCriteria, used Nielsen's NetRatings data on b-to-b Web sites to determine the b-to-b sites with outstanding "accessibility." Accessibility is defined as the time and effort it takes to navigate and the intuitiveness of site design. The top five listed in mid-2000, based on these criteria, were UPS (*www.ups.com*), FedEx (*www.fedex.com*), GTE (*www.gte.com*), IBM (*www.ibm.com*), and Intuit (*www.intuit.com*).

There are many other ways to assess the best b-to-b Web sites, and there is no shortage of lists of sites that rise to the top. One of the more useful lists is "The Net Marketing 200," which can be found at *www.netb2b.com*, the Web site of *BtoB* magazine, published by *Advertising Age*. The most recent list, published in September 2000, identified the best sites in 15 categories. The top rated sites were:

Category	Company	Web Site
Agriculture/Food	Monsanto Co.	*www.monsanto.com*
Automotive	Cole Hersee Co.	*www.colehersee.com*
Construction	Deere & Co.	*www.deere.com*
Energy and Power	Enron Corp.	*www.enron.com*
Financial Services	Merrill Lynch	*www.ml.com*
HealthCare/ Pharmaceutical	Baxter Healthcare	*www.baxter.com*
Manufacturing: High Tech	IBM Corp.	*www.ibm.com*
Manufacturing: Industrial	General Electric	*www.ge.com*
Outsourcing	ADP	*www.adp.com*
Petroleum/Chemicals	Eastman Chemical	*www.eastman.com*
Professional Services	KPMG Intl.	*www.kpmg.com*
Software	RealNetworks	*www.realnetworks.com*
Telecom Services	AT&T	*www.att.com*
Transportation/ Shipping	Federal Express	*www.fedex.com*
Wholesale/Retail	OfficeMax	*www.officemax.com*

4

Generating and Qualifying Leads with Online Advertising

In this chapter, we will consider the various types of online advertising, and explore how b-to-b marketers can best use them.

Online advertising continues to be a major growth area on the Internet. The Internet Ad Revenue Report for 2000, issued by the Internet Advertising Bureau (*www.iab.net*), shows 1999 ad revenues of $4.62 billion, a 141 percent increase over 1998. In the first quarter of 2000, ad revenues reached almost $2 billion, according to the IAB. Banner advertising accounted for 56 percent of that total, with sponsorships following at 27 percent.

In June 2000, eMarketer (*www.emarketer.com*) predicted $21 billion in U.S. online ad spending by 2004, up from $6 billion in 2000. That same month, Jupiter Communications (*www.jup.com*) predicted online ad spending would reach nearly $28 billion worldwide by 2005, with $17 billion for North America, over $5 billion for Western Europe, and over $3 billion for Asia. Research firm AdRelevance (*www.adrelevance.com*) looked at b-to-b online advertising specifically in May 2000, finding that the growth rate from October 1999 to February 2000 was 58 percent, vs. 17 percent on average for all other industries. Based on average number of ad impressions per company, it appeared that b-to-b advertisers had increased online ad spending by 66 percent, and that b-to-b advertising accounted for 5 percent of all online advertising in the fourth quarter of 1999.

The Changing Online Advertising Environment

Online advertising, unlike traditional media, is still new enough that advertisers with clout (those willing to commit to on-going spending) can stretch the boundaries of what can be done. Web site owners hungry for advertising revenue will sometimes allow advertisers to go quite beyond the ordinary, allowing large advertisers to even modify their home pages. That means you may be able to do some breakthrough online advertising if you are willing to pay for it.

Banner ads remain as the most popular online advertising medium, yet you can expect banner ad popularity to drop as time goes on. While the banner ad celebrated its fifth birthday in October 1999, industry experts continue to look beyond the banner for advertising effectiveness. eMarketer predicts that banner ads will *decline* from over 50 percent of online advertising revenue in 1998 to only about 25 percent by the end of 2001. Instead, sponsorships are expected to get the majority of advertising revenue. Sponsorships are typically referred to as "affiliate marketing programs," which we will talk more about in a later chapter about partnering.

Unlike other areas of the Internet consumer marketers rather than business-to-business marketers have pioneered online advertising—because large consumer advertisers and their agencies recognized the mass media potential of the Internet early. Consumer marketers have created a variety of advertising formats, many of which have now been adopted for use by business-to-business marketers.

- **Advertorials.** Advertorials are a form of paid advertising created to take advantage of the look and feel of a particular Web site. They are typically integrated with the other copy and graphics on a Web page, offering the appearance of editorial matter even though the message is advertising.

- **Interstitials or Pop-ups.** Interstitials appear between Web site pages. As the new page loads, an interstitial pops up to convey something about a company and its products or services. Because of their intrusive nature, there is a significant annoyance factor, yet interstitials have been shown to out-pull banner click-through rates in a number of online advertising studies. One company, Unicast *(www.unicast.com)*, has developed the Superstitial, a "polite" interstitial that only plays when it is completely loaded. It is now available on a number of Internet advertising networks, including Engage's AudienceNet, an online profile-driven ad network *(www.engage.com)*. Recognizing the b-to-b ad surge, Engage launched a new division in May 2000, "Engage Business Media." The Superstitial occupies nearly the full screen and utilizes rich media (more on that later). There is also a variation to interstitials which some advertisers are testing—a "Webmercial" which essentially is an under 10-second commercial played over the Web. Growing evidence seems to indicate that interstitials are proving to be more effective than banner ads. eMarketer, in its 1999 eAdvertising Report, said click rates for interstitials were 5 percent versus 1 percent for banner ads.

- **Games, Incentives, and Online Coupons.** Increasingly, e-mail sweepstakes and games are being used to advertise products on the Internet. Also on a growth curve are the use of incentive programs (rewards for providing information or buying on the Internet) and online coupons. These approaches are discussed in detail later in this chapter.

- **Content Sponsorships and Promotional Opportunities.** Some Web sites allow advertisers to sponsor content on pages or within entire sections of the site. Such content sponsorships may be in the form of promotional buttons, mastheads, banner ads, or other promotional vehicles. For example, two of the leading IT super-sites, CMPnet *(www.cmpnet.com)* and ZDnet *(www.zdnet.com)*, offer a wide array of promotional opportunities which fall under this category. Several of CMP's individual sites provide advertisers with "extramercials," vertical ads that run along the right side of the editorial space on the Web page. They are intermingled with editorial matter; visitors click on a bar that says "Expand Ad" to make the entire ad appear. ZDnet offers a similar advertising format it calls "skyscrapers;" these elongated ads also run on the right side of the page. Both CMPnet and ZDnet augment these online advertising formats with a number of other promotional opportunities, ranging from sponsorships of online seminars to creation of promotional micro-sites.

Banner Ads. Banners ads are still the leading form of online advertising, but that appears to be changing. Banners are like little electronic billboards or flashing neon signs on Web sites, appearing at the top, bottom, or sometimes within a Web page. The advertising area is restricted to a small horizontal or vertical space—hence the name "banner." Basic banners use several frames, or individual sequential views seen by the consumer. The last frame of the banner leads to a Web response form or other Web page. Banners typically incorporate some form of graphic movement through simple "GIFs" (Graphic Interface Format). More and more, banner ads are relying on rich media, which is discussed in more detail below. Because the majority of online advertising today remains banner advertising, we will concentrate on this format.

Although the banner ad may seem almost insignificant as an advertising medium, its importance as a technique for both creating awareness and driving traffic to a Web site or a Web response form should not be dismissed. As with building Web sites, entire books have been written about Web banner advertising. The purpose here is not to repeat that information, but rather to cover the basics of banners as they specifically apply to business-to-business Internet marketing.

How Effective Is Banner Advertising?

For some advertisers, banners may not be effective; for others, they are producing results. Yet the trend seems to be towards declining banner ad response rates. A 1999 study by Nielsen Media Research (*www.netratings.com*) suggested that the average click-through rate (the percentage of clicks compared to the number of impressions) had dropped from 2 percent in 1998 to under one-quarter percent. Along with it has come a general drop in banner advertising media costs, which is good news for advertisers. Of course, the more important statistic for direct marketers is what percentage of those "clicks" become real leads, but if the click-through rate is so low to begin with, you need to carefully scrutinize the true effectiveness of banner advertising.

Is there a secret to using banner ads effectively? A lot of it has to do with the marketing mentality of the advertiser. If the banner ad is designed as general advertising, then it will do what general advertising does best—generate awareness, not response. One 1999 study by Ipsos-ASI, a market research firm, in collaboration with America Online, indicated that online banner advertisements apparently matched television commercials in consumer awareness. The study suggested that both banner ads and 30-second TV spots were recalled by survey respondents just about equally. On the other hand, if the banner ad utilizes solid direct marketing techniques—sound media selection to reach the right audience, a compelling offer, and response-oriented creative—chances are it will generate responses and, potentially, qualified leads.

A study released by Andersen Consulting in November 1999 found new hope for banner advertising as an e-commerce influencer. According to *The Wall Street Journal*, the study of 1,500 experienced users showed that "25% of Internet users said they went shopping on a Web site after seeing a banner ad, compared with 14% of the users who said they clicked onto a site after seeing a television or magazine advertisement."

You should approach the creation and placement of banner advertising in much the same way you would implement a traditional direct response advertising campaign:

- Set advertising goals and measurable objectives.

- Establish budget parameters.

- Determine your target audience.

- Research available media targeting that audience.

- Develop a media schedule.

- Create the advertising.

- Place the advertising.

- Measure the effectiveness.

- Analyze the results.

- Refine the advertising program.

Of course, that is easier said than done. With traditional media, some business-to-business marketers execute and place their own advertising; others would not think of it. In this case, you are probably better off using skilled outside resources, such as interactive agencies, for banner advertising. That is because it requires specialized expertise in media placement and creation.

There are several electronic media placement services, some of which might be useful for the business-to-business marketer to investigate. Perhaps the most prominent of these services is DoubleClick (*www.doubleclick.net*), a company that had a successful IPO in early 1998. DoubleClick uses its network of Web sites to place advertising that you pay for *only* if you actually get click-throughs, responses, or sales. DoubleClick also offers extensive testing, and reporting services, but the company generally represents consumer-oriented Web sites with the highest traffic—and therefore the highest cost. In mid-1999, DoubleClick caused quite an industry buzz by acquiring Abacus Direct, a company with the nation's largest database of consumer catalog buying habits. The move was expected to put DoubleClick into the e-mail marketing business. Then in July 1999, DoubleClick announced the acquisition of a competitor, NetGravity.

Another advertising network, Flycast (*www.flycast.com*), focuses its approach on ROI by using sophisticated media planning and behavioral targeting models to pinpoint banner ad effectiveness. In fact, Flycast has the ability to determine the geographic location of a user's computer and, as a result, has helped pioneer "local" advertising on the Internet. Several regional telephone companies are working with Flycast to target their local areas with banner advertising. In November 1999, Flycast announced a relationship with AdForce (*www.adforce.com*), which provides centralized ad management, and Engage, referenced earlier. At the same time, Flycast introduced "Flycast CPCnet," a new advertising network based on "cost per click," a pay for performance pricing strategy. By early 2000, more consolidation took place as Engage announced it would acquire Flycast and Adsmart in a deal worth $2.5 billion. Adsmart earlier announced an expansion into business-to-business e-commerce by launching a multicategory online advertising network. All three companies are majority-owned by CMGI, one of the most successful Internet investment firms.

The adVENTURE Network (*www.ad-venture.com*) claims to be a true direct marketing network, offering advertisers targeting by site, affinity group, and network. The B2BWorks ad network (*www.b2bworks.net*), launched in mid-1999, focuses on business-to-business and features leading Web sites from more than 70 industries. The advertising network 24/7 Media (*www.247media.com*), which markets advertising and sponsorship programs, may be the first to signal a consolidation trend with its acquisition in early 1999 of an e-mail marketing service.

In June 2000, VentureDirect launched B2BfreeNet (*www.b2bfreenet.com*), the first service to integrate direct mail, Web site advertising, and e-mail into a single media buy. A b-to-b marketer could run the same promotions across all media, reaching targeted audiences in 23 different industries.

There are also numerous Internet media buying services, such as WebConnect (*www.webconnect.com*), as well as services which bring together Web site owners who want to exchange free banner ads, such as Microsoft's LinkExchange (*www.adnetwork.linkexchange.com*) and small business specialist SmartClicks (*www.smartclicks.com*).

You should be aware that the banner advertising environment is undergoing significant change. There is general agreement, for example, that banner ads have lost their novelty. In some cases, Web users may view banner ads as nothing more than an annoyance, since they can sometimes slow down a page from loading and be distracting. In responding to this attitude, a number of software companies have created filtering products that actually block banner ads from downloading. While this could be a real cause for concern to advertisers, the software must obviously be installed by the end user. This means that individuals who were not good prospects for banner ads anyway are now being eliminated from the media mix. This could actually improve banner ad effectiveness in the long run.

There are also some interesting innovations in online advertising that could extend the life of banner ads. One example is ZDNet's attempt to re-format the banner to make it more attractive to advertisers. This technology super-site offers a banner that "wraps" around the top of one of its Web pages and then runs down the right margin. It costs more than a traditional banner ad, but the site says it is getting higher click-throughs as well. ZDNet also offers an "extramercial," advertising that actually pops out from the right hand side of the page and moves over some of the editorial content.

A unique innovation comes from Alexa (*www.alexa.com*), a service that sells ad space based on "smart links" and individual Web site statistics. The service is being used largely for competitive purposes, because it can place an advertiser's banner ad on a rival company's Web page. These ads can only be delivered to people who download Alexa's special free toolbar, but as of early 1999, there were close to 1.5 million of them.

Will Rich Media "Save" Banner Advertising?

If anything will "save" banner advertising, it is likely to be rich media. Rich media—the ability to build sound, motion, and interactivity into online advertising—hit its stride in 1999 and proved, at least, that there is life left in that old banner ad.

Forrester Research says that 20 percent of all banner ads will have used rich media by the end of 1999, and Jupiter Communications predicts that by 2002, one-third of all ad spending will be in rich media. This growing popularity means that Web sites will increasingly need to accommodate the technology.

The acknowledged leader in the field is Enliven (*www.enliven.com*), formerly Narrative Communications, which was acquired by and made part of the @Home Network in 1999. Enliven delivers banner ads using its special server over Web sites that will accept them. The banners do not require any plug-in, and they are not limited by file size as are ordinary banners. However, they are more expensive to produce, and not every user will have the bandwidth necessary to support them.

Enliven ads do some interesting and novel things. (Fig. 4.1.) In addition to incorporating sound and motion, Enliven ads have the ability to offer heightened interactivity, directly from the banner. For example, an Enliven banner could offer a prospect the option to immediately print a data sheet by clicking a "Print" button in the banner. Another feature is a banner that "expands" into a form which a prospect can fill out and send immediately. Enliven banners even allow prospects to place an order for a product directly, thus enabling "instant" e-commerce.

Other ways to implement rich media include IBM's "HotMedia" technology, and Macromedia's Shockwave and Flash technologies. A relative newcomer to rich media, Bluestreak *(www.bluestreak.com)*, scored a coup in November 1999 by winning AT&T's rich media ad business. AT&T announced it would use Bluestreak's technology to create ad campaigns designed to attract consumers and allow them to request information and place orders via the banner ads. Bluestreak offers On-The-Fly technology that allows advertisers to create, produce and change rich media ads easily, on their desktop, so campaigns can be

MAKE YOUR BRAIN BIGGER.

Who is the **RICHEST** under-40 web entrepreneur?
Ⓐ Bill Gates Ⓑ Jerry Yang Ⓒ Michael Dell

CORRECT!
Michael Dell is worth $21.49 billion.

MAKE YOUR BRAIN BIGGER.

Get 3 Free Issues of FORTUNE
the #1 Business Magazine!

Just fill out this form to receive your FREE trial.

Name

Address

City

State/Province   Zip/Postal

E-Mail

Click here for Privacy/Offer Terms and Conditions

Figure 4.1. This ad for Fortune allows viewers to answer a question and then order a free trial directly from the expandable banner.

modified in real time. Bluestreak's E*Banners expand when the consumer clicks on them, so more advertising content can be conveyed. Another firm, IQ.com (*www.iq.com*), promises to energize ordinary banners with its Click & Stay feature which allows prospects to make a purchase from a banner from within a pop-up window.

The advertising implications of rich media could be significant. A 1999 study sponsored by Wired Digital (*www.wired.com*) tracked the impact of rich media advertising for Barnes and Noble, Intel, and Novell. The three advertisers together reported a 340 percent increase in click-throughs with rich media ads.

Best Practices in Business-to-Business Banner Advertising

With the primary goal of generating leads or orders, banner advertising is best used as a "feeder" medium. A banner ad can incorporate a link to any Web page, so if a prospect clicks on your banner ad, he or she is instantly transported to the page of your choice.

Used appropriately, the banner ad combines the best attributes of advertising and direct marketing. Think of the banner ad as an electronic direct mail envelope with interactive teaser copy. It "pops up" on a Web site page, usually either at the top or the bottom, depending upon the nature of the site and the price you paid for placement. Just as your direct mail piece competes with others for the attention of the recipient, your banner ad competes for attention with other banner ads on that same site, as well as with the information resident on the site. In fact, your banner competes with anything else that crosses the visitor's path during a Web session—and that could be hundreds of Web pages.

Your first challenge, then, is to make your banner graphically stand out in some way. Most banners use a variety of colors, large type, and graphics—often animated graphics—to distinguish themselves. Most banners have several "frames" that change to attract attention. Rich media, as discussed, adds a whole new dimension to banner ads.

In direct marketing, of course, you need to go beyond standing out. You need to get response. So your banner ad should also *make an offer* and include a *call to action*. With a banner ad, you will not have the luxury of a lot of copy space, so you will have to be clever about it. If your objective is to generate a lead, your offer should have high-perceived value to the target audience. Ideally, the target prospect sees the offer in your banner and is intrigued enough to click on it ("click-through"), but it helps to *tell* the prospect what to do ("Click here for your free demo" or "To get your report, click now").

Click-throughs are nice, but they are a measure of advertising *awareness*, not advertising *responsiveness*. A click-through is not much of a commitment—a site visitor can click on a banner, take a quick look at your offer, and back up or move on in a few seconds. Converting that click-through to a "complete," or a response, is the direct marketer's primary objective. So the real issue is, *where does that click-through lead?*

There are three basic options for the terminating point of a banner ad:

1. **The In-Banner Response.** As the "banner evolution" progresses, building in a banner-based response will become more common. That means someone who clicks on your banner can take an action instantly—get an answer to a question, receive a piece of information, or actually place an order. At this stage, even if the visitor goes no further, the technology exists to capture not just the incident, but also the e-mail address of the respondent. This action does not provide you with any real qualification information if the visitor stops there. However, instant response with little or no qualification requires the least amount of commitment on the part of the respondent—so you could generate a high number of responses, even if they are unqualified. As for banner-driven electronic commerce—that is, online ordering driven by banner advertising—it is still somewhat early to tell how successful this will be as a direct marketing channel for business-to-business use.

2. **The Web Response Form.** If you make an offer of value that elicits a response from a qualified prospect, you obviously want to capture information about that prospect. Your second option, then, is to have the banner ad lead directly to a special Web response form. The Web response form should continue to entice the prospect with the offer, encouraging him or her to complete the form and answer some qualifying questions to obtain the offer. If the offer can be fulfilled online (as with information that the respondent receives, or a demo that unlocks and can be downloaded once the form is sent) so much the better. Similarly, if you are using the banner ad to generate

orders, the Web response form should offer the prospect the opportunity to learn more about the featured product and provide the ability to order it online.

3. **The Web Site.** Most banner ads terminate at the advertiser's Web site home page. The objective is to tease the prospect with the banner ad and then, engage him or her at the home page of the Web site. This is fine if you are measuring the success of your banner advertising campaign by the amount of Web site traffic it generates, but Web site traffic is meaningless to a direct marketer unless it can be converted into measurable results—identifiable responses and qualified leads.

   Of course, if your Web site home page does a solid job of highlighting a response area and making an offer to capture a prospect's interest, you could ultimately elicit a qualified inquiry. In that case, you could accomplish a lot by leading the prospect directly to your Web site. However, you may be better able to focus your prospect's attention by giving him or her a limited number of options, and that could make the Web response form more suitable for direct marketing. Even if the Web response form resides on your Web site, you can lead the banner ad respondent there by linking to the response form's specific URL.

Knowing where to send prospects from a banner is the most important decision you need to make from a direct marketing perspective. But using the banner properly in the first place is also essential. Given the decline of banner ad click-through rates, a business-to-business Internet marketer should be extra careful about usage. Here are a few "best practices" for making the most effective use of banners.

1. **Test banners against e-mail newsletter sponsorships.** Find one or more e-mail newsletters with sizable circulations that appeal to your target audience. Compare the cost per thousand for the banner advertising on a comparably targeted Web site to the e-mail sponsorship. Test banners and sponsorships head-to-head and judge them in terms of lead quality rather than quantity. Include a link to a Web response form in the e-mail

ad, and link the banner ad to a different Web response form so you can accurately measure response to each.

2. **Test rich media banners against animated GIF banners.** Rich media banners cost more to produce and place, and not all Web sites will accept them. If you find a Web site targeted to your audience that will accept rich media banners, test them head-to-head against a traditional, animated GIF banner. Determine if the increased cost is paying you back in terms of an increased click-through rate and qualified leads.

3. **Test media, offer or creative approaches.** Pick Web sites that effectively target your audience and negotiate aggressively for the most attractive rates. Test Web sites one against the other. Also test at least two different creative approaches on the same site by asking the site to randomly rotate the banners. Keep the offer consistent to test the creative (or alternatively, keep the creative consistent to test the offer). Different banners should lead to different Web response forms so you can track responses to each.

4. **Use banners as pre-campaign teasers.** Banner advertising has shorter lead times than traditional print or direct mail campaigns. Use this to your advantage by placing banner ads strategically on sites that reach the same prospects as your forthcoming campaign, *before* the campaign runs, leveraging the creative work but using it to "tease" the audience. The banner will then act as an electronic "advance man," preparing the audience for the traditional media advertising to come.

5. **Promote an Internet event.** Banners can be effective alone, or in conjunction with direct mail, e-mail, or e-mail newsletter sponsorships, in driving traffic to online seminars or events. The banner acts as a teaser invitation, pushing the prospect to an online promotion page with a registration form.

6. **Use banners to launch and support affiliate-marketing programs.** Affiliate marketing (see the subsequent chapter on Internet partnering) is projected to grow beyond banner advertising. If you have products or services that can be resold by affiliates on the Internet, consider creating an affiliate

program and providing your affiliates with free banners they can place on their sites so they sell more of what you have to offer.

7. **Extend Banner Effectiveness by Extending Your Media Buy.** Look for opportunities beyond the banner and you could dramatically improve your online advertising effectiveness. As mentioned earlier, some sites offer promotional opportunities such as contests, online seminar sponsorships, "extramercials," and micro-sites. In addition, many sites may offer subscription e-mail newsletters, which provides yet another promotional opportunity, or opt-in e-mail lists. When you find the right sites for your banner ad campaign, also find out what these sites offer beyond the banner. By extending your media buy, you could reap the benefit of discounted prices or promotional add-ons, thus extending the overall effectiveness of your banner advertising.

Banner Ad Placement Is Critically Important

We have been concentrating on the creative and direct response aspects of banner advertising, but let us not forget that placing your banner ads appropriately is just as important to your lead or order generation success. Media research will uncover a multitude of potential sites for placement, and selecting both the right media and the right placement schedule takes skill. This is where some of the advertising networks and media services, referenced earlier, can be very helpful.

Obviously, you will want to select sites that you believe appeal to, or target, your ideal types of prospects. As with traditional print media and direct mail or telemarketing lists, you should work your way down in priority from most to least targeted Web sites. An easy way to start if you have had success with traditional media is to map those media to what may be available on the Web. The growing popularity of the Internet has paid off in the fact that virtually every publication with any kind of sizable circulation either has a Web site or participates in one. Similarly, many direct mail lists on the market have Internet counterparts—chances are the list owner is on the Web or the mailing list is available with e-mail addresses. At the very least, the types of individuals found on that list would have an affinity to a Web site somewhere.

Use this marketing information to point yourself in the right direction. Again, start with the most targeted Web sites—those that seem to perfectly target your audience—and work your way down to Web sites that may only in part target your audience.

If you are targeting software developers, for example, you would first concentrate on Web sites that appeal directly to software developers—sites sponsored by developer associations or user groups, specialized publications, developer conferences, and so on. You could either stop there or extend your research to the next category—Web sites that appeal, in part, to software developers. These might be sites sponsored by more generalized information technology publications and conferences, or some of the technology "supersites" such as IDG, ClNet (*www.cnet.com*), CMP's TechWeb, or ZDNet, referenced earlier.

You might then choose to go one step further, supplementing your media buys with specific pages on search engines that software developers are likely to use. In many cases, you can arrange for your banner ad to appear on a search engine only when certain keywords are searched on by the visitor.

Purchasing the media can get complicated, because not all sites sell banner advertising in the same way. This is yet another area in which the Web is a unique medium: It cannot be sold on the basis of *when* a banner ad appears (the day or time) because time is irrelevant in cyberspace. It is also difficult to "guarantee a circulation" as in print advertising, or to determine a quantity as in direct mail, so most banner ads are sold on the basis of *number of impressions*—how many times your banner ad actually appears. That does not mean the number of people who see it, just the number of times it shows up. That is an important distinction. To see why, try this experiment some time: Visit a Web site that accepts banner advertising, and go to a single page on which a banner ad appears. Instead of navigating around the site, just keep reloading the page several times and keep your eye on the banner ad. Each time you reload, it is likely that the banner ad will change, because it is in rotation with other banner ads. After several times reloading the page, you will probably see the first banner ad again. Each time you see that same banner ad counts as one impression.

Some banner advertising media are sold using other criteria. In some cases, for example, you pay for click-throughs, not for impressions. Be sure to understand how the pricing works when you are planning your media strategy.

The whole area of media pricing is now undergoing change due to new ways in which banner advertising is being analyzed. A report on online advertising issued in May 2000 by AdKnowledge is an example of this trend. The report analyzed over 150 million banner ad views from the results of numerous online ad campaigns. Interestingly, only 24 percent of the conversions to sales came from prospects who clicked on the banner ad. Thirty-two percent of the sales came from users who had *viewed* an ad, but *did not click*. The remainder of the sales came from repeat customers, whether or not they had initially clicked on the ad.

This fact brings up the need for a different perspective on banner ad effectiveness tracking and analysis. The report suggests that *non-click conversions to sales* are an important component of banner advertising. And yet, most media, and most advertisers, analyze and depend on "cost per click" data.

Banner advertising can be placed on traditional Web sites, but there are Internet service providers and networks which are so huge that they hold real promise for targeted online advertisers. Obvious examples include America Online, CompuServe, Prodigy, AT&T's WorldNet, and MSN. But there are other services, which may be lesser known but could be useful as new advertising outlets. One example is Juno (*www.juno.com*), which filed an IPO in March 1999. Juno began offering free e-mail service with no Internet access required in early 1996, and by 1999 had over 6-1/2 million accounts on record. Every time users open their e-mail, they receive highly targeted e-mail advertising, including banners, pop-ups, and "product order micro-sites."

Other Important Facts about Banner Advertising

- Banner advertising can be purchased directly from the Web site owner or through Web advertising networks. There are also services that facilitate free banner advertising through trade, exchange, and reciprocal link programs, such as LinkExchange, mentioned earlier.

- Banner ads have a promotional life of about *15 days*. Prepare several banner ads in advance of a campaign and ask for your ads to be rotated periodically.

- Banner ads can be created and placed on very short time frames. That makes it easy to pull ads that are not working or add them to new sites very rapidly.

- Banner ads and direct mail can be tested similarly. Consider testing not only media placement, but also different offers and different creative approaches. Because of short time frames, you can change entire banner ad programs quickly, so testing and program modifications can almost occur in real time.

- Try placing your banner advertising on your *own* Web site. This is useful if you want to draw attention to a special promotion, offer, or contest by providing a prominent link to it. You could also benefit from placing a banner ad on your own site that integrates visually with an ad you are running. The on-site banner ad will reinforce your advertising and provide a convenient link to a Web response form from your home page for visitors who came to your home page as a result of the ad.

- Check with media sources for technical restrictions on banner ads. You will generally need to keep graphics simple and file sizes small. You may also need to resize the banner ad for use on different sites.

- Make banner ads more dynamic and eye-catching by incorporating motion and multiple frames.

- Incorporate new technology into banner ads as appropriate, but do not assume every prospect will have the software or hardware necessary to take advantage of it. Given the rise of rich media, consider testing rich media banners against traditional banners.

- Always test banner ads and their links before going live. Look at banner ads through different browsers and on different computers. Be sure to check to see that your banner ads are appearing on the sites as contracted, and that the links you specified are working properly.

- Find out in advance what the site or advertising network offers you in terms of tracking capabilities so you can measure and analyze the effectiveness of your banner advertising.

- Use banner advertising in association with other media. For example, coordinating the placement of banner advertising with traditional media, such as print advertising or direct mail targeting the same audience, can lift awareness and response. After the campaign is running for a while, the banners can be used to reinforce the advertising and provide a means for on-line inquiry generation.

- Analyze the results of banner advertising campaigns as you would any other media. Turn banner ads into response-generators by using direct marketing techniques and measuring the results of all of your efforts.

Newsletter Sponsorships: For B-to-B Marketers, It Could be the Better Way to Advertise

One of the fastest growing areas of the Internet is e-mail newsletters, which will be discussed in further detail in the next chapter. An important aspect of these newsletters is that more and more of them accept advertising, commonly called "sponsorships." E-mail newsletters are often free to the subscriber, but they include a limited amount of advertising from sponsors to offset the distribution cost. Advertising is usually in the form of a small segregated area at the top or bottom of the newsletter, or sometimes embedded into the newsletter text. The ad is usually a text-only ad set off by itself. Some newsletters permit advertisers to sponsor an entire issue of a newsletter so no other ad is seen in that issue, only the sponsor's.

There are some distinct advantages to this type of advertising:

- Advertising that appears in an e-mail newsletter, even though it is text only, is almost guaranteed to be read. This is because newsletter subscribers tend to read the newsletter carefully; otherwise, they would not subscribe to it. As they read the newsletter, they cannot help but come across the sponsor's ad.

- While most e-mail newsletters are free to subscribers, and their publishers ask for nothing more than an e-mail address, the newsletters cover certain very narrow topics. Because of this targeted content, readers self-qualify as a legitimate targeted audience. Newsletter publishers can certainly give you circulation figures, but they typically will not release specific data about any subscribers. In some cases, newsletter publishers will share subscriber data with you in aggregate form so you know more about the types of readers. Some newsletters might also rent their subscriber lists.

- A newsletter ad can become even more effective when it incorporates a link to a specific Web response form or other Web page that further promotes the advertiser's product or service. Many e-mail programs provide the ability to directly link to Web pages, but to accommodate those that do not, it is wise to include the complete link address (including http://www if it is a Web link). Industry reports suggest over and over again that such links from newsletter ads are very effective. I have seen a number of reports of banner ads testing against newsletter ads, with the newsletter significantly out-pulling the banner in most cases.

- Some newsletters are somewhat of a hybrid between e-mail and HTML, and with these, there are additional advertising possibilities which may prove effective. Here, you can place a text-only ad in the e-mail newsletter, but you can also place a more graphic ad in the newsletter's HTML version. You may also be able to sponsor an entire column or page in the HTML newsletter.

Incentive Programs: Another Form of Online Advertising

A growing aspect of online advertising is incentive programs. These programs reward the prospect or customer for providing information, taking an action, or making a purchase. This phenomenon deserves its own section because it is proving for some marketers to be a way to increase banner ad click-throughs, acquire prospects, and even increase customer loyalty.

Incentive programs come in a variety of flavors, with the most common incentives being sweepstakes and contests, volume deals, and price breaks, according to Forrester Research. Also becoming increasingly popular on the Internet are online coupons and other forms of "instant payback" programs.

Contests and sweepstakes are growing at a rapid rate, being legitimized by big name marketers. For example, Fidelity Investments, a household name in the financial market, launched its first sweepstakes in November 1999 in an effort to drive traffic to *www.fidelity.com*. The prizes: free stock trades for life. In December 1999, Compaq Computer Corp. (*www.compaq.com*) cut a deal with Promotions.com (formerly Webstakes) to create custom sweepstakes-style promotions to run on Compaq's Online Services site.

It appears that both consumers and business users on the Internet respond favorably to incentive programs. Just as important, upscale individuals like them, says researcher Jupiter Communications. In a November 1998 survey, Jupiter found that 64 percent of consumers with more than $75,000 in income were likely to make repeat purchases from Web sites offering rewards for doing so. As for online coupons, Forrester Research reports that they can send banner ad click-through rates as high as 20 percent. In fact, a study by NPD Online Research released in November 1999 showed that almost a third of the Internet population used online coupons in October, up from 23 percent early that year. The top two sites where coupons were being obtained, according to the survey, were Coolsavings (*www.coolsavings.com*) and Valuepage (*www.value page.com)*. There is even a place where you can search out a free offer in the category of your choice—it is called The Free Forum Network (*www.freeforum.com).*

There are a wide variety of incentive programs, some initiated by marketers themselves. As you might expect, there are also numerous organizations on the Internet that specialize in online incentive programs. Here are just a few of the leading ones:

ClickRewards *(www.clickrewards.com)*

ClickRewards, operated by Netcentives, Inc., appropriated the frequent traveler miles concept and applied it to the Web. Hence, they offer

"ClickMiles" for shopping at participating Web sites. These ClickMiles can be converted into frequent traveler miles on a one-for-one basis in several leading airline and hotel programs, as well as for other types of rewards. ClickRewards reported in May 1999 that their membership had reached one million.

Flooz (*www.flooz.com*)

Flooz positions itself as "the online gift currency." In 2000, Flooz launched "Flooz for Business" to encourage companies to use their e-mailed gift certificates for employee and customer rewards. Flooz certificates can be used at over 70 online stores. One of the twists to Flooz is that the company offers its b-to-b customers personalized home pages. That way, companies can send Flooz over a site that is customized to their own needs.

MyPoints (*www.mypoints.com*)

With about eight million members and over 200 advertisers and partners participating in MyPoints and MyPoints BonusMail (e-mail advertising), MyPoints offers "rewards points" for purchase. Points may be redeemed for a variety of products and services from some 50 rewards providers. MyPoints also offers completely customized Private Label loyalty rewards programs used by such companies as American Express GTE and ZDnet. In 2000, MyPoints announced that it would acquire another leading online incentive company, Cybergold. In May 2000, MyPoints Connect!, a service which provides free Internet access, was ranked the Internet's top free ISP, according to independent Web rating service TheBullseye.com (*www.bullseye.com*).

Online Advertising is Undergoing Continuous Innovation

The dynamic nature of the Internet means that online advertising will be ever-changing. New strategies, techniques, and tools will continue to be introduced in an effort to improve the effectiveness of online advertising.

Some would say that affiliate marketing itself, which we will discuss in detail in a later chapter, is really a form of online advertising. Affiliate marketing largely uses banner ads placed on affiliate Web sites to drive traffic to sponsoring Web sites. In this context, affiliate marketing can be seen as a major online advertising innovation.

There are other innovations coming. In a May 2000 survey of ad agencies, Arbitron Internet Information Services found that Webcast advertisements—ads that use the Internet to broadcast a multimedia message—will grow rapidly. The study indicated that 1 out of 5 agencies who buy online advertising are using Webcast ads, and 81 percent of the respondents said their use of Webcast advertising would significantly increase in the coming years.

Will banner ads be better in the future? New technologies and advertising approaches almost guarantee it. In mid-2000, StickyAds by Spidertop (*www.spidertop.com*) were introduced. StickyAds are banners that keep clickers on the Web site where the banner appears, instead of leaving to go elsewhere. According to Spidertop, marketers can "position, brand, promote and even close the sale within the ad."

In a *New York Times* article on May 7, 2000, two other emerging innovations in online advertising are mentioned: "follow-me ads" and "piggyback ads."

With follow-me ads, an Internet user is identified as the customer of a particular company. The customer's activity on the Web can then be tracked, and appropriate advertising can be served up to the customer as he or she moves from site to site. In this way, a customer of a particular advertiser will actually see different advertising from others using the Web.

Free Internet access services, and other sites which give something valuable away, require that the user of the service accept advertising. Piggyback ads might appear over any Web site visited by the user as a result. This technique could be effective in providing a distinct competitive advantage to the advertiser. Now the advertiser could have a banner ad appear at the top of a competitor's Web site.

Online advertising will continue to evolve ... and the b-2-b marketer will benefit from these advancements.

5

Generating and Qualifying Leads with E-mail

This chapter covers the usage of e-mail as an inbound and outbound marketing medium for generating and qualifying leads. After an early period of distrust by Internet marketers, e-mail has regained status among consumer and b-to-b marketers alike as an important means of lead generation, e-commerce, and customer communications.

E-mail received negative attention from marketers initially because of "spam." Spam (not to be confused with the famous canned product), as almost everyone knows, is unsolicited e-mail, that is, e-mail sent to but not requested by the recipient.

Unsolicited e-mail became such an annoyance by late 1999 that numerous states had already enacted anti-spam legislation. During that year, however, the notion of "permission marketing" gained in popularity, driven in part by the best selling book of the same name by Seth Godin. The idea struck a chord with Internet marketers everywhere, and it held special relevance to e-mail marketers. In its simplest form, permission marketing means sending e-mail only to those people who give the marketer permission to send it. Such permission is granted when a prospect or customer subscribes to a newsletter mailing list, or answers a specific question in the affirmative, for example, "May we communicate with you via e-mail?" Then the individual should be re-qualified periodically.

Even so, the controversy over unsolicited e-mail has continued. As a result, "opt-in" e-mail continues to gain in popularity. This form of e-mail is directed to only those individuals whose e-mail addresses are on opt-in lists. These individuals have granted permission to receive promotional e-mail. The question is whether or not these lists legitimately include people who really want to receive promotional e-mail. It seems that some are not as carefully controlled as others. As a result, the more conservative Internet marketer might refrain from using any opt-in list, while the more aggressive marketer actively obtains and uses such lists.

In this chapter, we offer you guidance so you can make your own informed decisions about the most sensible use of e-mail marketing.

Why E-mail Marketing is Exploding

The Direct Marketing Association (*www.the-dma.org*) reports that, for the first time in 1999, more e-mail was sent in the U.S. than U.S. Postal Service mail. An August 2000 survey by Pitney Bowes confirmed that e-mail was the most common communication tool in U.S. and Canadian businesses. According to Messaging Online(*www.messaging online.com*), 569 million active e-mail accounts existed in the world by the end of 1999, an 83 percent increase over the previous year. Every one of those accounts represents an individual who can be reached with a promotional e-mail message. Messaging Online suggests that it would be only two to three years before the number of e-mail accounts surpass the number of telephone lines and televisions. Roper Starch Worldwide said e-mail is preferred by 48.5 percent as the primary business communications vehicle, vs. 39 percent for the telephone and 3.5 percent for traditional mail.

The eMail Marketing Report for 2000, published by eMarketer (*www.emarketer.com*) said U.S. e-mail marketing expenditures were $898 million in 1999, with a projected increase to $4.6 billion by the end of 2003. Forrester Research says e-mail will be a $4.8 billion industry by 2004, with more than 200 billion e-mail messages to be sent by that year.

Because of the current economics of Internet usage, e-mail direct marketing can be even more cost-effective than traditional direct mail lead generation. After all, there are no materials or postage costs. Jupiter Communications (*www.jup.com*) says e-mail costs from 1 cent to 25 cents each to distribute, vs. $1.00 to $2.00 apiece for direct mail. It takes just two days to receive responses with e-mail vs. six to eight weeks (the time it takes to produce and send a typical direct mail piece) for direct mail. In 1999, average e-mail response rates were 5 percent to 15 percent vs. 0.5 percent to 5.0 percent for direct mail. eMarketer claims that permission e-mail response rates average 11.5 percent, with an average cost of 25 cents each.

At an April 2000 e-mail conference, Rick Bruner of IMT Strategies (*www.imtstrategies.com*) presented some intriguing statistics attesting to the increasingly attractive marketing ROI of e-mail. Bruner looked at the cost of acquiring customers via e-mail, traditional direct mail, and banner advertising. Using a 1 percent click-through and a 1 percent conversion, Bruner estimated that it would cost $100 to acquire a customer with banner advertising. Assuming 10 cents per name, 50 cents per mailing and a 1 percent direct mail response, it would cost $50 to acquire a customer with traditional direct mail.

For e-mail, the numbers are very different. Bruner claimed that e-mail typically produces a 10 percent click-through and 10 percent conversion rate. With a cost of about 20 cents per name for e-mail, that translates into an acquisition cost of only $20 per customer.

There is an added bonus to Internet direct marketing in general and e-mail specifically. There is nothing to physically produce, so your production time line is compressed. Instead of waiting to print and mail something, you can distribute even thousands of e-mails very fast, and you can make modifications to programs just as fast. That means you can see the results of your efforts very quickly as well. In fact, responses to e-mail programs start to come in immediately and may be completed in just days, as compared to weeks with direct mail.

Although the Internet can be proven to enhance the traditional media used in your lead generation programs, it is probably premature to assume that e-mail can replace direct mail or telemarketing entirely. For one thing, the Internet is not yet a precision medium for targeting. It has not reached the level of maturity of direct mail in terms of your ability to hone a prospect list by using key criteria to select exactly the right individuals for a mailing program.

In addition, access to individual names and titles via the Internet is problematic. As you will see in the following discussion of e-mail, prospecting via the Internet presents a whole set of unique challenges to the b-to-b marketer.

You must also consider the fact that Internet lead generation and qualification is still in its youth as an acceptable marketing practice. Some target audiences may be comfortable with it; others may not be. Generally, those in IT and technical professions are fairly accepting of e-mail and Internet marketing. Not all individuals in all areas of business are as accepting. For example, marketing professionals tend to be more accepting than financial professionals. With consumers, acceptance tends to vary. Consumers who are active users of the Internet will obviously be more accepting, but acceptance of the Internet as a means of self-qualification will vary from prospect to prospect. Nevertheless, now is the time to think about augmenting traditional lead generation media with e-mail.

As evidence of the increasing acceptance of marketing e-mail, consider the results of a market research study released by IMT Strategies in November 1999. The firm surveyed more than 400 consumer and business e-mail users in the U.S. and looked at performance data from 169 companies doing e-mail campaigns. While 64 percent of those surveyed had very negative perceptions of spam, more than half of them felt positively about *permission* e-mail marketing, and three-quarters of them said they responded to permission e-mail frequently. In fact, over 80 percent of these e-mail users had granted marketers to send them e-mail promotions.

There are even e-mail communities. ONElist (*www.onelist.com*) enables you to explore and create e-mail communities where you can share views, ideas, and common interests with others, similar to the newsgroups mentioned in the previous chapter. In late 1999, ONElist merged with eGroups.

Integrating E-mail into Your Marketing Programs

One of the easiest ways to take advantage of the transition to Internet direct marketing is to integrate e-mail into your existing direct marketing lead generation, qualification, order generation, and customer relationship programs. E-mail can be an effective way to receive responses from prospects and to reach prospects and customers with promotional messages—*as long as they want to receive them via e-mail.*

Inbound E-mail

Inbound e-mail is e-mail that comes in from prospects or customers. You should consider offering an e-mail address as a response path in direct marketing programs. (Better yet, offer a URL leading to a Web response form. See Chapter 3 for more about Web response forms.) An e-mail address can be reached by virtually anyone with Internet access, because e-mail is still the most popular Internet application.

The mechanics are simple: You set up an e-mail address through your online service or your Internet Service Provider (ISP) and use it as one of the response paths in your direct marketing promotions. E-mail addresses used for marketing purposes are often labeled *info*@[e-mail box location] so that prospects and customers can respond electronically to a general post office box instead of an individual's e-mail address.

The downside, however, is that the e-mail response vehicle is relatively passive. Most e-mail boxes are just that—electronic repositories that have no greeting, no call to action, and no way to qualify the respondent. When prospects respond to an e-mail box, they have to know what information to leave and what to ask for. Although you will know which e-mail address the response came from, you will not know much else—including the source of the response (unless you set up an e-mail response path for a specific mailing or campaign).

If you are interested in capturing qualifying information, asking questions, conveying information, or making an offer—and measuring the results—inbound e-mail is the least desirable response path. If this were your only electronic option, it would probably be more effective to use traditional response paths—a mail or fax-back reply card or form, or a special telephone number, preferably a toll-free one. The better electronic response option is a Web response form.

Nonetheless, inbound e-mail is an essential component of Internet marketing. You should always include your e-mailbox on business cards, letterheads, and corporate literature. And you should always have an e-mail response path available on your corporate Web site.

Outbound E-mail

If you "follow the rules" of outbound e-mailing, this aspect of Internet marketing can have a substantial positive impact on your existing lead generation and qualification program. *But there are rules.* E-mail began as the primary method for one-to-one electronic communication—similar to a personal, private letter—but there are some distinct differences:

- *E-mail is delivered directly to a user's mailbox.* It contributes to "filling" that mailbox and always stays there, unless it is deleted or opened by the recipient. In that respect, it is more intrusive than direct mail, which can be easily discarded.

- *E-mail costs the end user money.* If the end user is an individual subscriber to an online service or buys Internet access from an ISP, e-mail is one of the items he or she buys. (More and more, e-mail is bundled in as a free service from ISPs, Web search engines, and other Internet services. However, the end user often has to pay for Internet access.)

  If the end user is at a business e-mail address, the business is "paying" for the e-mail address as part of its Internet access. Unlike the receipt of direct mail, which is free to the end user, the receipt of e-mail therefore has a cost associated with it.

- *E-mail was not designed for unsolicited promotions.* E-mail was first intended to be an electronic communications vehicle, not a marketing vehicle. You could say the same thing about early direct mail, but it took decades before direct mail became an accepted form of advertising.

  Today, *unsolicited* e-mail already has a poor reputation. Known as "spamming," it can create nothing short of fury on the part of recipients. In fact, some recipients of unsolicited e-mail have been known to give spammers a taste of their own medicine by overloading senders with countless e-mail replies. A word of caution: If you choose to use *unsolicited* e-mail to promote something to someone, you should be aware that not all recipients will be favorably predisposed to the practice. If in doubt, **do not do it.** In some states unsolicited e-mail is illegal.

- *E-mail is virus-prone.* E-mail is the way in which dreaded viruses are distributed throughout the Internet. The "love bug" virus, for example, caused major damage and loss of data worldwide in mid-2000. Generally, viruses are transmitted as e-mail attachments which, when opened by unsuspecting recipients of the e-mail, do their dirty work. This factor can serve to discourage recipients from opening any unknown e-mail, which means promotional e-mails can be screened and discarded unopened.

There are already strong signals from state and Federal legislators that unsolicited e-mail and Internet privacy is an issue for concern, and restrictions on its promotional usage are already in place. By 1999, California, Maryland, Nevada, and Washington had already enacted anti-spam legislation. The California law in particular has national implications. It basically says that sending unsolicited commercial e-mail to an individual in California without that person's consent is illegal. It goes further by saying that an ISP with an anti-spam policy can sue anyone, anywhere, if an ISP's equipment located in California is used to deliver that unsolicited e-mail. This effectively makes it illegal to send spam nationwide, because the sender is likely, one way or the other, to reach California names, or use an ISP with equipment in California. In addition to a flurry of state regulatory legislation, several federal laws are also under consideration. In June 2000, the "Unsolicited Commercial Electronic Mail Act of 2000" was introduced by the U.S. House of Representatives. If passed, this bill would be the first true anti-spam legislation at the Federal level. Even internationally, e-mail is subject to scrutiny. In mid-2000, the United Kingdom was about to pass legislation that would make e-mail public, so that police could gain unrestricted access to e-mail in that area.

Limit Your Risk

The real issue with outbound e-mail is finding ways to limit your risk when you use it for direct marketing. Here are some suggestions:

Always Ask Permission to Send E-mail

You have every right to ask for and collect e-mail addresses, just as you collect other pertinent information about prospects and customers. However, when you ask for an e-mail address, it also makes sense to ask the question, "May we communicate with you via e-mail?" If you receive a "Yes" response, it is assumed that the individual will accept your e-mail in the future, and you have a legitimate name. If you receive a "No" response, however, take it seriously and code that individual on your database so you will not send him or her unwanted e-mail messages. In fact, "permission e-mail" and "permission marketing" popularized by Seth Godin's book, *Permission Marketing*, is the accepted "right way" to engage in e-mail. A comprehensive guide to permission marketing, published by e-mail expert WebPromote, can be found at *www.webpromote.com/pmguide*. Some marketing experts believe the concept of permission marketing will extend outward from the Internet to all media, becoming a standard marketing practice in the future.

Always Provide the Recipient with the Ability to "Opt-Out"

Even if you have received permission to send someone promotional e-mail, it is good practice to let the recipient opt-out (tell you he or she does not want to receive future promotional e-mails from you). The most common way of doing this is to include some copy at the beginning or end of any promotional e-mail that, in effect, asks the recipient to simply respond with a word, such as "unsubscribe," to prevent receiving future promotional e-mails from you. Some Internet marketers believe you should include a Web page link in your e-mail for opting out. At this link, you could offer the individual an opportunity to change his or her mind about opting out. You might want to test this approach yourself.

Be Very Cautious if You Choose to Share, Sell, or Rent a List of Your Own E-mail Addresses

Some organizations generate substantial revenue by renting name and address lists of prospects and customers to others for commercial usage. Other organizations share or swap lists to broaden their prospecting efforts. These practices are common in the direct marketing industry, but they have led to such a proliferation of mail and telephone calls that the industry's major trade organization, the Direct Marketing Association (*www.the-dma.org*), now offers mail preference and telephone preference services that allow consumers to elect *not* to receive solicitations. The DMA is actively involved in electronic privacy initiatives.

The "P" word—privacy—is one of the largest looming issues in Internet marketing. Do not underestimate its importance when it comes to your Web site or your house list of e-mail addresses. You would be well advised at this stage to hold any e-mail list you may own "close to the vest" and treat it as the confidential and valuable marketing asset that it is. Keeping it private and for your use only is probably a wise decision at a time when privacy on the Internet is being scrutinized by the consumer and government alike.

Opt-in E-mail

As with direct mail, the rapidly increasing popularity of promotional e-mail has led to an entire business of providing e-mail names for rental. These e-mail lists are often referred to as "opt-in" lists, meaning that the individuals on them have indicated in some way that **they have given permission** to receive e-mail. While opt-in e-mail lists may sound like the acceptable alternative to sending unsolicited e-mail, keep in mind that just because you are told these lists are opt-in, they may not always be opt-in. It is essential to verify with any e-mail list owner or service that any list being represented as opt-in is guaranteed to be just that. Additionally, it is a good idea to verify the list owner or e-mail service's practices. The provider should have a written privacy policy, and should also be committed to the earlier referenced concept of permission e-mail. Individuals on e-mail lists should always have the ability to opt-out of participation on any given list.

In many cases, e-mail list vendors do not release the actual e-mail addresses on a list to third parties. Instead, you write a promotional message (typically not more than 500 words), give it to the e-mail list vendor along with your list selections, and the vendor delivers the e-mail to the recipients within a few days. Depending on the list source, there may be selection criteria available, so you may be able to target a specific audience.

Typical specialized e-mail lists, such as those in the Information Technology marketplace, rent for $250 to $300 per thousand names, with an additional $150 per thousand names for e-mail delivery. There may be a minimum of 3,000 to 5,000 names per list order. The reply-to address is generally the service provider's, and responses are handled for an additional fee, typically $50 per thousand names. Your e-mail promotional copy should encourage a reply-to response, or better yet, you could drive response to a Web link embedded in the e-mail as a direct response path.

Unlike direct mail, you will not be able to obtain a magnetic tape of the names and addresses—which means you will not be able to eliminate duplicates from multiple list sources. As a result, your e-mailing strategy may be different from direct mail—you may want to test one well-targeted e-mail list first and mail to another later, rather than to two similar lists at the same time.

Some of the better known opt-in list owners, managers, or brokers serving the b-to-b market include: 21st Century Marketing *(www.21stcm.com)*, Direct Media *(www.directmedia.com)*, ALC *(www.amlist.com)*, IDG List Services *(www.idglist.com)*, PostmasterDirect *(www.postmasterdirect.com)*, WebConnect *(www.worldata.com)*, and YesMail *(www.yesmail.com)*. YesMail, which announced it was to be acquired by CMGI in March 2000, claims to top the industry with some seven million people who have opted to receive information and offers via e-mail. A new service, *www.lists.com,* provides a search engine and directory for the thousands of e-mail lists available on the Internet. Another service, Topica *(http://www.topica.com)*allows you to find, manage, and participate in e-mail lists.

Responses to an e-mailing begin immediately. You could receive as much as 85 percent of the total response to your e-mail campaign within the first week. E-mail response rates in general tend to be considerably higher than traditional direct mail response rates. According to statistics obtained in 2000 by research firm IMT Strategies, response rates for house list e-mail average 15 percent, vs. 10 percent for opt-in e-mail. If you use an e-mail list that you obtained from another source, it is probably a good idea to acknowledge this fact in e-mail copy when you give the recipient the ability to opt-out.

There is value in outbound e-mail *when you use it responsibly* as part of an integrated, comprehensive direct marketing program. What are some of the most effective ways to use outbound e-mail for direct marketing? Here are some suggestions.

Customer Communications

Customers tend to be receptive to e-mail marketing, especially if the e-mail is used as an alert service to give them advance notice or an "inside track" on new product developments or late-breaking news. As such, e-mail can be a very effective way to pre-announce products or upgrades to customers, send a flash about a product update or a problem, inform customers about changes in service, announce important news about the company, invite them to a customer-only event, and so on. As with any good direct marketing, a call to action should be included, even if it simply states, "To take advantage of this offer, respond to this e-mail today." It is generally safe to assume that customers will find e-mail acceptable if they have given you their e-mail addresses. Even so, some of these customers may be upset by your use of promotional e-mail, so you should offer them the ability to "unsubscribe."

Follow-ups

Both customers and prospects will be more accepting of e-mail marketing if it is used to follow up on inquiries or orders, especially inquiries or orders that were electronically sent by them to your organization. If the e-mail message clearly states that it is in response to an inquiry or order, it is generally acceptable if that message also includes some marketing information and a call to action.

An increasingly common practice in direct marketing is to use a direct mail, fax, or telemarketing follow-up to an original promotional contact. In direct mail, the follow-up can be as simple as a double postcard or a one-page letter. Direct mail testing supports the fact that such follow-ups usually generate an additional one-half of the original response rate. For example, if an original mailing generates a 2 percent response, the follow-up will typically generate an additional 1 percent response. The added bonus is that most follow-ups can be executed at a very low incremental cost because you are reusing a list and the physical piece itself is inexpensive to produce.

E-mail holds great promise as a replacement for or enhancement to the follow-up strategy. If you have a prospect's or customer's e-mail address, sending an e-mail that reiterates the offer and messaging of an original contact (whether it is by mail or phone) could be effective. E-mail may break through in a way that a follow-up mailing or phone call may not—and at a much lower cost than mail or phone contacts.

E-mail can also be very effective as a means to quickly follow up on a personal meeting, summarize what was discussed, and offer an opportunity to respond. E-mail is also a personal, immediate way to just say thank you when you cannot reach someone by phone.

Major Announcements or Alerts

It may be appropriate to do a "broadcast e-mail" to a large number of customers and prospects when you have something very important to say. Of course, "big news" may be a matter of interpretation, and not every e-mail recipient will react the same way, but if it really *is* big news (such as a merger, an acquisition, a new president, going public, or something similar) then nothing can beat the immediacy of e-mail. It is likely that customers and even prospects would subscribe to an "alert service" that keeps them in the know about such developments.

E-mail Newsletters

Shrewd electronic marketers have figured out a way to implement e-mail in a non-objectionable format that reaches target individuals on a regular basis. It is called the *e-mail newsletter*. The e-mail newsletter is basically a long e-mail that is regularly and automatically sent to a customer or prospect "by subscription"—*upon request*. The best e-mail newsletters contain information of high-perceived value about a pertinent topic area, but they are, of course, marketing vehicles as well. Although most are free, some e-mail newsletters are sent on a paid subscription basis.

E-mail newsletters are hugely popular. They have become the acceptable method for using e-mail as an on-going form of promotional communication. For example, every major high-tech information provider, including CMP (*techweb.cmp.com*), ClNet (*www.cnet.com*), IDG (*www.idg.net*), and Ziff-Davis (*www.zdnet.com*), publishes a variety of free e-mail newsletters, some on a daily basis. Reportedly, some of the more popular e-mail newsletters have circulations as high as one million subscribers.

But that is only the tip of the e-mail newsletter iceberg. Now e-mail newsletters have pervaded every business and industry. E-mail newsletters have proliferated to the extent that there are likely to be many to choose from in even the narrowest of interest groups. And the majority of these newsletters are free. An increasing number of marketing Web sites offer free newsletters as part of their promotional strategy.

Why do organizations and individuals distribute these free e-mail newsletters so widely? For one thing, it keeps their names in front of a very large number of people, all of whom have given the information providers their e-mail addresses. As a result, *they are building their own opt-in e-mailing lists for free*, and the e-mail addresses they acquire will be available to them for ongoing use. The cost to e-mail these names is very low and, when compared with the cost of other promotional means of reaching prospects, e-mail is downright cheap. Newsletters are, in effect, one of the best ways to build your own house list of e-mail prospects.

Publishing an e-mail newsletter and collecting subscriber names is a smart business strategy. As the regulatory environment changes, unsolicited e-mail has become either unethical or illegal. Even opt-in lists are not completely foolproof. *As an e-mail newsletter publisher, however, you are building your own e-mail list.* You can continue to use it to send e-mail ethically and legally, because the recipients have *asked* for it. Of course, it is still good practice to offer e-mail newsletter subscribers the option of deleting their names from your list.

There are other benefits to publishing e-mail newsletters. As an e-mail newsletter publisher, you are constantly promoting yourself. Many e-mail newsletters drive subscribers back to linked Web pages to learn more about a particular topic. E-mail newsletters can be distributed at a very low cost. Imagine the cost for printing and postage to send one million paper newsletters. Even if they were simple one-page documents sent by fax, the newsletter publisher would have to pay to call every recipient's fax machine.

E-mail, on the other hand, can be broadcast across the Internet via automated methods at a very low cost. As long as you have the proper e-mail addresses and the necessary software and systems support, you can send e-mail to hundreds, thousands, or even millions of individuals instantly. In fact, with advanced database-driven technology, you can *personalize and customize* e-mail newsletters. E-mail newsletters can include an individual's name but, more importantly, you can even tailor e-mail newsletters to the needs of individual target audiences. Some e-mail newsletters even customize information within the newsletter itself to specific audiences.

E-mail newsletters can be revenue generators in and of themselves. Many of the larger circulation e-mail newsletters are also important vehicles for Internet-based advertising. Some e-mail newsletter publishers accept paid advertising messages and append them to the newsletter text. In some cases, the advertiser is positioned as a "sponsor" of the newsletter and can embed a live link to a Web site in the promotional message. Most e-mail programs accept Web links, so this can be a very effective way of driving a target prospect directly to a specific URL.

In some cases, HTML versions of e-mail newsletters published on the Web offer additional opportunities for advertising sponsorships. The HTML newsletter can be attached to an e-mail, or it can be posted on the Web and linked via a hyperlink in the e-mail.

One example of this is ClickZ (Figures 5.1, 5.2). ClickZ (*www.clickz.com*) is a combination e-mail newsletter and Web site that serves online marketers. More than that, it is actually a network that provides online marketing information and uses e-mail notifications to its subscribers with links to each of its articles, which are then published as HTML pages. Advertisers sponsor several of the recurring columns. ClickZ cleverly ties in the column to the sponsor by utilizing the advertiser's logo and corporate color to "brand" the information.

ClickZ publishes articles, hosts online discussion forums, and sponsors live conferences about online and e-mail marketing. In 2000, ClickZ published its first printed guide, "The ClickZ Guide to E-mail Marketing," a compendium of articles from the ClickZ network. For information about the guide, go to *http://www.clickzguide.com.*

Advertising in e-mail text newsletters may not be fancy, but industry sources say it is very effective. My direct and e-marketing agency has extensively tested e-mail newsletter ads against outbound e-mail and banner ads. The newsletter ads have almost always out-pulled both e-mail and banner ads. I have seen numerous industry reports supporting this data. E-mail newsletter advertising is such a significant business that now Internet advertising networks and service providers are working them into their offerings. For example, Flycast (*www.flycast.com*) announced

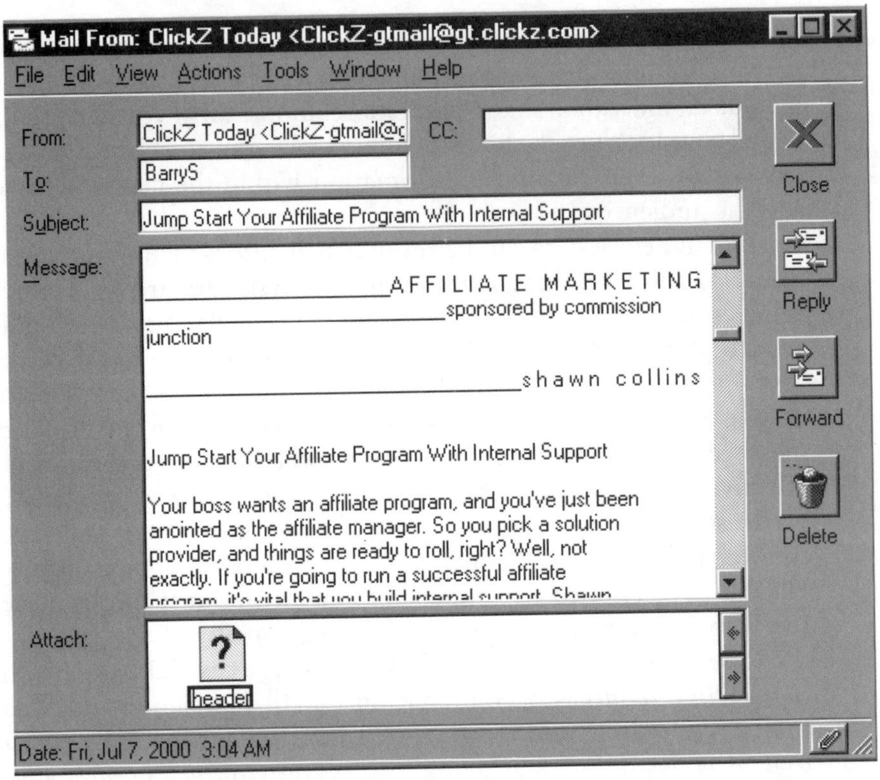

Figure 5.1. ClickZ E-mail.

in January 2000 that, through its new Flycast eDispatch Newsletter Network, it would offer advertisers the option of running banner and text advertisements across multiple newsletters with a single media buy.

There is a logical reason that advertising in e-mail newsletters works. Newsletter subscribers are looking for high-value content and they have requested the newsletter. Chances are the subscribers are reading each issue closely. Text-based ads are generally placed within the body of the newsletter. Although they are separated from the text itself, the reader can't miss them. If the ads embed Web page links, all the reader has to do is click to go to the advertiser's Web page. It's simple, effective direct marketing...and it works.

I subscribe to a wide variety of IT and marketing e-mail newsletters, most of which are free. (You will find my favorites in Appendix

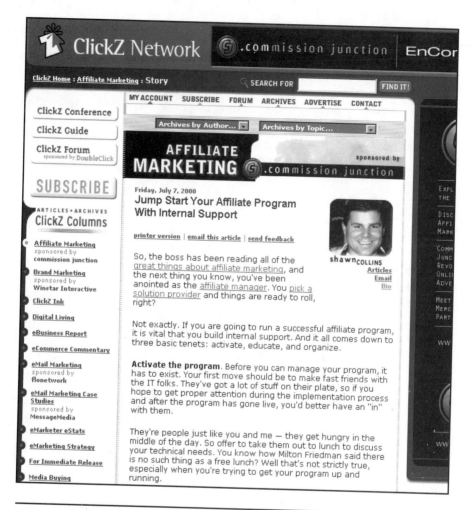

Figure 5.2. ClickZ Web page.

A.) These newsletters are typically rich in content and very useful to me. It is the way I personally keep up with what is happening in Internet marketing. In addition to ClickZ, mentioned above, I subscribe to INSIDE 1to1, a free weekly newsletter published by the Peppers and Rogers Group (*www.1to1.com*), the consulting organization that popularized the concept of one-to-one marketing. By early 1999, INSIDE 1to1 had 30,000 subscribers worldwide. And when the organization polled 200 random subscribers, it learned that INSIDE 1to1 is reaching an audience of over 100,000 readers weekly due to pass-along readership.

This newsletter is an excellent example of Internet direct marketing. As a marketing professional, I appreciate receiving it because it has real value and it is interesting to read. I get it delivered free to my electronic mailbox—I do not have to go anywhere to get it, or even ask for it ever again. It just appears automatically.

Online Surveys

Surveys that ask the opinions of customers or prospects, allowing them to respond by copying and answering the survey questions, can be as effective as surveys conducted via mail, phone, and fax—maybe more so. E-mail surveys are easier to respond to and less intrusive than phone surveys, so they may ultimately prove to generate a higher level of response. E-mail surveys can also contain a link that takes respondents to a Web response page to facilitate response. This is an increasingly popular way to execute online surveys, because a form-based survey is much easier to answer.

Customer surveys that use traditional media such as direct mail and the telephone are known to generate response rates as high as 20 percent or more, and online surveys are achieving results just as impressive.

Zoomerang (*www.zoomerang.com*) is a useful service that allows small companies and individuals to create and send online surveys, free. Created by Web researcher MarketTools, Zoomerang uses professionally designed templates that make it easy to create and customize surveys on anything from customer satisfaction to new product testing to event planning.

My company used Zoomerang to create an online survey about online seminars. We sent an e-mail to a house e-mail list of customers and prospects and asked them to complete the survey by clicking on a link to the survey page. We offered to send the survey results to all respondents, and we also offered a drawing for several e-gift certificates. We asked fifteen questions about the use of online seminars by these companies. We got a 23 percent response and some very valuable insight which guided us in the way we structure and sell our services. Online surveys should have the potential to do the same for you if they are used appropriately.

E-mail Discussion Groups

Discussion groups about virtually every subject exist on the Internet, so chances are one or more of them relate to your product or service. Some of these groups allow free or paid "advertising" or sponsorships by appending some copy about your company, product, or service to discussion text. It must be done appropriately, in the proper context, and always with permission—but it does present you with another way of reaching a very targeted audience via e-mail. A good source of discussion groups is *http://www.deja.com*

Making E-mail Work Harder

Numerous technologies are being introduced almost daily to make e-mail work harder. There are products and services available to enhance your ability to personalize and customize e-mail, and e-mail service bureaus who can provide you with start-to-finish services, including building and managing your own e-mail list.

Basically, you can decide to outsource your e-mail or manage e-mail lists and programs in-house. Two of the better known firms in the outsourced e-mail business are MessageMedia *(www.message media.com)* and Digital Impact *(www.digitalimpact.com)*. MessageMedia makes available ten "SmartMarketer" lessons in e-mail marketing on its Web site, free. These short lessons are a useful primer to direct e-mail marketing.

A number of products and services, from simple to extremely sophisticated, are available if you want to handle e-mail yourself. Interact from Responsys *(www.responsys.com)* is one of the more sophisticated systems. Responsys Interact provides support for dynamic personalization so marketers can personalize messages based on customer contact and profile data. It supports text and HTML e-mail, provides list and data management, and has a complete response management and tracking capability. TargetMessaging from Exactis.com *(www.exactis.com)* allows users to mine customer data and build targeted lists, create personalized offers or communications, use Exactis.com to build and send the offers, and analyze the tracking data provided to construct reports and improve later campaigns.

Personalized, targeted e-mail is on the rise. For example, an issue of the previously mentioned e-mail newsletter, INSIDE 1to1, distributed in mid-2000, reported on a personalized e-mail system established by Onsale. Onsale, now part of Egghead (*www.egghead.com*), moved from standard, non-personalized e-mails sent to customers in 1998, to e-mails that targeted customers with specific product recommendations, based on their purchase history. Information from the customer's registration record, transaction data, and click-throughs on the site was used to create a one-to-one e-mail strategy. According to INSIDE 1to1, Onsale improved its response rates by more than 40 percent...and 74 percent of the company's orders were from repeat buyers after Onsale began using the personalized e-mail system.

The Rise of HTML E-mail

More and more e-mail systems are moving to "visual" e-mail. While the predominant form of e-mail is still text-based, e-mail is increasingly becoming HTML-based. The result is that messaging might soon resemble mini-Web pages, complete with formatting and graphics, rather than standard text-based communication.

The lingering issue with HTML e-mail is that not all e-mail systems can receive it. In fact, even America Online does not currently support HTML e-mail. But as systems are upgraded, HTML e-mail is sure to become a far more common format. Today, the e-marketer would do well to consider creating e-mail in both text and HTML formats to accommodate this shifting market.

While the HTML attachment is the quickest route to HTML e-mail, a more conservative alternative is to introduce HTML gradually by using Web page links in text-based e-mail to send readers to an HTML newsletter or promotional page. As mentioned earlier, e-mail newsletters are using this hybrid strategy to mix the advantages of traditional e-mail and HTML pages.

My agency, Directech | eMerge (*www.directechemerge.com*) uses this strategy in publishing our own direct and e-marketing newsletter. We send out a text-based e-mail periodically to our house list of clients and prospects, which includes overview of articles in the latest issue of our e-letter, "Direct Insight Online." In the e-mail are hyperlinks to each of the newsletter articles, as well as a link to "subscriber services." The newsletter itself is HTML-based. You can subscribe to this newsletter free on our Web site.

E-mail Innovations are on the Way

Innovative e-mail tools and techniques are being introduced at Internet speed. Here are just a few examples:

- e-dialog (*www.e-dialog.com*) provide e-mail merge/purge and a service to append e-mail addresses to traditional address records.

- MessageMates (*www.messagemates.com*) are kind of like banner ads that attach to e-mail. They are part of a product line of e-mail attachments and other multimedia innovations from a company called AdTools, which in June 2000 was acquired by e-mail marketer Infobeat, who changed its name to Indimi (*www.indimi.com*). Rich Media e-mail features sound and animation, and is available through Media Synergy (*www.mediasynergy.com*) and its "Flo Network," which offers the ability to create, deliver, personalize, track, and report on e-mail campaigns.

- RadicalMail (*www.radicalmail.com*) is a streaming e-mail service that sends e-mails with sound and video to recipients...no plug-ins required. Rich media advertising vendor Bluestreak (*www.bluestreak.com*) offers RichMail, which allows e-mail to include rich media and, interestingly, permits the advertiser to change the offer in real-time, right up until the recipient opens the e-mail.

- In March 2000, FireDrop introduced the Zaplet (*www.zaplet.com*). The Zaplet resides on top of e-mail, arriving in the e-mailbox and acting like e-mail. Once opened, however, a Zaplet acts more like the Web, incorporating graphical and interactive capabilities. Zaplets can be created by anyone, updated as individuals respond, and analyzed as responses come in.

Keep in mind, however, that any new e-mail technology should be pre-tested and verified prior to use. Also realize that not every recipient's e-mail system will be able to accept e-mails or attachments using newer technologies.

For serious e-mailers, e-mail management systems are becoming a necessity. These systems not only handle outbound e-mail, but process inbound e-mail in much the same way as a call center or direct mail lead processing center would do. E-mail management systems identify, route, and sometimes automatically answer incoming e-mail. Many such systems also include full reporting capabilities and the ability to survey e-mail respondents on the quality of service received. One such provider of e-mail management systems is eGain (*www.egain.com*), whose customers include Microsoft Web TV, Nortel, and Real Networks.

What About Viral Marketing?

There is even new terminology associated with the emerging importance of e-mail marketing: "viral marketing." This somewhat unfortunate moniker wrongly associates e-mail marketing with viruses. The intended meaning, however, is marketing that spreads rapidly via e-mail or other Internet communications.

Writing in *Red Herring* (May 2000), Steve Jurvetson says viral marketing got its start when Hotmail, a Web-based e-mail service, included a promotional message about its service with a URL in every message sent by a Hotmail user. The result, says Jurvetson, was that "every customer becomes an involuntary salesperson simply by using the product." He says that Hotmail's subscriber base reached 12 million users in only 18 months, with a meager advertising budget of just $50,000. It was all because of viral marketing.

Given the nature of the Internet and e-mail, it is easy to see how marketing messages can spread just as rapidly as can computer viruses themselves. By simply adding a promotional message to an e-mail, that e-mail becomes a promotion that can then be forwarded to one, or one hundred, or one thousand individuals in no time. For viral marketing to be most effective, there should be a valuable reason why someone should want to forward your e-mail. Maybe it is a discount or a freebie, a brief test or a free report, or maybe it is just something with sound or motion. Whatever it is, if you offer both the sender and the recipient something of perceived value, viral marketing will be that much more potent.

Dr. Ralph Wilson, a noted e-commerce consultant, talks about viral marketing in great detail in two articles posted at *www.wilsonweb.com/wmt5/viral-principles.htm* and *www.wilson web.com/wmt5/viral-deploy.htm*. Wilson offers such tips as encouraging word-of-mouth recommendations, making it easy to e-mail or fax a Web page, encouraging people to forward your e-mail newsletter, enabling visitors to e-mail post cards from your site, and so on.

Other Important Facts About E-mail

- Various software tools are available to help you automate e-mailings. You can use these tools to build e-mail lists, do "broadcast e-mail" (send outbound e-mailings in quantity), and automatically respond to inbound e-mail ("autobots"). There are numerous firms advertising on the Web that will rent you e-mail lists or help you implement full-scale e-mail campaigns from start to finish.

- E-mail addresses change even more rapidly than business addresses, so expect at least 10 percent of an e-mail list to be undeliverable at any point in time. Obviously, starting with a clean list and scrupulously maintaining it will help.

- Response to e-mail campaigns can be fast, even immediate, so be prepared to handle the "back end"—acknowledgment, processing, and fulfillment—*before* you execute an outbound e-mail campaign.

- Response to customer e-mail campaigns can be very high—sometimes much higher than direct mail. Some customer e-mail campaigns will result in response rates as high as 20 percent or more.

- Expect e-mail to generate some *negative* responses. Even if you are e-mailing to customers, or to an opt-in prospect list, there may still be a few recipients who resent receiving promotional e-mail and will not hesitate to let you know about it. It is good business practice to send these people an apology and suppress their e-mail addresses from future promotions.

- E-mail can be—and should be—personalized whenever possible. As with personalized direct mail, if you can use an individual's name, recognize any relationship the individual has with your organization, and incorporate pertinent information in an e-mail, it could increase response. E-mail can also be customized to the needs of the recipient via database technologies now available.

- Use the Subject Line of an e-mail appropriately. The Subject Line is like teaser copy on a direct mail envelope, or the headline on a print ad—it could determine whether or not the recipient reads the e-mail. The Subject Line should be a few words of intriguing copy, but it should not mislead the recipient or misrepresent the content of the e-mail.

- E-mail is "short form" communication, except for the e-mail newsletter format. Paragraphs and sentences in e-mail should be short and concise. E-mails should generally be no longer than 500 words.

- E-mail is still primarily an informational vehicle. Some readers may react negatively to overuse of very promotional language. You need to be careful with tone, because e-mail comes across as "flat" copy without graphic signals to emphasize certain words or phrases. For example, anything in CAPITAL LETTERS is usually seen as SHOUTING when used in e-mail. Avoid overuse of exclamation points. Don't over-sell. Make use of good direct marketing copywriting techniques, such as incorporating a call to action into your e-mail, but be aware that all words may appear the same. So, using larger point sizes, bolding, underlining, or italicizing will not necessarily be seen.

- Send e-mails "raw"—do not format the text, change fonts, or use attachments, tables, graphics, or artwork. E-mail campaigns should be designed for the lowest common denominator, which today is plain text only.

- Use e-mail to drive recipients to specific Web pages with more information, or to reference your Web site. It is very likely that individuals with an e-mail address will also have Web access. You can embed a link to your Web site in an e-mail, but some readers may not be able to access the link directly through their e-mail programs. Include it anyway so that they can visit the link if they are interested.

- Use good sense in executing e-mail direct marketing. Integrate e-mail appropriately with other techniques in your direct marketing lead generation programs. Be sure you use e-mail wisely. Build your own e-mail list and keep it current with the addresses of individuals who give you permission to communicate with them via e-mail. Do not use unsolicited e-mail. Test opt-in e-mail cautiously. Respect the privacy and needs of your target audience.

Automated E-mail Response

It is easy to build in a "mail to" e-mail link so that visitors can instantly inquire about your products or services, but it is just as important to respond promptly if not instantly. There are a variety of auto-responder or autobot tools available that can respond automatically to such requests. On good electronic commerce sites, for example, your order can be instantly acknowledged as soon as you place it. An e-mail message is sent to your mailbox verifying your order and providing you with an order number and shipping information. This is also a good way to prevent fraud, because if the recipient did not place the order, he or she can immediately inform the sender of the e-mail.

Note

1. To subscribe to the Peppers & Rogers newsletter, send an e-mail to *subscribe@1to1.com* or visit the "one-to-one online resource center" at *www.1to1.com*.

6

Using Internet Events for Marketing

Event marketing plays a significant role in many b-to-b marketing programs. Marketers have long attended trade shows and conferences in an effort to get in front of "live" prospects. Many companies also use their own marketing and sales seminars to attract prospects to hear about products and services or see product demonstrations.

The Internet presents a compelling opportunity for marketers to transform live events into Net events. Early on, Internet visionaries imagined electronic learning places, and distance learning is now growing rapidly and becoming an Internet reality. Applied to marketing, this specialized area of Internet technology is already revolutionizing the manner in which meetings and events occur. This chapter explores the potential for "net events" and guides you through the dos and don'ts.

Are Live Events Still Good Marketing Investments?

In my early days as a marketing communications manager, I remember doing the "conference circuit" and the "convention route." Attending these events as an onlooker was far better than those dreaded times when my boss was a conference speaker or my employer had a booth. It meant countless hours spent on pre-event logistics, materials preparation, and shipping. When that nightmare was over, another began with booth duty on the floor of some nameless convention in a city that should have been fun if I had had the time and energy to see any of it. If you have "been there," you know how unglamorous and exhausting event marketing and the travel associated with it can be, despite rumors to the contrary.

Actually, there was something even worse than conventions: company-sponsored seminar programs. The headaches were multiplied across cities that spanned the country—and so much more could go wrong.

All of these national events were expensive. Seminars, especially, were a financial drain. Fees, travel, and accommodations for guest speakers, along with travel and accommodations for all company personnel involved in the seminars, mounted up quickly. Add to that the cost of slide shows, handouts, signs, meeting rooms, coffee, and snacks, not to mention the cost of promoting the event beforehand and following up with attendees afterwards.

Of course, it is not very different today with live event marketing. Many b-to-b companies still rely on conferences, conventions, seminars, and other such events to market their products and services. The motivation for doing so is basically sound, especially with seminars. Traditionally, b-to-b marketers have long believed the simple notion that prospects who attend seminars are more highly qualified than prospects who do not attend. The theory is that someone who gives up time to attend a half-day event (the typical length of a free seminar) has a compelling need for the product or service, or at least enough of interest in it to make a commitment of a few hours of time. And time, as we all know, is a precious commodity.

However, the reality is that experiences with live seminars vary widely from company to company. When a company is successful, it means that seminar rooms are filled with "butts in seats." More importantly, the attendees are the people the company wants—prospects whom the sales force considers to be quality leads. In this case, the company will keep investing in live seminars.

Yet seminar disasters are not uncommon, either. There could be any number of reasons for bombing out. Perhaps the audience is not well targeted to begin with or the seminar content (which is the offer) is weak. Maybe the weather in a particular location is lousy or traffic is bad on the day of the seminar. Maybe the seminar is in downtown Manhattan, New York City—where most seminars seem to do poorly— or it could be that the product being promoted is a dog, so even a great speaker or an action-packed agenda will not save the day.

The Typical Seminar Series

More and more, it seems that companies are scrutinizing their participation in live seminars. They need to justify that seminars are worth the investment because the expense associated with a seminar program can be significant. Let us put this into perspective by examining a breakdown of estimated costs and the anticipated results for a ten-city seminar series. We will make the following assumptions:

- The seminar will be a live, half-day event with free admission, held in ten U.S. cities at hotel meeting rooms.

- The sponsoring company will have to prepare a presentation, hire one or more guest speakers, and send a marketing coordinator and one speaker from corporate headquarters to every seminar.

- Handouts will need to be produced for an anticipated audience of about 500 people.

- A direct mail invitation will be sent to 3,000 prospects within 50 miles of each seminar site (30,000 prospects).

- The invitation will achieve a 2.5 percent response.

- Fifty percent of the respondents will *not* attend the seminar, even though they signed up for it. (This is a fairly typical "no-show" rate—the percentage of individuals who say they are coming to a seminar but do not show up.)

The accompanying chart (Figure 6.1) shows the costs and results for this ten-city live seminar program.

Depending on the costs and results of other qualified lead generation activities you might conduct, this may or may not seem to be a reasonable cost. To get a true read of any event's marketing value, you should track not just "cheeks in the seats," but also:

- The number of event attendees who were converted to customers,

- The length of the sales cycle associated with event attendees versus other types of prospects,

	Typical Costs/Results
Seminar promotion: direct mail invitation to 30,000 prospects (3,000 each of 10 sites), not including follow-ups, confirmations, or fulfillment	$45,000–60,000
Seminar presentation: One original of a typical slide presentation plus 10 copies for laptop or slide projector use	$3,000–5,000
Hotel meeting rooms, including AV support and breakfast	$7,000–10,000
Presentation hand-outs and promotional materials	$3,000–6,000
Guest speaker fees and travel	$20,000–40,000
Travel and accommodations for 2 people: 1 marketing person to be present at all 10 sites for registration/ coordination, and 1 speaker from company headquarters	$15,000–30,000
Total costs	$93,000–151,000
Number of invitations mailed	30,000
Response rate from the direct mail invitation	2.5%
Number of respondents	750
Total number of attendees (50% "no-show" rate)	375
Average number of attendees *per seminar*	37
Cost per attendee	$248–403

Figure 6.1.   Live seminar costs and results.

- The average sale from event attendee customers versus other types of customers, and

- The lifetime value of the event attendee customers versus other types of customers.

In some cases, what companies learn about their event marketing can be nothing short of shocking. Here is one scenario that is based on a true story:

A company has routinely attended several trade shows for years. Someone in marketing analyzes the results and discovers that the most expensive show is actually generating the lowest quality leads. When the costs of supporting that particular show and fulfilling the leads are added up, it is clear that the company has an ROI disaster on its hands. The marketing manager talks to the sales manager about it. He just shakes his head, laughs and says, "Oh yeah, the leads from that show are junk. My salespeople do not even pay any attention to them." Truly chilling—a b-to-b direct marketer's worst nightmare.

I hope this does not sound familiar, but it should be food for thought. Conventions and trade shows in particular should be carefully evaluated. These events tend to be far less effective than seminars in generating *qualified* leads, because the venue is very different.

If you have attended such shows, you know the score. You can go from booth to booth and pick up a slew of very expensive literature and a variety of giveaways free and without obligation, and in most cases you can remain totally anonymous while you scoop these goodies into a gargantuan convention bag. You can even participate in various games and contests and actually win something valuable—although you have not got the slightest interest in the exhibitor's product or service. At the end of this major trade show, all the exhibitors truck home with hundreds, or maybe thousands of "leads"—only to discover that most of them are about as qualified to purchase as the people manning the hot dog concession stand at the trade show.

This kind of shotgun marketing is not easy to justify to management. The cost of booth space, promotional materials, handouts, and travel is just part of the picture. The waste of staff time and the cost of fulfilling junk leads further magnify the problem.

Of course, not all trade shows leave a bitter taste in marketers' mouths. I can recall stories of technology companies whose marketing and sales staff come back from shows flush with hundreds of thousands of dollars worth of business booked in a few days. Just as important, some very significant products are launched at trade shows. With shows, as with marketing seminars, fabulous success stories abound—as do unmitigated disasters. The trick is to learn how to use event marketing in a targeted, results-oriented way so you can achieve the former, not the latter.

The Net Event

Even if your company is achieving substantial success with traditional event marketing, you cannot help but be intrigued by the "net event." The concept of replacing or augmenting traditional live events with Web-based online or "virtual" events has caught on quickly with b-to-b marketers. In fact, virtual events are booming on the Internet. To explore why, we will use the traditional seminar program as a point of reference. Despite the substantial face-to-face benefits of a live seminar, such a program can be:

- **A Logistical Nightmare.** Speakers and hotels need to be scheduled and managed, materials have to be in the right place at the right time, and prospects need to be invited in advance and registered on-site. The seminar is also dependent on things you cannot control, such as local traffic and weather conditions.

- **A Substantial Investment.** Costs for speaker fees, hotel rooms and food, travel, presentation output and equipment, and seminar promotion add up quickly. The seminar may also need last-minute support via telemarketing or fax if registration numbers are low.

- **A Quality Control Challenge.** Ensuring that presenters are well prepared and materials are well executed, especially when the seminar takes place at numerous national or worldwide locations, is a difficult task.

- **A Risky Venture.** Even if everything is handled properly, the typical no-show rate at a live seminar can be 50 to 60 percent. Free seminars have become somewhat of a "commodity item," because there are now so many of them offered. As companies downsize and managers become overburdened, attendance at off-site seminars becomes difficult to fit into the workday. In fact, senior business executives rarely attend these events due to the intense demands on their time and their heavy travel schedules.

Here is the difference between a live seminar and a virtual seminar. The virtual seminar can:

- **Virtually Eliminate Logistical Hassles.** Prospects are invited to come to a special URL in cyberspace instead of a physical place. You do not need to arrange for hotels and you do not need to ship anything anywhere. In fact, you do not even have to show up anywhere other than on the Web. Web traffic may be heavy, but it is better than the roads—and the weather is irrelevant.

- **Provide You with Foolproof Quality Control.** The online seminar is totally controlled by you. The format, content, and timing are uniform and singular, and therefore completely consistent. You only have to create it once, no matter how many times someone sees it. Even if you execute the online seminar as a live event, it can be archived and repeated.

- **Attract Qualified Prospects.** The online seminar is more convenient for prospects or customers; they do not need to leave the office to attend. As a result, the virtual seminar has the potential to attract not only larger audiences, but also a greater number of senior executives. The online seminar is also a more novel and intriguing approach than a live seminar. As such, prospects might find it more compelling to attend.

- **Cost Substantially Less Than Live Seminars.** Online seminars compare favorably to live events.

Earlier, we looked at the costs and results for a ten-city live seminar program. Now we will compare the costs and results for an online seminar program, using the following assumptions:

- The seminar will be a one-hour session, conducted entirely over the Web. The sponsoring company uses an outside firm to create and host the seminar.

- The sponsoring company will hire one guest speaker, who will provide a presentation for use on the Web. The guest speaker will also be available for an interactive question-and-answer session, which will be held during a few pre-appointed times via teleconference. Seminar visitors will be able to call a toll-free number to listen to the presentation which Web content is "pushed" over the Web. They will also be able to ask questions and listen to answers via telephone.

- A direct mail invitation will be sent to 30,000 prospects. They will be selected based on geographic areas that mesh with the live seminar program. We will also assume the same cost to execute the direct mail as with the live seminar program.

- The call to action in the invitation will instruct recipients to respond by coming to a special URL to "attend" the virtual seminar. That means a respondent is an attendee, so there is not a "no-show" rate, as with a live seminar. All respondents are attendees. Even if you want to pre-qualify prospects further by sending them first to a registration page, the typical no-show rate for an online seminar will probably be lower than with a live seminar.

Figure 6.2 indicates the costs and results for the online seminar.

Analysis of Live Seminar Program versus Online Seminar Program

1. *The cost for the direct mail promotion is the same for both seminar programs.* However, notice the difference in cost between the live seminar (Figure 6.1) and online seminar (Figure 6.2) programs themselves. The online seminar costs $15,000 to $31,000 *less* than the live seminar ($78,000–$120,000 vs. $93,000–$151,000).

	Typical Costs/Results
Seminar promotion: direct mail invitation to 30,000 prospects (3,000 each of 10 sites), not including follow-ups, confirmations, or fulfillment	$45,000–60,000
Seminar presentation: creation of the complete online seminar, including design, content, and interactive session	$30,000–50,000
Seminar Web hosting for one month	$1,000–5,000
Guest speaker fee for the online seminar	$2,000–5,000
Total Costs	**$78,000–120,000**
Number of invitations mailed	30,000
Response rate from the direct mail invitation	2.5%
Number of respondents/attendees	750
Cost per attendee	**$104-160**

Figure 6.2. Online seminar costs and results.

2. *Although the response rates are the same for both programs, there is a significant no-show rate for the live seminar program.* That is because generating attendance at a live seminar is basically a two-step process—prospects respond to an invitation first, and then they have a second opportunity to decide whether or not they will actually attend. Typical no-show rates at live events range from 40 to 60 percent. With the virtual seminar, *a respondent is an attendee,* because the individual responds by going online and entering the seminar.

3. *This means that the number of attendees to the online seminar is twice the number of attendees to the live seminar. As a result, the cost per attendee for the online seminar is less than half that of the live seminar.* In addition, if the online seminar program proves to be as successful as indicated in this analysis, it can be *reused* at an extremely low incremental cost—unlike the live seminar program, whose costs continue to go up every time it is presented at a new physical location.

This analysis of live seminars vs. online seminars makes an extraordinarily compelling case for the use of Internet events.

Replacement or Enhancement?

Do you need to eliminate all live seminars and conduct online seminars instead? Not necessarily. You may still wish to hold live seminars in a few key cities so that you can tell your story face-to-face and your salespeople can "press the flesh." However, you can *supplement* your live seminar schedule with an online seminar that you promote only in secondary cities—so you can "be there" even if your live seminar is not.

You also can use an online seminar as a follow-up to a live seminar, inviting individuals who could not attend the live seminar to share in the experience online. Also, you can suggest that attendees to your live seminars tell their colleagues that they can attend a virtual seminar version of the live seminar.

After you create an online seminar, you can easily version it for partner or reseller usage. And, by archiving the online seminar, you can extend its value and use it for subsequent promotional efforts.

The Net Event Is Not Without Technological Challenges

Early models for the Internet event were largely informational Web sites with a healthy dose of high-value "objective" informational content. Educational institutions, museums, scientific consortiums, and the like sponsored such sites. The Web is still populated with such informational sites, but commercialization has quickly taken over. Now companies with something to sell sponsor many informational sites. That is not a bad thing, necessarily—you can still find some incredibly valuable, data-rich sites if you are willing to wade through an occasional sales pitch.

The marketing version of the Internet seminar or event combines the best of both the informational site concept with the concept of Internet-based education. Internet events can be anything from online trade shows and conferences, to Web-based seminars and symposiums, to Internet "talk shows" and presentations. Some of these are widely promoted and open to the general public, while others are invitation-only, private access events. For the most part, these events are intended to promote something, so they are offered at no charge.

A major barrier for such events has been Internet technology itself. You cannot, of course, access Web sites without Web browser software. The two leading browsers are Netscape Navigator and Microsoft Internet Explorer. Current versions of these software products incorporate the Java programming language, which facilitates interactivity and multimedia. "Plug-ins," which enable sound and images to be sent across the Web, are also being built into current browsers so that they are already available without the need to download the plug-in. In some cases, limited sound and multimedia can be experienced on the Web *without* plug-ins using Java-based servers and other real-time technologies.

The most common implementation is "streaming," which replaces the need to download and launch a file to see or hear it. With streaming, after the applet is launched or the plug-in is installed, audio, or full-motion video can be delivered in real time to the computer desktop.

The rapid adoption of streaming media promises to fuel the market for Internet collaboration, meeting and events. The Internet Research Group says the market for streaming media services will reach $2.5 billion by 2004, twenty times what it was in 2000. Vastly improved streaming technology, in combination with much faster Internet connections, will converge to turn Internet events and even e-learning into mainstream markets.

As just one example of the pervasive presence of e-learning, in June 2000 Barnes & Noble (*www.bn.com*) announced it would develop its own "Barnes & Noble University" on the Web. This "free online education resource" will offer e-learning taught by book authors. Obviously, it is also an opportunity for authors to sell more books. Behind the concept is a distance learning organization, notHarvard.com (*www.notharvard.com*), who creates "eduCommerce" Web sites.

The de facto standard for audio and video streaming is Real Networks' RealSystem software (*www.real.com*), although Microsoft's Media Player is gaining ground. RealSystem software is used to deliver content on more than 85 percent of all streaming media enabled Web pages, according to the company. In June 2000, Real claimed that over 125 million unique RealPlayer users had been registered. The user base grows by over 200,000 users per day, an increase of more than 300 percent since the end of 1998. Users can download a free RealPlayer, through which RealAudio (sound) and RealVideo (full-motion video) can be received. RealPresenter permits PowerPoint slide shows to be enhanced with a synchronized audio track, and RealFlash enables animations that can be synchronized with RealAudio. Real products can stream both pre-recorded and live presentations over the Web.

Real took another step towards dominating multimedia on the Internet with its purchase of Xing Technology in April 1999. Xing was the developer of MP3 software, used to stream music across the Web. At the same time, RealNetworks announced a partnership with IBM to create a universal standard for digital distribution of music.

Services such as Activate (*www.activate.com*), Yahoo's Broadcast.com (*www.broadcast.com*), Education News and Entertaiment Network (*www.enen.com*), and Webcasts (*ww.webcasts.com*) offer the ability to send "Webcasts" (live or pre-recorded video presentations) in real time over the Internet, or take a telephone feed of audio, translate it, and broadcast it in real time over the Internet. Other companies are quickly entering this market. For example, high-flying Internet content delivery service Akamai Technologies (*http://www.akamai.com*) announced in June 2000 that it would offer online conference call services to telecommunications giants AT&T and Worldcom, among others. Earlier in 2000, Akamai acquired Internet conferencing company Intervu, whose product NetPodium was popular for online conferences and seminars. This is particularly useful for virtual seminars, because it means a speaker can be using a telephone and his or her voice can be seamlessly transmitted to Web "listeners."

The speaker can also be pre-recorded, so the event can be staged "live" and it can be archived for ongoing use as well. Numerous technology conferences, trade shows, and symposiums have used live video streaming to put a unique twist on their offerings.

The most common form of Internet event presentation is currently the combination Web/teleconference event. While there are a variety of technologies used for implementation, the basic concept is the same: The attendee goes to a URL to see Web content, but calls an 800 number to hear a synchronized presentation. Web content is "pushed" to the attendee's computer while the audio is sent via a telephone. The benefit is that no plug-in or sound card is required to participate, only a basic Web browser and a telephone, which is likely to be available to virtually any audience. Some technologies permit additional features, such as computer-based chat, instant polling, and live demonstrations.

Numerous providers of software and services have entered this market, and it is growing exponentially. For example, PlaceWare (*www.placeware.com*) (Figure 6.3) provides live, interactive Web presentations for business use that can include hundreds and even thousands of attendees at a single event. PlaceWare is based on a "meeting room" concept that goes beyond passive Web-pushed content. It also allows participants to "talk" via online chat, while permitting the presenter to not only push Web pages, but also to conduct online demos and instant polls, and to use an electronic whiteboard to enhance the online presentation.

Other solutions are provided over the Internet as a service, while others are software products. An essential difference is the combination of Web and teleconference, as described earlier, versus what is commonly known as "voice over IP", which is voice delivered via the Internet. While voice over IP quality has dramatically improved, it does require both a sound card and a computer headset, if the participant wants to both hear and speak. Some solutions offer the option of both the teleconference and voice over IP.

WebSentric's Presentation.net (*http://www.presentation.net*)and MShow (*www.mshow.com*) function as online event service bureaus, while companies such as Centra Software (*www.centra.com*) and Latitude Communications (*www.latitude.com*) offer Web-conferencing software products. Expect this area of Internet technology to expand dramatically in the next several years as service providers and software companies rush in to serve the market.

The Internet broadcasting market in general is growing rapidly. *NetMarketing* magazine (*www.netb2b.com*) reported in June 1999 that

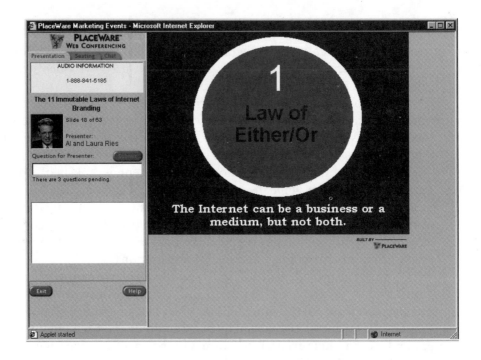

Figure 6.3. PlaceWare Online Seminar presented by Al and Laura Ries.

about 10 percent of U.S. businesses used Internet broadcasting in 1998, according to market research firm Dataquest. Helping to fuel that growth is Microsoft Office 2000, which includes a version of PowerPoint, the popular presentation software, that, according to *NetMarketing*, "will enable a presentation to be transmitted over the Internet/intranet, with users viewing it on their Web browser in conjunction with the Microsoft Media Player program."

The marketing world has been waiting for a Web that can truly support full-blown multimedia, live audiovisual presentations, interactive live chat, and live videoconferencing. Streaming media products take a giant step forward towards that ultimate goal. This technology is still in part dependent upon the vagaries of an Internet that is bloated with traffic, and the inadequacies of data transport pipes, delivery devices, Web servers, and receiving computers. But dramatic improvement is on its way. Broadband, which uses both cable and telephone lines, will increase the Internet's ability to handle the load, as will newer technologies such as DSL. Nevertheless, until these technologies are commonplace and available to the Internet majority, it may be risky to execute a virtual seminar that is completely live or wholly multimedia on the Web. The conservative strategy of using sound and motion selectively, supplemented with more traditional communications such as a teleconferencing component, is likely to be a better bet until the technology advances even further.

Interacting live via a computer or by voice during the virtual event requires "chat," voice over the Internet, or online videoconferencing capabilities. Technologies that allow visitors to interact and ask questions live and online are being perfected. Interim solutions, such as the use of traditional telephone teleconferencing in combination with the virtual event or employing e-mail to respond to questions, are being used with considerable success to overcome early adopter issues.

All of these advances are critically important to the proliferation of virtual events and virtual learning. Most marketers want to be in a position to replicate the content of a live seminar or leverage the investment they have already made in a CD-ROM, a slide show, or a videotaped marketing presentation for use on the Internet. Previously, the Internet was not the right venue for such heavy sound-and-motion content, but that is rapidly changing, and IT marketers will be the direct beneficiaries of advances in this area.

Types of Internet Events

It is possible to adapt virtually every kind of live event into a virtual event that either *enhances* the live event or stands on its own. Here are some specific examples that are appearing in one form or another on the Web.

The Online Trade Show

These events seem to be most popular as enhancements to live shows, but they are even being used to replace live shows. One example of online trade show usage is that the show is already running as a live event, and the show sponsor wants to extend its value to non-attendees. The sponsor creates a show-specific Web site and features some of the content from the live show. Aggressive sponsors offer special incentives to the exhibitors to advertise on the show site. An online trade show could be used as a "hook" for a live trade show, or it could completely replace a live trade show if desired.

The Online Seminar or Presentation

This is probably the most popular format, and the one with the most variations. These are the basic formats for the online seminar:

- **Scheduled live seminar.** The online seminar or presentation can be a "live" event held at an appointed time, during which a speaker is heard via a teleconference phone call or via audio streaming technology over the Web. The speaker can be heard *and* the presentation can be seen over the Web with audiovisual streaming. The speaker typically leads the visitor through a "slide" presentation of individual screens which are "pushed" over the Web. The speaker answers questions asked by participants via telephone, or takes questions via e-mail and answers them via e-mail, chat, or streamed audio over the Web. Audio portions can be recorded digitally for archiving purposes. This type of event can be enhanced with a mini-site or "resource area" (Figs. 6.4 and 6.5).

- **Scheduled pre-recorded seminar.** The pre-recorded format offers more flexibility in that it can be held at more times than the live session without the presence of the speaker. It is less flexible in that it does not allow for live interaction. Some presentations mix pre-recorded sections with a live question-and-answer period to gain the benefits of both formats.

- **On-demand seminar.** This type of event has the most flexibility, in that it is available to the attendee at any time. Audiovisual content is typically available on-demand; for example, a video of a speaker can be played at any time. It can be appended to an existing Web site or run as a special, invitation-only seminar or presentation. Typically, the on-demand seminar does not include a scheduled session or provide the ability to ask questions "live" online, except through e-mail. One option is to add a scheduled event, or to schedule a question-and-answer period at specific times as an enhancement to this format. Another possibility is to accept questions online and answer them via return e-mail. Generally the content of the on-demand seminar is organized into sections that can be easily navigated, so attendees can move through the seminar at their own pace.

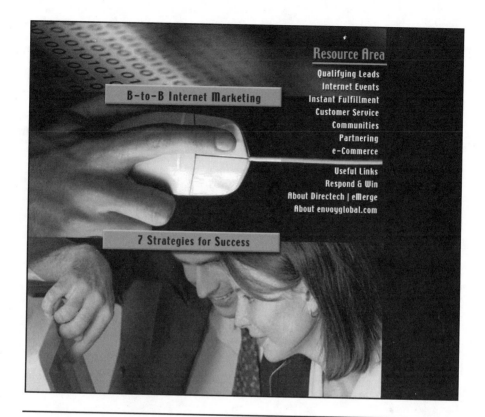

Figure 6.4. Resource area from an online seminar, "B-to-B Internet Marketing: 7 Strategies for Success."

The Online "Webcast"

This event is really a television or radio program broadcast over the Internet. It typically features a panel discussion or several speakers who offer short presentations, followed by a question-and-answer session, most often conducted via teleconference.

The Online Meeting

The online meeting can be anything: a sales meeting, user group conference, analyst meeting, press conference, and so on. A number of companies now routinely use the Internet for sales meetings and press

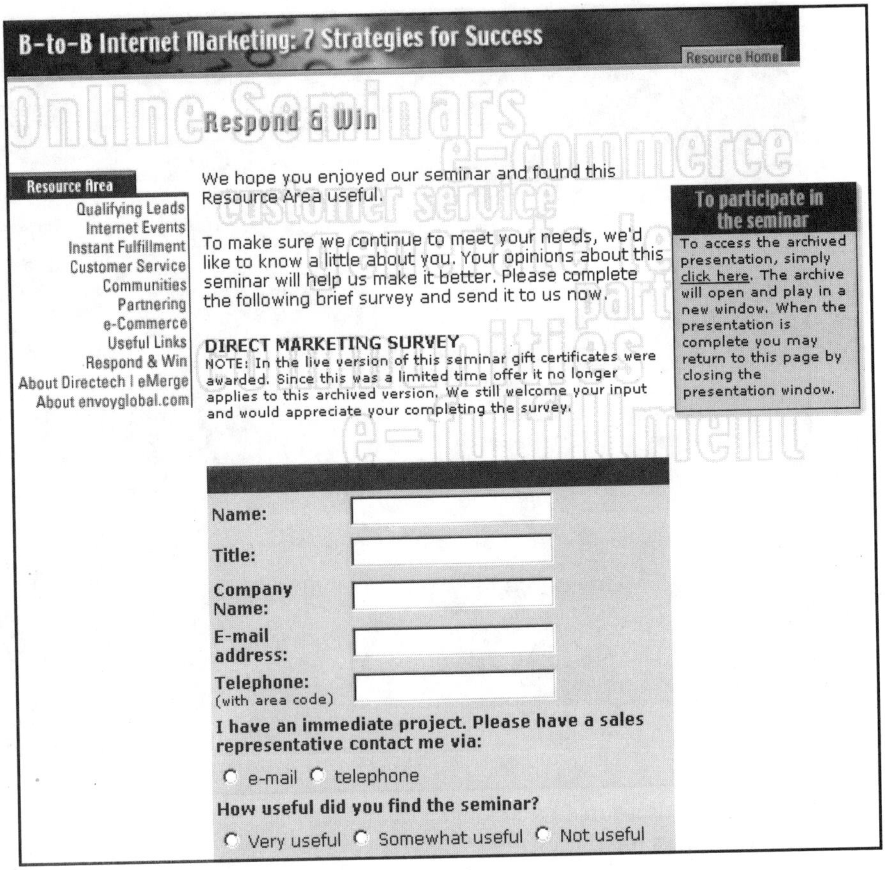

Figure 6.5. Web response form from an online seminar, "B-to-B Internet Marketing: 7 Strategies for Success."

conferences, and several companies have even experimented with on-line annual meetings.

"Crossing Over" with Online Events

A developing trend is the increasing connection between offline and online events. B-to-b trade shows, for example, are moving towards not just promoting live events on the Internet, but sometimes running live Webcasts from the event, or posting videos of the event on the Web soon after its conclusion. Live seminar programs are also being captured on video and archived for Web use. For example, the Direct Marketing Association (*www.the-dma.org*) held two live seminars, one on e-commerce and one on e-mail marketing, in several cities during the spring of 2000. In late June, once these seminars were no longer offered live, the DMA sent an e-mail to members promoting the seminars again, this time as online seminars. The DMA had adapted the live seminars, added chat rooms so classmates could converse and bulletin boards to connect with the instructors, and offered them as on-demand Web events at a 20 percent discount for both.

Developing and Hosting the Internet Event

Before you rush off to cancel all of your live seminar programs, do yourself a favor: *Test* the online event on a limited basis with your target audiences. Admittedly, it is almost a "no-brainer" when it comes to comparing the costs/results from an online seminar to that of a live seminar program. A seminar held on the Web looks like the clear winner, but although the Internet event may seem to hold great promise, it is important to know if your audience will be accepting of this new marketing format.

Today, the Internet event seems to have its greatest appeal for audiences such as technical professionals—IT managers, networking managers, software developers, and the like. But as Internet usage increases, usage of Internet events will increase. As a result, such events could become attractive replacements for live events.

The Internet event should also be a particularly attractive venue for senior executives, who often do not have the time to attend an event in person. If you want to reach a high-level audience via the Internet, compare the pros and cons of a virtual event to these other "live" formats:

- **The Teleconference, or Teleforum.** This format is basically a seminar held via the telephone. It typically lasts about an hour, rather than the traditional half-day event, and is offered early in the morning so the executive can grab a cup of coffee and listen, perhaps with *The Wall Street Journal* at hand, before the responsibilities of the day distract him or her. With the right speakers and topic, the teleforum is a very powerful format—perhaps even more attractive than virtual events for high-level decision-makers. If appropriate, teleforums can be enhanced by directing the listener to a URL to view Web-based content during the event.

- **The Executive Roundtable or Briefing.** This variation of the seminar is a small live event with a restricted invitation list. It is usually open to senior executives by invitation only from the sponsoring company's CEO. The executive roundtable is positioned as an opportunity to participate in a discussion with peers. Sometimes the invitation to such an event is as exclusive as the event itself—it may be engraved, hand-addressed, or even include an executive gift.

- **The Executive Retreat.** The "retreat" is typically an executive symposium that includes one or more renowned speakers and is held in a world-class resort—with ample time for golf and other recreational opportunities. These formats, if well executed, can attract top executives who want to rub shoulders with "stars" like themselves. Of course, the expense associated with such events is significant.

If you are successfully holding teleforums, roundtables, or retreats for executives such as the ones described, do not scrap them all in favor of Internet events—test such an event first to see if it has the same appeal and staying power.

Guidelines for Developing and Hosting Your Own Internet Event

Here are some of the things you should think about when you are planning and executing your own Internet event.

1. Plan Your Event

What kind of event do you need? The Internet event is a customized Web application, and it will vary substantially based on the type of event you wish to execute, as well as the audience for the event. First, map out your available options. Decide whether you will create the event entirely in-house or with the help of outside resources. Determine early whether you or another organization will do the Web hosting.

2. Develop the Event

Evaluate the needs of the target audience and develop an event well suited to the audience. Technology considerations are important, and they should be assessed during the development stage. Each of the following questions should be asked, because each requires a different kind of technological support:

- **Database Integration.** Will you pre-assign individuals an access code and greet them at the "door"—or will you simply identify attendees when they arrive and sign in? Do you wish to pre-qualify attendees by asking them to register in advance, or is it acceptable to send them directly to the event?

- **Audiovisual Requirements.** Do you intend to have one or more "live" speakers make a presentation or guide attendees through a section of the event? Will you use traditional telephone for the speaker(s), or will you do it all online using streaming audio? Do you wish to include sound and motion, and are you prepared to do so?

The "event concept" will ultimately guide the structure of the event, where the event is hosted, as well as the copy and creative execution.

In the case of a Web seminar, you may be adapting the content of a live seminar. Replicating the content is not as easy as it sounds: You will have to modify slides, scripts, and other materials so they are optimized for presentation on the Internet.

Critical Success Factors

In general, the same critical success factors that apply to live events apply to virtual events:

- **Guest Speaker(s).** Guest speakers add credibility and prominence to a seminar. The guest speaker should ideally be a noted authority in the field, an analyst or consultant, or a journalist. The guest speaker can provide an aura of objectivity and impartiality to a seminar and helps draw a crowd. It is also appropriate for guest speakers to be from organizations that are partners or customers of the sponsoring company. There should be an opportunity for a question-and-answer session if possible.

- **Success Stories.** Success stories, either told by customers or by the company sponsoring the seminar, are typically well received at seminars. Seminar attendees like to hear about how problems were solved and challenges overcome.

- **"Exclusive" Information.** Seminars that share some sort of exclusive information—such as the unveiling of survey results—have high-perceived value, especially if this information is conveyed by one of the guest speakers.

- **"Hot" Topics.** Current in-vogue topics of interest to the target audience, combined with success stories or product demonstrations, can add to a seminar's success.

- **Interactivity.** For the virtual seminar, interactivity of some kind is essential. A demo that the prospect can control and a worksheet with a calculator are examples of interactive elements that work.

3. Establish a Structure for the Event

It is critical to construct an effective structure for your event with an intuitive navigational flow and organized content. The structure should be mapped out on a flow diagram that outlines the path that visitors will take from the time they enter the event. Factors to consider in creating a structure include the likelihood of repeat visits, the frequency of information "refreshment," and the segmentation of the site's content. Generally, each page of the event should be short and clean to minimize the need for excessive scrolling.

Depending on the event's complexity, it is generally a good idea to follow a modular layout. This allows the visitors to go to different areas based on their needs, interests, and time constraints. If the event is on-demand, attendees may want to check in at several times on several different days, in order to fit the event within their busy schedules. If you want the event to include any type of real-time presentation or a live "chat room" for online questions and answers, you will probably want to schedule these parts of the event at various specific dates and times, just as you would a live event.

4. Create the Content for the Event

All of the content for an Internet event should be "Web-ized." There is nothing worse than loading an event with copy and graphics that have not been modified for electronic consumption. Copy should be crisp, informative, and conveyed in readable, digestible chunks. The navigation template should be clean and attractive. Graphical elements should be designed to facilitate navigation.

If you are doing a Web seminar, using the content from a traditional seminar is probably a good place to start. Use the speaker's slides as a basis for the virtual seminar's graphics, and his or her notes as copy input. Do not try to use the materials as is—graphics will typically need to be rendered especially for the Web in an appropriate program, with the final graphic resolution at 72 dots per inch (dpi).

Simple animations, such as movement of type and graphics, should be used to enhance the visitor's experience. Most animations should be universally viewable without any special software. Graphic files should be kept small and manageable. Interactive forms should be designed for the lowest common denominator.

5. Research and Add Appropriate Technologies

Incorporate only those Internet technologies that will enhance your event, not detract from it or cause undue complications for event visitors. Options include database connectivity, dynamic HTML, use of cookies, push technology, Java applets, streaming audio and video, and electronic commerce.

When used appropriately, multimedia offers the visitor an enhanced experience, with the ability to click on images and interact with animated text and images. However, essential content should be available to the lowest common technological denominator. If you require plug-ins to hear sound or view motion, they should be optional, not required. Mirror any content so that participants will not miss anything if they do not use the plug-ins.

A word of caution, especially if you are targeting your event to individuals who work in larger corporations: Some corporate networks have firewall technology that might block certain plug-ins. Always suggest that the participant do a browser test prior to the event if plug-ins are used. It is important not to assume that everyone can see and hear your event as you intended it. Designing the event for maximum audience attendance is important.

Database integration adds an additional personalized dimension to Web events. Merging Web pages with online information provides data that can be used to dynamically generate Web pages on the fly, offering the option for heightened personalization and user feedback.

You have a wide range of databases from which to choose. Many of the larger, more robust database products, such as Oracle and Sybase, can integrate with the Web, as can smaller programs such as Microsoft Access. Others, such as ColdFusion, are designed especially to acts as a database interface to process database scripts and return the information within HTML.

Implementation options include password access, user profiles, and interactive online qualification forms for individual users. Such mechanisms allow for rapid and accurate tracking of attendance, as well as gathering information on attendees and their opinions. All of this information will be valuable in improving future virtual events.

6. Determine How the Event Will Be Hosted

The decision to host a virtual event hinges on several issues, including expected traffic, database requirements, multimedia technologies employed, and site security. If, for example, you are using streaming media, you will need a special Web server to accommodate the traffic, or a broadcasting service who can stream it for you. Examine and compare the options for internal versus external hosting.

When evaluating outside hosting services, look at the following criteria:

- Server hardware and software

- Redundancy and reliability of servers

- Connections and bandwidth available

- Space restrictions

- Data transfer restrictions

- Availability of e-mail and autoresponders

- Availability of FTP

- Quality of access statistics

- Security

- CGI availability and support

- Java availability and support

- Database access

- Search capabilities

- Audio, video, and multimedia support as required

- Technical support

- Fee structure

7. Program and Test the Event

Before "going live," test all components of the virtual event thoroughly. Program and test all links, forms, and graphic files. Test all pages and any database integration from multiple Web browsers on different computer platforms. Test and evaluate all multimedia components to ensure they are functional on the widest possible range of platforms. Evaluate the content for general clarity and readability. If possible, try out the event on staff, customers, or "friendly" prospects before making it widely available.

It also might be a good idea to post technical information at the event's URL to be certain that attendees can take full advantage of the event. I saw an excellent example of "covering all the bases" when I went to a company's event address to sign up. This company had included a page of instructions for "testing and optimizing" participation in the event, as well as a link to "test your browser." The company listed all the technical requirements for the event, along with a description of firewalls and how to work around them so the data portion of the online seminar would function properly.

8. Promote the Event

Promote the Internet event. See the next section of this chapter for suggestions on event promotion.

9. Evaluate the Results

Establish measurement criteria in advance so that you know how many individuals attended the event. Use qualification forms with offers within the event to identify and track quality leads. Compare the ROI of virtual event programs to the ROI you have achieved with traditional events. You may find that it varies based on the type of audience and the type of event. Use this analysis to plan and refine future Internet event programs.

Promoting Events Using the Internet

The Internet brings a whole new spin to promoting both traditional and Internet-based events. And as you might expect, services already exist to help event producers promote and host their events with little effort. If you hold a substantial number of events, you might want to look at these services: EventsHome (*www.eventshome.com*), which extends "offline" events online, iNetEvents (*www.inetevents.com*), which provides a Web-enabled event management application that puts a "Web wrapper" around your event, b-there.com (*www.b-there.com*), an attendee relationship management engine, and iconvention.com (*www.iconvention.com*), providing associations with the means to extend physical shows into online vertical trading communities.

It is also a good idea to keep track of both live events and online events so you can be aware of trends. Here are some valuable resources:

- AllMeetings (*www.allmeetings.com*)– the best locations for meetings

- Go-events (*www.go-events.com*) – comprehensive listing of business events

- EventWeb (*www.eventweb.com*) – extremely useful event newsletter with a lot of Internet coverage

- MeetingEvents (*www.meetingevents.com*) – industry-related events

- SeminarFinder (*www.seminarfinder.com*), Seminar Information (*www.seminarinformation.com*),

- SeminarPlanet (*www.seminarplanet.com*), SeminarSource (*www.seminarsource.com*) – databases of seminar events

- TechCalendar (*www.techweb.com/calendar*) – technology-related events

- TSCentral (*www.tscentral.com*) – comprehensive listing of worldwide trade shows

Suppose you are promoting a traditional event, such as a free half-day seminar in ten cities. This might be what the promotional plan looks like:

1. Establish the dates and locations. Select list sources and target the appropriate audience within 50 miles of each city.

2. Create and mail an invitation. Include the traditional phone, mail-in, and fax-back response paths.

3. Follow up with fax and telephone confirmations to registrants.

4. Cross-promote the seminar with advertising and public relations activities.

Now see what happens when you enhance your promotion by using the Internet as a registration facilitator. You execute the same four steps, but you add a special seminar registration URL to the mail piece and promote it prominently. You urge the prospect to visit the URL to receive further seminar details and to register online.

When the prospect arrives at the Web response area, you offer:

- A more detailed agenda and description of the seminar, along with speaker photographs and biographies if appropriate,

- Directions, including printable maps, for each seminar location,

- Information about other events of potential interest to the prospect, including a list of Internet-based events for those prospects who are not in the ten-city area or cannot attend the live seminars but want more information about your company's product,

- An interactive registration form—perhaps with a special offer just for online registrants—so that prospects can register online and receive an instant acknowledgment. (Collect an e-mail address here and you can use it to remind the registrant of the seminar several times before the event. Use a Web-based database tool and you can capture the marketing information you obtain from the prospect "one time" instead of re-keying the information. Use it for future promotions and to track the prospect's activity.)

This relatively easy enhancement could have a significant impact on your seminar program—and your marketing ROI. Here are the six reasons why:

1. You may be able to reduce the cost of your direct mail seminar invitation by making it less elaborate and driving response to the Web—where they get full seminar details. Typical direct mail seminar invitations include a full agenda, speaker biographies, and location information. That takes considerable space to accomplish in a mailing piece. With the Web as your electronic information center, perhaps even an oversized postcard invitation would suffice.

2. Overall response to the promotion could increase because you have added a Web response path that some registrants may prefer to use. On the Web, they can get more information about the seminar without the need to speak to anyone, and they can easily register online.

3. Online registrants may be higher quality prospects because they take the time to visit the URL, review detailed information, and complete the registration form.

4. Using a series of e-mail confirmations and reminders, which you send prior to the event, could reduce your "no-show" rate (which is typically 50 to 60 percent for live seminars).

5. Even if prospects visit the URL and do not come to the seminar, they have been made aware of your company, your seminar series, and other events you sponsor which may interest them.

6. Individuals who are outside the ten-city seminar area could visit the URL to learn more about your company and products and, as a result, become new prospects for you.

The incremental cost to your seminar promotion to achieve these potential benefits should be very low. If you have a Web site, the seminar URL could "hang off" of it. Creating the seminar response area is not a complicated task—it can be done by your in-house Web staff or outsourced to an interactive resource. If you need comprehensive response management support, there are firms that handle online seminar registration and confirmation, along with maintaining your marketing database.

Use a similar strategy to promote other live events, such as your appearance at trade shows or conferences, sales meetings, press tours, and so on. Consider these additional promotional ideas:

- Place a Web banner ad on your own site to promote your appearance at a conference or trade show. Prominently feature your booth number and consider offering Web prospects something special if, when they visit your booth, they mention that they saw the promotion on your Web site.

- When you book any booth space or speaker from your company at a conference, be sure to see if the show's sponsor offers a Web site with links or special rates for exhibitors or speakers. Also see if you can offer "virtual" exhibit area admissions tickets to prospects, printable from your Web site.

- Collect e-mail addresses of trade show and seminar attendees and ask if you can communicate with them via e-mail. E-mail a questionnaire after the event to get their opinions and further qualify their interest.

- Collaborate with co-exhibitors at shows or cosponsors of seminars to promote events via the Internet. Cross-promote each other's products via e-mail and your respective Web sites.

Promoting the Net Event

All of the techniques you would use to promote traditional events apply to promoting virtual events as well. You can invite people to a virtual event in the same way you invite them to a live event:

- Direct mail is generally the most effective medium for seminar invitations.

- Telemarketing can be effective when you are inviting a small number of people, or to follow up on direct mail.

- Print advertising can supplement direct mail for trade show and conference promotions.

- E-mail sent to prospects and Web banners placed on your own site, or on carefully selected sites, could be used to augment mail and telemarketing efforts.

- You could also use public relations to publicize your event, which might lead to mention in trade publications or even free links on appropriate Web sites.

With the likelihood that virtual events and seminars will become more common in the future, it might be interesting to test various methods of inviting prospects and customers to such events. For example, if you can obtain an opt-in e-mail list, you might want to test traditional direct mail against e-mail invitations to a virtual seminar to see which is more effective in generating attendance.

With a virtual event, you can eliminate the need for an "I will attend" mail, fax, or phone response. Instead, you can offer prospects the ability to register online when they arrive at the special URL of the event. If the event is exclusive, you can pre-select a targeted list of people to invite, assign them individual access codes, and provide the codes on mailed or e-mailed invitations. Then, using a Web database program, you can actually "recognize" and greet them at "the door," when they come to the event. You can even encourage the prospect to share the access codes with colleagues, if you so choose, to extend the reach of the event.

Imagine receiving an elegant invitation to a virtual seminar with your own personal access code. Go to the seminar's special URL, enter your access code, and instantly, your name, title, company name, and address appear. You can verify it, or make changes as needed, online. The Web database records the changes and instantly updates the marketing database.

This technique is very appealing, because it suggests to the prospect that he or she is important to you, and that the event really is exclusive. In fact, it is the beginning of a marketing relationship that starts with the prospect coming to the event and taking responsibility for updating his or her own database record.

Obviously, there is considerable value to you as the direct marketer, because you are getting the prospect not only to attend your virtual event but also to engage in a dialogue with you. If you include qualification questions for the prospect to answer, you will get to know even more about the individual. You will be able to use that data to help prioritize the prospect's interest, and you will continue to market to that prospect over time.

Unlike the traditional event, the virtual event is more "anonymous" and certainly not as personal. As a result, you do not have the same opportunity for your marketing and sales staff to meet the prospect face-to-face. That is why promoting the virtual event should extend beyond the initial contact. Once a prospect comes to your virtual event, you should immediately engage him or her, offering compelling reasons to "sign in" and stay awhile. You may not want to ask a lot of questions of the prospect at the beginning of the event because this may discourage continued interest. Instead, use a questionnaire during the event or at the end—and make a substantive offer for completing it.

Use the event as an opportunity to cross-promote other virtual and live events, and give the attendee the ability to return to the event by keeping it available on the Web for a period of time. After that, it is a good idea to archive your virtual event, perhaps on your Web site or at another special site, so that prospects can come back in the future. The virtual event also has the potential to continue a marketing relationship that can ultimately turn a prospect into a customer.

Examples of B-to-B Online Seminars

There is widespread use of online seminars for marketing purposes among b-to-b companies. Some of the most aggressive users are IT companies and companies who are marketing Internet conferencing products or services. Since the target audiences of both of these types of companies tend to be heavy Internet users, they are likely to be early adopters and therefore comfortable with the online seminar venue. Here are just a few examples of b-to-b online seminars:

Centra BCN (Business Collaboration Network) (*www.centranow.com*)

Centra Software provides an online conferencing solution that incorporates the ability to do visual presentations with voice over IP technology—you hear the sound through your computer, and if you have a headset, you can also interact by speaking through your computer. While the software does not require a plug-in, your computer must have a sound card and speakers, although a headset is recommended to use the full capabilities of the software. To showcase its technology, Centra features numerous online seminars through its "Business Collaboration Network."

iPlanet netforums (*www.iplanet.com/netforums/*)

iPlanet is the flagship product area of the Sun | Netscape Alliance. iPlanet's series of "netforums," each a scheduled one-hour interactive seminar, addresses topics such as strategic Internet procurement, Internet trading communities, and remote access software/network security.

Oracle Internet Seminars (*www.oracle.com/seminars/*)

Oracle provides a very comprehensive "iSeminar" program through Oracle Internet Seminars, an entire area on the Oracle Web site. The seminar home page points you to an impressive list of scheduled seminars or "on demand seminars"—replays of previous events. The scheduled live seminars lead you through Oracle's "See, Try and Buy" process. In February 2000, Oracle raised the stakes in online seminars by introducing an "e-Business Network" that carries live "e-casts" of events and other streamed broadcasts on a regular basis. For example, its "View From a Suite" series features applications experts and other e-commerce leaders.

Placeware Seminars (*www.placeware.com/seminar*)

Placeware, an early leader in online conferencing, is particularly well-suited to online seminars. This is because the Placeware "room" offers presenters the ability to not only show slides, but also to annotate those slides, create new slides on the fly, use a whiteboard, conduct instant polls, demonstrate anything on the presenter's desktop, and lead audience members through tours of Web sites. Placeware also lets audience members ask questions via conventional telephone or a chat function. Placeware is "firewall friendly" and does not require a plug-in. To promote its product capabilities, Placeware runs an extensive program of free online seminars, many of which cover general business, e-business, and marketing topics and feature well-known speakers.

Results of an Online Survey About Online Seminars

My agency, Directech | eMerge (*www.directechemerge.com*), conducted a survey in March 2000 to gauge the use of online seminars by b-to-b marketers. We contacted over 800 marketing professionals via e-mail and invited them to come to a Web page and take the survey. We offered to send them the survey results, and also entered all respondents in a drawing to win several e-gift certificates.

We received 85 responses—over 10 percent response. Here are some of the highlights:

- 40 percent of the respondents were from companies with sales under $50 million

- 49 percent of the responding companies were using online seminars for marketing.

Of those using online seminars:

- 69 percent used slide presentations with a telephone conference call

- 67 percent had used a combination of in-house and outsourced services to produce their online seminars

- 84 percent had outsourced hosting the seminar, and 56 percent had outsourced the registration management process

- 47 percent had run more than 12 online seminars annually

- 38 percent had received response rates of 2.0 percent to 4.9 percent to their seminar promotions

- 34 percent had experienced "no show" rates of 40 to 49.9 percent

- 89 percent rated the quality of the leads generated from online seminars as good or excellent

- 63 percent rated e-mail as very good or excellent in promoting online seminars, the highest of any media used. Second was mentioning the seminar on their own Web sites, which achieved a 46 percent very good or excellent rating.

Case Study of a B-to-B Online Seminar Program

To demonstrate the effectiveness of a real online seminar program, I am using my own agency's experience, since our clients are sensitive about releasing results data. I believe our experience is fairly typical, because we have a need to reach a non-technical, marketing audience in business-to-business companies.

Promotion

We did extensive testing of direct mail and e-mail promotion for this online seminar, which was held in May 2000. A total of 14,010 individuals were reached using the following media:

- *Direct Mail:* 1,857 self-mailers were sent to our in-house prospect list, and 8,844 self-mailers were sent to three outside mailing lists. The direct mail invitation was a two-color self-mailing piece that featured the seminar "B-to-B Internet Marketing: 7 Strategies for Success." The invitation said the seminar was based on my book, *Business-to-Business Internet Marketing, Second Edition.* To respond to the direct mail, the prospect had to visit a special URL and sign up in advance of the seminar. The individual was asked to enter a "priority code" for list tracking purposes. No other response path was used other than the online response form.

- *E-mail:* 687 e-mail invitations were sent to our in-house prospect list of permission e-mail addresses, and 3,309 e-mails were sent to two guaranteed opt-in e-mail lists. The e-mail briefly described the seminar and invited the prospect to a special URL, which was unique to each e-mail list. Again, the prospect needed to sign up in advance using an online response form. All registrants received confirming e-mails, as well as e-mail reminders the day before the seminar.

Seminar

I conducted the seminar using Placeware, who also managed the seminar and registration process. The seminar was a one-hour free event, a 45-minute presentation followed by about 15 minutes of questions. I presented the seven strategies and showed direct mail and Internet marketing examples via static Web-pushed slides. Attendees listened to my audio presentation via telephone. During the seminar, I used instant polling, slide annotation, whiteboarding, and the live demo feature. Attendees were able to ask questions at any time during the seminar via the online chat feature, but these questions were hidden from view and held until the end of my presentation. At the close of the seminar, attendees were "sent" to a special Resource Area Web site, which included additional information about the seven strategies, along with links to Web sites and online seminars referenced during the presentation.

Results

The results of the seminar promotion were as follows:

- Direct mail for the house list pulled a 2.7 percent response, vs. a 7.3 percent response for the e-mail house list.

- Direct mail to outside lists averaged 1.4 percent, vs. 1.75 percent for the opt-in e-mail lists.

- The overall response rate for the seminar was 3.3 percent, with 456 individuals registering for the seminar. A total of 207 individuals attended, which translates into a no-show rate of 55 percent.

- We were extremely pleased with both the overall response and the number of attendees. Moreover, the quality of the respondents and attendees was extremely high. We attracted a significant percentage of marketing management titles at medium to large size companies—definitely the kinds of prospects we were interested in. We considered the program to be very successful in achieving our marketing goals.

Holding Online Marketing Meetings

Could the Internet also change the nature of meetings, perhaps making face-to-face meetings, and the travel associated with them, a thing of the past? Services such as WebEx (*www.webex.com*) might lead you to believe that could happen. WebEx is one of the leading Application Service Providers in a growing number of companies entering the emerging Web-based collaboration services marketplace. WebEx claimed by late 1999 to be "the world's most popular Web-based meeting service," providing its basic "Instant Meetings" service free for a small number of business users. Its paid "Premium Meeting" service adds participants and additional interactive features.

WebEx is successfully penetrating the b-to-b market. In November 1999, WebEx began partnering with MindSpring to offer "WebEx Office" to that ISP's small business customers at a new portal, MindSpring Biz (*www.mindspringbiz.com*). A small business user can "open" a WebEx Office in moments and begin conducting meetings on the Web, collaborating and exchanging information in real time. WebEx Office features include linking to existing Web sites to serve as a private conference room, instant messaging, meeting scheduling, calendaring, and more.

Clearly, this is another opportunity for the b-to-b company to leverage the Internet for both external and internal marketing-oriented meetings and events.

Using Distance Learning for Marketing

The natural evolution of online meetings and events is distance learning. While distance learning and online training has been around for years, the explosion of the Internet has increased its penetration of the marketing world. It is now on the verge of mass adoption for general marketing use. According to IDC, Web-based training is expected to exceed $6 billion by 2002, growing at a compound annual growth rate of almost 95 percent. By that year, says IDC, technology-based training is likely to overtake instructor-led training. In a survey of corporate training managers, Corporate University Xchange (*www.corpu.com*) found that as much as 96 percent of corporate training will be conducted online by 2003.

In this area, it is the IT market driving early adoption because of the ever-increasing demand for technical training. While educational programs may be beyond the scope of today's b-to-b Internet marketer, it is not difficult to imagine a future which involves extended customer service in the form of marketing-based online tutorials for prospects, modeled after earlier distance learning efforts. One of the reasons this will become more commonplace as a marketing technique is because of the widespread availability of multimedia tools, such as Flash and Shockwave, and the ever-increasing bandwidth to facilitate multimedia transmission.

Numerous companies have served the "e-learning" market for years, even before the Internet reached its current hot status. Typically, early leaders focused on IT technical training. One such company, CyberStateU (*www.cyberstateu.com*), today offers its "Synergy Learning System" to help reduce a student's total study time. The system combines multiple teaching mediums into a structured learning environment, combining online lectures, reviews, assignments, and interaction with more traditional books and video tapes. CyberStateU serves hundreds of leading companies, offering fully certified courses on behalf of Cisco, Microsoft, Novell, and others.

Now, e-learning is broadening its base and becoming a more accepted means of general business training. Newer organizations such as Digital Think (*www.digitalthink.com*) and SmartForce (*www.smartforce.com*) are typical of the "e-learning" trend. These and other services are expanding their offerings beyond IT learning as the education demands of general business continue to grow.

Another entry into this market, ZDUniversity, was originally an IT-oriented educational service, but it has evolved into the centerpiece of a new service launched by Ziff-Davis in October 1999 called SmartPlanet (*www.smartplanet.com*). According to the company, SmartPlanet is a "personal online learning community–a uniquely rich and diverse Web destination for people seeking continuous personal and professional growth on virtually any topic or interest." The former ZDU will become part of SmartPlanet as the base for the "Computers & Internet Learning Zone." SmartPlanet has registered members, both free and paid, and will grow its user base via distribution and partner agreements. Time will tell whether such online learning communities will become models for the future of marketing-driven distance learning

To apply distance learning as a marketing technique to reach larger organizations, the best solution might ultimately be establishing learning programs within each company. Here, such products as LearningSpace from Lotus (*www.lotus.com*) hold promise. LearningSpace Anytime 3.0, introduced in mid-1999, was the first Web-based product to give users the flexibility to learn either through self-paced materials, live interaction with others in a virtual classroom, or collaboration with others independent of time and place. This server software application can be accessed either from a Web browser or the Lotus Notes client. LearningSpace has been adopted by such organizations as Siemens Corporation, American Express, and online business education provider UNext.com.

7

Executing e-Fulfillment

Fulfillment—the process of responding to an inquiry or order—has always been a knotty problem for marketers. Since the early days of direct marketing, marketers have realized that answering a prospect's inquiry, or fulfilling a customer's order, can be a logistical nightmare.

The basic inquiry and order fulfillment process has not really changed much from those early days. A prospect or customer receives a solicitation, inquires, or places an order, and then the fun begins. The marketer responds to a prospect's inquiry via direct mail, sending data sheets, a catalog, or some other literature in a large envelope, sometimes with a personalized letter, often via first class mail. To fulfill a customer's order, the marketer receives and must verify payment and assure that the order is completed and shipped with the appropriate merchandise. Returns, of course, are a necessary evil of the business.

Whether it is inquiries or orders, speed is of the essence. Industry studies show that, if a prospect's inquiry is not fulfilled within 48 hours, interest cools. If an order is not fulfilled promptly, a customer is likely to become an ex-customer shortly thereafter. While managing the inquiry and order process is largely database-driven and automated, it still involves a back-end that is labor-intensive and often expensive.

Over the past several years, vendors have responded by introducing inquiry and order fulfillment software, systems and services. Yet, in the case of information requests, they could never solve the requirement of physically sending something out to the prospect.

Then the Internet came along, and e-fulfillment was born. While e-fulfillment is not appropriate in every situation, it does go a long way towards instantly responding to an inquiry. In fact, the Internet presents the b-to-b marketer with the unique ability to instantly fulfill inquiries online—no paper required! It scales beautifully, so hundreds, thousands, or even millions of inquiries can be handled electronically.

The Internet is revolutionizing order fulfillment as well. The Internet provides b-to-b marketers with the ability to instantly acknowledge orders via e-mail, and it allows customers to track their own shipments online. In addition, if the product being fulfilled is electronic information or software, a customer's order can actually be "shipped" online.

In this chapter, we will explore the growing area of e-fulfillment. You will discover how you can use e-fulfillment to dramatically reduce your costs, increase your efficiency, and improve prospect and customer satisfaction.

Traditional Fulfillment: An Aging Process

If your product or service is sold through any kind of sales channel, you deal with inquiries. Although most b-to-b marketers have a process for inquiry handling, it differs significantly from company to company.

Inquiries come in from a variety of sources—advertising, direct mail, trade shows, public relations, and the like, but until the company determines the quality of the inquiry, it should not be considered a "lead." A classic case in point is the reader service number that appears at the bottom of ads in many trade publications. The original purpose of the reader service number was for the publication to prove to the advertiser that the ad was working—in effect, to protect ad revenues.

You know the way it works: The publication assigns a reader service number to your ad. The reader circles that number, along with numerous others, on a "bingo card." The card is returned to the publication, which enters the informational data and then distributes the leads to you and the other advertisers.

It sounds great in theory, but in practice, reader service numbers often leave much to be desired. The commitment on the part of the reader of the ad is minimal. He or she circles a few numbers and is rarely asked any additional qualification questions. The inquiry goes into a large pool and is probably data entered by the lowest cost resource available. (After all, this is a free service provided by the publication.) That means the chance for error is high. Then, even if you receive an accurate inquiry, you have no idea whether it is from a qualified prospect or not.

This is the point at which some marketers make either of two critical mistakes:

1. The marketer disregards the inquiry altogether, assuming it is "junk," or

2. The marketer fulfills the inquiry through the standard fulfillment process, which generally means sending a costly full-color literature package, sometimes packaged in a presentation folder, via first class mail.

Both of these responses are wrong. In the first case, discarding the inquiries means that the marketer is potentially losing some good leads—maybe even qualified prospects—which could be buried in a pile of generally unqualified inquiries. The problem is, the marketer will never know.

The alternative is not much better: By fulfilling the inquiry as if it were a qualified lead, the marketer wastes a lot of money. Some marketers even exacerbate the process by then sending these inquiries to their sales force. There is nothing worse for a salesperson than spending valuable time chasing an unqualified inquiry. If the salesperson continues to receive unqualified inquiries, he or she will lose all faith in the marketing organization.

That is why the most sensible way to handle inquiries at this stage is with a *two-step* process. It is okay to respond to unqualified inquiries. It makes more sense, however, to do it with a far less expensive mailing—perhaps a simple #10 envelope with a printed letter that acknowledges the inquirer's interest but asks several qualification questions on an accompanying reply card before additional information is sent. This simple strategy can save thousands of dollars.

Even so, numerous industry studies suggest that fulfillment is the Achilles' heel of a majority of b-to-b direct marketers. Some companies do a shoddy job of it, hurting their corporate image in the process. Others may send the right materials; however, the turnaround time is anything but prompt.

Although they may not openly admit it, the fulfillment process of many b-to-b companies is in a shambles. Sometimes, it is because a company is overwhelmed with response. Sometimes, the fulfillment process itself is flawed, or the system is inadequate, or the quality control is poor, or it is simply human error. Whatever the reason, the result is the same—an inquiry is mishandled, over-fulfilled, or simply lost. That means a lead could be receiving inferior treatment and a potentially good prospect could be alienated. This is just on the prospect side. You can just imagine the impact of inferior order fulfillment on the customer side.

The Transformation of Traditional Fulfillment

Fulfillment experts say that 48 hours should be the *maximum* amount of acceptable lag time between the time an inquiry is received and the time a contact is initiated by the company. Basically, that means something should be on its way to a prospect within two days.

Interest in a product or service wanes from the moment a prospect or customer asks for more information to the moment it is received. The competitive environment is such that, if that individual has a choice, he or she is just as likely to go to any company that provides the requested information first. Business is so time-driven today that *the speed of information delivery is often as crucial as the information itself.* Buying decisions are sometimes made on that basis. That is why experienced direct marketers know that they should never underestimate the positive and negative effects of fulfillment. This brings into question the whole process of traditional fulfillment itself. Today, b-to-b fulfillment is still largely executed in the following standard ways:

Direct Mail

Direct mail remains the primary means of inquiry fulfillment. Typically, an inquirer receives a basic fulfillment package—a letter, literature, and a reply card—by mail.

Traditional inquiry fulfillment seems to be a remarkably wasteful process. Examine your own fulfillment materials and those that you receive from other companies. You will notice that many b-to-b direct marketers "over-fulfill." They mail folders packed with expensive, glossy literature to anyone, even unqualified inquiries. Companies who should know better are sending bulging literature kits to reader service inquiries, sometimes via first class mail. This is a colossal waste of money and natural resources.

Traditional direct mail fulfillment has been improved with the use of electronically distributed fulfillment requests and inventory control procedures. Some marketers have set up automated 800 numbers connected to voice response systems or autofax machines. Such systems accept an inquiry and electronically transmit it to the fulfillment operation, which picks and sends the appropriate literature pack within days or sometimes hours. The direct mail fulfillment material itself may be pre-kitted, waiting for alaser-personalized letter and mailing label to be generated and affixed. In extraordinary cases, literature or other fulfillment materials may be sent via priority mail or overnight delivery services. Overnight delivery is less common in inquiry fulfillment, but it is becoming more common in order fulfillment. Larger mail order companies contract with an overnight delivery service to reduce the shipping cost so that low-cost one- or two-day delivery can be offered to customers as a service enhancement.

Fax

Facsimile transmission is increasingly used to supplement or even replace direct mail fulfillment. Common among larger b-to-b companies is fax-on-demand, or autofaxing. The inquirer calls a toll-free number and enters his or her fax number and a product code. The responding fax-on-demand system immediately generates a data sheet on the corresponding product and faxes it to the inquirer. This type of fulfillment is inappropriate if a color brochure or multi-page booklet or manual must be sent, but it is acceptable for fast distribution of simple information. Its overwhelming benefit is the speed of response, which does offer a significant advantage in many cases. Sometimes, autofaxing is used to precede direct mail fulfillment.

Telephone

In the context of providing essential information immediately, the telephone can be a viable fulfillment medium. If an inquirer makes an inbound call to a toll-free number, the telemarketer can be trained to provide the caller with the necessary information by phone or offer to send additional information via fax or direct mail. Outbound telemarketing should only be used if the marketer believes the inquirer is a highly qualified prospect.

Behind each of these media is an inquiry handling process of some kind. Some companies choose to handle inquiries themselves, while others farm out the chore (and what a chore it can be) to fulfillment services.

Because direct mail is the predominant method of fulfillment, here is a quick look at the steps that are typically involved in the process.

1. An inquiry is received from any source.

2. Most of the time, the inquiry must be data entered, unless it is from a respondent for whom a name and address record already exists. The contact information is entered into a marketing database, along with answers to qualification questions, keycodes, and other identifying data.

3. The data is used to generate a label for an envelope or, in some cases, a directly addressed envelope or a piece that shows through the envelope. The data also might be used to address a personalized letter.

4. The labeled envelope, along with any other personalized material, must be matched.

5. Added to the personalized pieces is any non-personalized literature, such as data sheets and brochures. Even if this material is pre-kitted, it must be picked and packed along with the personalized pieces.

6. The material is inserted into an envelope and sealed. Then it goes through a mail preparation process—metering, bundling, delivery to the post office, and so on.

7. The material enters the mail stream—a scary thought in and of itself! Meanwhile, the data becomes part of a larger marketing database.

8. Many marketers continue the process with periodic follow-ups in an attempt to further identify the ongoing interest of the inquirer. These may be by phone, fax, or mail, and may occur on a regular basis.

This process probably sounds pretty familiar—it is similar to the way in which most b-to-b companies handle inquiry fulfillment.

The e-Fulfillment Difference

E-fulfillment is fulfillment that is facilitated by the Internet. In its most basic form, e-fulfillment is a simple e-mail response to an e-mail or any other kind of inquiry. Although e-mail is for all practical purposes still a text-only medium, it is useful in that you can send an immediate response directly to the inquirer's electronic mailbox. You can also embed Web links in your e-mail response so that the inquirer can visit a URL to receive additional information. While not all e-mail programs support Web links, it is still good practice to mention URLs in e-mail.

Responding via e-mail can be effective and desirable, as long as the individual made the inquiry via e-mail or gave you permission to respond via e-mail. (It is generally recommended that you ask the question, "May we communicate with you via e-mail?" on a reply card or during a telemarketing call.) Products are available to automate e-mail so that you can respond to multiple inquiries at once. With some e-mail communication products, you can "autorespond" to inquiries without human intervention.

Recent industry data suggests that customers are more accepting of e-mail fulfillment than prospects. However, an electronic inquirer would probably appreciate an e-mail response because it is immediate. Again, one of the biggest issues with fulfilling information requests is the time lapse between the act of inquiring and the receipt of information. E-mail is one way to dramatically close that gap and feed the need for instant gratification so prevalent today in marketing and in life.

One application of e-mail fulfillment that seems to be accepted and appreciated is the e-mail newsletter, which has broad appeal to both customers and prospects. A prospect who is receptive to e-mail and is interested in a product or service is likely to subscribe to an e-mail newsletter that keeps him or her informed on a periodic basis about that product or service. This method of fulfillment is far less threatening than receiving a telemarketing call. The e-mail newsletter is likely to receive more attention and get read more often than traditional direct mail.

As discussed in Chapter 5, the e-mail newsletter is in itself becoming a primary means of generating leads for b-to-b marketers. In the context of e-fulfillment, it is a remarkably efficient medium. Consider the fact that much of what you may now send in traditional printed form could be converted to e-mail newsletter format. It may not have the same appearance; today's e-mail is predominantly raw text with no bold, underlining, bullets, or graphic images. But that could be changing soon. E-mail programs are catching up, and it may not be long before they routinely incorporate HTML-like graphics. In addition, e-mail newsletters often have links to HTML pages so that recipients can click to a page on the Web which can have a more pleasing graphic design and include photographs and illustrations.

Even with the basic e-mail newsletter, you have an opportunity to translate marketing material into a format that is widely accepted and read. As long as the e-mail newsletter has information of perceived value, and it is not merely a sales pitch, prospects and customers alike will read it. Just as important, you can rapidly build an e-mail list of subscribers who, at the very least, share the commonality of being interested in your e-mail newsletter topic. Sending your e-mail newsletter periodically not only gets your message to a target audience more than once, it also positions you as an expert. And e-mail newsletters are very inexpensive. After you automate the e-mail process, the cost associated with e-mail distribution is almost insignificant. Compare that to traditional direct mail fulfillment.

The reader service number itself is undergoing change in the era of the Internet. Now several trade magazine publishers are providing Internet-based reader service numbers so that inquirers can respond online. Some of these services allow an advertiser to post electronic information at a special Web address, with a link to the advertiser's Web site. As a result, the inquiry can literally be instantly fulfilled instead of waiting days, weeks, or months, as might be the case with the traditional bingo card inquiry handling process.

Dell Computer (*www.dell.com*) created an Internet version of the reader service number that it calls an "E-Value Code." While Dell builds computer systems to individual specifications, they also know that certain pre-configured systems will be popular. Dell runs print ads promoting these systems and shows an E-Value Code with each of these systems. The interested prospect goes to the Dell Web site, enters the E-Value Code in the appropriate box on a Web page, and the site instantly returns information to the prospect about that particular system. That is e-fulfillment at its simplest, and its best.

Other innovations promise to keep the Internet on the cutting edge of fulfillment. In May 2000, Digimarc (*www.digimarc.com*) announced a technology called MediaBridge which permits an invisible image to be embedded in a printed ad, brochure, or CD. Suppose the prospect is reading an ad with this invisible image. He or she can hold the ad up to a camera connected to the computer, and the invisible image will point the computer to the URL of a Web page. Print ads using this technology appeared for the first time in the July 2000 issue of *WIRED*. The magazine ran 30 of the ads and included an explanation with that issue. Digimarc ran a promotion giving away 25,000 "PC cameras." The technology has been licensed by several other publishers as well. GoCode (*www.gocode.com*) uses barcode technology to achieve the same purpose. A barcode is placed in printed content, and then a barcode reader attached to the computer translates the barcode into the appropriate URL.

Creative use of imagery technology is also revolutionizing the visual quality of fulfillment. For example, MGI (*www.mgisoft.com*) offers the MGI ZOOM server, an imaging server that enables users to zoom in and examine items in very fine detail regardless of the bandwidth. The technology is being used by Internet retailers to give prospects and customers online close-ups of products.

The largest technology information providers have virtually made a business out of integrating their print publications, conferences and events, and the Internet—all in an effort to consolidate information and do a better job of serving prospects and customers.

IDG (*www.idg.net*) is a good example. IDG publishes *COMPUTERWORLD*, *Network World*, *PC World*, and countless other magazines and books, including the successful *...for Dummies* series. IDG also sponsors numerous industry conferences and events, such as ICE, the Internet Commerce Expo.

One of IDG's big success stories on the Web is Network World Fusion (*www.nwfusion.com*). This sister Web site to the Network World publication requires separate registration. Web site visitors must complete an eight-page qualification form to gain access to the content, but the form is hardly a barrier: The Web site garnered 94,000 registered users in just its first 18 months. All of this Web activity caused IDG to develop its own search and access service, IDG.net, which now permits registered users to personally navigate over 140 Web sites.

IDG's integrated use of traditional publications, Web sites, conference events, e-mail newsletters, and online surveys is a model for the future of b-to-b Internet marketing. This whole concept of involving the online "reader" in a literal web of communications is a significant trend in the information technology market that applies to all b-to-b marketers. E-fulfillment is a logical alternative to direct mail and fax fulfillment for numerous reasons, not the least of which is the incredible cost-saving potential. Not only does e-fulfillment drastically reduce the cost of fulfillment, it also removes the time-to-market factor.

E-fulfillment can quite literally happen instantly, at least on the Web. A prospect comes to a Web site, completes a Web response form, and clicks the Send button. With e-fulfillment, information can appear as an instant direct response to the request. There is no time lapse. Nothing has been available to the b-to-b marketer that even comes close to such an idea. What is even more significant is the relative ease with which it can be implemented.

Means of E-Fulfillment

E-fulfillment can be implemented in two basic ways: "pull" and "push."

"Pulling" the Prospect to You

1. The Web Response Area

In Chapter 3, we discussed the effectiveness of Web response forms. A Web response area with a Web response form is the termination point for a campaign-specific URL. The inquirer visits the URL and finds information about the offer and the product or service being promoted, along with a Web response form.

The Web response form can really function as a gateway to a company's e-fulfillment process. Here is an example. Suppose a prospect receives a direct mailing from a company promoting a line of modems designed for small business usage. The informational offer is a white paper, promotionally enhanced with the offer of a discount on the modems for an order placed within the next 30 days. The direct mail heavily promotes a special URL as the primary response path.

When the prospect visits the URL, there is a "welcome" page including links to pages with brief information about each of the available modems. Each page shows a picture of the product and highlights its specific benefits and features. At this URL, there is also a qualifying form that the visitor must fill out to get the white paper. The form has certain required fields. After these fields are completed and the form is sent, the visitor can receive the white paper via ordinary mail. However, the visitor also has the option of receiving the fulfillment electronically because the completed form leads to a page that allows the visitor to unlock or download the white paper.

Now what about that discount offer? This can be fulfilled in a number of ways. After the visitor completes and sends the form, a discount coupon can be dynamically generated. By linking the visitor's ZIP code with a directory of resellers, the names and addresses of several dealers can be generated on the fly—so the visitor can actually be directed to the closest reseller.

With the addition of electronic commerce, the visitor could also use a credit card to purchase any of the modems online at the discounted prices—right from an order page. Alternatively, the visitor can be given an 800 number to ask questions, place an order, or inquire about where to purchase the products locally.

Internet telephony promises an even more intriguing slant to this kind of e-fulfillment. In this scenario, e-fulfillment can include an interactive online conversation with a live sales representative. If the visitor has questions while navigating the site, they can be answered on the spot, through the computer itself, or via a connection between the computer and the prospect's telephone.

2. The Web Site

Your corporate Web site can also be used to "pull" a prospect to your site with an e-fulfillment center. In the preceding example, the incoming URL would terminate at a special "electronic door" into the e-fulfillment center of your corporate Web site. The e-fulfillment center is a designated area of a corporate site, set up to collect leads and generate information in response to inquiries. In this area, the visitor would locate information about the modems and request the white paper or take advantage of the discount offer. Online ordering could also be offered in the e-fulfillment center.

The response path to an e-fulfillment center is not as focused as with a Web response form, but it provides you with the ability to handle fulfillment in a centralized place, while exposing the visitor to a broader line of products.

3. E-Mail

E-mail itself can act as a pull–push medium. After you begin to correspond with a prospect or customer via e-mail, you have established an ongoing dialogue. As part of that dialogue, you can encourage the individual in the context of e-mail to visit a Web site to get more information or to sign up for an e-mail newsletter. Advertisers who place their promotional messages in e-mail newsletters are for the most part advertising a Web site address.

One innovator in this area is eCommercial.com (*www.ecommercial.com*), who, in 2000, introduced a way to send interactive "commercials" via e-mail. According to *iMarketing News* (November 19, 1999), the company's "Virtual Prospecting" system delivers a company brochure via e-mail and then analyzes which elements are most popular with viewers. The system has the ability to notify salespeople as to when prospects are reading the brochures and can track how long they looked at them and which products they found to be of interest.

B-to-b Internet marketers can make excellent use of e-mail in support of pull Web site areas by continuously reinforcing URLs in the body of e-mail messages.

"Pushing" Information to the Prospect

"Push" means sending information electronically, or pushing it, to the prospect or customer. In this respect, e-mail is the simplest kind of push technology a marketer can use. Any promotional e-mail delivered to a prospect or customer is, in effect, pushed to the individual's mailbox.

However, it is really the regular delivery of such e-mail, as with e-mail newsletters sent on a periodic basis, that turns e-mail into a push vehicle.

Push technology is most often defined as the process of pushing Web pages to someone's computer. The acknowledged pioneer of push is PointCast Inc., which was acquired in May 1999 by Launchpad Technologies, developer of the eWallet consumer shopping utility and an Idealab! Company. The acquisition led to the formation of a new company combining PointCast and eWallet called EntryPoint (*www.entrypoint.com*).

EntryPoint is a free advertising-supported service that provides a personalized bar that sits on a user's desktop. EntryPoint offers instant access to news and information, e-commerce, resources and search. A customized ticker delivers headline news and stock data to the desktop, and the eWallet feature is integrated with the bar so users can shop online with the convenience of not re-entering data at each merchant's site.

In November 1999, EntryPoint announced an agreement with 3Com (*www.3com.com*) to include its application in the company's modem installation CD package and availability via 3Com's Web site. A similar agreement was announced with Internet Service Provider Freei.Net (*www.freei.net*). By bundling the free toolbar with other products and services, EntryPoint hopes to dramatically extend its reach.

The push concept is not without its problems and controversies. In fact, by mid-1998, several push technology vendors had gone out of business, and of the remaining companies, some had moved away from the push label. One of the reasons push may have run into trouble was that it ran into a technology wall. Early derivations of push were slow and intrusive. Because most targeted end users were in corporations or other organizations, information was sent across the Internet through a corporate network to the end user's desktop. The problem was large files were being transferred, in some cases several times a day, to a corporate end user. If many corporate end users were using a push service, it was the corporate network that had to handle the load.

Despite these apparent shortcomings, push technology has been somewhat rejuvenated by new and improved products and services. In its new market-driven form, push technology could once again be an important way of reaching prospects, customers, and other constituents on an automatic, ongoing basis. The Yankee Group forecasts that push-related revenue grew from $10 million in 1996 to $5.7 billion in the year 2000.

How would you apply push technology to your own e-fulfillment? Instead of offering prospects or customers a few promotion pages to review when they visit your Web site or sending a periodic e-mail newsletter to their electronic mailboxes, you could deliver "personalized" Web pages with highly valued information to prospects and customers on a regular, complimentary basis. Prospects or customers would not have to go anywhere to gain access to the information they want—it would simply "appear" on their computer desktops.

This delivery method is already being used by major technology companies to automatically deliver software updates to customers. If push has a new life, it will probably be in the area of individualized corporate intranet and extranet use.

One vendor who has helped push move in this direction is Marimba (*www.marimba.com*), which filed an IPO in the second quarter of 1999. Through its Castanet product suite, Marimba provides the ability to deliver what it calls "Internet Services Management" products for use across intranets and extranets. Specific customer examples include:

- Seagate Technology, which uses Castanet to deliver and update business applications such as sales forecasting and pricing information to its internal sales management, mobile sales force and external OEM and distributor partners

- Nortel Networks, which employs Castanet to provide uniform delivery and maintenance of its manufacturing test applications shared among internal employees and external contractors

- Intuit, which embedded Castanet into its Quicken 99 personal finance software so millions of online users could receive software and information updates quickly and transparently.

In this context, push becomes an extension of a comprehensive Internet-based customer service strategy. From a marketing perspective, what push really does is turn fulfillment into *cultivation*. Applied appropriately, push puts information into the hands of people who want it, regularly and automatically. They do not even have to ask for it more than once; it simply appears. With traditional media, a marketer would need to send a printed newsletter on a quarterly or bimonthly basis to accomplish this. The cost of database maintenance, print production, and mailing would be substantial. With the Internet, on the other hand, delivery is immediate and far more cost effective.

This is no small issue for b-to-b direct marketers. Products and services tend to be purchased by committees or groups in a business environment. The timing of purchases tends to correspond more to a company manager's available budget than to when that individual receives a promotional message. In the case of more sophisticated, expensive products, there is often an evaluation and review process that could take considerable time before a purchase decision is made.

All of these factors contribute to the reality that, for many companies, the fulfillment of an inquiry is just the very first step in an ongoing mating dance between marketer and prospect. In some cases, a sales cycle can extend to 6, 9, 12, 18 months or more. Periodic contact with the prospect during this extended period can be costly via traditional mail, and even more costly via telemarketing or sales calls, yet cultivating the prospect is imperative. Continuing to re-qualify the prospect's interest becomes just as important in an effort to push him or her closer to purchase.

With the inevitable dominance of the Internet as the core of business communication, it is likely that more and more business people will likely prefer to get their information electronically. IDC says over 50 percent of online business people download information from the Internet several times a week.

Push technology offers a whole new form of fulfillment to marketers. Pushing information pages, special offers, and re-qualification forms to a targeted group of prospects could prove to be an expedient, low-cost method of direct marketing. It could extend the life of direct marketing campaigns and make them much more effective at an attractive incremental cost.

Push technology could offer a real service to prospects, fulfilling a need for automatically delivered information readily provided by marketers who "sponsor" its creation and delivery. If it is well executed, push technology could affordably and easily create a unique one-to-one relationship with prospects—a goal that many traditional high-end direct marketing programs strive for, but that is costly and logistically difficult to achieve.

The Unique Benefits of e-Fulfillment

Regardless of the delivery method, e-fulfillment can perform valuable functions that replace the need for paper-based fulfillment. These functions fall into several categories, listed here in order of "relationship intensity."

Acknowledgment

Just the simple act of immediately acknowledging an inquiry or order is a powerful communication technique. When a prospect or customer completes a Web response form and presses the "send" button, an acknowledgment page can instantaneously appear in response with the simple text, "Thank you. We have received your inquiry and will process it immediately." In a marketing world that has become depersonalized and automated, getting this type of acknowledgment in direct response to an action is reassuring. The impact of an Internet thank-you should not be minimized.

Confirmation

E-fulfillment can go beyond simple acknowledgment. The next step of a business relationship typically requires confirmation of specific information. When you call a toll-free phone number and place an order from a catalog, you interact with another person. This individual not only takes your order, but confirms it over the phone. He or she will typically repeat your credit card number, verify your name and address, confirm the items you just ordered, and tell you the total amount that will be charged to your credit card. You will also know, before you hang up, when you can expect to receive the items you ordered. Often you will be given an order confirmation number in case you have a problem with receiving the order.

This level of personal interaction is not yet possible via the Internet, although that is certainly where e-fulfillment is headed. If the same scenario just described takes place at a Web storefront today, the customer still has a need to know that the order has been confirmed. In fact, the need is greater, because there is no person-to-person voice contact—the order is being placed computer to computer.

Today's leading Internet-based order generation companies recognize this. Most of them therefore build in a number of confirmation contacts that help to reassure the customer that the order has been properly filled. At the point of sale, for example, the customer is led through a question and answer process, entering necessary data along the way. At the end of this process, a built-in autoresponder feeds back all of the data at once, asking the customer to review it and make necessary changes before pushing that Send button one last time. This is an important step in the confirmation process, because the customer is taking responsibility for the accuracy of the transaction.

The next confirmation contact point is typically an e-mail to the customer restating the specifications of the order—now confirming that it was understood by the company, and completing the confirmation loop by sending it directly to the user's mailbox. Confirmation at this stage is important for another reason—if the customer did not place the order, or the order is incorrect, the individual can take action at that point.

Finally, some Internet marketers take the confirmation process one step further, informing the customer that the order was shipped and when to expect its arrival. This step is obviously essential if there is a delay in the order, but it is just as useful and reassuring if the order is a normal shipment. Some marketers will include instructions for tracking the shipment at this stage.

We have used an order confirmation process as an example here, but confirmation just as easily applies to an inquiry from a prospect. It is particularly useful in confirming a prospect's attendance at a seminar, for example.

"Instant" Fulfillment

At its highest level of relationship intensity, e-fulfillment functions as the channel for actual physical fulfillment. Again using traditional media as an example, fulfillment of an inquiry is most often handled through a paper-based transaction. In some cases, an inquiry may be fulfilled via fax, but most often, the inquirer receives paper fulfillment, which may include a letter, data sheets, and brochures, perhaps packaged in a folder, all enclosed in a large envelope, and mailed or sometimes delivered via a package delivery service.

Even if the inquiry goes through a two-step fulfillment process, the individual receives, at the very least, a mailing with some additional information and a reply device designed to further qualify that person's interest. If the individual responds to this step, he or she will receive additional information from the marketer. Whatever the marketer sends, there will be a time lag unless the fulfillment is by fax only. That means a potentially hot prospect will continue to cool off as days or even weeks go by.

As previously discussed, traditional fulfillment is one of the weak links of the marketing process for many b-to-b companies. Although it may be unrealistic to convert the entire paper fulfillment process to e-fulfillment, moving towards fulfillment over the Internet has to be an attractive long-term alternative.

For one thing, e-fulfillment is environmentally friendly. Traditional fulfillment is paper- based and labor intensive. E-fulfillment, on the other hand, wastes neither trees nor ink. It does not have to be produced in quantities of one, ten, fifty, or one hundred thousand. It does not have to be cut, folded, stapled, and inserted into folders and envelopes. It does not burden your staff or Postal Service workers. In short, it saves natural resources, time, and money.

Now printed literature can have a longer shelf life, because time-sensitive information can be just as easily conveyed electronically, on the Web. Collateral materials can be mirrored electronically to leverage copy and artwork.

This extends far beyond the point of a casual convenience for prospects and customers. E-fulfillment is a desirable means of delivering information almost instantaneously—at a cost that is too low to ignore. I have heard and read industry stories about large companies that are saving thousands and sometimes millions of dollars by replacing much of their printed fulfillment with e-fulfillment. The need for printed literature still exists, but it can be substantially reduced with e-fulfillment.

E-fulfillment provides customers and prospects with a new kind of "instant gratification." They can receive information instantly in an electronic form that can be viewed online or printed out and saved. They can just as easily unlock or download information of high-perceived value or software that they can demo, try, and buy, right from the computer desktop. Information can even be personalized to meet the individual's specific needs and delivered free and on a regular basis to the individual's computer. Based on the individual's feedback, e-fulfillment can be further tailored.

E-fulfillment thus becomes the beginning of a relationship. You can engage your prospect or customer in a dialogue, which allows you to continuously learn more about the individual's real needs. You can collect data from the prospect or customer by asking questions on electronic surveys and response forms, and then turn the answers into *marketing intelligence*. You can then use this intelligence to build a highly effective communication program, tailored to individual needs. Database-driven e-fulfillment ultimately meets the informational needs of many individuals, one person at a time.

Meanwhile, you drastically reduce the costs and lag time of traditional fulfillment. You develop an ongoing one-to-one relationship with the prospect or customer, learn more about that person's specific needs, and reap the financial and timesaving benefits of e-fulfillment.

Instant Online Help

For IT companies in particular, the help desk is a necessity, but it is becoming just as important for general b-to-b marketers whose products and services demand a customer service and support function. Now the traditional help desk can be fully Internet-enabled through the "intelligent" Web page, which knows what a visitor is doing, and can provide assistance on-demand. Intelligent software agents can respond to a visitor's question and even "learn" from the questions, offering more accurate answers as the process progresses. With the addition of such intelligent or active agents, marketers have the ability to feed individualized information to Web site visitors, based on the information visitors provide. For example, every time a prospect revisits a site, active agent technology recognizes the visitor, calls up the visitor's profile, and guides the visitor to specific pages that would be of interest to him or her. Ultimately, targeted content can be delivered to each visitor to a site who is in the site's database.

Using push technology, the visitor does not even have to be online at the time. Active agent technology also allows the marketer to communicate with that person proactively and automatically, transmitting relevant information to them as it becomes available.

Another form of instant online help is the comprehensive self-service system. Primarily for customer use, this system essentially allows a Web site visitor to resolve problems via a structured, intelligent online process. This is discussed in more detail in the next chapter.

One area of online help that is intriguing is "call me" technology. Here is how it works: A visitor is navigating a Web site and comes across a product that seems interesting. The prospect has some questions that he or she wants to discuss with a salesperson immediately. The prospect clicks on a "Call Me" button found on the Web site. A dialog box pops up and requests the prospect's phone number. Meanwhile, the technology is alerting a salesperson and automatically calls the prospect.

When the sales person engages the prospect on the phone, the technology can go a step further in the sales assistance process. Now the sales person can "take control" of the prospect's Web browser and actually walk him or her through product information, or re-direct the prospect to other more appropriate Web pages. It is really functioning as a virtual sales call. Obviously, the sales person attempts to convert the prospect to a customer at the close of the session.

As these Internet telephony products and services become more available, usage will expand and extend into the area of online fulfillment. Imagine a marketing future in which both prospects and customers will largely be able to get all the assistance they require via the Internet, self-directed when necessary, and enhanced by live sales support as needed.

Moving to Web-based Information Dissemination

Even if you acknowledge the need to move your paper fulfillment to the Web, how do you actually accomplish what could be a daunting, even overwhelming task?

Start by doing a thorough inventory of all of your corporate literature and other collateral information. Determine which printed materials you currently use for fulfillment and how many different types of fulfillment packages you might have in existence.

Do a reality check: Are you sending too much literature to unqualified inquiries? Are you sending the right materials to qualified leads? Lay out all of the physical pieces you use for traditional fulfillment. Look them over and classify them as follows:

- General information about your company.

- General information about product lines, services, or support.

- Specific information about products or services, including data sheets, bulletins, and catalogs.

Now reclassify the above categories into "time-sensitive information" and "other." Put all the time-sensitive information in a priority pile. (Time-sensitive information is anything that will need to be updated periodically because of changes in specifications, deadlines, time limits, etc.)

After you have completed the classification process, you can begin to transition the printed literature to the Web. Convert the time-sensitive information first. It makes a lot of sense to look at e-fulfillment as value-added fulfillment: Instead of arbitrarily loading all of your fulfillment literature onto the Web, focus on the information that is most time-sensitive and critical for the prospect to have immediately.

You have two basic options for electronic conversion of printed information: HTML pages and PDF files.

HTML Pages

To produce HTML pages, your printed literature will need to be converted to or written in HTML. Any graphics, illustrations, diagrams, charts, or photographs will have to be scanned or re-created. Depending on the way your information is currently stored, and the HTML tools you use to convert the documents, this could be a relatively easy task, or a time-intensive, complex process.

Printed literature does not always transfer perfectly to the electronic medium. Dense blocks of text are difficult to read on a computer screen, some colors do not look the same, and photographs in particular can lose a lot of their definition on the Web because they must be converted to a lower resolution. You would probably be wise to enlist the services of a creative resource skilled at electronic media.

HTML will probably continue to be the standard way of creating Web pages in the near term. Even with the proliferation of new technologies, HTML is prevalent across so much of the Web because it is universally viewable by any Web browser. As a result, if you are creating e-fulfillment from scratch, you can probably use HTML as the safest "language" of choice. Now "dynamic HTML" (DHTML) is becoming more common. Basically, dynamic HTML adds more interaction and animation to HTML, breathing new life into it. One example of DHTML: When you go to a Web site and roll over a main link, you may see the contents for that link pop up on your screen. Then you can click on any of the sub-links. While only the latest versions of Web browsers can view DHTML, its increasing usage probably means that HTML is likely to be with us for a while.

The "competitor" to HTML is XML, the eXtensible Markup Language. XML usage is growing and it, too, could emerge as a standard way for exchanging data across the Internet. XML is an even more powerful language that incorporates document management technology.

PDFs

PDFs, or PDF files, are documents that are readable by the Adobe Acrobat Reader *(www.adobe.com)*. Adobe Acrobat has become the de facto standard tool for translating and posting printed literature to the Web. Once a piece of literature is in a PDF, it can be viewed in its "exact" format—with all typefaces, graphics, illustrations and photographs in place—electronically. Adobe even provides an online service that automatically translates documents in most formats to PDFs. For about $100 annually, you can get an unlimited number of documents translated via the Web.

To view a PDF, the visitor must have Adobe Acrobat Reader, but this program is free and can be downloaded from Adobe's Web site (through a link from your Web site, if you want). Typically, the visitor downloads the PDF of interest and then opens it with Acrobat Reader on his or her desktop for viewing. The document can also be printed—but it cannot be modified in any way unless the visitor has the full version of Adobe Acrobat.

The PDF format avoids the time-consuming task of converting fulfillment literature into HTML, because converting printed documents to PDF is a fairly simple process of scanning and saving. You will notice that a majority of sites with heavy-duty information content that originated in printed format offer that content as PDFs.

After you have transitioned to e-fulfillment, it is much easier to modify and disseminate content on the Web than via traditional methods. You can continue to convert printed literature into Web-based formats via HTML or into PDFs. Modifications can then be made in electronic format.

Electronic information dissemination has a number of benefits associated with it:

1. *Updating is easy and fast.* Unlike printed literature, you can update product information in real time and publish it to the Web on a moment's notice. This is a major benefit to companies who now depend on product data sheets and price lists. This type of information typically undergoes constant change. Printed formats take time to produce and the cost is high, especially for small print runs. Data sheets and price lists should be primary candidates for the transition to electronic information dissemination.

2. *Electronic product catalogs can be offered to prospects and customers.* As with a traditional catalog, the electronic catalog is a compendium of product information. Unlike a printed catalog, however, you can update the electronic catalog frequently and keep it current all the time. A properly designed electronic catalog can also be much easier to navigate and cross-reference than a printed catalog. Even if the catalog is for reference rather than for online purchase, it provides prospects and customers with an easy way to access information—and it provides you with a far less expensive and more timely marketing publication.

3. *Lead generation offer fulfillment is a natural for the Web.* You can encourage a prospect to respond via a campaign-specific URL and ask for a Web response form to be completed. When the form is sent, the prospect can instantly receive a copy of the offer, if it is information, or a demonstration or trial, if it is software. Electronic offer fulfillment can eliminate the need for physical fulfillment or, at the very least, dramatically reduce the cost of traditional fulfillment as more prospects respond online. If you collect a prospect's e-mail address and ask permission to use it, you can then establish an e-mail communications program, again reducing the need for traditional mail contacts.

    You could also use the Web to facilitate an online contest. A simple postcard mailing I received from one b-to-b marketer offered to enroll me in a monthly contest with cash prizes. The card carried a special number that, if entered on the company's Web site (along with other information, of course) would qualify me to win. This type of promotion is likely to generate a high number of "false positives"—individuals interested in winning, but not necessarily interested in the company's product—but it is an interesting concept that may have merit depending on the circumstances.

4. *The Web facilitates individualization of online fulfillment.* Here are a few examples:

   – Online fulfillment can be easily individualized by relating the response received to a question to the corresponding information. For example, when a prospect or customer responds to a certain question using multiple choice answers, each of those answers could be linked to a particular Web page, or several answers could be combined to dynamically generate the specific information of interest to the inquiring individual.

   – Web sites with search tools allow visitors to find the specific information they are looking for, quickly and easily. The built-in search engine uses key words to search a database of Web pages and reports the result of the search to the visitor. Then the visitor can select the appropriate page from the list provided. Some sites license search technology from other vendors for use on their own sites. In fact, search engines are increasingly common on Web sites. As the amount and depth of content increases, search functionality will become a necessity for many sites.

   – "Solution databases" are increasing in popularity as marketers build areas into Web sites that help prospects and customers customize their search for solutions. In this online fulfillment application, a database of potential solutions is created and the visitor is invited to define certain criteria to execute a search. The search then picks the most appropriate solution(s) and delivers the proper Web pages to the visitor. The visitor gets the impression that the solution has been customized to his or her needs when, in fact, it was simply assembled from information residing in a searchable database.

The CD/Web Connection

Now that virtually all PCs are being manufactured with high-speed CD drives, it is a rare software program that is delivered on diskettes. Most software, from operating systems to applications to games, is disseminated via CD or over the Internet. As a result, the CD is enjoying new popularity among business-to-consumer and b-to-b marketers alike.

Do you know anyone who *has not* received an America Online CD in the mail? AOL has grown its subscriber base to over 17 million, largely because of this direct marketing technique. I bought a music CD recently, only to find that America Online had worked a deal with the music company to put its software on it.

The CD, as a marketing medium, has great value due to a number of significant benefits:

- CDs hold a huge amount of data, so a marketer is unlikely ever to run out of room, no matter how much information must be conveyed.

- Depending on the speed of the user's CD drive, a CD can contain remarkably sophisticated programs, incorporating everything from sound to motion to movies to fully integrated multimedia productions. With newer CD drives, speed will not be an issue; in fact, a CD-ROM that runs at "20X" is twice as fast than a T1 Internet connection. The implications are that CDs can offer much faster delivery of graphics-rich, data-intensive content than can the Internet for most users.

- CDs take advantage of the "one-to-many" software manufacturing principle: The first one, or the master, is expensive to produce, but subsequent copies are cheap. That is one of the reasons America Online can distribute millions of CDs through the mail.

CDs are durable, lightweight, stable, non-magnetic, and nearly indestructible. This makes them ideal for mailing purposes. They can be silk-screen printed with colorful graphics and packaged in everything from CD cases to simple paper covers. Because they are "hard goods," they have a perceived value associated with tangible items.

- CDs can be built as "hybrids"—they can feature "collaboration" between the content on the CD and content on the Web. A CD can be programmed to provide seamless access to a Web site through the user's Web browser.

Here is an example of how this works. Suppose a b-to-b marketer produces a promotional CD utilizing a multimedia presentation that has lasting value, but wants to include product information on the CD that may change periodically. The CD can be segmented into distinct areas. The product area would include just an overview of the products; the prospect would be instructed to click on a built-in Web link for updated information.

When the prospect clicks on the link, the program on the CD detects the presence of a Web browser and, if one exists, automatically launches the browser and locates the URL specified by the marketer. The prospect sees updated information on the Web that coordinates with the information on the CD.

This is a particularly useful technique when applied to catalogs or price lists. It makes it possible for a marketer to produce a "master" catalog on a CD and, through a built-in Web link, update the catalog periodically. The benefit to the marketer is that the CD catalog retains its shelf life. The benefit to the prospect is that the CD is a semi-permanent reference that can be continuously updated online.

Another useful way to employ the CD/Web connection is to provide the prospect with a link to an online Web response form. This potentially turns a prospect who is reviewing a marketer's CD into a qualified online respondent with a need for additional information.

Suppose you want to go in the opposite direction and deliver Web content on a CD? That is possible, too. By designing the CD content as if it were on the Web, you can deliver Web-style pages in a CD format. In fact, you could copy and deliver entire Web sites in "local" form so that a prospect could navigate the Web site without being on the Web. You avoid Web download delays associated with bandwidth problems and provide CD-based browsing while you retain the look and feel of your Web site content.

Some marketers have figured out a way to turn this into a direct marketing concept. They utilize the CD as the core of a promotional mailing to select prospects, using Web-style content on the CD, and tell the recipients to go to a Web site or call an 800 number to unlock the CD content. Of course, the CD content better be worth it. This is no different than getting a "key" from a software vendor to unlock and use a program from a CD, but it is a novel way to leverage the CD/Web connection.

The Kiosk/Web Connection

Although kiosks are primarily used in a retail environment, their time may be coming as a viable b-to-b tool that puts even more prospects in touch—literally—with your products. Interactive kiosks with touch screens are now in use as informational vehicles in malls, retail stores, and airports. A shopper with no computer skills can walk up to a mall kiosk and locate stores. In the retail store, the shopper can locate departments and read about the day's sale items.

Now there is a growing trend for kiosks to be Web-enabled. A kiosk can be designed to house local versions of Web sites and pages so that a connection to the Internet is unnecessary. Web-enabled kiosks suggest a host of future possibilities for b-to-b marketers. They may be particularly effective in reaching the growing SOHO (Small Office Home Office) shopper.

Suppose just such a shopper walks into an office superstore during a lunch hour. He or she finds that there are not enough salespeople, so he or she walks over to the touch kiosk prominently displayed at the front of the store. With a few touches on the screen, the shopper can find and compare products and their prices. For example, let us say the shopper is looking for office furniture. Your company, which manufactures office furniture, happens to be running a special that month, and you have purchased advertising space on the chain's kiosks.

The shopper notices your on-kiosk banner ad and touches it. The banner ad links to local Web pages that you downloaded from your corporate Web site. Those pages were electronically transmitted earlier that month to the chain's advertising department, which distributed the pages to the store kiosks.

The shopper sees that you are offering a special in-store discount on a particular chair. The shopper touches an area on the screen, and an in-store coupon instantly comes out of the kiosk's thermal printing unit. He or she looks for and finds the chair, likes it, and likes the discount even better. The shopper decides to buy the chair and take advantage of the special price.

In fact, the Internet is now being used to enhance the traditional in-store retail experience. *InformationWeek* reported in May 1999 that by late that year, Sears expected to place in-store kiosks in its Michigan and Connecticut stores, offering shoppers access to more than 4 million items in its online catalog.

Internet-enabled kiosks are making their move not only in stores, but in places where businesses can reach business people—like airports. Typically, these are kiosks that are really enhancements to phone service, offering business travelers the ability to send a fax or check e-mail, but it may not be long before they also allow travelers to request information online or even place orders for products online.

Telecommunications carriers are also using touchscreens with telephones and mini-kiosks to enhance telephone service. These interactive devices may not be Internet enabled today, but they could be in the future. The technology to turn kiosks into freestanding Web stations is already here—it is just a matter of implementing it.

And it will not end there. The Internet is making its appearance in the most interesting, and sometimes unusual, places. Some bank ATMs now offer Web browsing. And Web pages are even popping up in office building elevators.

Future Information Dissemination Channels

You are likely to see many variations on the theme when it comes to future information dissemination. Some emerging concepts promise to make future e-fulfillment even more effective. One area of fast growth on the Web in the b-to-b space is the *Web community*—a kind of online mall, but with true community components, such as discussion forums, chats, newsletters, job banks, and more.

The Web community is a place where information—lots of it—is shared by companies with common interests or goals. The information providers pool their information to an information publisher, which sponsors a single "supersite" to disseminate the information.

Web communities function as large electronic directories or catalogs of information for a rich variety of sources, each of which is available on or accessible through a single site. Communities also offer information providers the ability to interact with their constituency and effectively expose new audiences to the providers' messages. In most cases, communities are free to users, as long as the users register (and therefore provide contact information that can be used by both the community and the participating information providers).

In addition to communities whose primary goal is to disseminate information, there are now b-to-b communities whose primary goal is to sell products from a single location. These communities are especially interesting because they are redefining the rules of e-commerce. Typically, a consortium of companies agrees to place its products for sale on a single site, providing customers with a single point of contact, a single invoice, and centralized order processing. Theses companies extend their presence, their buying power, and their market by collaborating. Communities have become such a significant trend, in fact, that an entire chapter is devoted to the topic.

Another Internet growth area that has ramifications for b-to-b marketers is the information consolidator or reseller, referred to by some experts as the "infomediary." These are companies who leverage information and either distribute it in new ways, or sell it in the form of packaged services. B-to-b marketers can use these sources to gain access to important information, but also as possible advertising and promotion outlets. Here are two such companies that have taken interesting approaches to Internet-based information dissemination.

1. **About.com** *(www.about.com)*
   Formerly The Mining Company, About.com (Figure 7.1) is a combination search tool/collection of online communities that directly positions itself against Internet search engines and directories. The company's approach is unique in that it adds a new component to information search—live people. A comprehensive network of Web sites for over 650 topics, each is run by an expert "Guide," who, says About.com, is "a company-certified subject specialist who is responsible for helping you get the most out of your time online. When they are not posting informative weekly features or combing the Net for fresh links to other useful online resources, many About.com

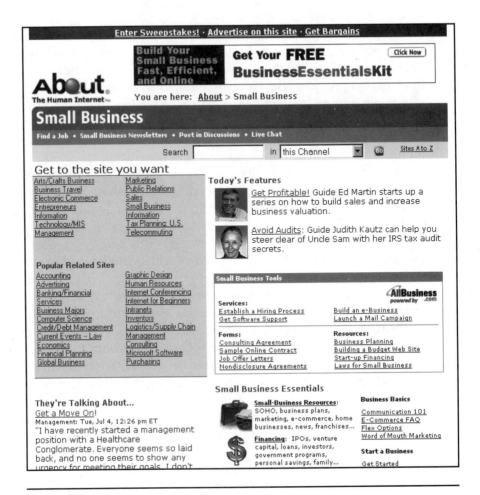

Figure 7.1. About.com.

Guides are hosting live chats, managing bulleting board discussions, recommending books, keeping abreast of relevant news, updating links, publishing newsletters and responding to email." About.com has established separate URLs for each topic area so that the user can go directly to the topic if desired, instead of wading through a single home page.

Like a number of hot Internet sites, About.com went public in early 1999. Only months later, the site already ranked third among all news and entertainment sites, according to

MediaMetrix. *PC Magazine* recognized the site as a "top 5 portal."

2. **Northern Light** *(www.northernlight.com)*
   Northern Light (Figure 7.2) is a search engine with a twist: It combines Web results with information from "premium material" in one search, giving users access to books, magazines, databases, and newswires not available from other search engines. Northern Light's "Special Collection" offers more than 5,400 full-text articles not commonly available, including reports from WEFA (Wharton Econometric Forecasting Associates), the organization which has conducted numerous statistical studies for the Direct Marketing Association. Northern Light

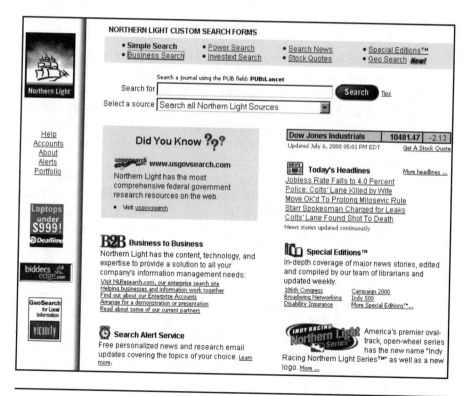

Figure 7.2.　Northern Light.

searches the Web in addition to this collection, and it offers users the ability to access full articles for a cost of $1 to $4 each. Users can preview articles by reading the free summaries and choosing only the ones they wish to order. Northern Light offers a unique money-back guarantee. The service is also unique in that it uses "Custom Search Folders" to organize searches into subject, type, source, and language—pretty handy for faster, more organized information retrieval.

Creating Online Demos and Trials

E-fulfillment holds great promise in the context of printed information that is converted to the electronic medium, but there is an even more exciting aspect to e-fulfillment—online demos and trials. The Web has become a major marketing medium for information technology marketers—primarily software companies—who use it as a giant arena for delivering online product demonstrations and trials. An "online demo" of a software product can be executed in a few different ways. Probably the least desirable is an actual interactive demo that happens on the Web in real time. A "live" demo can be affected by too many factors beyond the marketer's control—the Internet connection or Web traffic, the nature of the user's transmission device, the target computer's capabilities, and so on. Nevertheless, some marketers execute fast-running live demos in real time over the Web.

An alternative is the online demo that simulates the product's capabilities or includes a partially live demonstration. This type of demo is more of a guided tour or walk-through of the software—it allows some limited, preprogrammed interaction by the prospect in an effort to convey the basic product benefits and features. A demo of this sort is effective if it is tied together with an offer of a full CD demo—which the prospect can request in return for a completed Web response form.

The most common demo format is the download. (And yes, there is an entire Web site devoted to software downloads at, where else, but CINet's *www.download.com*.) The download is typically a compressed file that the prospect copies, expands with common utility software, and then opens on the computer desktop in "offline" mode. The download has several advantages:

- The prospect does not have to be online to interact with the demo. The demo runs off of the prospect's computer, not off of the marketer's Web site.

- The demo can contain multimedia (sound and motion), as well as interactivity, which is unencumbered by technology issues surrounding electronic media transmission.

- The demo can be delivered online, instantly, and free—the prospect does not have to wait for a disk or CD to arrive.

- The demo can also be set up as a *trial*—it can be the real software product that the prospect tries for a period of time and then purchases if desired. In such cases, the software is programmed to time out after 30 or 60 days.

That is all well and good for software companies, but what if you are a b-to-b direct marketer selling something else? You have the ability to use the online demo or demo download as well—just think creatively. For example, music companies now allow prospects to sample CDs on the Web prior to purchase. Movie companies encourage fans to download clips of forthcoming feature films.

Does your product lend itself to a multimedia presentation? How about creating a multimedia, interactive offer that relates to your product or service? Or maybe you can collaborate with another marketer and offer something of value together. The possibilities are endless with this kind of e-fulfillment.

Order E-Fulfillment and Distributing Live Products Over the Internet

Order e-fulfillment is crucial to the success of any e-commerce operation. It appears, however, that for many companies, e-fulfilling orders is no easy task. In May 2000, Bain & Company in association with Mainspring issued a series of studies that suggested order e-fulfillment needed to be significantly improved. During Mother's Day 2000, the studies said, as many as 30 percent of all orders were unfulfilled.

The ultimate in instant gratification is when a customer can receive a live product online. Entire companies are being built around the concept of electronic product delivery—some at the outset, and some because they have no choice.

Consider the case of Egghead, a company that, at its high point, sold software in 250 retail stores. But then, on the verge of bankruptcy in January 1998, Egghead announced it would close its remaining 80 stores, change its name to Egghead.com (*www.egghead.com*), and move its entire sales operation to the Web. The company literally re-invented itself as an online merchant and aggressively marketed its products through affiliate programs (discussed in a subsequent chapter). Now Egghead.com offers a discount software superstore, a computer products superstore, an online liquidation center, and online auctions at its heavily trafficked site. In July 1999, Egghead.com merged with Internet rival Onsale.com (*www.onsale.com*) in a deal valued at $400 million.

While there are endless numbers of companies selling and delivering software via the Internet, more than a few are inventing entirely new ways to fulfill their customers. CyberMedia (*www.mcafee.com/cybermedia*) was so successful at it, they were purchased by the McAfee Software Division of Network Associates. CyberMedia saw the potential of e-fulfillment and created a novel product called Oil Change, which has become a software bestseller. You install Oil Change on your PC and it checks the software you have, goes on the Internet, and finds, downloads, and installs the appropriate updates, patches, and bug fixes for more than 6,500 software programs. Oil Change costs less than $50 and is continually updated via the Internet on a subscription basis for a few dollars a year. It could represent a new class of facilitating software that will make the Internet all the more useful for the businessperson and consumer alike.

Anything that can be committed to an electronic format can be distributed live over the Internet. Any product with information at its core can be delivered over the Web. Information products—research reports, survey results, white papers, subscription e-mail newsletters, and the like—are all being sold electronically.

It is not only IT companies that are succeeding at selling information electronically. One of the non-high tech b-to-b success stories on the Internet is *The Wall Street Journal Interactive Edition* (*www.wsj.com*). The venerable business daily has aggressively marketed its Internet version with a two week free trial, offering print subscribers the special price of $29 annually, versus $59 for new, non-print subscribers. Dow Jones, the publisher, wisely made sample content from the Interactive Edition available free on the Web site so non-subscribers could see its value. The Interactive Edition already has a paid subscriber base of several hundred thousand.

The line between electronic inquiry fulfillment and order fulfillment continues to blur. B-to-b marketers are anxious to find new ways to qualify prospects, shorten the sales cycle, and, if possible, get prospects and customers to purchase over the Internet. Even if the product itself is not Web-deliverable, product update and service information can easily be electronically delivered via e-mail or over the Web.

Internet-enabled delivery of products obviously goes beyond the scope of electronic lead fulfillment. It is an area the b-to-b marketer should carefully watch. As information and services become products, the Internet becomes a powerful delivery channel for them.

Ultimately, the potential for order e-fulfillment is virtually unlimited for b-to-b marketers. The cost reduction associated with order e-fulfillment is tantalizing. According to the Organization for Economic Cooperation and Development, it costs just 50 cents to distribute a software product electronically versus $15.00 traditionally. And it doesn't just have to be software.

Airlines and e-travel services are seeing enormous benefits from order e-fulfillment. Airlines encourage online customers, particularly business travelers who order last-minute tickets, to use electronic ticketing instead of paper tickets. E-tickets have substantially reduced the cost of doing business for airlines and the growth of e-ticketing by airlines and travel services such as Biztravel (*www.biztravel.com*), Expedia (*www.expedia.com*) and Travelocity (*www.travelocity.com*) is expected to skyrocket. By eliminating the physical packaging and documentation for a software product, the entire cost structure of marketing and sales can shift dramatically. For IT marketers, e-fulfillment could be a dream fulfilled.

E-Fulfillment Resources and Services

Listed here are just some of the many services available to b-to-b marketers which may help facilitate e-fulfillment. An excellent additional source of information is the "e-fulfillment directory" offered by Digitrends (*www.digitrends.net/digitrends/dtonline/features/sections/fulfillment/*). Numerous customer relationship management (CRM) products and services now include e-fulfillment components, so if you need a broader solution, you would be wise to expand your search to CRM tools. We will discuss CRM in further detail in the next chapter.

DHL (*www.dhlmasterclass.com*)

DHL, an air express company that specializes in international package delivery, offers a site called DHL Masterclass to assist small and medium size companies transition from traditional to e-business. The site includes resources, information and tips on fulfillment, logistics, customer relationship management, and supply chain management.

FedEx (*www.fedex.com*)

FedEx has taken a new turn in e-commerce and fulfillment by announcing a service to help small and mid-size companies build online stores. The FedEx service links the company's electronic delivery and tracking capabilities to each online store, which can be set up in a matter of minutes.

MarketFirst (*www.marketfirst.com*)

MarketFirst is a software company that claims to be the first to offer a true end-to-end, comprehensive automated marketing platform. MarketFirst offers a marketing knowledgebase, campaign design and execution technologies, workgroup collaboration, real-time media preference management, and reporting and measurement capabilities in an integrated, open computing environment. Their "eMarketing Blueprint" applications are templates that get systems up and running quickly. MarketFirst also offers Web hosting services to allow immediate implementation of automated marketing programs. B-to-b users include Autodesk, NorthPoint, Quantum, and SalesLogix.

MarketSoft (*www.marketsoft.com*)

MarketSoft has a solution that it says solves the lead management problem. MarketSoft's eLeads is an Internet-based system that combines e-business with traditional selling models to ensure that the right leads get to the right people art the right time, measuring results as part of a closed-loop process. MarketSoft's eOffers improves the timeliness and relevancy of offers and promotions delivered to customers. Both products combine to form The Marketing Network, which the company says can accelerate buying cycles and sustain the growth and retention of new customers. B-to-b users include Compaq, Covad, Ingram Micro, and Microsoft.

NetQuartz (*www.netquartz.com*)

If you use trial downloads or CDs to sell software, NetQuartz offers an interesting product called LinkStudio that lets you track, control, and communicate with your prospects over the Internet while they are running your trial. When prospects actually run the trial, LinkStudio informs you, and a built-in e-mail service allows communication with each active user during the trial. LinkStudio also handles beta feedback, online software rental, license management, and secure rights management.

Netship (*www.netship.com*)

Launched in 1999, Netship allows small and medium size businesses to set up their own nationwide distribution network. Netship has networked over 450 Netship centers across the U.S. through its Web site to provide local support, competitive rates, and service through major shipping carriers. Netship centers act as virtual warehouses, holding inventory and picking, packing and shipping orders on demand. Using Netship.com, a company can get instant online quotes and up-to-the-minute shipment warehousing, packaging, fulfillment, tracking, and inventory control. Netship is operated by a major package delivery franchiser, Parcel Plus, Inc.

SubmitOrder (*www.submitorder.com*)

Claiming to have coined the term e-fulfillment, SubmitOrder.com is a pure play e-fulfillment service provider. The company provides e-fulfillment customers with everything from Web site development to inventory management, order fulfillment and processing, "pick, pack and ship" services, and integrated call center services. E-fulfillment strategic planning and integration, e-tail distribution, customer response, and e-tail business support are also parts of the service. Users of SubmitOrder.com include ZanyBrainy.com, MuseumCompany.com, and indulge.com.

UPS (*www.ups.com*)

UPS, the world's largest express carrier and package delivery company, has doing nothing short of re-invent its traditional business to become an e-fulfillment and e-commerce leader. In April 2000, UPS received the prestigious MIT Sloan School of Management "Clicks & Mortar" Award for "the greatest advancement in integrating both physical and online business practices." UPS has developed the fastest and most advanced Internet-based package tracking system, along with UPS Document Exchange, the digital Internet delivery service, eVentures, an e-business incubator for Internet start-ups, and UPS OnLine Tools, which enable businesses to integrate transportation information throughout their Web operations and other business processes. In April 2000, UPS Capital Corporation, the financial services arm of UPS, announced that it would offer b-to-b customers the first fully integrated means to link the delivery of goods with information and the accelerated delivery of funds via EBPP (electronic bill presentment and payment) solutions.

8

Building Customer Relationships

Customer relationship management (CRM), second only to e-commerce, has become the fastest growing area of Internet marketing. In January 2000, AMR Research estimated that the market for CRM will grow to $16.8 billion by the year 2003, from $3.7 billion in 1999.

In many ways, the Internet has become a symbol of the ultimate customer relationship for both business-to-consumer and b-to-b marketers. That, at least, seems to be the case among many of the top e-commerce players. Over 90 percent of these leaders are committed to customer loyalty programs, according to a February 1999 research study by IDC. Close to three-quarters of the firms researched use personalization and mass customization to help increase customer retention, and almost half of them are modeling the Lifetime Values of their customers.

Numerous studies support the fact that building customer relationships is far and away the most important undertaking for the Internet marketer. April 2000 statistics from the Boston Consulting Group indicate that 28 percent of all online purchases are unsuccessful. 23 percent of online shoppers who have unsuccessful experiences say they will not buy again from the site at which they encountered a problem. March 2000 studies jointly conducted by Bain & Company and Mainspring show that online retailers lose money on shoppers who visit only once, but that repeat purchasers spend more money over time.

Customer loyalty went beyond dollars alone. The studies found that an online shopper who purchased apparel from a Web site referred three people to that site after his or her first purchase. A purchaser of consumer electronics, after ten purchases from a Web site, referred thirteen people to that Web site. In short, happy online customers are a great source for word-of-mouth advertising.

The notion of electronically serving a single customer's needs in an individualized fashion, 24 hours a day, 7 days a week, anywhere in the world—even with a customer base of thousands or millions—is mind-boggling. But innovations such as customer self-service areas, Internet-based help desks, intelligent search engines, solution databases, and "call me" buttons on Web sites are making this kind of customer service a reality. The Internet presents a new, cost-effective, and lasting way of building all-important relationships with customers. As a result, many believe the Internet will fulfill the promise of a true one-to-one marketing medium.

In this chapter, we look at what the Internet has to offer to b-to-b marketers who want to build and enhance relationships with their customers.

Building Better Customer Relationships

The timing is uncanny. The business world in general has been focusing on the importance of the customer for the past several years. Such concepts as customer lifetime value, customer loyalty, customer relationship management, relationship marketing, one-to-one marketing, and mass customization now demand the attention of business executives. Then, the Internet—the ultimate relationship marketing panacea—arrives on the scene. It's almost too good to be true.

Before we consider the specific impact of the Internet on customer relationships, here is a basic question you should ask:

How am I going to protect and preserve my customer base?

The business reality of today and tomorrow is that customers have many choices—and they are exercising their options aggressively. As one piece of evidence of the dramatic shift in customer loyalty, you would be hard-pressed to find any IT manager at a sizable company in the world today who would brag about his or her fierce loyalty to a single computer manufacturer. There still may be "IBM shops" or "HP departments"—but commingled hardware is as common in most IT organizations as coffee and creamer are in the company cafeteria. That is why one of the fastest growing businesses in the computer industry is systems integration. If anything, hardware and software companies are developing products that work better together with their competitors' products than ever before. Now, a major computer company's service organization is often as skilled in servicing its competitors' products as it is at servicing its own gear.

This is just as true of any customer-driven business. Unfortunately, your customer is just as likely to be your competitor's customer. Business buyers are simply not exhibiting the kind of loyalty that may have anchored their purchases in the past. Products are more commodified, and choices are many. Where loyalty does exist, it is frequently connected to the service and support provided by a company rather than to the product itself.

The issue of customer loyalty has pervaded business to such an extent that perhaps the number one business book topic in the past few years (other than the Internet) is customer service and customer loyalty. There are business conferences and seminars devoted to customer service, magazines that highlight it, and Web sites that discuss it, such as CRMCommunity *(www.crmcommunity.com)* and CRMDaily *(www.crmdaily.com).*

Even among advertising and marketing service firms, relationship marketing is in vogue. Such terms as relationship marketing, frequency marketing, loyalty marketing, and one-to-one marketing are thrown around constantly. Some advertising and direct marketing agencies have even modified their corporate names to include the word "relationship."

B-to-b marketers use numerous programmatic techniques to attack the issue of customer loyalty. Arguably the best-known customer loyalty program in existence is the frequent traveler program. Pioneered by major airlines, frequent traveler/frequent buyer programs now abound. Hotels and rental car companies have them. Restaurants participate in them. Some credit card companies turn them into "Membership Miles" (American Express) or other kinds of frequent purchase rewards programs.

To what extent do the airlines' frequent traveler programs really create loyal customers? Opinion is mixed. Although frequent business travelers will often select an airline because they are building mileage credit, they will just as often join numerous airline frequent traveler programs so that they can switch airlines with little downside effect when the need arises. Industry data seems to suggest that the top priority of most frequent business travelers is flight schedule, not the mileage credit accumulated in an airline's frequent traveler program, which brings into question the effectiveness of such programs in truly cementing customer loyalty.

Brand preference in the airline industry may be a bad example. Domestic flights have so proliferated that one airline's schedule is sometimes indistinguishable from other airlines. Frequent travelers complain that the same is true of the service. The fact is that the traveler has so many choices that no airline is a clear-cut winner. That phenomenon is pervasive in other businesses as well. Look at the credit card, automobile, and gasoline industries.

For most b-to-b marketers the competitive environment may not be quite as severe, yet competition always seems to exist, whether it is direct or indirect. Even channel conflict can play a role in fostering unwanted competition.

The trick, then, is to create reasons, even opportunities, for your customers to gravitate toward you when the need arises. More to the point, your goal should be to *create loyal major customers*—buyers who continue to do business with you, preferably building a more important mutually beneficial relationship with your company over time.

Remember the Marketing Pyramid

It is worth reviewing the customer-marketing pyramid that we discussed in Chapter 1. Here is another look at it, using a software company's customer base to illustrate the audience segments in the pyramid (Figure 8.1).

Software Company's Customer Base

A: Purchasers of a site license of the customized version of the software product, running on a minicomputer, using four to six applications. These purchasers have also signed a service and support agreement.

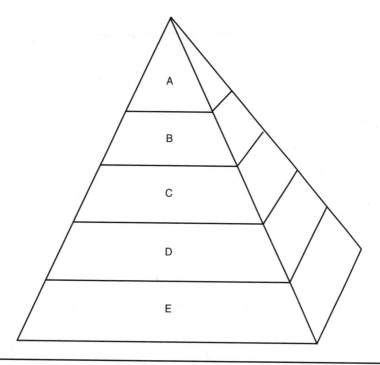

Figure 8.1.   Marketing pyramid revisited.

B: Purchasers of a single copy of the customized version of the software product, running on a minicomputer, using up to three applications. No service and support agreement.

C: Purchasers of a single copy of the non-customized version of the software product, running on a minicomputer, using only one application. No service and support agreement.

D: Purchasers of multiple copies of the PC version of the basic product.

E: Purchasers of a single copy of the PC version of the basic product.

In this example of a software company's segmented customer base, the segments of the pyramid get smaller as we go from the base of the pyramid to the tip of the pyramid. More important, *these customer segments increase in terms of their value* to the software company.

By the time we get to the top of the pyramid, the relationship with the major customer in the small triangle—the Golden Triangle—at the tip of the pyramid intensifies significantly. The customer in that triangle becomes worth much more to the company. The individual customer at the top of the pyramid is of higher value than the customer at the very bottom of the pyramid, both in terms of products and services purchased, and customer loyalty and longevity.

Notice that we are dealing with numerous customer segments, each of which has their own characteristics. Also notice that only a small segment of customers—perhaps 20 percent or less—composes the top customer segment. That is the segment that may be contributing as much as 80 percent of a company's revenue. (The "80/20 Rule.")

The only way you will ever know any of this information about your own customer base is by analyzing each customer's buying history. That is the essence of customer-driven database marketing, and most experts agree that, after you discover who they are, it pays to identify and reward your most highly valued customers:

> *The higher a customer's lifetime value, the greater the need to create brand awareness, reward loyalty or create a consumer behavior. Once you identify the most lucrative customers, it is important to reach them as many times as your budget allows—and with a consistent message.*[1]

Using the Internet to Learn About Customers and Build Better Relationships

Assuming you agree with the most-valued-customer premise, there are two basic strategies you will need to employ concurrently to build better customer relationships with the Internet: maintaining ongoing relationships with your most valued customers and moving other customers up the marketing pyramid so that they can reach most valued customer status.

1. Maintaining an Ongoing Relationship with Your Most Valued Customers

What do *you* value most about a business relationship? Is it the fact that the other party knows you personally? Understands your needs? Keeps in touch? Makes you aware of valuable offers, new products, and other useful information? Provides you with superb service? Solves problems quickly and to your satisfaction? Remembers what you like? Makes it worth your while to continue the relationship? Shows appreciation for your business?

It is probably all of these things—some of which may be more important to you than others. It is that complex thing called the business relationship, and understanding all of the attributes of the business relationship is the beginning of successful customer relationships.

One-to-one marketing experts Don Peppers and Martha Rogers of the Peppers and Rogers Group (*www.1to1.com*) say it is the *individuality of the customer relationship* is the key to its success:

> *The one-to-one marketer recognizes that every relationship is different, that it is based on the inputs of both parties, and that its context continues to build and change over time. A relationship marketer should never ask a customer the same thing twice, any more than you would ask your spouse how she likes her coffee. Traditional marketing is in its death throes—true one-to-one relationship marketing is just beginning what promises to be a long, successful life.*[2]

If this assessment is accurate, how do you begin to implement one-to-one customer relationship marketing, especially with your most valued customers? Use the information in a customer database to "learn" what a customer wants, say Peppers and Rogers:

> *...in a Learning Relationship the firm uses an individual customer's input and feedback to continually adjust and update its own behavior toward that customer (perhaps mass customizing its product or tailoring its service). As a result, customer loyalty rises dramatically.*[3]

Peppers and Rogers do not stop at theory, however; they put into practice what they believe by helping companies implement one-to-one marketing strategies, and by studying companies who do it well. In May 1999, Peppers and Rogers Group issued the first of a series of reports, *The State of One to One Online*. The ongoing reports track best practices of companies that use the Web to build a loyal customer base, identifying 21 capabilities that enable leading sites to build competitive advantage.

Based on a study of more than 500 Web sites, the first edition of *The State of One to One Online* selected 32 sites as "the best of the best." The report then offered the "top five secrets" for competing online profitably. Not surprisingly, all of them are centered on the customer relationship:

- Customer privacy should be protected, and customers should be informed how the marketer will protect privacy.

- A company's motives should be explained for wanting to create a customer relationship.

- A company's Web site should be organized around customer needs, not products.

- Customers should be given individual control; they should be able to request and receive personalized, individualized pages and information.

- A company should motivate customers to collaborate, so they provide input and information that helps build and reinforce the relationship.[4]

This may sound far-reaching, but by combining database marketing technology with the customer-enhancing power of the Internet, enhancing customer relationships is within reach of every b-to-b marketer. In fact, it is the Internet that now offers marketers the missing piece of the customer relationship puzzle: real-time interactivity.

You can start at the most basic level of Internet customer marketing by implementing an *e-mail customer survey*. Collect customers' e-mail addresses, construct a simple survey that polls them about their needs, and send it out. Make it easy for customers to respond—tell them to simply put X marks next to multiple choice answers. Provide a space for additional comments, but keep open-ended questions to a minimum. Then ask your customers to reply to the e-mail survey by a specified date.

Better yet, invite customers via e-mail to participate in the survey by visiting a special URL. Set up a Web page of questions, similar to a Web response form. That way, you can employ a user-friendly format to take the answers to survey questions.

Your customers have a vested interest in providing you with feedback. Some companies spend thousands of dollars holding in-person focus group sessions with a small number of customers to learn about their needs. Others invest in telemarketing surveys that never get through to a majority of their customers. A customer e-mail survey offers you the opportunity to inexpensively break through to many customers at once and get useful data quickly. Traditional direct mail customer surveys are known to generate 15 percent, 20 percent, or even higher response rates. You should be able to achieve that kind of response with a customer e-mail survey.

If you are in a position to go beyond the e-mail survey, you should consider building some sort of customer relationship program via the Internet, if only with your most valued customers. Your program could be as simple as a periodic e-mail newsletter delivered to a customer's e-mail box each month or as elaborate as a menu of customer-driven information choices, personalized to each individual's special requirements and needs, or it could become the Internet version of a *customer loyalty program.*

Customer loyalty programs come in numerous "flavors," but the most widely recognized is probably the frequent buyer program. Essentially, this type of program rewards the customer for continuing to do business with you. Although the basic principle of a customer loyalty program is sound, the very idea of "customer loyalty" is a misnomer. The program's real goal is to provide continuing incentives for customers to purchase from you rather than from someone else. The business reality is that they *will* purchase products or services similar to yours from a competitor occasionally, and there is little you can do about it. Nevertheless, a properly structured Internet-based loyalty program could do much to encourage your valued customers to show a preference for doing business with you.

Amazon.com (*www.amazon.com*) is legendary for its techniques in building customer relationships. In addition to a Web site that is easy to use, Amazon.com's ability to service millions of customers at a time is essential. Amazon.com uses intelligent agents to feed personalized recommendations to customers when they visit their Web site. These recommendations are based on their previous purchases. The company's Web site "learns" its customers' preferences and makes suggestions for books, music, and other items based on what each customer buys. The fact that Amazon.com does this with over 10 million customers, day in and day out, is almost inconceivable.

An Amazon.com customer can also receive e-mail notifications regularly when books are published in topics of interest. Every once in a while, an Amazon.com customer will receive a special gift either via e-mail, or packed in with his or her purchase. Maybe it will be a gift certificate good towards a purchase at an associated Amazon.com site, or an incentive to try a new area of Amazon.com. It doesn't really matter—whatever it is, Amazon.com is saying customers are important to them.

When an Amazon.com customer places an order, he or she receives a confirming e-mail immediately, sometimes before leaving the site. E-mails are sent to update the order status, and to confirm when the order is shipped.

Amazon.com started with books, and books are certainly available from numerous retail outlets and online stores. In some cases, an Amazon.com customer could even get a particular book faster by visiting a bookstore, but Amazon.com has one of the strongest customer bases on the Internet: about two-thirds of Amazon.com customers make repeat purchases. When Amazon.com treats its customers in a preferential way and provides them with exceptional customer service, the company is establishing a strong bond with its customers. It is only natural for them to come back for more.

Amazon.com is more consumer than b-to-b marketer, but other b-to-b marketers are executing Internet-based customer programs that are models for success. For example, IBM (*www.ibm.com*) has created a customer contact program called *Focusing on You* that makes methodical use of a customer marketing database and uses the Internet as the information delivery vehicle. IBM diligently captures customer data and aggressively applies it in a "consensual database program" to understand and meet customer information needs on a completely individualized basis.

Focusing on You is not based on pie in the sky technology—it relies primarily on e-mail and the simplest of Web site pages. The real key is the strategy behind *Focusing on You*, as Michelle Lanter Smith, direct marketing manager for IBM, explains:

> *It is very tempting as the marketer of a product or service to try to control the messages you want delivered to your customers. However, in today's reality of competition and easy access to numerous sources of information, it is not a strategy that will work very long or very well. Customers know that they have much more power than they had yesterday, so they expect to be able to control the information they receive, especially from a large vendor like IBM. With the* Focusing on You *program we give them that power. We ask them to tell us what they want to hear about (they select from topics listed on an interest profile) and then we store this information along with demographic data on a relational database.*[5]

You can see from this program description that IBM's philosophy is to *empower* the customer in the relationship. The company lets customers make the decision as to what they want to receive in the way of information, and even how they wish to receive it.

The benefits of a program such as *Focusing on You* extend beyond the value inherent in building solid customer relationships:

- The data received directly from the customer is "much more valuable than purchased data," says Lanter Smith, because it is straight from the source. Because the data is not being filtered through another party or purchased from an outside source, IBM gets to hear what its customers want, first hand.

- Lanter Smith reports that the company has seen "significantly higher responses in many instances" when comparing e-mail campaign messages to direct mail results. Results are fast too— one e-mail campaign generated one third of all responses in just 24 hours. Additionally, there is some evidence that pass-along of e-mail is beating direct mail pass-along by two to one.

- The program is extremely cost-effective because it relies heavily on e-mail marketing. Lanter Smith estimates that sending customers traditional printed materials, such as brochures and binders, as part of a one-to-one customer relationship program is "at least 10 times more expensive" than e-mail communications.

2. Moving Your Other Customers up the Marketing Pyramid

The second basic strategy is to move other customers up the marketing pyramid—until they reach most valued customer status. Some customers may never get there, but cultivating customer relationships will surely move others into the Golden Triangle at the top.

One logical way to move customers along is "upselling." Upselling is a technique that b-to-b marketers can use to encourage customers to purchase additional products or services. An upselling model that has relevance to b-to-b marketing is the one adopted by major computer manufacturers.

If you purchase a computer system directly from a computer manufacturer, you will undoubtedly be a target for upselling. Not only will you receive notification of the availability of other computer systems, perhaps at preferred customer pricing, you will also receive a host of promotions from other company divisions. You may, for example, receive a catalog of software marketed by the manufacturer that relates specifically to the system you purchase. You may also be notified of supplies or accessories available directly from the manufacturer (sometimes called "aftermarket selling"). You will almost certainly be solicited by the company's service organization.

The customer upselling practice has been easy to implement through telemarketing, direct mail, and retail outlets, and it is now possible to implement it online with newer database-driven Web technologies. Marketers can use the information from their customer databases to dynamically generate Web pages that are individualized to a customer's needs. Pages can even be generated on the fly as a customer "walks through" a Web site.

The potential for upselling and cross-selling products to customers is sure to increase dramatically as the appropriate Internet tools become increasingly available. In fact, customized Web pages which provide customers with the specific purchasing information they need are becoming a strategy to keep customers involved and loyal.

Internet-Based Customer Service

Customer service is a primary area that can keep your customers satisfied and intensify their relationship with your company. Internet-based customer service can now incorporate customer call centers built on Internet telephony technology, interactive chat rooms, and 24-hour-a-day, 7-day-a-week customer service support areas with "smart" databases that help customers solve their own problems.

How important is customer service? A study released in November 1999 by Servicesoft indicated that 87 percent of online shoppers who spent $2,000 or more on the Web in the past six months will abandon a merchant's Web site and click to a competitor's site if they experience bad customer service. 79 percent of these shoppers said they have increased their patronage and spending on a Web site when the customer service experienced is favorable. The study, conducted by Socratic Technologies, surveyed a total of 836 online customer service users during October 1999.

New customer service products abound, some of which are nothing short of remarkable. A worthwhile list of software companies generally servicing the "one-to-one" market can be found at the Accelerating1to1 Web site (*www.accelerating.com*). Accelerating1to1, a Peppers and Rogers company, measures the results of one-to-one and personalization initiatives.

Here is a sampling of just some of the innovative companies offering products and services in this burgeoning area.

Acuity (*www.acuity.com*)

A leading provider of Web-based customer interaction solutions, Acuity's WebCenter product line offers self-help and live-help options so customers can choose the way they prefer to communicate with a company. More than 2,700 organizations use Acuity software, including such business-to-business companies as Ascend Communications, Fisher Scientific, Harte Hanks, Lucent Technologies, Peregrine Systems, and Western Digital.

Aspect (*www.aspect.com*)

Aspect's approach is to create a "Customer Relationship Portal," a package of software products that perform a range of Customer Relationship Management tasks. The company says its "multimedia" portal makes it possible to accept contacts from customers via fax, e-mail, the Web, and the telephone and route them to a single contact center, where agents can handle all media according to established criteria. Agents can then communicate with Web customers using text chat, IP telephony, or whiteboarding, or answer e-mail with software that allows them to reply using pre-written responses.

BEA *(www.beasys.com)*

The BEA E-Commerce Transaction Platform is used by Amazon.com to help its customers shop for an increasing variety of products over the Web. FedEx uses BEA for its package tracking and logistics system, which handles an average of 36 million transactions daily to track 3 million packages delivered to 211 countries every weekday. Other users include Kaiser Permanente, DIRECTV, and United Airlines.

Bowstreet *(www.bowstreet.com)*

Bowstreet's "Business Web Factory" uses templates that contain data, behavioral information, procedures, and business policies so that programmers can quickly establish Web pages. With the templates in place, non-technical managers can then create their own Web sites for a customer or groups of customers, simply by linking the templates that define customer relationships.

Brightware *(www.brightware.com)*

Intelligent agents are one of the keys to facilitating personalized customer service on the Internet. Brightware, offers Answer Agent, which fields questions from customers and replies itself via e-mail. Answer Agent generates information for the customer on the fly, based on the questions asked, right up to the point of ordering, if appropriate.

Broadvision *(www.broadvision.com)*

Numerous companies provide Internet-based personalized customer communications solutions, but it was Broadvision who first appropriated and trademarked the concept of one-to-one marketing on the Internet.

Broadvision One-to-One is a software application system for large-scale personalized Internet, intranet, and extranet business applications. The system is designed to handle larger user and content databases, high transaction volumes, and intelligent agent matching. Broadvision customers include Siemens, Sun Microsystems, and US WEST.

ePage (*www.epage.com*)

ePage (Figure 8.2) is a solution developed by HomePage.com, a home page Application Service Provider. ePage allows users to easily create a personalized Web page for each customer where product information is stored and managed. Customized information, such as product warranties, owner manuals, purchase and customer service records, is maintained to create a 1-to-1 relationship.

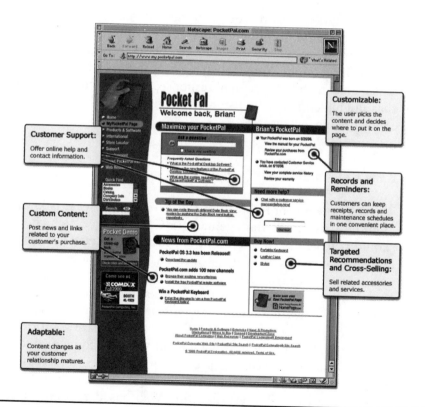

Figure 8.2.   ePage creates personalized Web pages for customers.

E.piphany (*www.epiphany.com*)

A comprehensive solution of interest to IT marketers might be the E.piphany e.4 System from E.piphany. This Enterprise Relationship Management suite of sixteen Web-based, packaged solutions is designed to "mass customize 1-to-1 interactions," says the company. With such users as Charles Schwab, Hewlett-Packard, KPMG and Wells Fargo, the company's technology is helping to drive the concept of 1-to-1 customer relationship-building. In March 2000, E.piphany announced it would purchase Octane Software for over $3 billion in stock. Octane's product analyzes data collected from Web sites, direct mail, and call centers.

eShare Technologies (*www.eshare.com*)

A total solution provider of Customer Interaction Management (CIM) solutions, eShare Technologies has more than 2,200 customers in over 30 countries, including AOL, AT&T Worldnet, and Lycos. The company offers unified Web and telephony interactive customer contact management, including e-mail response, real-time customer interaction, chat and bulletin boards, instant messaging, and inbound/outbound and contact management.

Kana Communications (*www.kana.com*)

There is now an entire breed of software serving what is known as the "Online Customer Management (OCM) market" which, by 2002, should reach close to $700 million, says Forrester Research. A leader in the OCM market is Kana, which has acquired a number of companies in pursuing an aggressive growth strategy. In December 1999, Kana announced the acquisition of Business Evolution, Inc. (BEI), a supplier of Web-based customer assistance and support software, and NetDialog, a provider of self-service customer care solutions. In February 2000, Kana announced a merger with a leading provider of customer self-service, Silknet. One of the first vendors to successfully enter the customer support market, Silknet created eService customer interaction software, an enterprise-wide Web-based customer interaction application that extends beyond a company's call center out to the customer. It integrates multiple means of customer interaction, allowing the management of phone, e-mail, and Web communications, all in one application.

LivePerson (*www.liveperson.com*)

LivePerson's technology allows visitors to e-commerce sites to engage in real-time text conversations with customer service representatives. Customers can instantly chat online to ask questions, make inquiries, and receive assistance from "live people." LivePerson acts as a service bureau or network, so no hardware or software installation is required. In just a few months of being founded, LivePerson had signed 50 major e-commerce sites as clients.

Net Effect (*www.neteffect.com*)

Acquired in November 1999 by search engine AskJeeves, Net Effect provides a live help service, using a client's own customer care agents or those provided by Net Effect in partnership with major national call centers. Net Effect's service enables real time, text-based conversations between e-businesses and their customers, and users include VerticalNet, The Right Start, and Southwestern Bell.

Net Perceptions (*www.netperceptions.com*)

In May 1999, Net Perceptions won the first-ever MIT Sloan E-Commerce Technology Innovator Award for "the technological innovation with the greatest potential to further revolutionize Web-based commerce." That technology is collaborative filtering: real-time recommendation technology that learns more about each customer's individual needs and preferences with every interaction and then makes increasingly personalized product and service recommendations.

PeopleSupport (*www.peoplesupport.com*)

PeopleSupport provides a suite of customized customer care services including live text chat, personalized e-mail reply, telephone services and interactive self-help. The company offers complete outsourcing, software and infrastructure hosting, customer care consulting, and training. PeopleSupport's clients include Time-Warner, GE Card Services, Toyota, and CarParts.com.

Servicesoft (*www.servicesoft.com*)

Servicesoft launched its eCenter solution in August 1999, claiming that it was the industry's only fully integrated, end-to-end Internet Customer Service solution available. eCenter integrates best-of-breed applications for self-service, e-mail management, and collaborative interaction, bringing together the company's Web Advisor, E-MailContact, LiveContact, and Knowledge Builder products. Servicesoft customers include Cisco, Eddie Bauer, GTE, Intel, Motorola, and Verio. Servicesoft filed an IPO in February 2000.

Internet Telephony and Customer Service

Internet telephony is poised to take off as technological barriers continue to fall. Frost & Sullivan says the "VoIP" (Voice Over IP) market will grow to close to $2 billion through 2001. Already several vendors have staked a claim in this arena, both on the product and service provider side. The area with the most activity in this space is "Call Me." Marketed by different companies under different names, the concept is basically the same: A visitor comes to your Web site. He or she is interested in learning more about a product or service—more than the Web page provides. The visitor sees a "Call Me" button or icon on the page, clicks on it, enters his or her phone number and a query, and receives a phone call from a live sales representative within moments. Even more interesting, the sales rep can then lead the inquirer through a directed Web session by "taking control" of the browser and pushing select Web pages to the inquirer at appropriate times. "Call Me" is being offered by an increasing number of telemarketing service firms who re-sell the Web-based software as part of a total customer service package.

Advanced forms of the technology will ultimately permit instant communication via the Internet, versus over a telephone, as computers are increasingly VoIP-enabled. While Internet telephony is spreading rapidly, a few companies became early market leaders in the "Call Me" market.

AT&T InteractiveAnswers (*www.iaexpress.com*)

AT&T InteractiveAnswers is a telecommunications service that allows marketers to integrate voice with the Web. The customer clicks a Call Me icon on the marketer's Web site, which generates a Welcome page. The customer enters his or her phone number and within seconds receives a callback from the marketer's customer service representative on a separate phone line. The service offers a number of options to the marketer, including the ability for the call to be immediately transferred to an in-house or outsourced call center.

NetByTel (*www.netbytel.com*)

NetByTel's Telephone E-Business Platform offers e-businesses an automated, speech-enabled interface to their Web site, so a customer can call from anywhere and transact business over any wire line or wireless telephone. NetByTel can automate inbound order purchase, order status, lead capture, contest entry, information access, and customer service, as well as outbound auction notification, market research, reminders, and direct response. NetByTel's customers include Priceline.com and Office Depot.

NetCall Telecom (*www.netcallusa.com*)

NetCall started in 1996 in the United Kingdom and expanded its operations to the U.S. market in 1998. The company's "Internet Controlled Telephony" controls the entire call process. This allows marketers to deliver personalized content to prospects via push-pull screen integration, route calls to the best qualified sales agent using intelligent virtual call distribution, and improve the sales conversion process by providing the agent with pop-up scripts, Web pages, or desktop applications. NetCall does not require special hardware or software and packages its offerings as services designed to meet specific needs.

WebLine Communications (*www.cisco.com*)

WebLine Communications' flagship product is WebLine Collaboration Server, a Java-based enterprise-class application that allows users to visually interact with remote prospects or customers over the Web during any telephone call, using any Java-enabled browser. Users can deliver Web-based content to individuals or large groups, navigate callers around the Web, demonstrate software applications, and transfer downloadable files instantly. Networking giant Cisco Systems obviously recognized the value of the technology when they acquired WebLine in November 1999. With WebLine, a marketer and customer can interact via voice over a traditional telephone connection, or using Voice Over IP (voice carried via the Internet) if the proper equipment is installed. The customer can be "led" through a Web site as the agent helps the customer navigate around the site or helps download files. In the IT industry, WebLine technology is being used by Cisco, HP, and others. One of the most consumer-friendly examples, however, comes from the apparel marketer, Lands' End (*http://www.landsend.com*). Lands' End employs WebLine to provide exceptional online service. Customers can either request an immediate telephone call, chat with a Lands' End representative via computer, or "shop with a friend" online. As an aside, in mid-2000, Lands' End began to aggressively build its database-driven customer-focused b-to-b capabilities on the Internet as well, launching a new corporate sales Web site.

Moving to the One-to-One Customer Relationship

The very idea of developing a "one-to-one" relationship with a customer was little more than a marketing fantasy before the advent of database marketing. With advances in computer technology, marketers now have access to even the most sophisticated marketing database products on their desktops. Nevertheless, the tools themselves are not enough: first, there must be a *commitment* to the concept of one-to-one relationship marketing, and then, there must be a *strategy* behind it.

Web site analysis firm net.Genesis (*www.netgen.com*) goes so far as to formalize a process for "understanding your online customer." In their Design for AnalysisÔ methodology, net.Genesis cites the need to identify goals, define metrics, assemble data, and build baseline business metrics. According to net.Genesis, the real path to understanding the customer is applying these metrics "to solving real-world business problems."

In a January 2000 research note on CRM, GartnerGroup (*www.gartner.com*) suggests that the customer database is at the core of any customer relationship management program. Gartner cites several key reasons for the prime importance of the customer database, including the fact that the customer database offers a "unified customer view" and permits "multichannel marketing."

There is little doubt that organizations have generally recognized the value of the customer. Many b-to-b marketers now realize that building a "customer-centric" company is vital to corporate health and profitability, but even the most superb customer-oriented companies may still be far removed from anything resembling one-to-one customer relationships. One simple reason is that it often means changing attitudes, then business practices, and sometimes even the corporate culture.

In the May 2000 issue of *1 to 1* magazine, Cisco is mentioned as a company that has "virtually" re-invented itself around customer needs. Already a pioneer in creating a customer-focused Web site, Cisco publishes a print and online magazine, along with dozens of e-mail newsletters which are industry and job-specific. Cisco says all of these publications are offered free to customers, but they are only sent with a customer's permission. According to the company, Cisco is pursuing a "personalized, dynamic, customer-driven content model."

Now, b-to-b marketers are realizing that it pays to get customers involved in solving their own problems. Customer "self-service" is a growing part of Internet-based marketing, and it is saving customers and companies time and money. The MathWorks (*www.mathworks.com*), the world's leading developer and supplier of technical computing software, is a good example. The MathWorks was one of the first 100 companies to create a Web site. Customers of The MathWorks include technology companies, government research labs, and more than 2,000 universities. The company's primary product is MATLAB, a fundamental tool for engineering and scientific work.

The MathWorks puts a major business emphasis on its services and support Web capabilities. Each month, the MathWorks Web site gets 220,000 visits from 120,000 users who can access 13,000 HTML pages of information. The number one destination of those users is the service and support area, which includes the ability to: get technical support, check order status and license information, get quotes for products and services, edit contact information, obtain prerelease "sneak previews," get downloads of product patches and updates, and gain access to the Help Desk and minicourses. The most popular part of the service and support area is the company's solution search database of over 10,000 cases, where customers can solve their own problems based on the experience of other customers.

The move to customer self-service has paid off handsomely for The MathWorks. Now 90 percent of the company's technical support happen over the Web. Users visit the site at least once every one to two months. "It is not just about sales and marketing," says Patrick Hanna, Web manager for The MathWorks. "Our Web site includes full service and support. Service is the secret. If you do a good job at it, loyalty and repeat business will increase."

One-to-one customer marketing doesn't have to be nearly that complex. A March 2000 issue of the Peppers and Rogers newsletter, *INSIDE 1to1*, reported on Hewlett-Packard's efforts to improve upon product registration rates. For manufacturers, getting a customer who just purchased something to fill in that registration card is a major challenge...yet if the customer does so, the company collects customer data which can be used for further promotions. Hewlett-Packard implemented an automatic registration link: Each time a customer installs HP software, a window pops up on the customer's computer screen suggesting electronic registration. Then, within a minute of registering, the customer receives a personalized e-mail with a link to a Web page offering a coupon for an additional related purchase. This process, says the report, moved HP's registration rate from 5 percent to as high as 20 percent, while registration costs fell almost 90 percent.

In your role as a b-to-b marketer, you can demonstrate your commitment to the concept of addressing customer needs individually. You can do this by establishing a relationship program that truly enables your organization to get closer to your customers, and you can use the Internet as a powerful relationship-building tool in your move toward one-to-one customer marketing.

The Personalization Phenomenon

Underlying one-to-one marketing is the rapid move towards Internet personalization, which accelerated in late 1999 with numerous product announcements, partnerships, and media attention. Of course, personalization is not a new Internet concept; such leading e-marketers as Amazon.com (*www.amazon.com*), referenced earlier, have made it an integral part of their success. Amazon.com's "instant recommendations," "1-click ordering," and their 1999 innovation, "purchase circles" (which show who's reading what by company and town) are all examples of customized, if not personalized, customer service. In 2000, Amazon enhanced their customer personalization engine by adding a "New for You" feature (Figure 8.3), which refined their instant recommendations even further.

As mounting evidence of widespread Web personalization, you will notice the presence of "my" pages at a growing number of sites. "My" pages give users considerable individual power to customize home pages and other Web pages to meet their specific needs. These pages typically use personalization engines and tools which provide users with choices, usually in the form of check boxes, from which to select personalization criteria. By answering a few simple questions, the user is instructing the Web site to "learn" his or her preferences, so a personalized page appears the next time.

Figure 8.3.   Amazon.com's personalized customer page, "New for You."

One good example of this is "My Sun" at *www.sun.com*. It uses a personalization engine called Dynamo from Art Technology Group (*www.atg.com*). With "My Sun," a visitor to the Sun Microsystems Web site can change the look and feel of the page; link to the Sun Store, the Product Configurator, the Spares Buying Guide, and an Online Order Status Report; customize their own stock portfolio; get customized Reuters news feeds; use their own quick links, and more. This creates a very personalized experience each time the visitor returns to the page.

One of the better explanations of Internet-based personalization can be found at C|Net's Builder.com Web site (*www.builder.com/Business/Personal*) in an online paper entitled "Personalizing your Web site." As the paper points out, there are varying degrees of personalization as well as various ways to measure its effectiveness. For a continuing dialogue about Internet personalization, check out the Web site *www.personalization.com*. It will provide you with more than you will ever want to know about the subject.

Another valuable source of information covering personalization as it relates to marketing and customer service is the print publication *1to1* (*www.1to1.com*). Launched in late 1999 by *DIRECT* magazine in association with Peppers and Rogers Group, the acknowledged one-to-one pioneers, the publication reports on 1-to-1 customer marketing innovations.

Also worthy of review is a report entitled "Best Web Support Sites" published by The Association of Support Professionals (*www.asponline.com*). The 1999 report, for example profiled the ten winners of the ASP's 1999 "best support sites" competition and included screen shots of key site features, essays by site designers, and hands-on advice about performance metrics, project management, promotion, navigation, and other aspects of support site development. The winning sites were those support sites developed by Iomega, Cisco, Sybase, Microsoft, Intuit, Intel, Symantec, CambridgeSoft, Dell, and Macromedia. According to report editor Jeffrey Tarter, "There's a clear trend toward personalization and audience segmentation, deeper use of clickstream data, better online forums, and greater intelligence in search tools and knowledgebase design."

In the context of building customer relationships, there does appear to be strong evidence that customizing and personalizing the Web experience leads to greater customer loyalty and higher customer retention rates. However, personalization, customization, and one-to-one marketing are not gimmicks to dazzle or Band-Aids to fix poor service; one-to-one marketing is a strategy to which a b-to-b marketer must make a serious commitment.

Five Ideas for Building a One-to-One Customer Relationship Program

1. Treat Customers Like Prospects

B-to-b marketers spend a lot of time, money and effort in the acquisition of new customers, yet too many times, these same marketers under-invest in customer retention. That is wrong—because building a long-lasting customer relationship starts *after* the sale.

Numerous industry studies show that the cost associated with customer retention is far less than the cost of customer acquisition—sometimes the cost of keeping a customer is as little as 20 to 25 percent of the cost associated with acquiring a new customer. This could mean that, for every dollar you spend acquiring a new customer, it will cost you just 25 cents to retain that customer.

This law of customer acquisition and renewal or retention is well known to fundraisers, subscription publications, and mail order companies. When they evaluate their marketing efforts, they often find that they actually acquire new donors, subscribers, or customers at a *loss* but renew them at a profit. It may therefore take a year or more to make money on a customer.

This is the principle behind LTV—lifetime value of a customer. A customer's LTV becomes an important measurement criterion when you evaluate customer acquisition and retention. Look at the average number of years you retain a customer. Then look at the average value of that customer over that period of time. You will get a good sense of what that customer is worth.

If possible, apply this analysis to each individual customer and use it to rank your customers; in effect, you build your own statistically accurate version of the customer marketing pyramid. Then you can compare this data with the amount of money you invest in customer acquisition and retention. If you find, as many companies do, that you are investing far less in customer retention than in customer acquisition, consider the ROI impact of even a modest shift in the ratio. By investing in customer marketing programs—and improving your use of the Internet as a customer marketing and communications tool—you could get a substantial payback.

Attitude is just as important as the money you invest. That is why you should start **treating customers like prospects.** When you treat customers like prospects, you never assume they are comfortably yours forever. You recognize that they always can choose to go elsewhere and that you need to do everything you can to make sure they do not. The key point here is: *You never take customers for granted.* Rather, you create opportunities to reward their loyalty, delight them with superior service, and ensure that their interactions with you are positive, satisfying, and rewarding.

With your customer as a prospect, you can think of new ways to keep the flame burning in that relationship. Direct marketing is an excellent way to cross-sell, upgrade, and extend a customer's business relationship with you—and to get that customer to refer other prospective customers to you as well. Use direct mail and telemarketing in combination with e-mail and a customer-only portion of your Web site to build an ongoing relationship with customers. These media should be used in combination to inform customers *first* about new products or services, make special offers, invite them to special events, and encourage their feedback.

The Internet can help you put a large emphasis on customer service and support and build real value into the customer relationship. Web-based customer service can be open for business 24 hours a day, seven days a week, anywhere in the world. Just as important, by servicing existing customers over the Internet and making it known on your Web site, you demonstrate to prospective customers the value you place on customer support.

2. Ask Customers What They Want—And *Give It to Them*

Companies that are responsive to their customers are companies that *listen* to their customers. These companies provide easy ways for customers to offer their feedback and opinions—via phone, fax, mail, e-mail, and over the Web. They encourage their customers to interact, they take customers' recommendations seriously, and they act on them.

With one-to-one Web technologies available, those companies who not only listen to their customers, but learn from their input and needs, will be the leaders in the Age of the e. These are the companies who will be able to respond quickly and give customers what they want in real time.

IBM's *Focusing on You* program, referenced earlier, was built on asking customers what they want—and giving it to them. One of the company's key findings was that customers wanted to "direct the dialogue based on their own needs." IBM took the responsibility to *reduce* the amount of information directed to the customer—giving him or her the choice of what to receive. That choice made it easier for IBM to provide the customer with the appropriate product information, based on specific needs.

Because customers directed the relationship and were involved in a meaningful dialogue, IBM benefited from an important side effect of the program: customers also updated their own records. This aspect of a customer relationship effort is just as significant, because database maintenance plays a large role in its successful implementation. When a customer updates his or her own database record, the data is more likely to be accurate.

3. Explore New and Innovative Ways to Encourage and Reward Customer Loyalty

You do not necessarily have to establish an elaborate frequent buyer program to encourage and reward customer loyalty. Sometimes, simply making customers feel special can be enough. One simple way to do that is to keep in touch with your customers via e-mail. Another way is to establish a customer service center on your Web site. A customer service center is a tangible way to reward customer loyalty, especially if you are providing added value to the customer relationship.

Web-based customer service centers obviously offer service and support to users of your products, but you can go beyond that in a number of ways. For example, you might post white papers, special reports, or benchmark studies only in the customer section of your Web site and provide links to useful Web sites just for customers. You may wish to build in a self-service area where customers can use solution databases to solve their own problems, or perhaps you will consider using Internet telephony to enhance communications with customers.

You could offer customers the option of signing up for e-mail newsletters or the option of receiving Web pages from you, delivered to their computers on a regular basis. You could use your Web-based customer service center as a "reward center" by offering customers incentives for purchasing certain products or for doing business over the Web. You could build a b-to-b portal that serves your company's business area or industry, and then give customers "special privileges" in using it. Whether you take small or large steps with Internet customer marketing, you are proving that you value the relationship you have with your customers.

4. Recognize the Differences Between Classes of Customers—And Treat Customer Classes Differently

If you utilize database marketing effectively, you can use the information you gather about your customers to segment them and rank them, and then build individualized programs based on classes of customers. For example, you may wish to treat customers at the top of the customer pyramid very differently from other customers. You may want to develop a special relationship with these highly valued customers, communicating with them more frequently via e-mail, enrolling them in preferred customer clubs, and making them special offers on a regular basis.

You may also wish to develop a special program for resellers or partners. Business partners are a customer audience in and of themselves, and they should be treated differently and communicated with separately. We will discuss more about how to enhance partner relationships with the Internet later.

5. Make One-to-One Fun

The idea of a one-to-one relationship is that you get to know each of your customers, their attributes, and their individual needs over time. The more you learn about your customer, the more you can use the Internet to target individualized communications to your customer.

Building that relationship is a serious marketing process, of course, but it should also be fun for the customer. Having fun—providing the customer with an opportunity to smile or even laugh—is a part of relationship building that can endear your company to the customer because you make him or her feel good. The Web can be a playful place. Some b-to-b marketers make use of this characteristic, offering customers games, contests, and "cafes" where customers can do the cyberspace equivalent of leaning back, putting their feet up, and just relaxing. You can use the informality and interactivity of the Web in a good-humored and informal way to make your customers feel that your company is friendly, down to earth, and easy to do business with.

We have discussed a number of ways to implement Internet-enhanced customer marketing, but the bottom line is *customer database integration*. You need to have access to customer data and use it in a proactive yet appropriate fashion to build a long-lasting customer relationship program via the Internet.

With Internet-enhanced customer marketing, you have the potential to keep your most valued customers buying more, the ability to push other customers up the marketing pyramid until they reach "golden" status, and the likelihood of improved productivity and profits that come from the cost-effective implementation of superior customer service.

Building Customer-Driven Extranets

The culmination of one-to-one marketing is the creation of a customer-driven extranet, a Web site established by a company to specifically offer private or preferred customer access to information and order entry. The extranet can be implemented as a restricted area on an existing corporate Web site, or it can be built as a separate site. Either way, it makes it clear that the company believes in the credo "the customer comes first."

As just one example, IBM reported at a 1999 Internet marketing conference that the company created extranets with some of its key customers to encourage them to do business with IBM online. The move contributed to moving IBM's e-commerce revenues from $35 million a month in early 1998 to over $1 billion a month by December 1998. As an aside, IBM saved some $300 million in call center costs in 1998 by handling more customer service inquiries online.

A restricted access customer service area of a corporate Web site is, in effect, a version of a customer-driven extranet. Many companies establish such areas for customers only, so that they can interact privately with the organization or gain access to information intended only for them. For the most part, access is permitted via a simple password, which the company assigns or the customer selects. Invitation-only Internet events, discussed in Chapter 6, are also a form of extranet, because they are often delivered via a special URL and require passwords to enter.

Private access customer areas and virtual events running over the Web may be acceptable solutions for some IT companies, but conducting business on an ongoing basis with customers and partners over the Internet could stretch the boundaries of any public Web site. An extranet may make more sense, if only because the load of real-time customer service and transaction processing could eat a Web server alive.

The customer-driven extranet is, of course, a major technological undertaking. The impact on the organization should not be minimized, as business processes themselves may undergo dramatic change. If systems serving customers within your company are not centralized, the extranet will likely not succeed.

However, if you have your organizational act together and you have the technology to back it up (either with in-house resources or through outsourcing), then the business benefits of a customer extranet can be huge. In larger companies, for example, the costs associated with customer service and support can be dramatically reduced by shifting much of the repetitive person-to-person contact to Internet-based communications.

There are also out-of-the-box extranet solutions that smaller companies can take advantage of, such as Intranets.com (*www.intranets.com*). Intranets.com offers a set of free services that allow you to establish private spaces where you can collaborate and communicate with external audiences.

Even if you believe in the value of a customer-driven extranet, where do you begin? Maybe it is obvious—but it all starts with what your customers want and need. As mentioned earlier, asking your customers what they want—and giving it to them—should be the driving force behind an extranet. Using database technology, you can accumulate profile data about each customer's relationship with your company, track the customer's interactions with you, and use this data to individualize communications with the customer. In addition, you can learn what customers might want built into an extranet to best meet their needs.

Internet-based customer service requires consideration of new forms of data. For example, transaction data is different from online interaction data. The customer's transactions represent the inquiries or orders you receive. Analyzing this data will help you understand a customer's need for information or buying pattern. But interaction data can offer insight into online behavior. This is the data that tells you how often a customer accesses your Web site, which pages they access most, how they navigate the site, and so on.

You can also bring together product data with solutions and applications information and what-if scenarios so that customers can interactively learn how products apply to their specific needs or how to solve problems with your products. Solutions-oriented content as part of an extranet is at once the most challenging and most exciting opportunity for both company and customer. Imagine, for example, a customer solutions extranet for your organization. It could take the form of a searchable database that cross-references solutions with your products. Customers could enter their desired parameters and be immediately greeted with a list of solutions that fit their needs. Web pages would be dynamically generated on the fly, based on preferences that customers establish in their user profile. New product information could be selectively displayed.

This solutions center could also be used as a sales tool to allow your direct sales force or partners to better match solutions with products your customers' should be purchasing. Electronic fulfillment can be added to the mix so that customers could unlock or download relevant information.

Extranets can also become the core of a highly successful e-commerce strategy. Dell Computer (*www.dell.com*) provides business customers with "Premier Pages"—extranets which display only the Dell products approved for purchase by the customers, along with the special pricing to which those customers are entitled. With over 15,000 Premier Pages, Dell expects to take the next logical step by facilitating the integration of its extranets with its customers' own accounting systems.

Extranets with highly personalized information are already widespread. Ultimately, you will be able to cost-effectively offer an even higher level of personalization to customers as Internet database technology continues to advance, and the Internet and the telephone continue to converge. Not only will you serve up highly personalized information over your extranet, you will also be able to "watch" your customers navigate the extranet and provide live assistance to them when required.

A Checklist for Developing Customer Extranets

From a marketing perspective, here are some of the things you need to consider as you create a customer-driven extranet:

- Learn what to build in to your extranet from customers. Listen to their input and give them what they need.

- Provide a *secure path* to your extranet that goes beyond password protection alone, especially if you will be using your extranet to transmit sensitive customer data or to accept orders. Be sure that your IT organization or outside service provider addresses any security issues up front.

- Utilize customer promotions to increase customer involvement with the extranet. Consider offering gifts or incentives to customers who provide you with case histories or successful experiences with your product that you can then post on the extranet.

- Actively promote the benefits of the extranet to the customer base. Get customers excited about it and build a business case for its ongoing usage. It will repay you many times over in time and money saved.

- Incorporate online forms that allow customers to easily create user profiles, change their profiles, and request information. Use a Web database that enables you to update customer data online. The cost of this database will be quickly offset by the time saved in one-step data entry.

- Create an online solutions center to provide added value to customers. Integrate the legacy customer database with the extranet so that you can generate customized content that is individualized to each customer.

- Create online fulfillment in conjunction with the solutions center. Allow customers to request and receive product literature in the way they prefer—via e-mail, fax, or traditional mail. Encourage them to go to the Web to unlock or download information directly from the extranet.

- Consider using "push" technology to deliver product information directly to your customers_ desktops by request, via periodic e-mail newsletters or Web pages.

- Explore emerging technologies that link the extranet with Internet-based telephony to provide customers with a new level of personalized customer support.

- Establish online measurement criteria and do periodic customer surveys to analyze customer usage of the extranet, understand which areas of the extranet are most and least popular, and continuously improve the extranet.

Why Enhancing Customer Relationships With the Internet Is Worth It

These are just a few b-to-b examples that dramatically tell the story of the measurable impact of the Internet on companies' customer relationships:

- Cisco generates over $8 billion of revenue annually electronically, with a significant portion of sales from repeat customers.

- Amazon.com serves over 17 million customers exclusively on the Internet, and more than half of them make repeat purchases.

- Dell's "build to suit" PC strategy has been transferred to the Internet, resulting in sales of over $2.5 billion annually.

- IBM generates $1 billion a month of online revenue, in part due to creating extranets for major customers.

- The MathWorks gets 220,000 visits from 120,000 users each month, the majority of them to the customer service and support area. The result is that 90 percent of the company's customer service is conducted online.

In addition to providing exceptional levels of customer service, promoting customer loyalty, and gaining competitive advantage, these companies and others are seeing a significant *return on their Internet investment*: measurable savings in employee time and money spent on customer service and technical support functions.

Beyond the customer service advantage, the company that invests in Internet-enhanced customer relationship programs could also become a "customer magnet," according to Internet e-commerce pioneer Shikhar Ghosh:

> *It is conceivable that some companies will attempt to control the electronic channel by becoming the site that can provide customers with everything they could want.[T]hey could control access to suppliers and subtly sway customers' choices by promoting or ignoring individual brands. Over time, a customer magnet could become the electronic gateway to an entire industry.*[6]

Although becoming a "customer magnet" might require an Internet technology investment beyond the means of some b-to-b marketers, the concept is an intriguing one. If a company could influence its customer base to the extent suggested by Shikhar Ghosh, the marketing landscape could very dramatically change in the future. In fact, in the next chapter, you will discover how b-to-b marketers are taking the next logical step towards becoming a customer magnet: building communities on the Internet.

Notes

1. Robert E. Hackett, "3 Steps to Lifetime Value," *TARGET MARKETING*, February 1998, North American Publishing Co., copyright 1998, Robert E. Hackett.

2. Don Peppers and Martha Rogers, "The Truth About Faux Relationship Marketing," *INSIDE 1to1* Weekly Newsletter, January 15, 1998, copyright 1998 by Peppers and Rogers Group/Marketing1to1.

3. Don Peppers and Martha Rogers, "Smart Customers, Smart Companies," *INSIDE 1to1* Weekly Newsletter, February 5, 1998, copyright 1998 by Peppers and Rogers Group/Marketing1to1.

4. Peppers and Rogers Group, "The State of One to One On-line," May 1999, copyright 1999, Peppers and Rogers Group/Marketing1to1. Available at *www.1to1.com*

5. Michelle Lanter Smith, "One to One: Put the Customer in the Information Driver Seat and Build Better Relationships," *DIRECT MARKETING*, January 1998, copyright 1998, Hoke Communications, Inc.

6. Shikhar Ghosh, "Making Business Sense of the Internet," *Harvard Business Review*, March–April 1998, copyright 1998, Harvard Business School Publishing.

9

Using Business Communities and Exchanges

Unlike any medium before it, the Internet creates a sense of community. Early on, there were newsgroups, bulletin boards, and chat rooms. At first, bulletin boards met the needs of technical audiences with a hunger for information and advice. But as information-sharing became commonplace, full-fledged communities started to populate the Internet. Now communities have advanced to the stage where there are classes of communities–portals, "vortals" (vertical portals), hubs, exchanges, marketplaces–a dizzying array of options, each with its own twist.

While many of these communities are designed for consumers to chat, trade, and interact, the fastest-growing area of community is business-to-business. There are an ever-increasing number of business-oriented communities that bring together sellers with information-seekers, prospects, and buyers. That's why it makes sense for the b-to-b marketer to think of business communities as a marketing opportunity. You can capitalize on the concept of community not only by participating in communities on the Internet, but by creating one if appropriate. This chapter explores the marketing potential of such communities and suggests how to make the best use of them.

What is an Internet Community?

An excellent frame of reference for the b-to-b marketer when it comes to community is the user group of an IT company. Most every IT company of substantial size has a user group, an organization of individuals, sometimes operated independently, who use the company's products. The user group typically has its own governing body, its own annual meeting, and today, its own Web site. An IT company listens hard to its user group, because this is a community that could do much good–or much damage–to the company's reputation. A user group is very much a community of people with a common bond–the company whose products or services these people depend upon.

A community on the Internet is, likewise, a group of people with something in common, getting together or collaborating in a particular area of cyberspace. But community on the Internet extends far beyond this basic definition. An Internet community seems to take on a life of its own and almost share the personalities of its members.

We could probably consider the first primitive Internet communities to be bulletin boards, newsgroups, and chat rooms. Each of these means of communication brought together people in a common bond. Bulletin boards allow posting of comments and questions for all to see, but they typically allow neither privacy nor one-to-one communication. <t>Newsgroups took the Internet concept of community a step further. Through a newsgroup, individuals can communicate interactively via e-mail. Most newsgroups "thread" the discussions so members can not only answer each other, but also read each other's answers. Since newsgroups tend to be formed around specific topics or interest areas, they function as mini-communities in their own right.

Chat rooms may be more like cocktail parties than communities. In this environment, individuals can spend time chatting interactively (in real time) with others.

Now we will bring our consideration of communities up to the present. Chat rooms were in part responsible for spawning full-fledged Internet communities—entire slices of the Internet which appeal to certain segments of society, or people interested in a particular subject. Today there are thousands of such communities, and many of them, as you'll see below, are relevant to b-to-b marketers.

Types of Communities

Online Service Providers

The first Internet communities with any kind of mass "membership" were the early online service providers (as opposed to Internet Service Providers, or ISPs, who provide Internet access but not information services). The most successful has certainly been America Online, or AOL (*www.aol.com*), with a burgeoning membership that, by June 2000, had exceeded 23 million. Early that year, America Online drove the consolidation of the Internet industry by acquiring CompuServe (*www.csi.com*) and scooping up one of the two giants in the browser war, Netscape (*www.netscape.com*). As mentioned at the beginning of this book, America Online pulled off the merger of the century when it announced its intent to acquire the much larger Time Warner.

America Online and CompuServe, itself with over 2.7 million members, are Internet communities in their own right, although CompuServe started as primarily a business-oriented service provider and still maintains that orientation. Both services have grown from basic fee-based online service providers to full-fledged communities that offer their own unique spin on the Internet. America Online, for example, features real-time chat rooms, in which members can hold ongoing "conversations" with each other. Some of these chats are business-oriented. America Online also organizes information areas for easy consumption, using some of its own proprietary content as well as drawing on information from available Web sites.

It appears that America Online will continue to operate CompuServe as a separate service, leveraging its business expertise as a separate brand. Under America Online's stewardship, CompuServe, stagnant at about two million members, may be poised for future growth.

CompuServe does a good job of organizing information into "Web centers" which cover such areas as Business, Computing, Personal Finance, Research, and Travel. CompuServe also features over 100 Forums, or special interest groups, clearly oriented to business professionals.

While the primary business objective of CompuServe is to sign up members for monthly Internet access, it is really their ability to provide value-added service to the CompuServe community that helps retain those members. In this regard, CompuServe, like America Online, is a classic membership organization, not just a community, with a need to continuously acquire new members, renew existing ones, and provide a never-ending array of new services to keep those members loyal.

But as communities, CompuServe, and America Online are two Internet giants serving millions of people, many of whom seek out others like them, or with interests similar to theirs. This is the essence of the Internet community that marketers must understand: The Internet uniquely encourages a very personal kind of community, even though individuals may only know each other's email addresses and never meet face-to-face.

As a b-to-b marketer, how can you take advantage of these special communities? As you might expect, both America Online and CompuServe accept online advertising and other forms of paid promotion.

In late 1999, Prodigy (*www.prodigy.com*) and SBC, the nation's largest local telephone company, announced they would combine their Internet operations, with SBC taking 43 percent ownership of Prodigy. This deal would immediately turn Prodigy, a once-failing ISP, into a powerhouse with more than 2 million customers. But more importantly, Prodigy would now have broadband access to the 100 million people served by SBC. This could help re-shape the ISP landscape fairly significantly.

In relation to promoting your product or service to people in business, where your greatest sales opportunity probably is, look at CompuServe, and the business-oriented portions of America Online, as real opportunities to reach "captive" audiences. These two services can deliver huge audiences to you—and their members are people who are already active Internet users. By understanding how to appeal to certain segments of these audiences, you could uncover new prospects and get more business for your company.

Portals, Hubs, and "Vortals"

One of the most significant Internet developments in 1999 was the rise of the "portal." The portal is a Web destination or gateway—a site which visitors start at, and come back to often. Even that definition is changing fairly rapidly. While a portal is one working definition, a "hub" is another. The hub might be more of a place that simply links to other Web sites without the clear objective of becoming a user's home page. In this context, some would consider America Online, CompuServe, and other ISPs' home pages to be portals. Portals are part search engine, part community, and part something else. "Vortals" emerged in early 2000 as a term used to describe vertical portals. There was so much portal activity from late 1998 through early 2000 that you needed a scorecard to keep track of it.

The Yankee Group viewed the rise of Internet portals as the beginning of "Internet Media Networks." The Yankee Group's December 1998 report on portals stated:

> *As portals, these sites have evolved into places that not only help people navigate through the Web but also provide a number of applications, services, and content directly on their own real estate. With such a wide array of services, portals have significantly increased their Internet user reach, frequency, and usage. By amassing a mass audience, portals have become key bases of power in the Internet market, and are attracting the attention and money of global leaders in communications, commerce, and media.*

Portals are designed to engage visitors, provide them with attractive services, such as free e-mail and free home pages, expose their eyes to online advertising, and create loyalty and repeat usage. Some of these portals have started to consolidate and make strategic moves in preparation for the future.

More and more, all of the leading Internet search engines are becoming portals. Some of the newer search engines or directories combine judgment with search—they actually evaluate your questions and answer them accordingly. The following is a list of search engines and directories, both the established players and some of the newer entries, that account for virtually all of the Internet traffic generated through search engines:

www.about.com

Formerly The Mining Company, About.com is a combination search tool/collection of online communities that positions itself against Internet search engines and directories. This search tool was discussed in Chapter 7.

www.altavista.com

Bounced from its creator, Digital Equipment Corporation, to Compaq, which acquired Digital and then Alta Vista, this search engine has now been purchased and re-invented by one of the Internet's leading investors, CMGI. Alta Vista was re-launched in late 1999 as both a search engine and a free Internet access company. It remains one of the more important major search engines.

www.ask.com

An up and coming intelligent search engine, Ask Jeeves, now known as simply Ask.com, uses a butler cartoon character to represent its "at your service" positioning. You can ask Jeeves any question and "he" will suggest places to find the answer. Ask Jeeves is more than a consumer site; it also provides technology to support e-commerce, navigation, and e-support services to Arthur Andersen, Compaq, DaimlerChrysler, and other companies. One of the more engaging search engines, Ask Jeeves filed its own IPO in 1999. In 2000, the company acquired Direct Hit (*www.directhit.com*), another search engine.

www.excite.com

In early 1999, Excite was purchased by @Home, which provides high-speed Internet access delivered via cable TV wire. Excite is one of the Internet's leading search and directory companies whose technology is licensed to other sites. @Home is a leader in "broadband," which many experts feel will be the answer to the Internet's future. Broadband services, which can be delivered over either phone or cable lines, permit users to get even video and audio over the Internet at very high speeds. As a result, many of the nagging issues related to sluggish downloads and slow access can be eliminated. Even so, @Home's subscriber base stood at under a half million in 1998, dwarfed by America Online and even CompuServe. But with Excite, @Home can now offer a compelling reason that tops the list for its subscribers to pay for high-speed access. (As an aside, @Home also purchased Narrative Communications, creator of Enliven, the leading technology used for "rich media" banner advertising.)

www.4anything.com

This search-by-topic engine is an interesting concept. Fourteen categories contain over 1,000 sites, and 4anything classifies them with a "4" in the front of a name. So, for example, you can find sites named 4advertising, 4baseball, 4the90s, and 4wine. Each becomes a self-contained search engine/directory, offering you specific information about the selected topic.

www.google.com

A new but rapidly growing search engine, Google was selected by Yahoo! in June 2000 to be the site's default search results provider. By mid-2000, Google's search engine services were in use by 76 portal and destination sites worldwide, including 20 countries. Google was named the Number 1 search engine in a search and portal tracking study conducted by research firm NPD.

www.hotbot.com

A search engine spun off by Wired, Hot Bot has been known to be at the top of the list in terms of numbers of indexed pages. It uses the same technology as Inktomi, one of the leaders in search engine technology.

www.infoseek.com

One of the early search engines, Infoseek launched the GO Network in January 1999 with a major advertising campaign designed to pump new life into the brand. With its search engine at the heart of GO, Infoseek sought to stake its claim in the portal wars by bringing together a number of high profile sites, such as Disney.com, ESPN.com, and Family.com, onto one accessible super-site. GO offers eighteen "centers" that integrates content (not unlike America Online) into shopping, news, sports, family, and other areas where online users can "go" to get what they need. By July 1999, Disney bought GO and decided to take Go.com public.

www.lycos.com

With its signature phrase "Go get it!" Lycos has positioned itself as a "retriever" of any information on the Internet. It consistently ranks as a top spider and has often been in a fierce battle with Yahoo! for the leadership position. In early 1999, Lycos became distracted when it announced its intention to merge with USA Networks. The on-again, off-again merger was one of the business world's most-watched stories of 1999, finally collapsing three months after the announcement. In May 2000, Lycos announced it would be purchased by Spain's Terra Networks for $12.5 billion. Terra is a provider of Internet service and content to Spain and Latin America, claiming to be the largest provider of Web services to Spanish-speaking users. The deal was expected to dramatically expand Lycos' international presence.

www.northernlight.com

Northern Light is a search engine with a twist in that it combines Web results with information from "premium material" in one search, giving users access to books, magazines, databases, and newswires not available from other search engines. This search engine was discussed in Chapter 7.

www.yahoo.com

Profitable from early 1996, Yahoo! has a devoted following for its search and information expertise. Yahoo! is the behemoth of the search engine/portal space, the largest of its kind on the Internet. By January 2000, Yahoo! had over 44 million unique users monthly, according to Media Metrix. The next largest portal was Lycos with over 31 million unique users monthly. Yahoo! took to the acquisition hunt in 1999, purchasing GeoCities (*www.geocities.com)*, the Internet's largest community of communities. Also in 1999, Yahoo! sealed one of the Internet's largest deals, the $6 billion plus purchase of Broadcast.com, one of the Internet's leading broadcast facilities.

All in all, the rise of portals represents a true convergence of the Internet and the media/entertainment business. And that, too, only supports the fact that the Internet is now reaching enough individuals to translate into VERY big business.

While searching for information is likely to be the main reason a visitor comes to a particular portal, there must be far more available than a search engine to entice the individual user to visit and *return*. Most if not all portals now offer free e-mail, free chat, personalized pages, and other attractive services that make their sites "sticky." (This is a phrase that Internet-watchers have coined to refer to a site's ability to keep users at its site for more time, rather than coming for just a brief visit. Time spent on a site is believed to translate into dollars, because the "stuck" visitor is exposed to more of the site's advertising and uses more of the site's services. This also promotes return visits and loyalty to the site, which are important factors in generating additional revenue.)

Some Internet observers believe sticky sites will become the only way to differentiate between the millions of options available to visitors. Ultimately, to keep sites sticky, portals, and other sites are expected to offer Web-enabled database, word processing, or scheduling tools—eventually creating competition for the programs that run on the PC desktop. As broadband becomes the preferred method of Internet access, portals can really burn rubber, offering heavy-duty applications previously only available on computers.

Are portals truly communities? Yes and no. Some of them are more like information networks than communities. But others, like Yahoo!, seem very community oriented. Yahoo! users can create their own "My Yahoo!" pages to personalize their experiences, while younger users can go to a special community just for them called "Yahooligans."

Here again, as with America Online and CompuServe, there are many opportunities for b-to-b Internet marketers to capitalize on each portal's popularity—including carefully targeted online advertising, purchase of space on pages which search for certain key words, page links, discussion groups, and the like. If nothing else, be sure your Web site is linked to the appropriate areas of each portal, and be certain to construct your Web pages so they can be easily recognized by search engines.

Why else should the b-to-b marketer care about portals? That is because in the Internet future, you could be part of one, or you could decide to eventually build one of your own. In a February 8, 1999 cover story, the publication *Information Week* suggested that "A growing number of businesses are adapting the portal's gateway-to-the-world model as an efficient way for their employees to access critical information online." The article went on to report that "enterprise portals" will make it possible for companies to not only share internal information, but for employees to use the portal as a "starting point...to access real-time and historical information...all from their browsers."

Virtual Malls and Auctions

Virtual malls and auction sites can be considered Internet communities in the sense that they bring buyers and sellers together with the common goal of conducting commerce. For the b-to-b marketer, virtual malls and auction sites may provide useful opportunities to more widely promote products and services beyond traditional audiences.

The business-oriented virtual mall offers merchants an opportunity to associate as part of a group of merchants who take advantage of the publicity and e-commerce engine of a larger site. One such mall, aptly named "The Virtual Business Mall" is the creation of HyperMart (*www.hypermart.net*), which claims to be the leading provider of free business hosting. HyperMart offers businesses tools to create a free hosting account. In return, the business agrees to become a member, display HyperMart banner ads, and participate in HyperMart marketing programs. (HyperMart itself recently launched an Internet network/portal called "Go2Net.") Other malls, such as business1.com (*www.business1.com*) not only consolidate wholesalers and retailers, but also provide business-oriented services.

While virtual malls may lack daily excitement, auction sites have brought a fast and furious brand of electronically enabled old time commerce to the Internet. As such, auction sites have become a hot commodity on the Internet. In particular, the growth of b-to-b auction sites has skyrocketed. *The Industry Standard* (*www.thestandard.com*), in its March 13, 2000 issue, categorized b-to-b auctions into "forward" auctions, in which sellers post goods or services and buyers submit competing bids, and "reverse" auctions, in which buyers post the items they want to purchase, with sellers competing to provide the items at the appropriate prices. *The Industry Standard* added "Internet Exchanges" to the mix, defining them as places where buyers and sellers trade bids and offers until they make a deal.

We will take a look at a few of the leading auction sites, focusing primarily on b-to-b, to see why many of them can be considered true communities.

AdAuction (*www.adauction.com*)

AdAuction.com is a business-to-business e-commerce service for buying and selling media. Advertisers can purchase ad space from Web, print, and broadcast media by placing bids on the site to receive competitive prices. Media publishers participate by indicating an inventory of available media. Over 2,000 media buying organizations participate in the service.

CompareNet (*www.comparenet.com*)

CompareNet's claim to fame is its ability to compare thousands of products online. In March 1999, CompareNet was acquired by Microsoft, who planned to integrate the site into its MSN Sidewalk buyer guides. MSN (*www.msn.com*) is itself a giant portal operated by Microsoft.

eBay (*www.ebay.com*)

Founded in 1995, it was eBay's successful 1998 IPO that validated the fact that auctions were one of the Internet's leading growth areas. eBay calls itself "the world's personal trading community".™. By early 2000, eBay had more than 7.7 million registered users, who added more than 375,000 items daily to more than 2,900 categories. The eBay concept pioneered online auctions, and it is eBay's model that is now being adopted by other auction sites, including those concentrating on business-related items only, similar to the way in which Amazon.com's success was leveraged by other e-commerce sites. In fact, Amazon.com adopted the successful eBay idea and launched an auction service of its own in 1999. In early 2000, eBay announced that it would launch the eBay Business Exchange to serve the needs of small businesses.

FairMarket (*www.fairmarket.com*)

FairMarket is not an auction site, but rather an auction service. FairMarket sets up and manages auctions for its clients, and also provides 24 hours a day, seven days a week e-mail customer service support so inquiries from buyers and sellers can be promptly answered. FairMarket's clients include CompUSA and Dell.

FreeMarkets (*www.freemarkets.com*)

FreeMarket is a "market maker," bringing together direct material purchasers from large consumer, high-tech, utility, and industrial product companies with sellers who manufacture or supply custom components and materials to the buyer's specifications. In the first quarter of 2000, FreeMarkets acquired iMark.com, an auction site for surplus equipment and inventory.

Onsale.com (*www.onsale.com*)

Onsale.com, which merged with Egghead.com in 1999, features both an "at cost" wholesale store and an "at auction" site. The At Cost store offers an inventory of over 35,000 computer products, obtained through participating distributors, and sold to the public at wholesale prices, plus transaction processing fees. Onsale's At Auction claims to be "the world's largest retail online auction."

Priceline *(www.priceline.com)*

Priceline.com is less of an auction site/community and more of a comparison shopping site. Here, users bid on select items, to see if they can "win" the item at the price that they wish to pay. Priceline achieved notoriety primarily for creating a market in bidding on airfares, but its success led to establishing similar bidding programs for hotel rooms, new cars, home mortgages, home refinancing, and home equity loans. In 2000, Priceline even added gasoline and grocery store products to its offerings.

TradeOut *(www.tradeout.com)*

TradeOut.com says it is the leading business-to-business exchange connecting buyers and sellers of business surplus. TradeOut provides an opportunity for sellers of excess inventory, overstocks, and other surplus goods to find buyers, who may be wholesalers, discounters, or just companies looking for a good deal. Using a model not unlike eBay (which is one of its major investors), TradeOut facilitates bidding on everything from office furniture to industrial equipment to computers and peripherals, charging its sellers a percentage of the transaction but allowing buyers to participate free. This is a rapidly growing area of business-to-business e-commerce, spawning a number of sites specializing in the surplus market.

The Information Technology Super-sites

A model for the information portal/community could well be the Information Technology super-sites. This collection of sites consolidates information, often from the various publications the sites represent, and makes it available in a single location. Some may consider them portals, while others may classify them as hubs. But they are communities in the sense that a visitor to one of these super-sites can typically obtain free e-mail accounts, receive free e-mail newsletter subscriptions, connect with others in special interest groups, and take advantage of online events and targeted programs. The most prominent IT super-sites are:

CMPnet *(www.cmpnet.com)*

One of the largest IT-focused super-sites, CMPnet consolidates information from more than 35 different Web sites, including *Computer Reseller News, EE Times, InformationWeek, InternetWeek, ISPs.com, Network Computing,* and *Windows* magazine. Start at the home page and you will find all of them, including CMP's three true communities, TechWeb, Ch@nnelWEB, and EDTN Network.

- **TechWeb** *(www.techweb.com)* Within TechWeb is "PlanetIT" *(www.planetit.com)*, a true community carved out of the larger network especially for IT professionals. As of December 1999, this one-year old community had 90,000 members.

- **Ch@nnelWEB** *(www.channelweb.com)*This community is very useful for IT companies with channel partners (is there an IT company who *doesn't* have them?). Ch@nnelWEB focuses on the specific needs of distributors, resellers and partners, offering deep content and extensive services for this audience and advertisers interested in reaching them.

- **EDTN Network** *(www.edtn.com)*EDTN specializes in Electronics Design and is organized into such areas as News Center, Design Center, and Career Center. More of a network than a mature interactive community, EDTN is a hub-like site which points to partner sites, such as Embedded.com, etown.com, and EE Product News.

C|Net *(www.cnet.com)*

C|Net is an extremely useful network for IT marketers. In itself, it is more of a portal than a community, connecting to other C|Net sites, including News.com (do not be fooled by the name, it is IT news), Builder.com, Download.com, Shareware.com, and Shopper.com. C|Net operates a technology auction area and offers over 25 "dispatches" (free e-mail newsletters) available in text or HTML.

EarthWeb (*www.earthweb.com*)

EarthWeb has grown rapidly, becoming one of the leading providers of online services to IT professionals. EarthWeb is a collection of over 20 very targeted sites, some of which function as communities. These include:

- **Dice.com** (*www.dice.com*) Dice.com is a major job search site for computer professionals, listing thousands of high tech permanent, contract, and consulting jobs nationwide.

- **Datamation** (*www.datamation.com*) The print publication Datamation was acquired by EarthWeb and turned into a Web publication, now providing information to IT decision-makers online.

- **Developer.com** (*www.developer.com*) This is a true community site for developers, providing them with a comprehensive resource on software development languages, tools, technologies, and techniques.

- **ITKnowledge.com** (*www.itknowledge.com*) ITKnowledge claims to be "the largest online collection of best-selling technical books, source code and examples from the leading publishers."

IDG.net (*www.idg.net*) and ITWorld (*www.itworld.com*)

IDG.net is a gateway to the more than 250 publications and services Web sites of this corporate giant. IDG publishes *Computerworld*, *InfoWorld*, *Network World*, and *PC World*, along with the Internet-focused magazine, *The Industry Standard*. IDG's ITWorld is a network of seven of its premier publications, including *CIO* and *Network World*.

Internet.com (*www.internet.com*)

Internet.com is an informational super-site with 79 "e-business communities" which provide different perspectives on the Internet. Internetnews.com is a must read if you want to keep up with Internet developments on a daily basis.

ZDnet (*www.zdnet.com*)

Rounding out the collection of major publishers serving the IT marketplace, Ziff Davis operates ZDnet as a portal/hub, linking to the sites of such publications as *Inter@ctive Week, Macworld,* and *PC Week.* In late July 2000, C|Net announced it would acquire ZDnet, so expect some significant changes here.

Marketplaces and Exchanges

The business-to-business community is a place where information—lots of it—is shared by companies with common interests or goals. The providers pool their information to a publisher or consolidator, who sponsors a single location to disseminate the information.

Business-to-business Web communities function as large electronic directories or catalogs of information for a rich variety of sources, each of which is available on or accessible through a single site. Communities also offer information providers the ability to interact with their constituency and effectively expose new audiences to the providers' messages. In most cases, communities are free to users, as long as the users register (and therefore provide contact information that can be used by both the community and the participating information providers).

Many of these communities are rapidly evolving into **marketplaces** and **exchanges**. In an October 1999 report, the Yankee Group (*www.yankeegroup.com*) said b-to-b e-commerce portals are trading networks that "have a shot at constructing the first true electronic supply chain for companies outside of the Global 1000."

Forrester Resesearch (*www.forrester.com*) says these "eMarketplaces" will capture 53 percent of all online business trade by 2004. GartnerGroup (*www.gartner.com*) reports that, as of January 2000, there were more than 300 such organizations, vs. about 30 of them a year prior. Gartner believes that they will account for almost $3 trillion in sales transactions by 2004. In April 2000, Forbes reported that there were more than 500 exchanges funded with at least $5 million and that, by 2003, there would be 2,000 of them.

Not all the predictions about b-to-b marketplaces and exchanges are rosy, however. Despite their dramatic expansion, potential problems ahead could hamper on-going growth. A high-profile meeting of e-commerce executives held in May 2000, the Association of Strategic Alliance Professionals Summit, said that a majority of b-to-b marketplaces will vanish within two years. They gave as their reasons anti-trust issues along with fierce competition and stealing each other's personnel.

Nevertheless, the year 2000 saw some spectacular e-alliances that promise to change the way business is done, even among the fiercest of rivals. In March, GM, Ford and DaimlerChrysler said they would form a b-to-b marketplace to buy and sell auto products. In May, IBM said it would form a b-to-b hub, *www.e2open.com*, that brings together the inventory of a dozen of the world's technology leaders, including Ericsson, Hitachi, Motorola, Nokia, and Nortel Networks. That same month, a dozen computer manufacturers, including rivals Compaq, HP, and Gateway, said they would form a b-to-b exchange to consolidate parts-buying. Numerous other exchanges were announced in 2000 involving everything from aerospace manufacturers to retailers to hotels to consumer packaged goods, each involving rival companies working together. This "coopetition" phenomenon is examined in the next chapter.

In addition to these large exchanges being formed, b-to-b marketplaces have grown exponentially on the Internet. Some vertical segments have found new business opportunities through marketplaces. Small business provides a rapidly growing market for b-to-b products and services, which could be more cost-effectively delivered via the Internet. As a result, there has been a dramatic increase in the number of marketplaces serving small business.

Listed below as examples are some marketplaces and exchanges in a number of b-to-b categories.

Small Business

AllBusiness (*www.allbusiness.com*)

AllBusiness.com services small businesses through a site that provides an advertising platform for companies who want to advertise their services, as well as a source of advice and resources for the small business owner.

bCentral (*www.bcentral.com*)

bCentral, launched in late 1999, is Microsoft's strong entry into the small business market. bCentral promotes Microsoft's own products and services, of course, but it is also a legitimate information site with plenty of helpful resources and useful links for the small business owner.

BizBuyer (*www.bizbuyer.com*)

BizBuyer.com matches up sellers and buyers by letting small businesses automate the RFP process. The buyer specifies what is needed, and then BizBuyer finds the potential sellers, gets bids from them, and returns the bids to the buyer.

BizProLink (*www.bizprolink.com*)

BizProLink is a network of over 100 industry-specific, business-to-business communities. Each community focuses on industry-specific content.

BuyersZone (*www.buyerszone.com*)

BuyersZone provides purchasing tools and advice for small to mid-sized businesses, covering over 75 types of business purchases, everything from 401(k) plans to fax machines to voice mail systems.

CommerceInc (*www.commerceinc.com*)

A content provider to small businesses, CommerceInc's mission is to model the entire U.S. procurement network online. As a result, the company says, it will create "the first validated e-commerce business community."

Inc.com (*www.inc.com*)

Started as the companion site to the successful business magazine, *Inc.*, this site has now become an independent small business portal.

Office.com (*www.office.com*)

A venture of Winstar Communications, Office.com (Figure 9.1) targets small and mid-sized businesses, offering them original content and selected third-party information for 150 industries, community areas, independent reviews, assessment tools, and one-click purchasing. In 2000, Office.com acquired Individual.com, a popular customized news service.

Onvia (*www.onvia.com*)

Quickly rising to the top as one of the leading small business service sites, Onvia offers the ability to review suppliers, products, and prices quickly and easily.

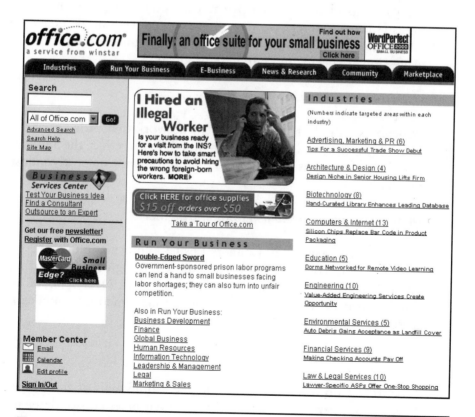

Figure 9.1. Office.com.

General Business

Ariba (*www.ariba.com*)

Launched in early 1999, Ariba.com claims to be "the largest worldwide business-to-business commerce network for operating resources on the Internet." Ariba.com creates a single network access point created for buyers and facilitates the transaction by acting as an intermediary. Such companies as Bristol-Myers Squibb, Cisco Systems, Federal Express, Hewlett-Packard, and Visa are client buyers.

Industry.net (*www.industry.net*)

Industry.net claims to be "the world's largest engineering-related, Internet-based technical information community." The goal of Industry.net is to offer a variety of free and paid editorial and technical information to help design and maintenance engineers and procurement professionals specify and purchase products.

iProcure.com (*www.iprocure.com*)

iProcure is an industrial procurement network that provides access to millions of industrial parts and supplies. It helps reduce the administrative costs of purchasing and saves time and money on costly industrial purchases.

Manufacturing.net (*www.manufacturing.net*)

Manufacturing.net, from Cahners Business Information, is one of the Internet's most comprehensive sites tailored to engineering, design, purchasing, logistics, and distribution professionals. Over 170,000 registered users gain access to content from 23 manufacturing publications, directories, searchable databases, and more.

ProcureNet (*www.procurenet.com*)

ProcureNet positions itself as "the electronic mall of the future for buyers, suppliers, and distributors." ProcureNet consolidates maintenance, repair, and operations materials from print catalogs. The buyer can search, compare products and prices, and purchase items at a single site.

Product News Network (*www.productnews.com*)

Product News Network is on online database and news service that covers industrial products. Sponsored by advertisers and free to users, the database contains over 50,000 industrial products of every kind, searchable by categories and manufacturers.

PurchasePro.com (*www.purchasepro.com*)

PurchasePro allows its users to build electronic catalogs of products, sell and purchase products and services, and bid on or offer products for bidding using PurchasePro's online marketplace.

SupplierMarket.com (*www.suppliermarket.com*)

This site is a leading marketplace for built-to-order products. Suppliers can browse requests for quotes, and buyers are matched to qualified suppliers by the site's "SmartMatch" system. Suppliers then have the opportunity to bid for the business in a live, online bidding session. In August 2000, SupplierMarket was acquired by Ariba.

Vertical Markets – Cross Industry

VerticalNet (*www.verticalnet.com*)

VerticalNet (Figure 9.2) is arguably the most aggressive operator of vertical trade communities on the Internet. By early 2000, VerticalNet had 55 vertical "communities" in such specialized areas as communications, electronics, environmental, food and packaging, service, process, and science. Each of VerticalNet's communities is individually branded by industry and caters to individuals with similar professional interests. VerticalNet updates its editorial content daily on each site, encourages professionals to exchange ideas, provides a targeted area for buyers and

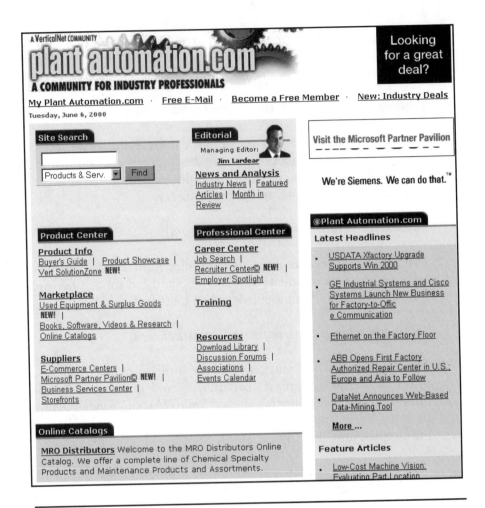

Figure 9.2. Plant Automation.com, a VerticalNet community.

sellers to do business with each other, and solicits advertisers for its "storefronts" on each vertical site.

VerticalNet became one of the first such sites to launch its own online auction service in 1999, when it filed a successful IPO. VerticalNet announced in late 1999 that it would acquire NECX, a leading e-commerce site, and that IBM signed a deal to buy 375 storefronts on VerticalNet communities in the year 2000. In early

2000, Microsoft announced it would invest $100 million in VerticalNet.

Vertical Markets - Chemicals, Medicine, Science

Chemdex (*www.chemdex.com*)

Chemdex is a leading "marketmaker," uniting life sciences enterprises, researchers, and suppliers via a Web site that represents the world's largest online marketplace of lab supplies. Chemdex aggressively expanded in 1999, acquiring SpecialtyMD.com, which enables delivery of objective information about medical products and procedures. In 2000, Chemdex made more strategic moves: The company formed a joint venture with DuPont called Industria Solutions to create an online marketplace for the fluid processing market, and then created Ventro (*www.ventro.com*), an operator of vertical marketplaces, to compete with VerticalNet.

Medcast Networks (*www.medcast.com*)

Medcast, targeted to doctors, provides the latest medical information through daily news broadcasts delivered to physician's computers each night. Medcast also provides medical courses and three-dimensional patient demos.

Plastics Network (*www.plasticsnet.com*)

The Plastics Network is a good example of how specialized a Web community can be. This network offers a new product center, a complete resource of plastics companies and products, and a purchasing center, as well as community services.

SciQuest (*www.sciquest.com*)

Positioning itself as the Internet source for scientific products used by the pharmaceutical, biotechnology, university, and industrial markets, SciQuest added online ordering in 1999 to its database of over 100,000 products from about 100 suppliers.

Energy

Enermetrix (*www.enermetrix.com*)

Enermetrix operates an active energy exchange and also provides Internet commerce solutions for companies operating in competitive energy markets. Energy buyers save money and sellers tap new markets as Enermetrix connects utilities, energy service companies, corporate energy buyers, and energy traders.

Vertical Markets - Government

eCitydeals (*www.ecitydeals.com*)

One of a new breed of exchanges focusing on better use of the Internet by government, eCitydeals (Figure 9.3) is for city governments who want to sell used equipment. Cities can also use eCitydeals as an Internet-based procurement system.

GSA Auctions (*www.gsaauctions.gov*)

Not an exchange, but a vast marketplace, this site offers surplus Federal government property for sale at one central Web site.

Vertical Markets - Information Technology

Midrangeuser.com (*www.midrangeuser.com*) and News400.com (*www.news400.com*)

These sites are included as good examples of vertical IT communities, focused on the needs of AS/400 and RS/6000 professionals. Midrangeuser.com includes an auction, catalog, education resource, news, and job search area.

MyHelpdesk.com (*www.myhelpdesk.com*)

Desribing itself as "the Web's largest computer help directory," MyHelpdesk.com is a support portal. The site covers service for over

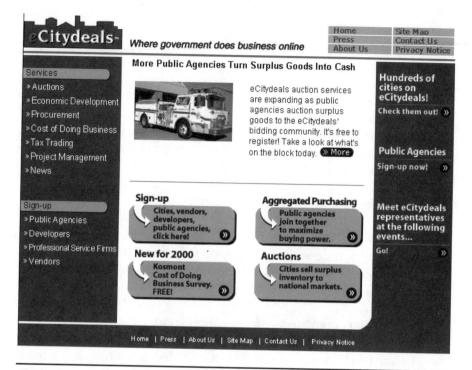

Figure 9.3. eCitydeals, one of a new breed of "B-to-G" (business-to-government) Web sites.

1,500 software and hardware products, independent of any vendor. The site is as much a customer service example as a community: users can create their own customized helpdesk where individual computer configurations are stored. As questions and problems arise, MyHelpdesk.com recommends only the specific, relevant products and services that are needed to assist the user.

WebHarbor.com (*www.webharbor.com*)

WebHarbor describes itself as "The ASP Industry Portal", serving the emerging class of technology companies that are known as Application Service Providers. WebHarbor is also a clearing house for ASP-enabled software (for both vendors and prospective customers).

Services

eSpeed (*www.espeed.com*)

A marketplace started by fixed income securities broker Cantor Fitzgerald, eSpeed is designed to be a trading place for commodities. On eSpeed, you can trade in electricity and natural gas derivatives, or if you are a customer of Charles Schwab, you can buy bonds. eSpeed plans to build its b-to-b portfolio to some 40 offerings by the end of 2000.

Guru.com (*www.guru.com*)

One of a new breed of services marketplaces that brings together companies with independent freelancers and consultants. Companies list assignment opportunities and consultants list credentials...and perhaps there is a match made in heaven.

Newmediary.com (*www.newmediary.com*)

This marketplace is an online resource dedicated to helping businesses locate highly qualified providers of Internet-related services. Participating vendors include companies who offer Web site design, hosting, e-commerce, public relations, and consulting services.

Becoming Part of a Community

You can become part of most communities, as an individual or a representative of your business, by simply "joining." In some communities, joining is free. It takes nothing more than the process of completing and sending an online application and getting a user ID and password. Obviously, you could also become a paid advertiser.

In other communities, you may have to pay a membership or participation fee, or you may have to contribute part of the revenue you receive from the community, if you sell something through that community. Some communities, such as virtual malls, may "rent" you virtual space on a contractual basis. Still others may ask you to "subscribe" for a certain period of time.

But this should not deter you from exploring the business viability of communities. Certainly, you can tell a lot about a community just by the companies it attracts. Typically, "name brand" companies will not participate in a community that is not a legitimate operation.

Below is a suggested plan of action to help you evaluate communities for potential business participation.

Find the Right Communities

There are so many kinds of communities that you must first do a broad search to locate those communities that may have business or marketing value for you. You can start with the communities mentioned in this chapter, but there may be tens or even hundreds more that apply to your particular needs. Go to several of the portals mentioned earlier and use their search engines to help you locate appropriate communities. Remember that communities are not always identifiable as "communities;" they could be portals, hubs, virtual malls, auction sites, or any site where Internet users congregate regularly.

Narrow Your Options

Armed with this preliminary list of communities, begin to narrow your options by critically evaluating each site. First classify the potential communities into free versus paid sites. Then make sure you understand whom the community serves. You want to be certain that the target audience is appropriate for your product or service. Finally, determine from the information on the site which companies are involved in the community. You want to learn if your competitors participate. You also want to know whether or not the buyers and sellers are from companies that fit your company's own profile, or they are the kinds of companies you want to do business with.

Then apply the following checklist to each community:

Which Free Services are Offered?

Does the community offer free services you could take advantage of, such as e-mail, home pages, chat, discussion groups, etc.?

What Opportunities for Free Publicity Exist?

Does the community have areas in which your company, product, or service can obtain any of the following free:

- Listing in member or supplier directories,

- Mention in discussion groups or chats,

- Posting of press releases or product information,

- Including a company profile,

- Having speakers participate in online forums or seminars,

- Posting of job openings,

- Listing of your events in a community calendar,

- Listing of your products or services in a buyer's guide, and

- Reciprocal linking to your site from the community and vice versa.

What Opportunities for Paid Advertising and Promotion are Available?

In evaluating paid opportunities, look at each possible activity from a media ROI perspective. In other words, analyze the potential number of prospects you will reach and ask yourself if the dollars you are investing in the paid activity are reasonable on a cost per thousand basis. The smart way to go about it is to test a particular activity on a limited scale and see if the results warrant continued investment. The kinds of paid opportunities that may exist on community sites include:

- Paid sponsorships of discussion groups or chats,

- Paid sponsorships of site features, such as job banks and events,

- Paid listings in directories and buyers' guides (some communities provide different levels of participation so your products can be highlighted or you can be a featured supplier),

- Fees/commissions for products sold,

- Banner advertising on the home page or specific pages,

- Paid sponsorship/advertising in a community e-mail newsletter, and

- Rental of e-mail subscriber lists.

As with any business decision, weigh all the positives and negatives before you get involved in a community, even if participation is free. If your objective is to use the community for marketing purposes, you will have to invest time as well as money. It takes time to make use of a community's resources and build relationships with community members.

Often, the highest value you get from a community is the *networking* value. View the community as a giant virtual meeting room. The networking possibilities are limitless. If you look at the community as a place where unlimited networking potential can result in unlimited business opportunities, you will probably get more out of one than you ever thought possible.

Building Your Own Sponsored Community

A much larger decision than participating in an existing community is whether or not to build one of your own.

As a b-to-b marketer, why should you consider building a community in the first place? One reason is to establish a peremptory leadership position in a particular field.

Examples of Company-Sponsored B-to-B Communities

Sales.com (*www.sales.com*)

Siebel Systems (*www.siebel.com*), a worldwide leader in sales automation software and one of the most successful companies to capitalize on e-business, launched a business portal called **Sales.com** in February 1999. Company chairman Thomas Siebel, author of the book *Cyber Rules*, called the site "the world's most comprehensive resource available to make sales professionals the most effective and successful they can be." Siebel partnered with Sun Microsystems, Dun & Bradstreet, and Miller Heiman to add content and value to Sales.com.

Sales.com provides, among other things:

- Sales tools to track and manage opportunities, accounts, contacts, calendars, and action items,

- Up-to-the-minute information about public and private companies, customers, prospects, and competitors,

- Personalized sales leads and fully integrated pipeline management, to build and manage sales opportunities,

- Skills enhancement services to help sales professionals continue to refine their sales skills by reading articles, daily tips, and participating in a wide range of courses,

- Networking services that allow sales professionals to build and leverage relationships through online communities and discussion forums, and

- A variety of online services including travel, a complete business center and online shopping.

Available first only to Siebel Systems customers, Sales.com was opened to all by the end of the first quarter of 1999. In December 1999, Siebel announced that it was spinning off Sales.com as an independent, private company, having secured $27 million in private financing. According to Siebel, Sales.com has become "one of the Internet's most successful and fastest-growing application service providers."

Sales.com probably leaves competitors scratching their heads and saying, "Why didn't we think of that?" This is a classic example of a visionary company staking out new territory on the Internet and applying the concept of a business-to-business community to its own marketing and sales objectives.

During 1999, numerous other b-to-b companies extended their presence by building stand-alone communities. Here are three other examples:

DeepCanyon (*www.deepcanyon.com*)

If you are doing market research for your own company, why not offer it to others? That is what happened when Hewlett-Packard started its own internal research site and then capitalized on a market opportunity by launching it publicly as DeepCanyon. This site specializes in delivering research reports to IT marketers and keeping them aware of the latest business information and data analysis related to the Internet. DeepCanyon also offers some very handy tools, such as a market calculator, company locator, and competitor alert.

mySAP.com (*www.mysap.com*)

A spin-off of SAP, the worldwide leader in Enterprise Resource Planning, mySAP.com aims to be the ERP equivalent of Sales.com. It includes news from Reuters, an extensive business directory, and an extensive community area serving such diverse industry sectors as discrete manufacturing, financial services, education, and process industries. Each community includes industry news and trends, upcoming events, a speakers corner, market information, a career center, and more.

Oracle Exchange (*www.oraclexchange.com*)

Oracle's aggressive move into e-everything is exemplified by Oracle Exchange, launched in mid-1999 as a hosted business-to-business trading network. Oracle first created "Auto-Xchange" for Ford, the world's first automotive online supply chain network, and the largest business-to-business electronic network, so the automotive giant could move its procurement operations to the Internet. Leveraging that experience, the database company then created Oracle Exchange, which offers "open e-business marketplaces that enable Internet supply chain networks to dramatically increase purchasing and operating efficiencies."

Tools to Help You Build a Community

Of course, such communities as Sales.com and Oracle Exchange are engineered on a much larger scale than many companies could ever contemplate. But remember, this is the Internet and the Internet has the enormous potential to scale to every need, making even the smallest of companies look bigger. Almost any smart IT company, no matter how small, can therefore build a modest community, or at least a "destination site," on the Web.

There are numerous tools already available on the Internet to help you build community into your existing site, or even build a whole new community. As with any Internet or software application, there are low-end versions (sometimes called "lite") and high-end versions. The services below are included as a few examples of some of the easiest, fastest ways to create the feeling of community, but they are really just the beginning. Some are quite sophisticated, but others may be appropriate primarily for consumers or very tiny groups of people, so evaluate them carefully before making any commitment.

321 Website! (*www.321website.com*)

321 Website! is an easy way to establish a virtual community. It can be used to add interactivity to an existing site, or to establish a stand-alone site. While 321 Website! is technically free, there is an annual cost to register or manage domain names, and a monthly cost for the shopping cart feature.

BuyerWeb (*www.buyerweb.com*)

BuyerWeb helps you set up your own buyer referral community that enables buyers to specify what they want and receive offers from sellers by e-mail.

Comercis (*www.comercis.com*)

Comercis forms industry-specific communities that network professionals, vendors, distributors, manufacturers, and suppliers in a secure trade environment.

Commerce One (*www.commerceone.com*)

Commerce One offers a number of e-commerce community solutions, including MarketSite, a "trade zone" which competes with the previously mentioned Ariba.com. Commerce One created the Internet purchasing system for General Motors.

Delphi (*www.delphi.com*) and Prospero (*www.prospero.com*)

Delphi has more than 750,000 registered members and 220,000 Forums. Delphi Forums allow members to create, control, and promote a virtual meeting place consisting of message boards, real-time chat, customized Web pages, integrated promotion and electronic commerce. In mid-1999, Delphi introduced a unique twist to its forums called "Mention Marketing." This technology monitors Delphi's message boards for particular words that users might enter. These words would relate to a potential banner ad. So, for example, if a user types in the words "hard drive," Mention Marketing will detect it and trigger a banner ad from a computer vendor to appear at the bottom of the message board. In early 2000, Delphi Forums and Well Engaged merged to form a new company, Prospero Technologies.

eGroups (*www.egroups.com*)

This service focuses exclusively on "e-mail groups," using common e-mail to facilitate interaction. With eGroups, small organizations in particular can easily disseminate information, debate issues, poll group members, make plans, schedule events, and generally communicate better. In June 2000, Yahoo! announced it would acquire eGroups.

eSociety (*www.esociety.com*)

A company with a noble mission, eSociety focuses is efforts on helping associations leverage their existing assets. eSociety assists associations in planning and building industry-focused online communities to increase the value of membership, improve membership acquisition and retention, and create new sources of revenue.

Excite (*www.excite.com*)

Excite, mentioned earlier in this chapter, is a portal that also provides the ability to start and join communities, as does the portal **Yahoo!** *(www.yahoo.com)*.

iBelong (*www.ibelong.com*)

iBelong creates customized, group-specific Web sites for professional and alumni associations, cause-related and special interest groups, and franchise-based organizations. iBelong is helping more than 50 groups representing about 27 million members go online, including the AFL-CIO's "workingfamilies.com" Web site.

Involv (*www.involv.net*)

Most suitable for intranet usage, this free business-oriented service with home pages, polling and voting, a discussion board, task management, calendar, and shared links is positioned as "Web Teaming."

Participate.com (*www.participate.com*)

Participate.com offers larger companies outsourced online community management services. Its clients include Arthur Andersen KnowledgeSpace, AT&T WorldNet, Quote.com, and The Street.

PeoplePanel (*www.peoplepanel.com*)

This novel concept, offered by CyberSites, places a customizable "PeoplePanel" on your existing site to instantly add a community. The concept is funded by selling merchandise and subscriptions, for which CyberSites collects 75 percent and you get 25 percent of the revenue.

Viewlocity (*www.viewlocity.com*)

Viewlocity provides b-to-b integration, trading community frameworks, and supply chain synchronization for large b-to-b online implementations. Viewlocity solutions allow trading partners to communicate while leveraging their existing technologies. Viewlocity has more than 3,200 installations worldwide with more than 1,000 customers, including DHL, DuPont, ECnet, Sony, and Volvo.

What to Build Into Your Community

Suppose you have decided to consider building a community. How do you really go about it? Here is a basic plan:

1. Determine the type of community you need

First decide if your community will target only employees (an intranet), customers or suppliers (an extranet), or a public community on the Web. Intranets and extranets will require special security measures to protect confidential information and limit access to authorized participants. You may wish to restrict access to a public community as well by establishing subscriber or membership rules. While your goal for a public community may be to gain widespread publicity, you may wish to allow only qualified individuals to make use of the community's services.

2. Set objectives for your community and establish an operating budget

Set some realistic specific objectives for your community. With a customer community, for example, set a goal for how many customers you expect will participate. Project customer service savings and revenue impact of the community. Also establish a community operating budget, both for start-up and ongoing development and maintenance costs. A community is more complicated to build than a basic Web site, and it potentially involves more back-end support because it is so interactive in nature. Be sure to anticipate the cost and manpower required to support the activity generated by a community.

3. Establish a community structure

Learn what a community is, how it operates, and what it includes by visiting other business communities and actively participating in them. Typically, you will want to consider including the following in your community:

Information Center

This is usually the heart of the community. Depending on the type of community you establish, this area would contain information about your industry, your company and other companies' products and services, white papers, special reports, directories (if appropriate), pertinent news, research links, tools, etc.

Community Services

As part of your community, you may want to provide value-added services to community members, such as a master calendar of events, selected links to other relevant Web pages, and an e-mail newsletter.

Interactive Areas

A key part of what makes a community a community is interactivity. The easiest way to offer interactivity is probably through the creation of a bulletin board. Beyond bulletin boards, interactivity can move from e-mail messaging to discussion forums to live chat rooms. It is recommended that you include at least one form of interactive technology, because this is a primary characteristic of a community. It is also a good idea to include an interactive feedback mechanism, even if it is a simple Web response form, to encourage community members to offer their comments and suggestions.

Conducting Business, or Using e-Commerce

You will need to incorporate some combination of database and e-commerce technology into your community if you want to conduct business. In this case, you should thoroughly review the chapters on "Internet Customer Service" and "Selling on the Internet."

Involving Partners

Some partners may want to participate in co-founding your community, while others may want to be sponsors. Others may see the community as a way to increase their own exposure and sales opportunities. Partners who have a "brand name" can enhance the credibility of your community and make it all the more desirable to users. For more about partnering, see the next chapter.

4. Set Up the Back-End

As indicated above, a community is a more complex and involved Web site. Do not underestimate the back-end. Establish processes and procedures to service and respond to community members. Have a good, integrated Web database in operation. Ensure that all technologies you deploy in the community are pre-tested and functioning properly. Verify that your Web server or hosting service is adequate and that all activity can be monitored. Make sure everything is working—*before* you go live!

5. Launch and Publicize Your Community

Launching a Web community is a lot like launching a new product—and most IT marketers know what that involves. Use the same marketing tactics for launching the community as you would with launching a new product: establish a publicity campaign, try to get press coverage, hold special events, and if appropriate, advertise.

6. Maintain and Grow Your Community

Once established, your community will require ongoing care and attention. A community is an active, vibrant place. Community members will expect content to be refreshed frequently, links to be working, discussion groups to be current, and interactive systems to be responsive. Maintaining the community is an essential part of its success. And it does not stop there—you should always be looking for ways to improve and grow the community.

10

Developing Internet Partnerships

B-to-b partnering is not a new concept. Strategic alliances, channel partners, and cooperative business ventures are common practices. However, the late 1990s saw some "coopetition" that previously would have been unthinkable. Arch-rivals built pacts and formed alliances in hopes of collectively increasing revenues. IBM was at the center of two such deals in 1999, reaching agreements with Dell and EMC. Both Dell and EMC compete fiercely with IBM, the first going head-to-head in PC sales, and the second steadily increasing market share in computer storage systems, once an IBM stronghold. Yet IBM apparently saw value in co-operating with these competitors, finding a way to turn their opposition into a business opportunity.

In the chapter on business communities, we discussed the phenomenon of Internet business exchanges. Here again, rival businesses are forming alliances to pool purchasing power and resources. While it opens up the question of anti-trust violations, the short-term effect is to fuel the Internet economy. The Internet is, in part, responsible for a whole new business environment in which partnering, even with competitors, becomes incredibly attractive. With its natural alliance-building architecture, the Internet has broken down business barriers and caused partnering to flourish. The Internet has even spawned its own brand of partnering—affiliate programs. The Internet is also becoming the core of entire information networks established by partnering organizations.

In this chapter, you will see how you can take full advantage of Internet partnering.

Partnering—The Traditional Way

"Strategic alliances" and other partnering relationships are an increasingly common way of doing business. Companies with compatible products or services find that they can reduce marketing and sales costs, provide a more comprehensive solution, and potentially increase revenues faster when they work together.

Information Technology is one industry that has seen great change because of partnering. Computer hardware and software companies often develop partnerships that are intended to present strong reasons to buy two or more products together rather than separately. These companies will sometimes involve a "channel partner," such as a VAR (Value Added Reseller) or a distributor, who typically adds a service and support component to the package. In the best scenarios, the partners deliver a superior solution of high value. But if the partnerships go awry, the customer can be caught in the middle of a lot of finger pointing or, at the very least, a lack of coordination.

Nonetheless, partnering has its distinct advantages, and it has been generally successful as a way of doing business for computer companies. It seems logical, then, that the Internet would not only adopt the partnering model, but capitalize on it. In fact, a whole new Internet-based business model—the ASP, or Application Service Provider—is largely built on partnering. ASPs typically provide services via the Internet for a monthly fee. These services often utilize select software applications from partner organizations as the basis for their existence. The business model would not work without partnering.

Before we explore Internet partnering, it might be appropriate to first talk about some of the ways you can get the most out of traditional partner marketing relationships.

Cooperate But Do Not Capitulate

Cooperative marketing programs should be just that—cooperative. You and your partner should develop programs together, and you should agree on common objectives, offers, messaging, and logistics. But it is generally best for only one partner to take the lead—and usually it is the partner who is putting in the most money. If that is your company, you need to diplomatically take control of the program. While you will work in a spirit of cooperation, you will also want to be sure that your company gets what it needs out of the relationship, that you can make the final decisions, and that you will get a reasonable return on your investment.

Accentuate Your Compatibility

Get to the root of what is fundamentally special about your partner relationship—and then highlight the benefits of it. You may want to develop special packages or offers that make it very attractive to purchase your products together with your partner's products. If the partner relationship involves service and support, this too could be a unique aspect of your sale. Whenever you sell jointly, convince the prospect that your partnership makes you stronger and differentiates you from the pack.

Centralize Lead Processing

If possible, centralize the lead processing and fulfillment. If you are the lead partner, maintain management of the lead generation process. If leads go directly to partners, you immediately lose control over those leads—and your ability to track responses and analyze results is lost as well. If you must de-centralize lead generation, at least establish and agree on methods to share, distribute, contact, and follow up on leads. This activity should be just as carefully managed and coordinated as joint sales calls.

Offer Resellers Turnkey Programs— And Make It Easy to Participate

Many business-to-business direct marketers are involved in *channel marketing*—marketing products and services through VARs (Value-Added Resellers), retailers, distributors, representatives, agents, or other marketing partners who resell products. Computer hardware, software, and networking manufacturers have widely adopted this selling model to more effectively reach diverse markets, often on a worldwide basis. Insurance companies have long distributed their products and services through captive or independent agents.

Resellers are a special kind of partner. They especially like programs that support their business, but take very little effort on their part. If you want to support reseller partners, it pays to design direct marketing programs that are fast, low cost, and easy to customize for resellers. Consider doing "VAR versions" of your end user promotions, and get larger VARs to sign on up front so you can simply tag them on to your existing program. It will be easier, faster, and cheaper for everyone.

Consider adding incentive programs for the sales teams of larger resellers—so they get excited about promoting your products over someone else's. Make sure the sales teams (yours as well as your partners') are informed of any direct marketing programs that you are executing on their behalf.

Supporting Partners with Traditional Direct Marketing

Supporting partners with traditional direct marketing is a commonplace practice. Companies working as partners may co-brand advertising or direct mail promotions to take advantage of market conditions and benefit from joint marketing. Alternatively, the sponsoring company may execute a direct mail program and offer partners the opportunity of participating by printing versions of the piece with each partner's logo and call to action information.

Many Information Technology companies execute partner versioning as a routine part of a direct mail promotion. Several years ago, I was involved in a significant effort that brought together a major computer manufacturer with more than 50 software partners and resellers. The computer company was promoting a new hardware platform, and it was important to demonstrate that software vendors were building applications for and supporting the platform. The company aggressively solicited the participation of leading partners and offered to fund the majority of the promotional costs.

A core-mailing package was developed. It included elements that could easily be versioned:

- The oversize outside envelope had a glassine window that allowed the cover of a full-color brochure to show through it. The flap of the envelope carried a return address of a third party vendor so mail returns could be managed centrally.

- The letter included the computer company's logo, along with a digitized logo of the partner company. The laser-generated copy was personalized to the recipient, and individualized to promote the unique benefits of the relationship between the sponsor and the partner.

- The reply form also included the identities of both the hardware company and its software partner. Questions asked of the recipient were individualized. The recipient's name, title and address, along with list code information, were included on the reply form. An accompanying business reply envelope carried the third party vendor's address so leads were returned to a central location. A telemarketing firm manned an 800 number. Each version of the campaign was assigned a unique extension number so partners could be identified.

- A full-color brochure used photographs that were common across all partners. The brochure was designed as a template: The first panel described the computer company's technology, the second panel the software partner's solution, and the third panel the offer. Only the black printing plate varied for each partner's version.

- A common informational offer was used for the program, but this offer was enhanced with a special purchase incentive, such as free training or free additional licenses, unique to each partner. The partners were required to make incentive offers as their payment for participating in the program.

A few of the partners wanted their own unique versions of the program. One such version was quite elaborate: It proposed a combined solution from the hardware company and a leading software partner, joined by a distributor who added consulting, service, and support. The mailing package was specially designed to highlight the partnership among the three companies. It included a die-cut, multi-page square brochure in a square envelope, along with a personalized letter and reply form offering free software from the software partner, and a free technology assessment from the distributor. The hardware company paid for the entire mailing as its contribution.

The package was sent via overnight mail to CFOs at the software company's customers and top prospects. Every mailing package was followed up with a call from a telemarketing firm to assure that the executive received the package and to reinforce the campaign. Despite the considerable cost of the promotion, the revenue directly attributed to the program was nothing short of remarkable. This single mailing produced an ROI of over 50 to 1.

Many marketing lessons were learned from this campaign:

1. The computer company could extend its reach well beyond its own customer and prospect base, reaching new audiences with an interest in specific software solutions. In fact, in many cases, it was the software that pulled the sale to the computer company.

2. The computer company could penetrate new vertical markets as a result of a software company's specialized product or industry strength. This opened new business opportunities that were not previously available.

Centralizing and consolidating the direct marketing campaign achieved a number of economies and efficiencies. Rental lists could be acquired at once, so duplicates could be eliminated across all mailings in advance. Materials could be printed at once for maximum efficiency. A single source managed the program, increasing program efficiency. All leads funneled through a single point of contact, increasing the efficiency of prospect contact and lead distribution...and resulting in the ability to consolidate response management and results reporting. This made it much easier to evaluate the success of each individual mailing, as well as the overall campaign.

Partnered direct marketing programs need not be this elaborate to achieve results. I have seen partner versions of self-mailers and postcards perform very effectively. As with any direct marketing program, the keys are good list selection, a strong offer, and audience-appropriate creative.

But today, there is another weapon—the Internet. Now traditional direct marketing partner programs can be enhanced with the Internet in a variety of ways:

1. Using a partner-specific URL, you can direct leads to a special Web page that reinforces the benefits of the partnered program and captures responder information.

2. E-mail can be used to acknowledge information requests, confirm orders, and embed Web links to partner's Web sites.

3. You can keep partners informed of program activities via e-mail and post direct mail samples for partners to review on the Web.

4. You can use a partner extranet to allow partners to view and order entire programs, distribute leads, track results, and monitor performance.

We will discuss these ideas further later in this chapter, but first, let's take a look at how partnering began on the Internet.

The Starting Point for Internet Partnering: Affiliate Programs

Amazon.com has delivered on the promise of e-commerce, building one of the first successful models for selling products on the Internet. Part of that model was the creation of an *affiliate program*, known as Amazon.com Associates, which now has several hundred thousand members. Amazon.com pioneered a method of partner or shared revenue marketing that has become one of the fastest growing types of business on the Internet.

What exactly is an affiliate program? While the particulars change based on who is offering it and how it operates, the basic definition is the same: An affiliate program is essentially a revenue-sharing program that uses the Internet to facilitate partnered selling.

Forrester Research (*www.forrester.com*) and Jupiter Communications (*www.jup.com*) both suggest that by 2003, more than 20 percent of all Internet revenues will be related to affiliate marketing. Forrester itself announced in early 2000 that it would form its own affiliate network, recruiting Web sites to offer Forrester research reports and online strategies. Jupiter says that an online merchant could reduce its marketing and sales costs by 10 percent by increasing affiliate sales to 20 percent of their total.

Let us use the Amazon.com affiliate model to explain the affiliate concept. It is a simple yet ingenious idea. Anyone with a Web site (as long as it does not have questionable content) can become an Amazon.com Associate, free of charge. You just sign up, agree to the company's terms, and link to Amazon.com's site through a variety of ways. For example, you can put a "button" on your home page, or use a search box link (which allows visitors to search Amazon.com for products from within your site), or link to individual products sold by Amazon.com. In all cases, links lead your Web site visitors directly to Amazon.com—through a unique URL that tracks activity back to your participation. This way, if a visitor purchases anything from Amazon.com through your site, you get paid a commission, based on the particular product purchased. You also get the benefit of an e-commerce "store" on your site, along with the legitimacy of the Amazon.com name.

You are simply an "agent" or a reseller for Amazon.com. You need not fill the order, collect money, or deal with customer service. Amazon.com handles all that. And since the company is so good at it, your Web site visitors have a positive buying experience through your site. It is an Internet variation of the old "drop shipping" model used by mail order companies. A mail order company would offer a product it did not manufacture and make an arrangement with the manufacturer to ship the product, from its warehouse, directly to the customer. The mail order company, as the middleman, would then bill the customer and pay the manufacturer.

The affiliate concept is so uncomplicated and easy for both parties that it is possible for everybody to be a winner. There is little risk on the part of either the affiliate program sponsor or the affiliate. Setting up links is technically simple and inexpensive, and the very nature of the Web makes these links easily traceable. An affiliate can be as aggressive or passive as desired in promoting the sponsor's products. In some cases, the affiliate's primary objective may be to enhance a Web site's service component, so the added income from the program is just an added benefit. Other affiliates may be looking for a fast, easy way to get into e-commerce.

From the site visitor's perspective, an affiliate program is an added benefit. The visitor can now purchase products or services from your site. If those products and services are relevant to your site's topic area, then the visitor's experience is enhanced.

Business-to-Business Affiliate Programs

Most affiliate programs can be adapted to meet the needs of the business-to-business marketer. Suppose you are a marketer of financial services targeted to businesses. If you were part of the Amazon.com Associates program, or another Internet bookseller's program, you could select appropriate books in the financial category and sell them on your Web site. You are providing your site visitors with a service and gaining additional revenue at no cost. It really is that simple to make money with the affiliate program model.

The same principle applies to other affiliate programs, from products to services to auctions. It is all in how you apply the affiliate program to your own specialized business-to-business marketing needs.

I have taken this approach with my own company. Through the Amazon.com Associates Program, I was able to add a direct marketing bookstore to my company's Web site. It is completely flexible and uncomplicated. We choose marketing books (including my own) that are relevant to our site and write our own descriptions of the books. Each book has a special order number, which links directly to the Amazon.com site, so visitors to our site can order these books through Amazon.com. We also have a search box link, which makes it possible for visitors to buy anything Amazon.com sells through our site.

For each item ordered through our site from Amazon.com, our company gets a small commission. We are providing a valuable service to our Web site visitors and enjoying the benefits of e-commerce—at no cost to the company. The income is modest, but the service we provide is invaluable. As an Amazon.com Associate, I can check on the hits and purchase activity generated through my bookstore via Amazon's associates' Web page, plus we get a check every quarter. This is but one tiny example of how an affiliate program can work in a business-to-business setting.

Second only to Amazon.com in terms of e-commerce leadership is Dell Computer. Validating 1999 as the year the affiliate program reached star status, Dell announced its first-ever affiliate marketing program in March 1999. With 50 charter members, the Dell program relies on LinkShare (*www.linkshare.com*), the owner of the largest affiliate network, to bring its products to more than 65,000 affiliate sites. LinkShare technology tracks and monitors all Dell sales through affiliates. Soon after the launch, Dell expanded its affiliate program to Gigabuys.com,

Dell's online store for software, accessories, and peripherals. In November 1999, LinkShare announced that it would develop and manage an affiliate marketing program for Dell's Asia Pacific business as well. In early 2000, LinkShare indicated it would launch a new affiliate network, B2B LinkShare, to specifically serve the business-to-business marketplace.

Affiliate programs are not without their critics. The backlash against affiliate programs is being fueled by such companies as Iconomy (*www.iconomy.com*) and Escalate (*www.escalate.com*) who build "ready-made" Web stores for e-businesses to counter affiliate programs. These vendors are looking to keep customers on a site rather than sending them to another site through an affiliate's link. Others are looking to improve affiliate marketing by using the model to focus on b-to-b. B2BRover (*www.b2brover.com*) works with 35 business exchanges which represent specialized product categories. B2BRover puts its search box on affiliate Web sites so visitors to those sites can search for merchandise across the business exchanges.

Tips on Becoming an Affiliate

In most cases, becoming an affiliate is as uncomplicated as signing up and linking to the affiliate sponsor's site. But there are a number of key considerations:

1. Choose affiliate programs carefully.

There are thousands of affiliate programs available. Start by doing a survey of these programs to determine which fit with your site. Two of the best places to look are Associate-It (*www.associate-it.com*), which claims to be the "Web's biggest directory of Associate Programs," and Refer-It *(www.refer-it.com)*. These two sites do an excellent job of both providing general information about and providing search engines for affiliate programs. Between the two sites, you will find well over one thousand affiliate programs to review. Pick several that appeal to you and then read the terms of every affiliate program very carefully. *They are not all the same.* Each may have its own unique twist. Be sure to understand the commitment required by the sponsor, and whether or not you will have to pay anything up front to participate.

2. Verify the legitimacy of the programs you are considering.

Do not assume that an affiliate program or its sponsor is legitimate, just because you find it in a directory. If you are familiar with the name and the reputation of the company, there is probably little cause for concern. However, many affiliate program sponsors could be companies you never heard of before. This does not mean they are not legitimate, but do your homework. Make sure you are comfortable with the types of products the sponsoring company offers. Find out how long the sponsor's affiliate program has been in existence and how many affiliates are involved. Ask for references and check them out. Try to learn if there have been any complaints about the company by checking them out with local Better Business Bureaus or other such organizations operating on the Internet. It may even be worth it to go to a few of the sponsor's affiliate sites and order product through them to see how the sponsor handles your order. Determine if you can try the program for a limited period of time without obligation. This is a serious business decision. Make sure you are affiliating with a company who will not damage your own reputation.

3. Select programs that meet your Web site visitors' needs.

Narrow down your selection to a few affiliate programs which you feel best fit with your site. Typically, your affiliate program will be more successful if the sponsor's products or services are complementary to your own. As in the earlier example of selecting specific books from Amazon.com that might be of interest to a site visitor, you should think about *drawing a relationship* between the sponsor's offerings and your site. Why do visitors come to your site, and what are they looking for? If the sponsor's affiliate program helps to answer these questions and support the theme of you site or the business you are in, then it is probably a good fit.

4. Test one program.

You will probably be tempted to add several affiliate programs to your site. If you are new to affiliate marketing, however, you may want to approach it conservatively and test one program first. It is important to understand how affiliate marketing works and to see if your visitors will be receptive to it. You also need to make a commitment to the affiliate program, promoting it on your site and keeping the information relating to the program fresh.

5. Continuously evaluate the program... and add other programs selectively.

Keep a close eye on how well the affiliate program is working. Evaluate the sponsor's service and make sure your visitors are satisfied. Determine if you are getting what you anticipated out of the program. Once you are comfortable with the concept of affiliate marketing, you could consider adding other programs to your site. But do so selectively. Typically, it is not productive to add multiple affiliate programs in the same category, for example. Make a commitment to one bookseller, or one computer products vendor. Otherwise, you may be offering your visitors too many choices and that could dilute overall ordering from your site. Affiliate programs should enhance your site, not take away from its effectiveness. If you fill your site with too many affiliate programs, your visitors may perceive that you are more interested in making money than servicing their needs.

Guidelines for Creating Your Own Affiliate Program

If you are interested in creating your own affiliate program, you will have a different perspective. Here our guidelines for such an undertaking:

1. Establish an e-commerce operation first.

Although some affiliate programs share leads rather than revenue, the vast majority of affiliate programs are e-commerce programs. Do not even try to institute an affiliate program unless you already have a successful e-commerce operation or you are willing to make the investment in such an operation. If your objective is to fuel your e-commerce effort with affiliate marketing, you probably should consider a packaged solution or an affiliate marketing service provider. Here are four of the leading providers of affiliate marketing programs:

- BeFree *(www.befree.com)* BeFree, which filed an IPO in November 1999, had over 2,800,000 affiliates signed up for some 200 merchants by December 1999. BeFree merchant clients establish "virtual storefronts" on affiliate sites, targeting specific merchandise to complement both the merchant and affiliate Web sites. The BeFree solution also provides real-time market intelligence on the effectiveness of each affiliate storefront. BeFree's clients include barnesandnoble.com, Network Solutions, and Yahoo!

- **ClickTrade** *(www.clicktrade.com)* Formerly LinkExchange, ClickTrade is a Microsoft offering that is now part of the company's small business portal, Microsoft bCentral *(www.bcentral.com)*. ClickTrade encourages small businesses to sign up as merchants in its "Revenue Avenue" area, a directory of over 7,000 affiliate programs. As of December 1999, ClickTrade had over 120,000 affiliates.

- **Commission Junction** *(www.cj.com)* Commission Junction manages online relationships between more than 340 retailers and more than 70,000 content sites. In 2000, Commission Junction launched "EnContext," a process of contextual selling which allows affiliates to embed retailer images into and around their content, rather than simply placing banner ads. In February 2000, Commission Junction announced a partnership with kinzan.com *(www.kinzan.com)*, which provides e-commerce solutions for deploying and managing very large networks of Web sites. Kinzan.com and Commission Junction together will provide a "build and grow" solution for e-communities. Kinzan.com customers, who build distributed Web networks, will be able to support the online marketing efforts of their member sites through Commission Junction's affiliate marketing solution.

- **LinkShare** *(www.linkshare.com)* Mentioned previously, LinkShare says it is the worldwide leader in affiliate marketing programs, servicing more than 400 merchants, including Borders.com, Dell, OfficeMax, and Outpost.com. LinkShare launched the first affiliate marketing network in 1996, and today its software tracks and measures user traffic and transactions made within the LinkShare Network.

Each of the above service providers offer start-to-finish services in terms of setting up and managing affiliate programs. In return, they typically collect 20 to 30 percent commission. While this may seem like a lot, it would be very difficult to set up your own affiliate program and manage the high level of affiliate interaction that is necessary for success. If your affiliate program had thousands or even hundreds of affiliates, you would need a specialized system to run the program.

The affiliate model itself has some variations that you should know about. Early on, most affiliate programs focused on the merchant's needs, recognizing that affiliates were largely another sales and promotion channel for an online store's products. Now some providers are putting the emphasis on the affiliate's ability to maximize revenue from these programs.

For example, Nexchange (*www.nexchange.com*), offers a different twist on the affiliate marketing concept. Nexchange helps companies build fully-stocked online stores "without charge and without any e-commerce hassles," says the company. Basically, Nexchange sets up the store using products supplied from its own network of merchants. Each store looks like the sponsor's Web site, and Nexchange handles the back-end. In return, the sponsor gets 10 to 25 percent commission on every sale, while Nexchange collects the rest.

Other service providers are entering this market with the same or a similar approach. Affinia (*www.affinia.com*) helps affiliates build their own stores around specific subject areas or niches. Affinia then "stocks" the store with items from merchants it services. In early 2,000, Affinia claimed to have over one million products available from more than 1,000 participating merchants. Here, affiliates are paid per click, even if a sale isn't made.

2. Construct an affiliate program that benefits everyone.

As the affiliate program sponsor, your primary objectives are probably to extend your own company's awareness and reach, and increase your revenue. But you have a business obligation to construct a program that also benefits your primary customers (your affiliates) *and* your secondary customers (your affiliates' customers). Your affiliate program should be easy and uncomplicated for an affiliate to implement. While you could charge an affiliate for participating in your program, most affiliate programs are free to the affiliate, so you may be less competitive if participation in your program costs money. Structure your compensation plan fairly so the affiliate benefits from your sales success. Typically, companies offer affiliates anywhere from 5 to 15 percent of the selling price of a product or service. Some programs may offer as high as 20 to 30 percent, but these higher amounts are usually doled out as special incentives or bonuses. While many affiliate programs are based on flat commissions, there is some evidence that sliding scale commissions are being adopted by merchants with products of varying value. A sliding scale may be appropriate if you want to reward affiliates for selling higher-priced products, and it could also differentiate your affiliate program from others. Remember, affiliates are really resellers who can contribute significant incremental sales at little cost to you, so make it worth their while to participate.

3. Work out all the details.

There are numerous operational details you will need to think about. For example, you could offer an affiliate program that has branding options. You may feel strongly about maintaining your identity on the affiliate program (as does Amazon.com), or you may want to allow affiliates the flexibility to co-brand or "private label" your program. Under the private label scenario, an affiliate could basically take your program and put his name on it. You could decide to implement a graduated revenue-sharing arrangement, whereby affiliates who sell more get a higher share of revenue. You need to determine what kinds of linking you will allow to your site, provide artwork and instructions, and set up a system that tracks affiliate activity. These are the kinds of details you will need to work out in advance, and each detail will have technical implications behind it.

4. Protect yourself with a legal agreement.

One of the advantages of affiliate programs is that you can grow a network of affiliates very rapidly via the Internet. If hundreds or thousands of Web site owners become your affiliates, it is unlikely you will be able to screen each one and get to know them individually. That is why a legal agreement is absolutely essential. Before you accept affiliates, they should be required to accept the terms of your agreement. The agreement should include, among other things, a discussion of the business relationship you are establishing, your stand on ethics, terms of payment, and conditions of cancellation. You will probably want some language in the agreement that protects you and your site against fraud, unethical practices, and use of your program in association with any illegal or objectionable business activity.

5. Service your affiliates.

After your program is up and running, keep your affiliates informed via e-mail and by posting information on a special affiliates' page on your Web site. Report activity to affiliates on a regular basis and be sure to issue payments *promptly*. Ask your affiliates for feedback on how you can make your program better, and what you can do to improve service. Affiliates are not only a valuable source of revenue, they can also refer other affiliates to you, and help you keep your finger on the pulse of Internet buyers.

6. Make a long-term commitment to affiliate marketing.

After you are in the affiliate marketing business, look at it as a *business*, not just a marketing program. As a major distribution channel for your product or service, your affiliates are as important a channel as distributors, resellers, retailers, or a direct sales force. Do not underestimate the care and attention affiliates will require. You will need to consider an on-going program of affiliate acquisition and retention, just as you would with prospects and customers. You will need to "police" your network as best you can to make sure affiliates are legitimate and that they are playing by the rules. You will want to work out the details of building and maintaining relationships with your "affiliate community." Of course, you will also need to have a solid structure for standard affiliate reporting (both internal and reports to affiliates) and affiliate compensation.

Examples of Affiliate Programs

Visit the two sites mentioned earlier, Associate-It and Refer-It, for an updated listing of affiliate programs. Here are some examples of b-to-b affiliate programs:

BidFocus *(www.bidfocus.com)*

Claiming to be "the #1 bid search company on the Internet," BidFocus provides sales leads and bid opportunity searches for businesses. BidFocus searches thousands of state, city, institutional, federal, commercial and industrial procurement agencies each day and matches sales leads and bid opportunities to the participating company. BidFocus will pay you a commission for both sales generated directly through your Web site, and sales generated through additional affiliates you sign up.

BuyTELCO.com *(www.buytelco.com)*

This unique site, with over 1,000 affiliates, sells BellSouth Business products and services online—everything from Internet access and frame relay circuits to ISDN packages. BuyTELCO.com pays $20 per ISDN line purchased through an affiliate. All billing is handled by BellSouth.

ebates *(www.ebates.com)*

This twist on affiliate programs is different—ebates pays commissions to online shoppers at its new e-commerce portal. Ebates will pass along the commissions it receives from sellers to the buyers and make its money instead from advertising on the site. Buyers need to register and provide ebates with information to take advantage of the program. Ebates guarantees safe shopping through their Web site by reimbursing consumers for any credit card loss due to fraudulent use through ebates or any affiliated merchant.

Newsstand Network's enews *(www.enews.com)*

The largest magazine selling affiliate program on the Web, the Newsstand Network lets you offer the lowest prices on magazine subscriptions and make money on each sale. The service includes magazine search engines, category, special interest area racks, and round-the-clock sales reporting.

iSyndicate *(www.isyndicate.com)*

iSyndicate is "the Internet content marketplace," aiming to syndicate content and make it available to anyone who wants it...and over 17,000 affiliates think it is a good idea. This service aggregates and delivers Web site content from hundreds of sources, such as Reuters NewMedia, CNET, The Associated Press, ZDNet, and CBS Sportsline.

Through its "iSyndicate Express" service, affiliates can offer standard or customized bits of news and images on their sites free. There is no payment; the affiliate gets the free continuously refreshed news service and, in return, is promoting the content providers. The other side of the business helps content creators syndicate their material across the Web.

ITKnowledge.com *(www.itknowledge.com)*

Part of the EarthWeb network, ITKnowledge is one of the largest online technical support databases. It features paid subscriptions which give users access to technical books, source codes, and examples from leading publishers. ITKnowledge pays a $10 commission for each subscription acquired through an affiliate.

Network Solutions *(www.networksolutions.com)*

The Network Solutions affiliate program lets an affiliate offer its visitors a Web address service. Every time a visitor registers or reserves a Web address, signs up for Network Solutions' "dot com essentials," or clicks through to the "dot com directory," the affiliate earns a referral payment. For each sale, the affiliate can earn from 10 to 14 percent for up to 100 Web address registrations per month. For more than that, Network Solutions offers a Premier Partner Program.

PromiseMark *(www.promisemark.com)*

PromiseMark provides an interesting service called the "Virus Service Plan," which protects individual computer users from the increased costs and frustration associated with destructive computer virus infections. The company offers a "Virus Repair Guarantee" and has alliances with Symantec, Aon, and Virginia Surety Company. Affiliates get a commission on each plan sold.

QSpace *(www.qspace.com)*

This unusual service delivers reasonably priced credit reports in seconds over the Web through its affiliates, which include Yahoo!, Autoweb.com, and Realtor.com. Qspace.com pays 10 percent on all credit report sales generated through an affiliate.

Sundial.com *(www.sundial.com)*

A November 1999 entry into the market, Sundial.com acquired 1,000 affiliates by mid-December 1999 by retailing wireless products and services online. Sundial.com partners with such well-known providers as AT&T, Omnipoint, Cellular One, US Cellular, AllTel, GTE, and SkyTel to offer wireless plans, phones, pagers, and even satellite TV systems. Affiliates earn 10 percent commission on all wireless products and services, and $20 commission on each satellite TV system sold.

VeriSign *(www.verisign.com)*

VeriSign is a leader in security products used to authenticate sites to visitors. The VeriSign affiliate program is targeted to Internet Service Providers and Web hosting companies, allowing them to integrate digital certificates into their service offerings.

WebTrends *(www.webtrends.com)*

Known for its e-business analysis and system management solutions, WebTrends launched its affiliate program in January 1999. WebTrends was selected by *Computerworld* in December 1999 as "one of the top 100 emerging companies." WebTrends makes Security Analyzer and CommerceTrends, among other software products, to help e-businesses do a better job of traffic and site management.

Using the Internet to Support Channel Partners

While the affiliate program is the prevalent partner model on the Internet, there is another kind of partnership that the Internet can impact—channel partnering. Companies using retail or reseller channels know that these forms of product distribution make it difficult if not impossible to capture the end user customer. Customer end users are sometimes held at arm's length—unintentionally or purposely—by distributors, dealers, resellers, or retailers. Even worse, these customers become vulnerable to a company's competition because the reseller or retailer often does not have an exclusive relationship with the company and can therefore market competitive products to these customers.

As a result the originating company misses out on the opportunity to communicate first-hand with a vast customer segment. These customers are no less important to the originating company, but they are "co-customers" of the channel partner. Marketing to this specialized customer base and building relationships with them becomes a complex and difficult challenge.

Just as important, the originating company needs to build an ongoing relationship with the partner organization itself. Large, global companies in particular could have a loose network of partners all over the world, some more loyal than others. How can a large company keep all of these various types of partners informed? And how can that company truly service their needs?

The Internet may help to solve this chronic business-to-business marketing problem. The Internet can help you know whom your customers are when you rely on indirect sales channels. And the Internet makes it relatively easy for you to collaborate with resellers and other partners, sharing resources and cooperating on electronic marketing initiatives that could result in a substantial payback for a modest investment on the part of all partners. If you are the originating company, you can go a step further and enlist the assistance of partner organizations in reaching out to its extended customer family.

Reaching channel customers could be just the beginning of a deepening Internet relationship between companies and their partners. It therefore makes sense to fully explore the potential of sharing information on each other's Web sites, cross-linking, and extending electronic marketing activities.

Building an Internet-based Channel Partner Program

There is little doubt that b–to-b companies will increasingly rely on the Internet to help them maintain partner relationships and service channel partners. Of course, these business relationships are far more involved than the previously discussed affiliate programs. For the most part, the affiliate program concept relies on large numbers to succeed. The affiliate concept chains hundreds or thousands of other Web site owners together, working on the basis of exponentially increasing the sales of the originator. While the originator "touches" the affiliates occasionally, the business relationship is more distant than with traditional partners. In most cases, the originator never meets or even speaks with the affiliate; the relationship is conducted via e-mail.

Here, on the other hand, it is likely that a business partner relationship has already been established, typically with a select group of companies. The partners are far more important in their relationships with the originating company. They were in place before the Internet was even considered as a marketing channel.

For Internet "pure play" companies, the affiliate program may, in fact, represent the sole partner channel. But for traditional b-to-b marketers rapidly transitioning to Internet marketing, the affiliate program is merely a nice bonus in terms of incremental revenue. For the traditional b-to-b company, channel partners are more integral to the success of that company's entire selling model. In some cases, as with companies distributing products through distributors or master resellers, channel selling could be largely responsible for the company's profit or loss.

For these companies, then, the Internet is being used to facilitate communication and interaction between the company and the partner. In fact, this application of the Internet is probably even more significant than affiliate programs in the long run.

It is important to realize that the Internet itself will not compensate for a channel partner program that is unstable or poorly run in the first place. However, if your channel partner program is on solid ground to begin with, then using the Internet can have a major positive impact on channel partner programs.

There are several ways you can combine the traditional principles of partnering with the benefits of new media marketing.

1. "Web-ize" the Partner Relationship

Whether you are the company with partners, or the partner, you can quickly begin to make the Internet an integral part of your business relationship by collaborating on the Web. Encourage partners to either link to your site, or to pick up and incorporate entire pages of information from your site into their sites. Provide partners with information from your Web site that you have re-packaged for their use or offer to customize Web content for their sites. Give partners a graphic "button" or small banner that they can use on their sites to link to your site. If you are the originating company, offer partners a place on your site where they can post their information, perhaps in a "partner showcase" section of your Web site. Provide partners with their own unique order page to facilitate e-commerce.

2. Link Your Communications Electronically

Encourage e-mail communications between your organization's employees and your partners' employees. With major business partners, you may want to agree on using portions of each others' networks selectively to facilitate communications.

3. Promote Your Partners in a Special Area of Your Web Site

B-to-b marketers with significant partner relationships may want to promote these relationships on their corporate Web sites. The most common way to do this is by creating a special area on the Web site. This section typically describes the company's partner program (so the company can potentially acquire new partners), highlights new partner participants, features news about partners, and provides links to partners' sites.

4. Establish a Partner Service Extranet

A partner extranet is a Web site that you establish especially for the use of one or more partners. There are two possibilities: You can create a private access area of your company's Web site just for partners, or you can establish a private extranet which uses a separate URL to "hide it" from public view. In both cases, the primary objective is the same: to provide a site that services your partners. This site can be as simple or as sophisticated as you wish. You can start by using it as a central repository of all partner information—program details, agreements, promotions, and so on.

Ultimately, however, the greatest value of a partner extranet is *service*. You can use the partner extranet to offer a full range of promotional and marketing services to your partners. By establishing an order, delivery, and monitoring process up front, you will be able to offer partners a complete, one-stop resource for support.

You can also use the extranet to service the partner relationship by transferring paper-based systems to the Internet. For example, consider moving program and product ordering, lead distribution, results tracking, program monitoring, invoicing, receivables, and inventory tracking to the Internet over time. Create a self-service center where partners can resolve their own problems to cut down on telephone and face-to-face support. In other words, use the Internet to conduct business with your partners, not just as a marketing support medium.

Examples of Internet Partner Programs

Since Information Technology companies lead the market in using partners and the channel to distribute their products, they tend to have the most mature Web-based partner programs. Here are some examples.

3Com (*www.3com.com/partners/*)

This networking leader has a partner page that provides a wealth of information about its numerous partner programs and program benefits. In addition, this page acts as a gateway to various private access partner sites, including PartnerAccess, the OEM Partners Place, 3Com Connected Program, Passport, and TOTALService OnLine.

IBM (*www.teamplayersprogram.com*)

IBM, whose name has intentionally become synonymous with "e-business," has developed a partner outreach program that is an excellent example of partner service. The program, called IBM TeamPlayers (Figure 10.1) offers partners a Web site that is a one-stop online resource for customized direct marketing campaigns using mail, fax, and e-mail to reach those customers. The IBM TeamPlayers, or Business Partners, can take advantage of customized catalogs, seminar invitations, and customer follow-up, retention, loyalty, and event-driven marketing programs. All of these programs can be ordered directly through the IBM TeamPlayers Web site. IBM also acts as a primary resource or a clearing house for other resources, such as help in managing partners' databases, online updating, developing Web pages, and executing telemarketing campaigns. IBM TeamPlayers is not just a program that helps IBM Business Partners do a better job of marketing. It was clearly established to ensure that IBM could identify and reach end users through

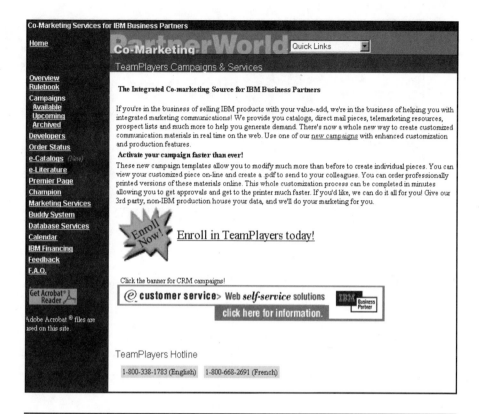

Figure 10.1. IBM's TeamPlayers Web site allows partners to order just about any support program online.

partners, and help ensure customer loyalty to both IBM Business Partners and to IBM itself. The IBM TeamPlayers Web site is itself a superb example of a company servicing another customer base— its own channel partners.

Intel *(channel.intel.com)*

Intel, the ubiquitous maker of the Pentium processor, has an entire sub-site off its corporate site just for the channel (Figure 10.2). The content page shows its depth, from a new visitor's center to general resources, including product and technical information, training, sales tools, glo-

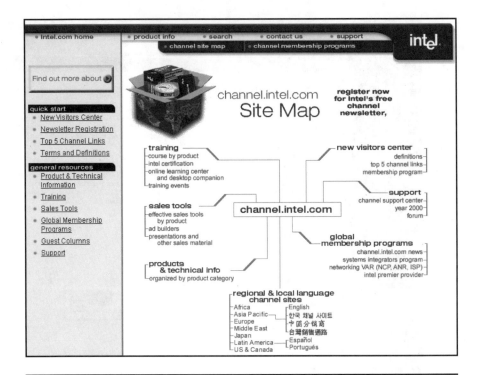

Figure 10.2. Intel's Web site for the channel is rich with partner tools.

bal membership programs, and more. In April 2000, Intel enhanced its partner program by introducing the Intel e-Business Network, a centralized mechanism for serving partners with certification, training, and business support. As part of the e-Business Network, Intel introduced a Business Market Place, where channel partners could locate and link up with one another, combining their strengths to offer customers more comprehensive, total solutions.

Novell *(partnerweb.novell.com)*

Networking software company Novell's "PartnerWeb" is a comprehensive area that services the company's partners in Europe, the Middle East, and Africa. In addition to standard links, the site allows partners to find information based on their functional areas: marketing, business manager, sales person, and technical person.

Oracle *(www.oracle.com/partners/)*

Oracle, the world's leading database company, has quickly capitalized on the Internet by orienting its entire site towards "iSolutions." The company says that its Oracle8i product is "the world's only database for Internet computing," extending its technology leadership in transaction processing data warehousing, content management and high availability to Internet usage. Oracle has a large network of partners which includes hardware vendors, independent software vendors, and systems integrators who deliver applications and services based on Oracle's database. Oracle makes heavy usage of the Internet in servicing these partners. In addition, the company provides a solutions finder (*solutions.oracle.com*) that allows users to search on a combination of any word, company name, product name, industry, geography, business function, and operating system to locate the appropriate solution, and partner.

Partnering, Internet Style: What the Future Holds

In March 1999, Amazon.com and Dell "affiliated" in an unusual Internet business relationship that could be a forerunner of future Internet partnering. Each company agreed to link their sites to the other at the point of purchase pages. In effect, the companies are "advertising each others' products at their on-line checkouts," reports Reuters. Dell customers are being given the option of purchasing a book from Amazon.com, and Amazon.com offers its customers Dell PCs on the way out of their electronic store. As these two online giants share customers, the results of their efforts could lead the entire e-commerce world into collaborative ventures.

The business reason for this partnership is simple—each company is gaining access to the other's customer base. In so doing, both companies share the potential to rapidly expand their businesses and attract new Internet buyers. The key word is "Internet" because, as Amazon.com and Dell realize, the old direct marketing adage applies even to electronic audiences: Buyers tend to repeat their purchases *using the buying channel with which they are most comfortable.* Since Internet buying is a relatively new and growing phenomenon, reaching a large base of new potential *Internet buyers* at a reasonable cost, in association with another premier Internet brand, is like striking a vein of gold in cyberspace.

Dell was involved in another partnership formed in October 1999 with the goal of helping a chemical company move aggressively into e-business. Eastman Chemical has begun a partnership with Dell to offer its customers an opportunity to purchase discounted Dell computers. Eastman at the same time announced a partnership with UUNET (*www.uu.net*), the leading business Internet Service Provider. Eastman customers can sign up for UUNET's Internet service through Eastman and get a credit on their purchase.

America Online (*www.aol.com*) aggressively pursues Internet partnerships as a way of growing and solidifying its subscriber base. In May 2000, America Online announced a five-year deal with Office Depot (*www.officedepot.com*) to build a co-branded Web site targeting small business. The Web site would provide small business customers with online office solutions as well as business-related content. America Online, who owns Netscape, put the new Web site into Netscape's Netcenter Business section and will feature Office Depot's name-brand office supplies in its shopping areas. In return, America Online will gain visibility for its brand in Office Depot retail locations around the U.S. and in all other company sales channels. America Online will also be Office Depot's preferred ISP. Office Depot customers will be able to sign up for AOL service in Office Depot's stores and on its Web site.

How Grainger Makes Internet Partnering Work

W. W. Grainger (*www.grainger.com*) is a classic story of a traditional, industrial b-to-b company that not only re-invented itself as an Internet leader, but also leveraged the Internet to build a massive partnered Web presence. Grainger is a $4.5 billion b-to-b distributor who offers an online catalog with over 200,000 items to more than a million commercial, industrial, institutional, and contractor customers worldwide.

Grainger's success with e-commerce is a model for other industrial companies. The company's online sales in third quarter 1999 were eight times their sales in third quarter 1998. Sales for 1999 generated via the Internet reached $160 million. Grainger's site makes it easy to review its catalog of industrial products and offers a Resource Center with advice about preparing a business for emergency situations, an area on safety awareness, and a chat room where visitors can join conversations with guests, management and operations experts, and celebrities. While Grainger's own site is impressive enough, the company extended its Web presence in 1999 by launching a partnered site called OrderZone (*www.orderzone.com*). OrderZone targeted small and medium-sized industrial companies with a Web site that brought together five industrial partners in addition to Grainger to sell more than 400,000 items, from office supplies to cleaning products to laboratory safety equipment. The real "magic" of OrderZone, however, is that Grainger and its partners recognize the power of a single source approach. OrderZone features consolidated buying across the six companies' product lines. That means a customer can enter the site and purchase products from any of the six companies with a single point of registration, a single purchase order, and a single invoice. The partners have even pooled resources to create a single customer service path for OrderZone.

OrderZone further evolved in June 2000 when Grainger announced it would merge OrderZone with the small business purchasing site, Works.com (*www.works.com*). Grainger took a 40 percent stake in the newer Works.com, which offers a Web-based purchasing service to the same size companies as OrderZone, but with a less industrial focus. As *Upside* magazine pointed out in its report on the merger: "The combined companies, which will retain the Works.com name, bridges (sic) the blue—and white—collar worlds and is another example of business-to-business partnerships between Old and New Economy companies." With the financial power of Grainger behind it, Works.com could become a significant force in consolidated purchasing for the small and mid-size market...and it all started with the concept of partnering.

The b-to-b exchanges discussed in the chapter on Communities go even further. They are indicative of an Internet partnering trend that transcends business competition. Some of the largest competing car manufacturers, chemical firms, airlines, and consumer package goods companies are partnering in unexpected ways that, prior to the Internet's existence, were inconceivable. For example, in June 2000, six major airlines, some who are fierce competitors, teamed together to form Hotwire.com (*www.hotwire.com*), a Web site that would offer discount air fares to complete directly with the pioneer of "name your price" air fares, Priceline (*www.priceline.com*). These companies have clearly recognized that their collective strength and purchasing power will bring benefits compelling enough to rise above their competitive positions in their respective industries. Some business observers could legitimately classify these new relationships as cartels, and their existence will undoubtedly be scrutinized by the judicial branch of the Federal government. Yet the fact that they were even conceptualized is a testament to the Internet's power.

You can expect to see many more of these partnerships, strategic alliances, and affiliations spring up because of the Internet. It is too large a business opportunity to ignore. The business-to-business portals and communities discussed earlier could have just as easily been included in this chapter because they represent Internet partnerships in the true sense of the word.

The growth of business-to-business buying portals and communities in particular suggest that Internet partnering will continue to advance rapidly. Many of these Internet-economy business arrangements share a common goal: bringing together non-competitive suppliers of products and services with qualified buyers who come to one place to shop. Several of these sites go beyond simply consolidating the information by also centralizing the purchasing process.

This phenomenon itself has far-reaching implications for b-to-b companies who may be suppliers and buyers alike. Suppliers can participate in a consortium that spreads the Internet infrastructure costs across non-competing "partners," achieves economies of scale by offering more and more products at little or no increase in promotional costs, and reaches a wider audience of prospective buyers than could be reached independently. Buyers gain the tremendous convenience of a single point of contact for locating and evaluating products, issuing purchase orders, procuring items, receiving invoices, making payments, and tracking orders. It is likely that, with the proliferation of such consolidated buying sites, suppliers can ultimately reduce their costs and buyers can get better deals. In theory, at least, everyone wins.

As a b-to-b marketer on the Internet, you have a whole new opportunity to extend the reach of your company through this type of Internet partnering. It might be as simple as linking your Web site to other partner sellers, or as serious as participating in a sellers' consortium. Whatever form of business venture you pursue, partnering could mean a new source of profits.

This is not the only form of partnering that will exist as the Internet economy matures. Licensing brands and information is a rapidly growing business on the Internet. Co-branding and sponsorships are spreading. These are opportunities that should be explored.

Chances are that, if you are not already, you will also be partnering with your customers in a very real sense. As numerous books on the Internet's future point out, customers will drive companies to build entire marketing and business strategies around them. Models for the most successful companies doing business on the Internet are already built and, not surprisingly, they are all customer-driven. These new age companies treat their customers as if they are strategic partners, encouraging them to play an integral part in molding the company's business.

Finally, as business and consumer prospective customers realize that they will have no choice but to navigate the waters of the Internet, they will turn to a new kind of partner—the "infomediary." As described by Hagel and Singer in their book, *Net Worth*, the infomediary, or information intermediary "...will become the catalyst for people to begin demanding value in exchange for data about themselves....By connecting information supply with information demand, and by helping both parties determine the value of that information, infomediaries will build a new kind of information supply chain."[1]

Hagel and Singer's infomediary of the Internet future could be the portal, community, or information network of today. Wherever the infomediary comes from, business-to-business Internet marketers will need to factor this new partner into the mix.

An infomediary that b-to-b marketers should keep an eye on is Respond.com (*www.respond.com*), launched in June 1999. This Internet matching service, the first of its kind, puts prospective buyers in touch with sellers anonymously. The twist is that Respond.com lists product categories connected to forms that the prospect completes and sends. The prospect indicates interest in a particular product. Respond.com *removes the personal information about the prospect* from the form and forwards it to participating sellers via e-mail. The sellers then respond to the e-mail with information, which goes through

Respond.com back to the prospect. Already, there are other services following this model.

One way or the other, a significant success factor in b-to-b Internet marketing is likely to be based on choosing the right partners. It is a strategy that should not be under-estimated.

Note

1. John Hagel III and Marc Singer, *Net Worth*, McKinsey & Company, Inc., 1999, Harvard Business School Press, Boston, MA.

11

Selling on the Internet

Selling on the Internet is, of course, the holy grail of Internet marketing. That is why it is the last, but certainly not the least, of the Internet marketing strategies discussed in this book. For b-to-b marketers, e-commerce is the culmination of every online marketing effort, the ultimate goal of every marketing activity. While not all products and services are appropriate for selling on the Internet, almost every b-to-b Internet marketer can find a way to sell something. The year of e-commerce mass adoption was 1999. It was then that we saw the beginning of a surge in Internet-based sales that would fundamentally change forever the way consumers and businesses purchased products and services. There is little question now that e-commerce is today part of the fabric of generating orders for both b-to-b and business-to-consumer companies. This chapter looks at some of the characteristics of successful users of b-to-b e-commerce and shows you how you can follow their lead, avoid some of the pitfalls, and profit from the e-commerce gold rush.

How the Internet is Changing B-to-B Selling

Early interest in the Internet went beyond a better way to communicate or a more effective way to generate, qualify, and fulfill leads. The real power of the Internet, according to early adopter visionaries, was in its as yet untapped potential to be a major sales channel for marketers. E-commerce—generating revenue directly from electronic storefronts—was touted as the "killer application."

Initial optimistic expectations did not quite match reality. 1997 saw the growth of e-commerce, but it was slower than expected. This may be best explained by some of the early significant issues surrounding electronic commerce:

1. **Security and Privacy.** Despite the attractiveness of online buying, considerable concern about the security of Internet-based transactions existed on the part of the prospective e-buyer. With the growing success of high-profile Internet merchants who use secure servers and the increasing number of security solutions now available, this issue began to diminish in importance. No less prominent, however, was the issue of privacy—not just privacy of credit card data, but the individual purchaser's privacy. It quickly became clear that organizations were capturing and accumulating personal data on prospective customers and buyers, and that in some cases, that data was being traded or sold. This issue continues to be one that could hamper e-commerce if it is not resolved.

2. **Infrastructure Cost.** Internet marketers quickly realized that taking orders electronically required a whole different information infrastructure. Initially, e-commerce solutions were prohibitively expensive for all but the largest of companies. Many early e-commerce leaders designed their own systems from the ground up, but this was not a viable option for mass implementation. The market reacted as a number of vendors introduced lower cost e-commerce solutions beginning in 1997. Now, many off-the-shelf solutions are available, even to small business. A whole new breed of solutions began popping up in late 1999: free e-commerce stores that basically use others' Web sites to sell-through products and services. E-commerce was further fueled by the widespread popularity of auctions and, in the b-to-b space, business exchanges, discussed in an earlier chapter.

3. **Regulatory Environment.** Internet marketers were legitimately wary of regulatory controls that apply to commerce, such as

the FTC's "30-day rule," and possible tax implications of doing business electronically. It was clear, however, that online sellers were able to achieve considerable e-commerce success despite these controls. By 1998, Internet commerce was fueled even further by a Federal moratorium on taxes, although taxing online sales continues to be hotly debated by state and Federal governments alike.

Actual business conducted online, as well as numerous predictions for future e-commerce sales, support the fact that the U.S. economy will increasingly depend upon the Internet as a leading commerce channel for goods and services. E-commerce has spread to worldwide markets as the Internet's penetration continued to grow exponentially. Here are just some of the validating statistics:

- An April 2000 report by the Boston Consulting Group indicates that over $61 billion would be spent by the end of 2000 by U.S. online shoppers.

- A major study by the Center for Research in Electronic Commerce at the University of Texas Graduate School of Business, funded by Cisco Systems and released in October 1999, indicated that Internet-related businesses accounted for over $500 billion in revenues by the end of 1999. This outpaces such American industries as autos, airlines, and telecommunications. The study found that over 2 million people in the U.S. were employed in Internet-related business in the first quarter of 1999, an increase of 43 percent from the first quarter of 1998.

- In January 2000, GartnerGroup forecasted that worldwide b-to-b e-commerce would top $2 trillion by 2002, reach close to $4 trillion by 2003, and move to over $7 trillion by 2004.

- Research firm IDC believes that 80 percent of business will be conducted online by 2003, and that $2 million per minute will change hands globally via the Internet by that same year. IDC's U.S. Small Business Survey, released in April 2000, predicted that over 70 percent of small business (fewer than 100 employees) would access the Internet by 2003, up from 52 percent in 1999. IDC says that 2.9 million small businesses, nearly half of them, will be selling online by 2003, up from 850,000 at the close of 1999.

- According to Forrester Research, b-to-b e-commerce alone will grow to $220 billion by 2003. The Yankee Group puts b-to-b e-commerce at $138 billion in 1999, projecting a compounded annual growth rate of 41 percent over the next five years.

- E-commerce growth worldwide will be significant. In April 2000, Forrester forecasted that 8.6 percent of worldwide sales in general will come from e-commerce by 2004. By that year, U.S. e-commerce will reach $3.2 trillion and Asia-Pacific e-commerce would reach $1.6 trillion, with most of it coming from the b-to-b sector. Forrester predicts that Western Europe will reach $1.5 trillion in online sales by 2004, and Latin America will reach $82 billion in online sales.

- Market research firm ActivMedia reported that 25 percent of the top 100 e-commerce Web sites had revenues above $100 million each in 1998, while over half of them topped $50 million each annually. Their September 1999 study of 200 b-to-b Web sites indicated that, of those sites selling for 3 years or more, 42 percent were profitable, averaging $30 million a year in sales.

Which companies are fueling this stunning growth? It probably isn't surprising that the predominant players are IT companies. Researcher Jupiter Communications says that, by 2001, online sales of PC hardware will grow to more than $5 billion from about $3 billion in 1999. Online sales of PC software will grow to about $1.5 billion in 2001 from about $500 million in 1999.

The numbers change so quickly in e-commerce that you can barely keep up with the latest reports. *Interactive Week's* "@500" list, published in November 1999, awarded the top spot to Intel, with annual online revenue of $10.5 billion. According to Intel, the company averages $1 billion worth of online orders every month from customers in 46 countries. Cisco ($9.5 billion), IBM ($8.8 billion), Dell ($6.1 billion), and FedEx ($5.6 billion) rounded out the top five in B2B e-commerce.

E-commerce is very serious business indeed. IBM is typical of an IT company that has not only embraced the Internet, but also made it an integral part of its long-term business strategy. IBM was the subject of a

December 1999 *BusinessWeek* cover story that reported that 25 percent of its revenue–about $20 billion–is "driven by e-business demand." The story indicated that ". . . about 75 percent of IBM's e-business revenue comes from sales of Net technology, software, and services...and not the old mainframe computers for which IBM is so well known."

The company adopted the term "e-business" and launched a massive advertising campaign in 1997. The campaign, which industry sources estimated to be in excess of $200 million, deluged virtually every media channel available (including television).

IBM was not just promoting e-business for others, the company aggressively began to practice what it preached. The company started the IBM Institute for Advanced Commerce, staffing it with over 50 scientists. In late 1999, IBM Global Services launched "e-business innovation centers" in four U.S. cities, with plans to open three more in the U.S. and four in Europe by mid-2000. These physical locations give e-business customers access to IBM business strategists, marketing specialists, application developers, integration specialists, and interactive designers in one place.

In late 1999, IBM announced it would launch a new enterprise information portal to allow its customers easily access and search data across numerous sources. IBM also announced a flurry of partnerships and relationships with such sources as Stamps.com and VerticalNet to bring value-added services to customers and prospects.

The kind of b-to-b e-commerce growth we have been talking about would not occur if it weren't for b-to-b purchasers buying into e-commerce. Research firm Aberdeen Group (*www.aberdeen.com*) reported in May 2000 that a company engaging in online purchasing can save up to 90 percent in administrative costs, up to 50 percent in inventory costs, and 25 percent or more in purchasing costs. These economies are due primarily to improving the efficiency of purchasing processes and eliminating off-contract purchases.

The Amazon.com Phenomenon:
A Look at the Company that Started It All

Perhaps the best way to understand the impact of everlasting e-commerce is to look at one of the companies whose very existence was spawned by it. Amazon.com (*www.amazon.com*) is generally recognized as the Dot Com company that has dominated all others.

The Amazon.com story has been told countless times in many media, so my intention here is not to repeat all the details. Instead, we will focus on the lessons the b-to-b Internet marketer can learn from Amazon's success.

Just to put it into context, here is a quick look at the company's meteoric rise. Amazon.com boasts the following impressive statistics:

- Amazon.com went live on the Web in July 1995 and went public in 1997. The company generated over $600 million of income in 1998. In first quarter 1999, sales reached $294 million and grew to over $574 million in first quarter 2000.

- Amazon.com's customer base rose from 3 million in June 1998 to over 8 million by the end of first quarter 1999. In June 1999, Amazon.com became the first Internet store to reach 10 million customers. The company began 2000 with 16.9 million customers and added another 3.1 million new customers in first quarter 2000. The company closed 1999 with a repeat customer purchase rate of 73 percent.

- In 1998, the company's revenue was 100 percent from books. Now Amazon.com sells books, music, videos, electronics, software, toys and games, tools, lawn and patio items, and kitchenware...tens of millions of products. Non-book items represent more than half the company's revenues in fourth quarter 1999. Amazon.com made a string of e-commerce acquisitions and investments in 1999, expanding its Internet presence, influence, and product line. That same year, Amazon.com launched its own auction service. In June 1999, Amazon.com announced that it was investing $45 million to launch a separate joint auction site with Sotheby's, bringing the strength and credibility of this brand name to the Internet auction business. Amazon.com has become "the Wal-mart of e-commerce," now owning interests in e-commerce properties that sell everything from drugs and vitamins to pet supplies. In July 1999, Amazon.com expanded its own product line once more to toys and electronics.

- The company pioneered affiliate programs (see Chapter 10) with the introduction of its Associates program in July 1996. It was the first, largest, most widely adopted, and most copied program of its kind. By Q1 2000, the program had more than 450,000 member Web sites selling Amazon.com merchandise.

As a book-lover, I was hooked from my first visit to the Amazon.com site. Amazon.com's concept seemed to be deceptively simple: positioning itself as "Earth's Biggest Bookstore," this virtual resource claimed to offer millions of book titles in every imaginable subject area. I was skeptical—how could anyone, anywhere, fulfill that promise?

I soon learned it was true. I could search for any book with amazing results using the site's fast, accurate search engine. I could browse the "shelves" or order products with equal ease, and contrary to the site's name, it was no jungle of confusing or overwhelming technical stuff. It was a lot like a bookstore—but better in some key aspects.

Let me advance the timeline to 1998 to continue my description, because at that time Amazon.com's Web site had undergone a significant facelift that made it even more user friendly and customer oriented. That is when I could begin to search for books seven different ways. The most intriguing way was "instant recommendations," today a cornerstone of Amazon.com's differentiation. Each time I returned to the site, Amazon.com greeted me personally by name, with a message such as this one:

> *Hello, Barry Silverstein. Based on the items you've bought at Amazon.com, we think you'll like these. This list changes daily, so check back often.*

The underlying technology of this handy little feature is remarkable. Amazon.com uses a database engine to maintain a record of my purchases along with its millions of other customers. With astonishing speed, that database triggers a totally personalized list of recommendations. To answer your next question, yes—I look at those books first and in some cases I purchase directly from this list.

When I click on the title of a book, Amazon.com quickly provides a page with a picture of its cover, all pertinent specifications, and a solid description. In many cases, the listing includes the book's complete table of contents and numerous reviews. It is also not uncommon to find reviews by readers and sometimes commentary by authors. Virtually all of my book purchases have been at a discount, some at up to 40 percent off. That more than covers the shipping charges.

Not one to stand still, Amazon.com further refined its purchasing and customer service capabilities in 2000, adding a "New for You" service that builds a personalized profile of a customer's purchase categories and e-mails recommendations regularly.

Customer Service That Sets Amazon.com Apart

A large part of what distinguishes Amazon.com is its customer service. Amazon.com goes beyond basic Internet commerce, still ahead of most in the area of superb personalized customer service. The company encourages me to select key categories of my own choosing. Then their "eyes" keep me informed of all new releases in those categories with regular e-mail notices and even reviews via e-mail of select titles.

Placing an order at Amazon.com is as enjoyable as the browsing process. You add books to your "shopping cart" with a simple click. When you are ready to check out, you review your shopping cart and make changes.

If you have previously placed an order, Amazon.com keeps a record of every pertinent piece of data so that your subsequent orders are even easier and faster. Your name, address, and all the credit cards you may have used are there on the secure server. A list of names and addresses of people to whom you have sent gifts is there. You can choose the gift wrapping of your choice and write a personal message to the recipient of your gift.

The company offers an even faster way to order, pioneering an expedited order process it calls "one-click ordering." You can standardize much of your personal information so that you can execute "one-click" ordering, eliminating the need to reenter recurring data. Not surprisingly, this too has been copied by other online retailers.

After you complete your order, you see it on the screen—the books, the shipping address, and the total amount, along with the shipping charge. A final click and the order is transmitted.

Usually, before I even leave the site, Amazon.com has already sent me a confirming e-mail, acknowledging my order and telling me when it will ship. Then, when the order does ship, another e-mail is sent confirming its shipment. Amazon.com provides instructions for tracking your shipment through UPS if you wish. The company keeps a record of your past orders, which you can review at any time. You also "control" your customer record by making changes to it at any time. It is not difficult to figure out why I quickly became a happy and enthusiastic Amazon.com customer. Actually, a fanatic might be a better word for it.

Amazon.com is not just a superb example of e-commerce, it is also deservedly legendary for its customer service. I have been asked for my opinion on Amazon.com improvements through e-mail surveys. I have on occasion received complimentary shipping upgrades. During one Christmas holiday season, Amazon.com invited me to take advantage of an additional discount, just because I was a good customer. I have received free unexpected gifts from Amazon.com to thank me for my continuing business.

The principles behind Amazon.com are the founding principles of any company whose goal it is to acquire and grow customers. Amazon.com seized the electronic commerce and relationship-building opportunity of the Internet early and held on. Yes, you could probably find faults with Amazon.com, not the least of which is the fact that to date, they still have not turned a profit. Nonetheless, Amazon.com has expanded so rapidly that it today owns the most coveted title in cyberspace of undisputed e-commerce leader. It is no wonder that Amazon.com has become on icon of e-commerce.

Applying the Amazon.com E-commerce Model to B-to-B E-commerce

One of the obvious realizations about Amazon.com's success at taking orders and keeping customers is that its greatest strength is in database-driven marketing. Amazon.com knows its customers, but more important, it recognizes its customers and develops ongoing business relationships with them. Amazon.com also has the ability to straddle the business-to-consumer and b-to-b markets. For example, I purchase books from the company both as a consumer and a business executive, using different credit cards and different shipping addresses.

But what does Amazon.com have to do with you if your products are targeted exclusively to the b-to-b market? I hope the personal experiences with Amazon.com that I shared with you reveals areas of commonality that you can easily apply to your own implementation of electronic commerce. Here are the primary attributes connected with Amazon.com's success:

- **Fast Access to Product Information.** Despite its large number of products, Amazon.com "slices and dices" the information on those products so that it is easy to find. You can sort the information by seven different criteria. If you do not have time to search for books yourself, Amazon.com will do it for you—with personalized "instant recommendations" at the site and by alerting you to new books in your key categories via e-mail. Regardless of the products you market and to whom, easy access to product information should be a prerequisite for an e-commerce site. Imagine this as a gigantic electronic interactive catalog and you will be able to relate the concept to any product line.

- **Ease and Security of Ordering.** Ordering products through the Internet competes with every other order generation channel, so e-commerce marketers must be especially sensitive to ease of use and security. Amazon.com uses the standard "shopping cart" concept—you add books to an electronic holding area until you are done, changing your order at any time up until purchase. Amazon.com enhances the ordering process by maintaining a full purchase history and record of all pertinent customer data so that you can refer to it as you order. In addition, Amazon.com offers faster ordering with its one-click service.

  In terms of security, Amazon.com uses a secure server and explains to customers why this is safe, but a customer has the option of placing an order online and calling in a credit card number if desired. Security is further enhanced because Amazon.com acknowledges orders immediately to the separate e-mailbox of the customer. This simple technique closes the loop on the order by verifying that the order was actually placed by the customer at that e-mailbox and provides a level of customer service that goes beyond just acknowledging the order at the Web site.

- **Personal and Attentive Customer Service.** Amazon.com turns customer service into an art form. Considering that the company is dealing with a multi-million record customer database, the customer service component of the business is exceptionally personal and attentive. Personalized instant recommendations, a "new for you" feature, and the ability to modify your own customer record on site, plus order acknowledgment, notification of book shipments, notification of new books of interest, book reviews, customer surveys, and Associates program reports—all executed via e-mail—are evidence of Amazon.com's exceptional service. These small, simple things in combination, enabled by Internet-based technology, are truly impressive.

• **Marketing Beyond the Site.** Amazon.com does not limit itself to its own Web site, it extends its reach outward to the rest of the Web with syndicate selling, or affiliate marketing, which has now been widely adopted as a key e-commerce growth strategy. Amazon.com keeps the requirements simple and the stakes low, making it easy for Associates to build their own electronic book-stores and become feeders for Amazon.com. In addition, Amazon.com has struck deals to become the exclusive bookseller on major search engines and other top sites, maintaining its high profile and adding to its multi-point distribution channel on the Internet. With its expansion into other product areas, Amazon.com has gone beyond its bookseller base, using the same successful e-commerce business model to sell other products.

Think carefully about how to apply all of these concepts directly to your own effective implementation of Internet-enhanced order generation.

How E-Commerce Works with Your Selling Model

Before you launch a serious e-commerce effort, consider how you sell now and how the Internet might affect your selling model. Next, we will examine the impact of electronic commerce on several common b-to-b selling models.

The Retail or Mail Order Model

Amazon.com is, at its roots, a retailer. The retail model is basically one in which the customer makes a direct purchase from a location—a store. The store sells its goods to a customer, who must physically come in to make the purchase. If the store has the item in stock, the customer can purchase it immediately; otherwise, the item needs to be ordered and the customer needs to return to get it, or to have it delivered when available.

The mail order model is a variation on the retail store model. It simply uses a different distribution channel to complete the transaction. Here, the customer does not physically come to a place to purchase but rather orders an item via phone, mail, fax, e-mail, or the Web. Representative of mail order, probably more than anything else, is the catalog. It is no accident that many retailers have mail order catalogs and many mail order companies have opened retail stores. Why? Because the products are the same, only the distribution channel is different—so the basic underlying business process can be retained and applied to both selling models.

In many respects, Amazon.com is both a store and a catalog. It is an electronic storefront with millions of items, which are classified and cross-referenced so that each product can be individually purchased by any number of criteria. Every product has its own description, its own order number (in this case, the standard ISBN by which books are identified), and its own price.

The Internet difference is that you can "visit" the catalog. You do not actually drive there, open physical doors, walk down the aisles, pick up physical books and leaf through them, or review products, pay at the cash register, and leave with your purchase. You can say it differs from a traditional book or retail store in that there is a loss of personal contact, the tactile and intellectual bookstore browsing experience, and the immediacy of getting your merchandise on the spot, but consider the other benefits of the electronic book or retail store. You do not have to get in your car, drive there, and park. You can find what you want without a salesperson. You can browse limitless "shelves" and visit whenever you want (even in your pajamas). You can find every book or item imaginable, and never wait in line to make a purchase.

Other major retailers (those with stores and mail order catalogs alike) have followed the lead of Amazon.com by opening storefronts on the Web. If you sell a large number of products through stores or other direct-to-the-end-user locations, or through catalogs and mail order, you can quickly see how to apply this retail or mail order model to your own brand of Internet-based order generation.

It is not surprising that on the b-to-b side, the first electronic merchants to succeed with Web stores were technology-based catalogers—sellers of multiple computer software, hardware, and networking products and services. Software merchants have even been able to fulfill the promise of instant product delivery by allowing customers to unlock and download live products upon purchase, but the marketplace has quickly extended far beyond that niche, and now virtually everything is, or will be, available for sale on the Internet.

A variant of the retail model on the Internet is the *virtual mall*. As with a traditional mall, a virtual mall is a collection of storefronts. Most malls are established primarily to sell to consumers, but an increasing number of malls feature business-oriented categories.

If you are considering participation in a virtual mall, be prepared to ask the mall manager a lot of detailed questions:

- How much *business* traffic does the mall generate?

- How many b-to-b advertisers are in the mall?

- Which categories are available, and do they appeal to business buyers?

- How is the mall promoted?

- How does the mall assist advertisers with Internet commerce in terms of technical support, activity tracking and reporting, and secure electronic commerce transactions?

- What costs are associated with being a mall participant?

Yet another Internet-based retail model is the auction. Auction sites are springing up on the Web to facilitate bidding on new and used products, services, and more. There are variations to auctions such as price comparison sites and "name your lowest bid" sites. In fact, auctions and these related sites are one of the hottest growth areas on the Internet.

While auctions are clearly designed to generate revenue for the sponsoring sites, there is a key characteristic they share that differentiates them from other e-commerce applications: many auctions are also Internet-based *communities*. That is because the auction encourages ongoing interaction between buyer and seller, and often between seller and seller, via bulletin boards, newsletters, and community activities. In b-to-b, the latest and perhaps most promising variant on the retail model is the b-to-b exchange. Part electronic catalog, part reseller (see below), the exchange offers b-to-b companies the huge opportunity to partner with others and achieve massive economies of scale in both selling and purchasing.

The Reseller Model

Many b-to-b marketers rely heavily on distributors, resellers, or partners to generate revenue. This is very common in the high-technology sector, and it is becoming an increasingly common model for numerous non-technical product, and service categories—especially in a global economy where selling products might be more efficiently done through indirect channels.

Depending on the type of product or service you offer and the industry you are in, the reseller channel may enhance or even dramatically change the item you sell. In the computer industry, for example, a computer manufacturer's business systems are often bundled with a distributor's, reseller's, or partner's own products or services to create a total package or solution sale. The reseller "adds value" to the sale (hence the term "Value-Added Reseller," or VAR). The reseller channel may just as easily become an extension of the company's direct sales force (which, if it is not handled properly, can create channel conflict situations—harmful to prospects and customers alike).

How do you apply the reseller model to Internet-based order generation? Part of the answer depends on the type of relationship you have with your resellers and how they sell and deliver your products or services to the end user. Consider the concept of populating your resellers' Web sites with information you supply if resellers will allow it. Also consider the possibility of funding e-commerce initiatives with the goal of obtaining "site prominence" on resellers' sites for your products.

If appropriate, you could use the Amazon.com Associates model to offer resellers the ability to generate revenue by becoming an electronic conduit to your order generation system. Amazon.com's Associates program simply passes through the orders from an Associate's site via a link to the company's central order processing. The link identifies the Associate with a code and the book ordered, connecting the two so that the Associate can be credited for the sale.

You could provide each reseller "associate" with a unique order page on the Web, reflecting the special arrangement you have with that reseller. This can be done by setting up a basic Web page, modifying it for each reseller, and then linking the appropriate page through each reseller's site. Alternatively, you could authorize your resellers to use special pricing and part numbers in their sites so that the orders automatically pass through to your Web site and order fulfillment system.

Another possibility is to explore partnership opportunities that link your organization together with key resellers. Joint e-mail campaigns, combination banner ads, cooperative lead and order generation Web sites, and Web communities or "supersites" benefiting several noncompetitive organizations are just a few of the possibilities.

The Direct Selling Model

If your company relies on your own telemarketers and/or a direct sales force to sell products, you are accustomed to the ongoing need to feed them qualified leads. In previous chapters, we discussed how the Internet can be used to generate and qualify leads, attract qualified prospects through Internet events, and instantly provide information to prospects and customers through electronic fulfillment.

Although the direct selling model is likely to survive, it is undergoing dramatic change as businesses feel the pressure to cut selling expenses and improve sales efficiency. Direct selling will always have its place in consultative and complex selling situations. It is difficult to replace a live sales call when it comes to selling highly technical or high-end products and services. Yet the Internet holds real promise as a tool for enhancing the sales process and for continuing the sales cycle in the absence of the salesperson.

Internet telephony offers one intriguing way to take advantage of direct selling. Technologies that integrate telephony with the Web make it possible for telesales representatives to intercede during a prospect's Web session and assist the prospect by answering questions immediately. The technology is still in its early stage, but more and more sites are incorporating "call me" buttons and other forms of Internet telephony. As a result, it may not be long before online ordering is enhanced with live voice support.

The Internet-enhanced direct selling model can also facilitate the traditional sales call. A salesperson could walk into a prospect's office and make a sales presentation that was absolutely guaranteed to be consistently the same, anywhere in the world, regardless of that salesperson's personal knowledge base. That could happen by adapting a Web-based presentation, such as an online seminar, for the specific selling situation.

After an online seminar is created, it can be captured and modified for any salesperson to use. Loaded onto a notebook computer and called up locally through a Web browser, the seminar becomes an interactive sales presentation. The salesperson has instant access to it, without the need for an Internet connection. The salesperson can lead a prospect through a personalized one-to-one presentation, and the company has the assurance that the selling message is uniform and consistent. By connecting the notebook computer to a projection device, the salesperson can make the interactive presentation to many individuals at a single prospect or customer location.

Similarly, while in a prospect's office, the salesperson could access the company Web site or a private intranet or extranet to inform and educate the prospect and facilitate the sales process. If the prospect is ready to buy, contracts and product ordering information could be available to the salesperson over the Web. The salesperson could even place an order and receive an instant electronic acknowledgment from his company—all while the salesperson is sitting right in the prospect's office.

Regardless of the selling model, Internet-enhanced order generation can have a dramatic beneficial impact on your sales process. You can either augment the way you sell products and services with the Internet, or transition to the Internet and eventually replace your existing selling model with an Internet selling model.

The way you approach it is up to you, but whatever you decide, generating orders through the Internet is already offering significant business benefits and productivity gains to b-to-b direct marketers. They are achieving increased reach into new markets, better support of customers, accelerated speed of order-taking and order fulfillment, and reduced selling costs.

A New Twist to E-commerce: The Shopping Bot

Enabled by powerful search-and-compare engines, the shopping "bot" brings a twist to e-commerce that has far-reaching implications for b-to-b and all e-sellers. The shopping bot is an agent that basically searches the Web for products you want and then can not only bring back the results, but compare features and prices for you. As these bots continue to improve in quality and increase in popularity, they could ultimately change the very nature of e-commerce, putting the buyer in total control of the transaction.

These are a few examples of bots:

www.mysimon.com

mySimon was selected by *Time Digital* as the best bot on the Web. mySimon was ranked by Nielsen NetRatings as the leading shopping bot during the 1999 holiday season. Over 70 percent of all mySimon shoppers went through to merchants listed by the shopping service. By the end of 1999, mySimon could analyze specifications and prices of products from over 2000 online merchants. You can compare prices by using model numbers or product names and, even better, you can get helpful "tutorials" on a product category, pick the features you want, and then compare available products and their prices, side-by-side. mySimon will even scour some online auctions as part of its service. In January 2000, C|Net announced it would acquire mySimon in a $700 million stock deal.

www.rusure.com

R U Sure, released in a beta version in December 1999, is a "shopping agent" that actually resides on your Windows desktop. On the downside, you have to download it and you may consider it intrusive. On the upside, if you are a serious e-shopper, you might like having a permanently available comparison shopping tool right there, all the time, which "turns on" when you visit a supported site.

www.dash.com

Dash is about cash. The approach of this shopping bot is the give you cash back, up to 25 percent, every time you shop online, along with special coupons and savings opportunities. Dash uses a "dashBar" which sits at the bottom of your Web browser and combines the typical comparison shopping with "coupon alerts," local weather and news, Web search, and other handy features.

www.respond.com

Respond.com is not so much a shopping bot as a new breed of shopping service. Started in July 1999, by January 2000, Respond.com had 45,000 participating merchants, each of whom pay varying fees for leads. The novel twist here is that a prospective buyer tells Respond.com what he or she is looking for and at what price. Respond.com acts as the middleman, e-mailing the appropriate merchants with the request. The prospective buyer then receives offers from those merchants who want the business, kind of like a reverse auction. Respond.com already has relationships with America Online and Excite.

How to Get an E-commerce Order Generation System Up and Running

The bottom line for b-to-b marketers who want to sell over the Internet is that, one way or the other, they will need to have an e-commerce order generation system available to them. While many b-to-b companies may choose to outsource the entire system, or use someone else's system (such as a virtual mall, an exchange, or a service that creates an online store), others may wish to make a long-term commitment to e-commerce by establishing their own system. To address this need, look at it from two different perspectives—modifying your existing order generation system versus creating a new order generation system.

Transitioning from an Existing Order Generation System

Transitioning to the Internet from an existing order generation system is no less challenging than building a system from scratch. You should conduct an audit of the existing system's order information and processing capabilities, as well as its technical infrastructure, to determine exactly what needs to be modified or added.

Of course, any order generation system, traditional or Internet based, should be comprehensive from the start. You will need a closed loop system that offers you the ability to:

- Easily enter and maintain prospect and customer data,

- Manage merchandise planning and product inventory,

- Pick and process orders quickly and efficiently,

- Provide responsive customer service,

- Monitor order shipments,

- Handle returns, and

- Invoice and reconcile payments and credits.

It is important that the basic system be grounded in a solid database that retains both customer data and a history of customer transactions. You should be able to use this information to continuously update customer records and segment customers by key product and Recency-Frequency-Monetary (RFM) criteria: which products are purchased when, how often, and for how much money.

The underlying technology is not insignificant. You will need to evaluate existing database software and systems to be sure that they can be Internet enabled. You may need to overlay new software tools onto parts of your system and replace other parts with new software. Equally important are the software and hardware servers and networking systems you will need to handle the anticipated e-commerce activity.

Although most b-to-b direct marketers conceptually understand that generating orders through the Internet is essentially the same body in electronic clothing, there are aspects of e-commerce that are decidedly different. Making a commitment to e-commerce will require a marketer to focus on these major areas at a minimum:

1. **The "Store" or Electronic Catalog.** The storefront or electronic catalog is the place you establish to let the visitor browse, learn about products and, potentially, purchase them. The most common customer purchase model is a store with products that can be put into a "shopping cart." A visitor adds or deletes products to his or her shopping cart—typically an electronic inventory list of product names, numbers, and prices. When the visitor is finished shopping, he or she checks out—the point at which payment is authorized and the order is placed.

2. **The System Behind the Store.** Behind the store is the electronic infrastructure the marketer needs to have in place to run the store. This is the system that processes the order, verifies the credit card payment, picks the items for order fulfillment, trig-

gers the shipping order, tracks the order, and updates the customer record. This system is also responsible for, or tied into, an inventory management system so that products can be replenished as necessary.

3. **The Customer Service Component Integrated with the Store.** A customer service component that creates a sense of confidence and responsiveness is important to e-commerce success. There is a need for almost instantaneous response, because the Internet compresses everything into real time. Customers who order through the Internet will demand feedback at once. From their perspective, they are enabling the order process and facilitating product delivery by being on the Net in the first place.

More than anything else, successful e-commerce marketers convey the perception that they are truly on top of customer service. Organizations such as Federal Express (*www.fedex.com*) and UPS (*www.ups.com*) have gone beyond the boundaries of simple Internet order generation—they allow their customers to play a role in the order generation and fulfillment process, and in many respects, it is the customers who actually drive the process. Try it for yourself: You can write your own shipping orders and track your own packages over the Internet.

Both FedEx and UPS are Internet innovators in their own right. FedEx pioneered online tracking and brought that capability to the Internet early on. Not to be outdone, UPS in April 1999 introduced UPS OnLine Tools, which e-commerce vendors can incorporate into Web sites so customers can calculate shipping costs, select and compare services, and track packages from order through delivery. In February 2000, UPS went a step further, forming an e-commerce subsidiary called eVentures that will perform back-end fulfillment functions for e-businesses. The Internet shipping business was further enhanced with the introduction of iShip.com (*www.iship.com*), a service that offers online buyers and sellers a one-stop package shipping and tracking solution. Online merchants can use iShip to ship packages cost-effectively and manage shipments. Online buyers can choose carriers and track deliveries through iShip.

In the same arena, the Internet will not only change the way we ship, but also the way we buy postage. E-Stamp (*www.estamp.com*) became the first online postage solution to be approved by the U.S. Postal Service for testing. As of early 1999, E-Stamp was beta testing online postage, which is ordered through the company and, upon payment, is downloaded via the Internet. E-Stamp verifies the mailing address and prints a "SmartStamp" with the correct postage, deducting the postage from an electronic account. The SmartStamps can be printed directly onto envelopes through standard word processing or business applications, or onto labels for usage on oversized mail. In August 1999, Stamps.com (*www.stamps.com*) joined E-stamp as the two companies authorized by the Postal Service to officially sell online postage.

What distinguishes outstanding Internet b-to-b direct marketers is their ability to personalize the business transaction. Behind the friendliness of Amazon.com is a marketing database strategy that clearly puts the customer first. Information must be available on a real-time basis so that pages, such as the personalized "instant recommendations" area, can be updated on the fly. Amazon.com and other sites use something called "collaborative filtering" to accomplish this. And it appears that collaborative filtering is, in part, responsible for turning e-browsers into e-buyers. In October 1999, research from Nielsen's NetRatings suggested that online merchants with personalized sites were converting browsers to buyers at a significantly higher rate, sometimes more than double than those with non-personalized sites.

In fact, as database marketing becomes a driving force on the Internet, e-commerce is likely to become a whole new ball game:

> *Instituting database marketing on the Web will be like making the leap from playing checkers to playing multi-level niches....The high level of segmentation granularity that can be achieved with interactive direct marketing is virtually unlimited....Direct marketers can determine not only what products to display to a particular customer or customer segment, and what products to group together to improve cross-sell opportunities, but they can even determine finite levels such as which color product to feature based on customers purchase history.*[1]

Starting a New Order Generation System on the Internet

What if your company is brand new to order generation? Then the Internet is a good place to start—perhaps the only place you will really need. Most early Internet order generation systems were home grown out of necessity, but now packaged systems are available that can get any business-to-business marketer up and running quickly and cost-effectively.

One of the earliest entrants and an acknowledged leader in the e-commerce business is Open Market (*www.openmarket.com*). Founded in 1994, Open Market was awarded three U.S. patents for Internet commerce technology in 1998. The patents granted to Open Market cover, among other things, the use of electronic shopping carts and the secure passage of purchases, payments, and receipts through URLs.

The company welcomed the action, saying that the patents "give Open Market broad intellectual property protection on its innovative technology" and announced plans to license the technology covered by the patents. The problem is, much of the technology is already in use by others. So, enforcing the patents may be difficult. Nevertheless, as the "inventor" of Internet commerce, Open Market's contributions to both the business-to-consumer and business-to-business markets have been substantial.

In early 1999, Open Market introduced LiveCommerce 2.0, which included the ability to scale to beyond 100,000 products, user tracking, ERP integration, and support for German, Italian, and Japanese. There are now numerous other products that make it possible for organizations to get an e-commerce operation up and running quickly.

E-commerce has now expanded so dramatically that there are a wide variety of packaged solutions offered by numerous vendors, priced from hundreds to hundreds of thousands of dollars. Some of these solutions are even being offered free, as long as the user agrees to utilize the seller's online e-commerce services.

One interesting example is Electrom.com (*www.electrom.com*) which claims to be the world's largest business-to-business e-commerce portal. Electrom.com, launched in November 1999, uses "SitePlugs" that work with Web design tools, such as Microsoft FrontPage 2000, to enable merchants to "plug in" e-commerce into their Web sites. Then the merchants can publish their site and Electrom will manage it from start to finish for up to 250 products, free of charge.

Even with the availability of such off-the-shelf products and all-in-one resources, however, the implications of e-commerce on an organization's existing systems should not be minimized. Legacy systems, such as financial and accounting, and possibly the entire order processing and fulfillment system, will need to be tied together with Internet-based operations. Ultimately, any e-commerce initiative will need to be integrated into a company's operations to gain maximum efficiencies. This fact has never been more obvious than in the experience of traditional retailers transitioning to the Internet. While 1999 was very much an e-Christmas, horror stories about retailers whose e-commerce systems crashed were not uncommon. It seems that the "pure play" Dot Coms knew something more about e-commerce than those bricks-and-mortar companies anticipated.

Of course, the cost of a fully enabled e-commerce system should not be underestimated, either. A May 1999 survey of twenty medium- to large-size corporations by IT research firm GartnerGroup found that building an e-commerce Web site from scratch costs an average of $1 million, with 79 percent of the cost being labor-related.

Another major issue that should be addressed early on is whether or not you want to commit internal staff and resources to a major e-commerce effort. Maintaining an electronic store or catalog is no small feat. Products need to be photographed, scanned, and uploaded. Copy needs to be written and published. Order numbers and prices need to be continuously reviewed and updated.

That is just the creative side. An e-commerce operation requires serious site management on an on-going basis. Maintaining pages and links and ensuring that all processes are in proper working order can be a laborious responsibility. At the very least, running an effective e-commerce operation will require a Web server that has the capabilities to facilitate online ordering and transaction processing.

Consider the following in evaluating Web servers:

- Languages and development tools,

- HTML editors, search indexes, virtual servers, and other administration tools,

- Security capabilities: protocols, authentication, and access control, and

- E-commerce features, such as credit card processing.

Should You Use a Web Hosting Service for E-Commerce?

Web hosting by an outside resource is an option that may make sense for some companies. If you choose to have your e-commerce site hosted by an outside service, you will want to review the full capabilities of the hosting Internet Service Provider (ISP). Do not assume that every ISP can provide e-commerce hosting. ISPs typically offer the hardware, software, communications access, and service to host Web sites, but not all ISPs have experience with e-commerce b-to-b applications.

Here are some of the key questions you should ask of potential Web hosting services:

- How many b-to-b customers do you have? How many of them are involved in e-commerce?

- What do you provide in the way of security? (firewalls, encryption, authentication, etc.)

- How do you handle secure transactions? (SSL, CyberCash, etc.)

- What other e-commerce services can you provide? (packaged solutions, back-end connections, analysis of site traffic, etc.)

- What support do you provide in the following areas?

  - Online store software and services

  - Database connectivity

  - Server disk space

  - CGI scripting

  - Java and JavaScript

  - Authoring tools, such as FrontPage

  - Support for multiple languages

  - E-mail standards

  - E-mail virus scanning

- What are your technical and service capabilities?

  - Guaranteed uptime

  - Technical support availability (days and hours)

  - Number of Web servers and number of sites per server

  - Access capabilities (Dial-up, 56K, 128K, T-1, T-3, ISDN, DSL)

  - Data backup

  - Site management

- What are your fees?

  - Setup

  - Monthly: based on which usage criteria

  - Other fees

Taking Orders Electronically

You do not necessarily have to transform your entire operation into an Internet-based business to take orders electronically. Today, scores of b-to-b direct marketers straddle traditional and Internet order generation by supplementing their printed catalogs and mail order marketing materials with the Internet.

The easiest way to start is to add the Internet as a response path to traditional order generation campaigns. If you generate orders via direct marketing, then you already have an established process to handle mail, phone, and fax orders. You could add an e-mail address, but that does not really facilitate the ordering process. Instead, consider adding a Web address that leads to a Web order form. Tell customers to refer to their printed catalog for complete product information while ordering on the Web. Set up a simple open-ended order form that pretty much mirrors one of your catalog order forms.

Even with this first small step toward full-fledged Internet order generation, you will have to establish security procedures so that the privacy of your customers ordering and credit card information is protected.

Secure transactions are essential across the Internet, and this aspect of e-commerce cannot be a weak link. There were initial concerns about online ordering, but they are quickly vanishing with technological advances from companies such as CyberCash (*www.cybercash.com*). CyberCash pioneered major electronic commerce payment advances on the Internet. CyberCash enables merchants worldwide to accept multiple forms of payment including Secure Payment/SET, CyberCoin, and PayNow electronic check. In early 1999, CyberCash unveiled "Instabuy.com" (*www.instabuy.com*), a one-click shopping service Web site, allowing consumers to sign up and make purchases from more than 85 online merchants. The consumer establishes an "InstaBuy wallet" which can be used to consolidate purchase information so it does not need to be re-entered each time the consumer buys with a participating merchant.

Numerous other electronic wallet services were introduced in late 1999 with the hope of increasing consumer and merchant interest in this nascent technology. Microsoft (*www.microsoft.com*) introduced "Passport," an e-wallet that allows e-buyers to input, edit, and send such purchase information as credit card numbers and shipping addresses to multiple merchants from a single place. Others, including American Express (*www.americanexpress.com*), EntryPoint (*www.entrypoint.com*), Gator (*www.gator.com*), and NextCard (*www.nextcard.com*), are vying for top spots in this arena.

Anxious to purchase online from anywhere? That, too, is coming. Also in May 1999, the "E-Station" online shopping terminal was introduced by Zoom Systems. E-Station is a kiosk that can be located in stores, hotels, airports, office buildings, even next to ATMs, so consumers can shop online to their heart's content. Hewlett Packard already uses the terminals to sell supplies at convenience stores.

Innovative technologies such as Instabuy, electronic wallets and E-Station will continue to fuel the explosive growth of e-commerce. There is even movement towards a standardized method of online payment using a new technology called ECML, Electronic Commerce Modeling Language. As of mid-1999, several leading companies, including America

Online, IBM, Microsoft, MasterCard, and Visa, were working together in an effort to standardize and simplify the online purchasing process.

Several forms of security promise to make online ordering safer than ever. An especially hot technology area is the *digital certificate*. A digital certificate is a way of identifying the sender of a message or transaction, protecting that message, and then verifying that the original sender sent the message.

Here is how it works. You want to send a secure message. Your identity is verified by an intermediary via traditional mail, telephone, or in person. You then receive a digital certificate with a private key and a public key that will be used by the party who is receiving your message. You encrypt the data to be sent. The party receiving the data decrypts it with a private key and your public key. As a result, the receiving party knows it is really you who sent the message.

It may sound complicated, but standards already exist that are supported by both Netscape Communicator and Microsoft Internet Explorer (versions 4.0 and higher for each). The use of digital certificates is already growing rapidly among financial institutions.

Want to avoid taxes on those Internet orders? It is a complicated issue, but to date, the Federal government is looking the other way when it comes to taxing goods sold over the Internet. States are rushing to include the Internet in mail order tax legislation. In June 1999, an organization called EOCnet.com (*www.eocnet.com*) came up with a novel approach to avoiding taxes, at least outside the United States. According to Reuters, the organization offers "e-suites"—legal entities for companies selling goods globally on the Internet. U.S.-based companies can classify offshore businesses as foreign sales corporations so they can tax advantages on overseas earnings.

Driving Traffic from the Internet to a Traditional Order Generation Channel

Another way to implement e-commerce is to use the Internet to provide incentives to prospective customers to go to a *traditional store* to purchase your product. You can accomplish this with Internet couponing.

Internet couponing promises to be a future growth area. According to research conducted by NPD (*www.npd.com*) in March 1999, 87 percent of online coupon users says they plan to use them again in the future, yet only half of Internet users know about online coupons. Surprisingly, over half of the online coupon users in the study were considered upscale, with household incomes above $45,000. One-third had incomes above $75,000.

Internet couponing is already available in the consumer market. SuperMarkets Online (*www.supermarkets.com*) offers a "ValuPage" to consumers who come to the site and enter their Zip code. Then, if there is a supermarket chain nearby, the consumer can print out a special ValuPage of items for which there are special discounts and take it to the store. At check-out, the ValuPage is presented to the cashier, who scans it and in return gives the consumer "WebBucks," which offer the consumer money off on any items purchased during the consumer's next shopping trip. (That helps to prevent fraudulent use, according to SuperMarkets.) SuperMarkets Online says it has signed up more than one million ValuPage subscribers.

With minor adaptation, b-to-b marketers could apply this model to their own selling situations. For example, you could offer a prospective customer an Internet coupon that is redeemable through any of your traditional order generation channels—a printed mail order catalog, a reseller, or a retail store. The coupon could be generated on the fly, based on answers to qualification questions. It could be accompanied by specific redemption instructions that include the catalog's 800-phone number, a reseller's local phone number, or the local address of a retail store.

In fact, in July 2000, Coupons.com (*www.coupons.com*) introduced a b-to-b print-at-home couponing solution called "Bricks." Bricks places a coded coupon link on a partner's Web page. When activated, Bricks securely transfers offer data directly to the consumers printer. The consumer can print coupons either online or offline and only a Zip code is required. Coupons.com launched the program with partners Quaker Oats and Veryfine Products as the industry's first Internet based, decentralized, coupon distribution channel.

The Business of Order Fulfillment

As part of even the most basic e-commerce operation, you will need a way to implement online order entry and fulfillment. Ideally, it will be an automated process so that the orders received over the Internet can be seamlessly handled through your existing order entry system.

It may actually make more sense for you to outsource the entire order generation process to an Internet order fulfillment firm. Outsourcing allows you to test the viability of e-commerce without committing internal resources to the operation, but it is generally a short-term strategy for any business that is serious about generating orders through the Internet.

It is more likely that you will want to provide customers with everything in one place on the Web—product descriptions, special promotions, pricing information, online ordering, perhaps even interactive customer service. Ultimately, that requires an investment that goes beyond a one-time trial or a simple Web order form.

The extent to which you provide online ordering is really up to you—and the variations are as unlimited as the potential. Insight Direct (*www.insight.com*), a b-to-b marketer of over 100,000 computer-related brand name products, is a case in point. The company has been doing business on the Web since 1995, which has helped fuel its growth. In April 1999, Insight reported its seventh quarter of more than 50 percent year over year growth in sales. Net sales for first quarter 1999 were over $338 million, a 64 percent increase over first quarter 1998. In late 1997, Insight transitioned to a true one-to-one marketing approach, offering customized pages to key customers:

> *Despite the amount of purchasing data the company has on its customer base, Insight is only giving custom Web pages to those customers who are recommended by one of its 60 account managers.*
>
> *Insight.com offers product listings, descriptions, specifications, and real-time pricing, including volume discounts for eligible customers. It also features "landing pads" from corporate intranets that allow multiple users to order from the site, special equipment configuration forms and Internet auction pages with bargain-priced items.*[2]

In 1999, Insight innovated again by moving from customized landing pages for customers to fully customer-customized "eCatalogs."

Given the almost continuous flow of innovations in Internet technology, you can expect that generating orders through the Internet will change shape before your eyes. In early 1998, for example, a new kind of Web banner ad was introduced to the market that essentially enables banner-generated e-commerce:

> *Typically, online merchants place banner ads on other heavily trafficked sites like search engines in the hope that users will click on them and visit their sites. ...banner ads with Enliven technology allow people to click on them and make a secure purchase without leaving the site they're currently visiting.*[3]

Now vendors such as Enliven and BlueStreak have turned banner ads into miniature electronic equivalents of solo mailings, offering the opportunity to purchase directly from the banner via a secure order form. Obviously, such a concept would be most appropriate for impulse purchases or items that require minimal description, but it certainly shows how pervasive e-commerce has become.

A new service introduced in May 1999 promised to enable e-commerce through e-mail. RealNetworks, the leader in Web multimedia software, has teamed with an online marketing company and an e-commerce software vendor to create "Buy@Once." This service will enable consumers to hear CD tracks, or watch movie clips within e-mails and then buy immediately without going to a Web site. In May 2000, RealNetworks announced it would integrate its software with Macromedia's Flash multimedia plug-in so e-commerce could occur within media presentations.

The implication of such innovations is that e-commerce will traverse the Internet in new and novel ways, not limited to e-commerce Web sites. In the b-to-b market, a whole new class of "light" e-commerce applications could offer even the smallest marketers the ability to sell their wares online.

Examples of B-to-B e-commerce Web Sites

B-to-b e-commerce is flourishing on the Internet. Here is just a sampling of some b-to-b sites that do a great job at selling.

Biztravel *(www.biztravel.com)*

Biztravel had the formidable task of carving out the business travel market for itself on the Web. Faced with competition from such heavy-duty competitors as Expedia *(www.expedia.com)* and Travelocity *(www.travelocity.com)*, not to mention the airlines themselves, Biztravel took a bold, breakthrough step in May 2000. That is when the site began offering refunds for late or canceled flights on five of the largest airlines. According to *The Wall Street Journal*, this high-risk move resulted in a five-fold increase in member registration and a 50 percent increase in ticket sales.

Boeing *(www.boeing.com)*

Wait a minute...Boeing? They're not selling airplanes online, are they?? No, but Boeing has become known as a leader in b-to-b e-commerce through its successful "Boeing PART Page." Launched in late 1996, this specialized Web site has grown more than 100 percent each year in transaction volume, and it supports nearly 75 percent of the world's jet transport fleet in spares-related business. The Boeing PART (Part Analysis and Requirements Tracking) Page provides airlines and maintenance firms with a direct link to half a million different types of spare parts stored in seven distribution centers worldwide. By the end of 1999, the site was processing about 18,000 transactions on an average day, including orders as well as inquiries about shipping status, inventory levels and pricing.

Cisco Systems *(www.cisco.com)*

One of the first networking companies to take the e-commerce plunge, Cisco has reaped the dividends. In 1999, the company logged $21 million a day of online sales. Early on, Cisco figured out (not surprisingly) that its networking customers would prefer to purchase networking products and services via the Internet, so it migrated customers to the "Cisco Connection Online." Now customers have online access to the same knowledge base used by its technical support specialists so Cisco not only sells more, but also provides better service. Now 85 percent of Cisco's orders, and more than 80 percent of customer inquiries, are transacted over the Web. Cisco has also embraced the e-business concept wholeheartedly. According to CEO John Chambers, all of Cisco's operations, from supply chain management to employee communications, are Internet-based. Cisco also utilizes virtual manufacturing to seamlessly manage 37 global plants as one, and executes a "virtual close" on the financial side, says Chambers. Down from 15 days only four years ago, the company can now close its books within one day.

Dell Computer *(www.dell.com)* and Gigabuys *(www.gigabuys.com)*

Dell (Fig. 11.1) may have been one of the most successful direct marketer of computers before it took to the Internet, but its e-commerce triumphs surpass an Internet marketer's wildest dreams. As of April 2000, Dell was selling $40 million a day of merchandise online, up from $1 million daily in 1997 and $14 million in 1999. Visit Dell Computer and you will find The Dell Store—a place where you can literally build your own computer system online. But The Dell Store is very aware that its business audiences' needs are unique, so it is segmented into "specialty stores" such as Business, Federal Government, Healthcare, and Education. At the Dell Store, you can "build your own system" by choosing the components you want and configuring the computer. After you build it, Dell instantly prices it for you online. You can view the details of your system, make any necessary changes, add it to your shopping cart and check out. You've just ordered a custom-designed computer, which will arrive in less than 30 days. You can watch as your computer goes through its various production steps and find out exactly when it will ship, all online. Now, Dell has expanded its services to include Web site hosting for small businesses at *www.dell-host.com*. In June 2000, the company announced it would launch additional online services, such as Internet access and e-mail, targeting small and mid-size companies. Dell also intends to introduce its own b-to-b marketplace so businesses can purchase almost anything on a Dell-sponsored site.

Dell made its first foray into non-Dell merchandise in 1999 with the launch of its site, Gigabuys. Gigabuys offers printers, scanners, software, accessories, multimedia, data storage, monitors, projectors, networking products, and even office products. The site follows the Dell

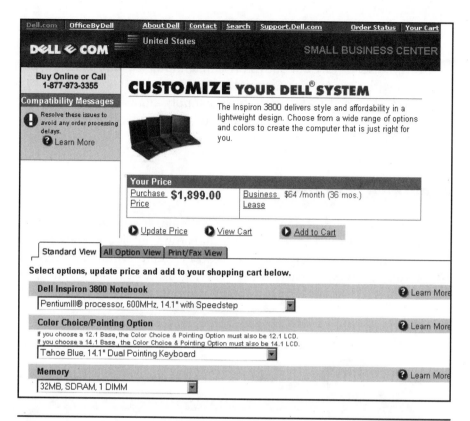

Figure 11.1. Dell customize.

model for ease of use and quick ordering. It is well organized and makes excellent use of its home page to feature specials and deals.

GE (*www.GE.com*)

This b-to-c and b-to-b giant was selected in 2000 as the leading e-business in the general manufacturing category of the "*InternetWeek* 100." GE has gotten up to speed quickly across all its many business divisions. Visit GEAppliances.com if you want to schedule appliance service online. Go to GESmallBusiness.com and you can get a credit card, industrial equipment lease, or vehicle lease. Visit GE.com/industry/ and you can buy select GE products, such as adhesives and silicones, online.

Go to GEGXS.com and you'll learn about GE Global eXchange Services, a division that supplies Internet-based supply chain solutions for b-to-b use. In July 2000, this division announced a far-reaching partnership with Commerce One, and in August, it launched Express Marketplace, designed to facilitate b-to-b supply chain collaboration for any size company. Who says an old-line company can't learn a few new e-tricks?

iPrint (*www.iprint.com*)

Can you run a traditional print shop online? If you are iPrint (Fig. 11.2), the answer is yes. Founded in 1996 and now a public company, this award-winning Web site has taken the lead in online printing, targeting small businesses with its easy-to-use ordering process. iPrint's "push-button" visual interface makes professional printing as easy as entering text, im-

Figure 11.2. iPrint turned the Internet into an electronic printing store.

porting graphics, and choosing colors. The self-service site allows visitors to quickly and easily create, proof, and order customized business and stationery products, promotional items, and custom-printed corporate gifts at prices that are up to 50 percent less than typical print shop rates. The company also private-labels its print services technology for the business market to such companies as 3M, OfficeMax, and Sir Speedy.

Marshall Industries *(www.marshall.com)*

Marshall Industries is among the largest global distributors of industrial electronic components and production supplies, serving 40,000 customers. Their major products include semiconductors, connectors, passive components, computer systems and peripherals, production supplies, tool kits, test equipment, and workstations.

Marshall was an early player in e-commerce and has consistently rated as one of the top e-commerce Web sites for years. Among its many innovations, Marshall offers "QuoteCart," a quick quoting service for a long list of parts or a Bill of Materials, and "Help@Once," a 24-hour a day chat service that offers online support from a Marshall Technical Support Engineer.

NECX *(www.necx.com)* and NECX Direct *(www.necxdirect.necx.com)*

NECX runs the Global Electronics Exchange, an exchange for buying and selling electronic components and computer products. The company says that, in 1993, it developed "the first Internet-based, transaction-capable online e-commerce site." In 1998, NECX had sales in excess of $420 million. By mid-2000, the Exchange had more than 10 billion items listed, with access to $30 billion in inventory. Over 20,000 trading partners worldwide and more than 300,000 registered users from 129 countries belonged to the Exchange. The company also offers the Enterprise Purchasing Network, the industry's first Web-based system for managing computer purchases throughout an enterprise, providing purchasing agents, IT professionals, and other business managers with the ability to track, manage, and generate reports online for computer purchases made throughout the enterprise. In 1999, the Global Exchange was acquired by VerticalNet, mentioned in Chapter 9.

The other side of the NECX business, NECX Direct, is an "Office and Personal Technology Center" that includes information on over 30,000 computer products from over 1,000 manufacturers. NECX features side-by-side product comparisons to benefit the buyer. The Office and Personal Technology Center has won e-commerce awards from *PC Magazine*, *PC World*, and *U.S. News & World Report*. In 1999, NECX Direct was acquired by Gateway Computer.

Office Depot (*www.officedepot.com*)

The b-to-b market for office supplies is red hot, and every major supplier is on the Internet. What's more, an increasing number of business marketplaces and service sites are offering office supplies. The biggest in the business, though, is Office Depot, with 868 stores throughout the U.S., Canada, France, and Japan. The company reached over $10 billion in sales in 1999. Office Depot uses the Internet in a big way, offering an online catalog of everything in the retailer's massive inventory, from supplies to furniture, to technology products. OfficeDepot.com also features a "resource guide" for small businesses called Office Solutions, as well as select links to partner sites who round out its business-oriented offerings.

Notes

1. Michael Rowsom, "Bridging the Gap from Traditional Marketing to Electronic Commerce," *DIRECT MARKETING*, January 1998, Copyright 1998, Hoke Communications, Inc.

2. Larry Riggs, "Made to Order: Insight Offers Business Clients Customized E-Catalog Pages," *DIRECT,* January 1998, Copyright 1998, Cowles Media.

3. Ken Magill, "Banners Say 'Buy' in E-Shift as Bauer Loads New Tech," *DM NEWS*, February 9, 1998, Copyright 1998, *DM NEWS*, Mill Hollow Corporation.

12

Integrating Online and Offline Marketing

The last chapter of this book demonstrates how you can put all of the strategies previously discussed to work. This chapter has another important goal, however: to prove that online and offline b-to-b marketing can and should be integrated. No b-to-b marketer should be under the impression that the time has come to completely abandon traditional marketing in favor of Internet marketing. Despite the growth and inevitable dominance of Internet marketing, other marketing channels such as advertising, public relations and direct mail/telemarketing will likely continue to be essential components of the marketing mix. What will change, however, is the mix itself. It is not difficult to imagine, for example, that the time will soon come when all other marketing media support the Internet, rather than the other way around. The wise b-to-b marketer will start preparing for this now.

We start with the premise that "online" and "offline" marketing must be integrated–and that the best principles of traditional marketing must be applied to Internet marketing in preparation for migration to the Internet. We also consider how Internet marketing will fundamentally change the way b-to-b companies market their products and services, and how you can get ready to take full strategic advantage of Internet marketing.

Online and Offline: The Reality of a Changing Marketing World

A little more than five years after the first commercial Web browser hit the market, the Internet became ubiquitous in business worldwide. It has been so widely adopted and is so pervasive that the press routinely refers to "the Internet economy." Nowhere has the impact of the Internet been more apparent than on the nation's stock markets, as Internet IPOs almost single-handedly fueled the Dow's record-breaking rise in 1999. The Internet has been the software industry's second-coming, as its rise has already spawned a slew of under-40 billionaires (that is "b", not "m"). A whole new breed of Internet-only companies have become a breeding ground for countless innovations.

From a business perspective, the Internet's impact has been nothing short of profound. Statistics quoted throughout this book bear witness to it. The Internet receives almost daily mention in the nation's press and on national television. Some newspapers, including *The Wall Street Journal*, devote regular columns and sections to the Internet. Numerous national weekly and monthly publications are devoted to the Internet, not to mention the countless Web sites and e-mail newsletters that cover the Internet in depth. There is a National Public Radio show about the Internet. The Internet has its own rapidly growing section in major bookstores. The Internet is becoming a necessity in a growing number of the nation's schools. Indeed, you can even earn a degree on the Internet.

Even with this unprecedented media attention, and the impact the Internet has had on daily life, the fact is that the Internet is nothing new to marketers. When you open up the electronic black box and look inside, Internet marketing is, basically, *electronic direct marketing*. It is not all that different from what direct marketers have been working towards all along, even though it has uniquely different qualities and requirements. The migration to Internet marketing implies many things for all of us in marketing, not the least of which is a fairly dramatic shift in the way marketing dollars will be allocated in the future. Internet marketing could turn marketing budgets upside down and even lead you to rethink how a marketing organization should be staffed. These are not insignificant issues for b-to-b marketers.

It may be somewhat reassuring, then, to look back upon the first foray into the marketing world by Dot Coms. By the end of 1999, you could not look up at a billboard, read a newspaper or magazine, listen to the radio, or watch television for more than thirty minutes without seeing an ad for a company with ".com" at the end of its name. This was a media invasion of sorts by a brand new class of dot-company, the Internet company. Those in the advertising business were struck by the irony that these e-companies were using traditional media to launch their e-businesses. Why? Because they needed to gain something even the Internet alone could not promise: broad brand awareness.

Somewhere along the line, some brash Dot Com marketing maven probably coined the term "offline" as a way of begrudgingly admitting that traditional media had its place in the "online" business world. "Offline" was likely meant to be a pejorative word; I know I have heard it used by people in the interactive advertising world in that way. It was almost as if these e-marketers forgot what business they were really in. But enough grousing. My point is simply that the Dot Coms, like any other emerging business, could not rely on just one medium to execute an effective launch–even if that medium was the Internet. They could scoff by calling traditional media "offline," but the Dot Coms used plenty of that offline marketing to build awareness for their brands. Without offline marketing, how many of these brands would have been noticed by the clicking public?

In the context of b-to-b marketing, heed this as an important lesson. The Internet is a grand and powerful marketplace, a medium that now reaches over 100 million people in the United States alone. But it is also an emerging marketplace, a very fragmented medium with millions of places people can go. Standing alone, it is not yet as effective as it can be in combination with other media.

Most b-to-b marketers would not use a single marketing medium to launch a new product. They know that trade magazines, for example, will accomplish one kind of objective, while direct mail and telemarketing will accomplish another. The most successful marketing programs still *combine and integrate* media to increase efficiency and maximize results.

No lesser a world-class marketer than IBM is proving the point. IBM combined TV, print advertising, direct mail, and online media to support its Global Business Intelligence Solutions Group in a major worldwide integrated campaign with a $30 million budget, reported *Advertising Age* (September 20, 1999). Advertising in business magazines and newspapers was carefully woven together with direct response television, radio, and banner ads on select Web sites, supported by a 250,000-piece mail drop.

If you consider the Internet to be *one* of your arsenal of marketing weapons, rather than the sole weapon, your chances of success will be that much greater. It is likely that, someday, the Internet will become the most powerful weapon available to you. But not many b-to-b marketers would be ready to risk abandoning every other form of marketing just yet.

How, then, can you most effectively integrate "online" and "offline" marketing today?

Your Market and Your Audiences Will Determine How You Integrate Online and Offline Marketing

As this book points out, Internet marketing is emerging as an inevitable way of doing business for b-to-b marketers. Yet, if you have ever done targeted marketing, you know that *audiences* drive the effectiveness of direct marketing activities. That is why it is essential to understand where your market is today, and how accepting your audiences are of Internet marketing.

First consider the market you are in. How actively do your competitors utilize Internet marketing? (You will find out a lot about that, just by visiting their Web sites.) How do they speak to their audiences?

Would you classify *your target audience* as early adopters of Internet technology, or laggards? How your various target audiences and constituencies respond to Internet marketing is a key consideration. You are probably familiar with the technology adoption curve, popularized by Geoffrey Moore (*www.chasmgroup.com*) in his landmark technology marketing books, *Crossing the Chasm* and *Inside the Tornado*. The curve basically defines the stages of acceptance of a technology product. Every product has a group of people who are its "early adopters"—individuals who will try the product before anyone else and, potentially, lead the market in the product's initial usage and ultimate acceptance. There is also a segment of the product's potential audience that will be far more conservative in adoption, lagging behind and, in some cases, never using it.

While the Internet itself is now in a stage of mass adoption, you need to apply the technology adoption curve to your target audiences. Which are the audiences who will be very accepting of Internet marketing—the early adopters? Which audiences will be less receptive or even resistant to Internet marketing?

Information technology professionals—software developers and programmers, for example—will obviously be early adopters, but what about other business audiences? Where do sales and marketing people fit in your target industries? Financial managers and purchasing agents? Human resources managers? CEOs? *Which industries* are more likely to accept Internet marketing? *Which size* companies? The fact is, no one can be absolutely certain, because Internet marketing is still relatively new.

That means you may need to do some solid research to determine how *your* audiences will react to Internet marketing. Closely follow the practices of your competitors and your industry. Watch where they are focusing their efforts. Also, keep a close eye on the traditional media that target your prospect and customer audiences. Are they reporting about the Internet and the Web more frequently? Do they have companion Web sites that serve your audiences? Are there other Web-based information providers beyond your competitors who target your audiences? Are Internet marketing conferences springing up in your target industries? These are all strong signals that Internet marketing is, if not already accepted by your target audiences, rapidly gaining acceptance. It will just be a matter of time before Internet marketing is commonplace, but you may have an opportunity right now to decide whether you will lead or follow with Internet marketing in your specialized area. Which will it be?

How to Integrate Online and Offline Media in the Internet Marketing Era

A second key factor to consider is how you will integrate the Internet with other media. Your media strategy—the way you use media and the mix of media you use—may change radically in the future. Begin the transition to Internet marketing *now*—by making the Internet a more prominent and integral part of your media mix.

Below we examine how media integration will shift from the use of traditional media to the increasing use of electronic media. Figure 12.1 is a classic example of media integration dominated by "offline" media. Note the following:

1. **Lead Generation.** Direct mail and print advertising are the primary media utilized to generate leads.

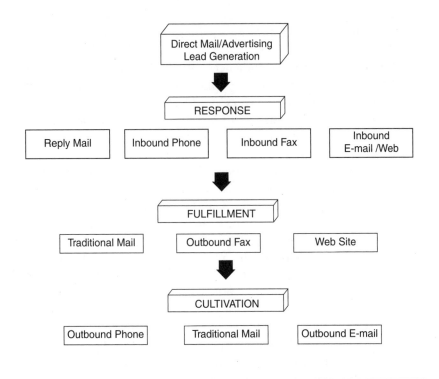

Figure 12.1. Media integration chart.

2. **Response.** Responses come in via reply mail, inbound phone calls to an 800 number, faxes of the reply device, inbound e-mail inquiries, or inbound Web via a Web response form.

3. **Fulfillment.** Fulfillment takes place using traditional direct mail or outbound fax. In some cases, the respondent can be fulfilled instantly by receiving information and/or an offer at the Web site.

4. **Cultivation.** The respondent's name, address, phone number, e-mail address, and answers to qualifying questions are collected at the response stage and used to initiate a cultivation process. This process uses outbound telemarketing, traditional mail, and outbound e-mail to periodically contact and re-qualify the prospect.

Next we examine media integration in the era of the Internet. Figure 12.2 is an updated version of the media integration chart with an emphasis on e-marketing. Note the following:

1. **Lead Generation.** Leads are generated from any source. In the future, e-mail and the Web may very well out-pull other media as the primary lead source, so electronic lead generation will become more essential as time goes on.

2. **Response.** Responses come in via reply mail, inbound phone calls to an 800 number, faxes of the reply device, inbound e-mail inquiries, or inbound Web, as before. It is likely, however, that the Web will become the primary response path in the future because it will be so much easier for the respondent. Web responses arrive via a designated, campaign-specific URL that leads to a Web response area with a Web response form that

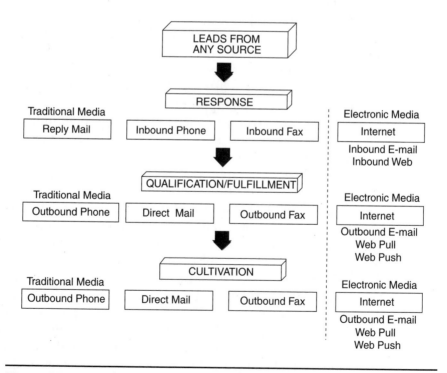

Figure 12.2. Media integration chart emphasizing electronic media.

collects not only basic contact information, but answers to qualification questions. Prepare for Web responses to be the predominant form of inquiry and, eventually, order.

3. **Qualification and Fulfillment.** Notice that the e-marketing future calls for a single-step qualification and fulfillment process. Today, traditional media are still being used to qualify and fulfill leads in a two-step process, but soon, the process will be more heavily weighted to the Internet, which will combine qualification and fulfillment. This transition is already taking place.

   With the online lead qualification process happening in real time, marketers will be able to instantly deliver individualized fulfillment content to all types of prospects based on their interest and qualification level. This content could be delivered via outbound e-mail or, more likely, through individualized Web pages targeted to the prospect's specific interests and needs. Standard text-only e-mail will suffice for fast acknowledgments and "instant response," but eventually, e-mail will routinely include graphics and embedded Web site links, enhancing the e-mail fulfillment process. Fulfillment on the Web will occur via a routine Web response area process, as well as at Web sites. Fulfillment will also be "pushed" via the Web to a prospect's desktop if appropriate.

   The cost savings implications of electronic fulfillment to marketers, and the ease of use to respondents, are so extraordinary that you should anticipate this type of fulfillment becoming the norm rather than the exception.

4. **Cultivation.** The cultivation process will be easier and more automatic with electronic media. Marketers will routinely use outbound e-mail for promotional purposes to communicate periodically, relying on e-mail newsletters, which will be sent to qualified prospects and customers who have consented to e-mail use. E-mail will routinely embed Web page links, which go to surveys, forms, and specialized Web pages. Prospects and customers will be pulled to Web sites and extranets via ongoing informational programs, which may include special promotions and content. Web content will also be pushed to the desktops of interested prospects and customers on a regular

basis. As part of the cultivation process, Internet-based customer service will rule the relationship.

An Example of How to Execute Online-Offline Marketing

You can apply the principles of online-offline marketing today to reduce the overall cost and increase the overall efficiency of your marketing efforts even if you are still at the beginning of the Internet marketing curve. Below is an example.

Suppose you are organizing a traditional in-person marketing seminar targeted to a particular audience. It is a free half-day event to be held in five key cities. You need to make sure the seminar is well attended by the right prospects. What is the best way to promote it? If you used offline marketing alone, as you've probably done in the past, here is what you would do:

1. Establish the dates and locations, select list sources (including any in-house lists) and target the appropriate audience within 50 miles of each city.

2. Create and mail a direct mail invitation including a full agenda, dates and locations, and all other pertinent details. Include the traditional phone, mail-in, and fax-back response paths.

3. Follow up to non-registrants with a direct mail postcard to encourage them to re-consider. Follow up with fax and telephone confirmations to individuals who registered and said they would attend.

4. Cross-promote the seminar with traditional advertising and public relations activities.

Now what if you add the Internet *as an integral part* of the promotional plan? Here is how your original plan would be modified:

1. Establish the dates and locations, select list sources (including any in-house lists) and target the appropriate audience within 50 miles of each city. During the audience selection process, research additional opt-in e-mail lists that may be available.

Also compile an in-house list of e-mail addresses for use in the promotion.

2. Create and mail an oversized postcard, considerably less expensive than the direct mail invitation referenced above, that promotes the seminar. Instead of including all the details, provide a toll-free phone number for more information, but strongly encourage the prospect to visit a special Web page that fully describes the seminar. Let the Web page act as an electronic invitation which provides:

- A more detailed agenda and description of the seminar, along with speaker photographs and biographies if appropriate

- Directions, including printable maps, for each seminar location

- Information about other events of potential interest to the prospect, including a list of Internet-based events for those prospects who are not in the five-city area or cannot attend the live seminars but want more information about your company's product

- An interactive registration form—perhaps with a special offer to encourage registering—so that prospects can register online and receive an instant acknowledgment. Collect an e-mail address here and you can use it to remind the registrant of the seminar several times before the event. Use a Web-based database tool and you can capture the marketing information you obtain from the prospect "one time" instead of re-keying the information. Use it for future promotions and to track the prospect's activity.

3. Follow up to non-registrants with an e-mail, if you have their e-mail addresses, or if necessary with a direct mail postcard to encourage them to re-consider. Follow up with e-mail at least twice to individuals who registered, said they would attend, and provided their e-mail addresses. Use fax and telephone confirmations only when e-mail addresses are not available.

4. Cross-promote the seminar using online advertising and public relations targeted to your audience rather than traditional advertising. Appropriate media might include mentions and sponsorships in e-mail newsletters, promotions on pertinent community sites, and banners/interstitials placed on targeted Web sites.

Notice in this example that there was a true inter-relationship of online and offline marketing. You did not completely eliminate offline marketing, instead you used it to push prospects to the Internet. By using online and offline marketing in this way, you are likely to have a significant impact on your marketing ROI as you take advantage of the growing dependence on, and preference for, the Internet. The bottom line is this:

1. You *reduce the cost of your direct mail seminar invitation* by making it less elaborate and driving response to the Web—where they get full seminar details. You provide additional helpful service to prospects by acknowledging their registrations instantly online, and by offering exact seminar locations with maps.

2. *Overall response to the promotion could increase* because you have facilitated response by adding a Web response path. This will probably become the preferred method of response in the future for most b-to-b audiences. On the Web, they can get more information about the seminar without the need to speak to anyone, and they can easily register online.

3. *Online registrants will likely be higher quality prospects* because they take the time to visit the URL, review detailed information, and complete the registration form.

4. Using a series of e-mail confirmations and reminders, which you send prior to the event, *could significantly reduce your "no-show" rate* (which is typically 50 to 60 percent for live seminars). E-mail is much less expensive than telephone calls and even faxes. It goes directly to the recipient and is likely to be read.

5. Even if prospects visit the seminar Web page and do not come to the seminar, *they have been made aware* of your company, your seminar series, and other events you sponsor which may interest them.

6. Individuals who are outside seminar cities could visit the seminar Web pages to learn more about your company and products and, as a result, *become new prospects for you, even if they cannot attend the live event.*

The incremental cost to your seminar promotion to achieve these potential benefits should be very low. In fact, you are replacing the cost of a direct mail invitation and potentially direct mail and telephone follow-ups with the much less expensive use of a modest direct mail piece, Web pages, and e-mail. If you have a Web site, the seminar Web page could "hang off" of it. Creating the seminar response area is not a complicated task—it can be done by your in-house Web staff or outsourced to an interactive resource. If you need comprehensive response management support, there are firms that handle online seminar registration and confirmation, along with maintaining your marketing database.

The Impact of Internet Marketing on B-to-B Marketing Organizations

Most b-to-b marketers are familiar with their role as a change agent in their companies. In recent years, database and direct marketing have catapulted the marketing organization to prominence, as an increasing emphasis on measurable results has struck a responsive chord with senior management.

B-to-b marketing managers are now as likely to be held accountable for generating and qualifying leads as sales managers are for closing them. Senior marketing strategists are no less important to a company's inner management circle than are operating officers. The title Chief Marketing Officer is emerging among larger companies as marketing gains prominence. It is only a matter of time before the word "Internet" is added to it.

The rise of the Internet can enhance the position of marketing executives, managers, and the entire marketing organization within your company. Most senior business executives already acknowledge that the Internet will fundamentally change the way their company does business. They are also likely to acknowledge that it is the marketing organization in the company who is on the leading edge of that change.

The vast majority of Web sites are, first and foremost, marketing and sales sites. That reality has already resulted in many b-to-b companies gaining a leadership position in Internet lead generation and electronic commerce. In fact, more companies today are moving rapidly towards becoming "e-businesses." It is therefore unlikely that you will meet with much resistance from a company's senior management *outside* the marketing organization when publicizing the notion that Internet marketing is necessary and desirable. After all, these same senior managers are in the midst of developing strategic business plans that will leverage the Internet as a means of business process improvement. IT executives are aggressively lobbying their companies for Internet-related dollars on a regular basis so that they can implement intranets and extranets. Corporate Web sites are reaching a level of importance well beyond the marketing area, especially for public companies. The Web site is becoming an "enterprise information portal"–the repository for all corporate information and the conduit to get that information out to every one of the company's audiences—not just prospects and customers, but investors, analysts, the press, business partners, suppliers, employees, and prospective employees. Even more so, the rush to e-commerce will put the Internet front and center as the primary sales channel for an increasing number of companies.

Ironically, the most skepticism or resistance to Internet marketing may actually come from *within* the marketing and sales organizations. Why? Because of the FUD factor: fear, uncertainty, and doubt. These are likely to accompany any fundamental change to business as usual—and the change will be dramatic and all encompassing with Internet marketing.

The Impact on Marketing

The company's marketing organization will likely face the challenge of re-examining marketing objectives, priorities, strategies, and tactics.

Marketing managers may need to recast their programs, reshuffle their media mix, reorient their staffs—and perhaps even replace some staff with interactive media specialists.

The entire marketing organization will need to learn, and to teach the company, new ways of information delivery and response management. Marketing databases and database marketing programs will revolve around the Internet. Fulfillment priorities will change as instant response and electronic fulfillment becomes the norm. E-mail is becoming an accepted form of external marketing communication. The U.S. Postal Service and others will get into the fray as they provide certification of e-mail delivery.

Advertising, direct mail, and telemarketing usage could shift dramatically as these media begin to play a more subordinate role to the Internet and the Web. Chances are traditional media will not disappear, but they will follow behind the Internet, relinquishing their former leadership position. Media convergence already exists. Web site addresses are everywhere, and the Web is fast becoming a primary response path for b-to-b marketers. Direct mail or direct response advertising is even now being aggressively used to lead a prospect to a Web response form, an Internet event, or a corporate Web site. "Integration" will take on a whole new meaning as the Internet emerges as the core of a company's marketing programs, with all other media revolving around it and playing a supporting role.

With it all, some difficult budgeting and staffing decisions will need to be made. Internet marketing will require the marketing manager to accommodate entirely new budget line items (e.g., e-mail delivery, development of virtual events, online advertising campaigns, participation in communities, management of affiliate programs, creation of Web pages, maintenance of Web sites, electronic fulfillment and response management, Web server expenses, etc.). Decisions will not always be clear-cut as marketing melds with information technology and budgets become the shared responsibility of more than one department.

On the staffing and resources side, Internet marketing could cause a massive shift in hiring or training the types of individuals who work in a marketing organization and the kinds of outside services that need to be procured.

Internal resources may very well be skewed toward the Internet. Instead of the typical advertising and media personnel, marketing communications project supervisors, marketing service managers, or even direct marketing specialists, a marketing organization may need a cadre of Internet marketing experts. This could be a team of Internet marketing strategists, interactive producers, new media specialists, Web writers, and interactive designers—but it also may need to include a new addition to marketing: a "marketologist." The marketologist is part marketer, part Webmaster—someone who understands the unique combination of marketing and technology that Internet marketing demands.

The Impact on the Marketing/IT Departments

The Internet has spawned some unholy alliances, not the least of which is between IT and Marketing departments. In larger companies, these two contrasting functional organizations already find that they must work hand-in-hand to deliver Web content over the Internet, and the need will soon go beyond Web sites alone.

The IT department could be a potential internal barrier to an Internet marketing initiative—not because IT managers want to derail marketing, but rather because they legitimately need to control network traffic and user needs. That is a major part of their responsibility. As Marketing "messes around" with e-mail and the Web, some IT managers may get more than nervous. IT's support of corporate intranets is a given—but Web sites, virtual events, or extranets that utilize heavy-duty marketing database engines, include online transaction processing, incorporate voice over IP, and require the implementation of electronic commerce are something else again. This is the kind of stuff that could choke bandwidth, melt servers, and bring a corporate network to its knees.

That is why the "marketologist" will be a key person in the Marketing organization. It is the marketologist who will need to speak IT's language, work the relationship, and make sure that the needs of Internet marketing can be accommodated by the corporate IT group. It is the marketologist who will need to understand what the internal IT organization can and cannot provide, and help make the decision, if necessary, to outsource Internet marketing to the appropriate Internet service providers.

The Impact on Sales

For the sales organization in any b-to-b company, the transition to Internet marketing will be no less dramatic and potentially, more traumatic. The lead generation and qualification process may not fundamentally change, even though the requirements for information input and dissemination may be drastically different. However, Internet-enabled partnering and electronic commerce initiatives could turn a company's entire sales process upside down.

As electronic commerce becomes easier and more cost-effective to implement, b-to-b companies are now shifting some if not all of the traditional telephone or face-to-face selling to Internet-based selling. "Call me buttons" and live text chat on Web sites will become the norm. Telesales may very well become Internet-based as telephony and the Internet converge. Sending voice over IP (Internet Protocol), is already technically feasible. As demand for these applications grows, prospects or customers will go to the Web instead of the telephone to ask for information, solve their own problems, and when necessary, engage in a sales or service dialogue on demand. In short, customers will drive the interaction process.

Banks of telemarketers may actually find their work shifting from inbound telephone calls to inbound e-mail and Web inquiries. Telesales specialists will be retrained to "watch" a visitor navigate a Web site, be available when the visitor clicks a Call Me button, and intercede when that visitor needs more information—pushing Web pages to the visitor if necessary. Outbound telemarketers will just as likely be communicating via the Internet as over a telephone.

The direct sales force in a b-to-b company is likely to change in complexion as well. In-person sales calls may still occur, but they will increasingly be enhanced or sometimes replaced by Internet conferencing. It may begin with just a telephone call that is enhanced with Web support. The salesperson will conduct a phone conversation but will suggest to the prospect that he or she go to the Web to view some information.

The salesperson of the future might arrange a virtual meeting over the Web with a prospect, perhaps including live videoconferencing. The prospect, of course, could be anywhere in the world. At this virtual meeting, the salesperson will make eye contact and walk the prospect through a visual presentation on the Web, leading him or her along with live voice. The salesperson will be able to stop at any point and take questions. The salesperson could show the prospect video clips of customer testimonials and success stories, or maybe the salesperson will invite the prospect to view and interact with a real-time product demonstration, right then and there.

If a face-to-face meeting is warranted, the salesperson will undoubtedly bring along a notebook computer that has presentations and demonstrations pre-loaded. He or she might connect to the Internet while in the prospect's office and guide the prospect through an online presentation, seminar, or demonstration on the Web. This might be an opportunity to have the prospect access an online calculator or analyzer to see the ROI benefits of the company's proposed solution.

Presenting the Case for Internet Marketing

In your role as a marketer, you will now become responsible for obtaining full management support and educating the entire organization about the inevitability of Internet marketing. You know the politics of your company—who the movers and shakers are, where the influence is, who calls the shots. You will have to use this intelligence wisely to elicit broad-based support for dramatic change.

You will, in effect, need to establish your own internal public relations program for Internet marketing. Plan it carefully and execute it wisely, for it will help shape the future of your marketing organization and your job. Your ally in all of this? The Internet itself. As you have seen in this book, the Internet is a business phenomenon of unprecedented proportion. IT marketing success stories are being written daily, and all of them can be found on the Internet.

In presenting the case for Internet marketing to your organization's management, use the Internet and its vast resources for credibility and validation. Rely on the major search engines and other information search sources, along with industry-specific sites, to get the ammunition you need. Use industry data and reports from the traditional press to enhance credibility.

Start with some of the gateway sites, which provide countless links to the relevant sites you will need to find. One such gateway is the outstanding site, *www.ceoexpress.com*. This "launching pad" for managers opens a wide door to all kinds of information and research about business in general. It is well organized, it is easy to use, and it offers plenty of links to sources that will be useful to you. Other valuable resources are listed in Appendix A of this book and linked on the book's companion Web site.

Focus on the Quantifiable Business Benefits of Internet Marketing

Selling the concept of Internet marketing to senior management and to the various groups, departments, or divisions within your company should be supported with facts. There is plenty of evidence, much of it presented in this book, to support the accelerated movement towards Internet marketing.

To make your argument all the more effective, focus on the *quantifiable business benefits* of Internet direct marketing[1]:

1. *The most successful Web marketers are integrating the Web with other media.*

2. *Internet direct marketing is 60 to 65 percent cheaper than traditional direct mail marketing.*

3. *Internet direct marketing campaigns can be changed in real time.*

4. *The Internet provides "unlimited shelf space" for products.*

5. *The Internet provides worldwide reach for your company.*

6. *The Internet makes one-to-one marketing a reality, if it is executed properly.*

Below we consider each of these benefits individually:

1. *The most successful Web marketers are integrating the Web with other media.* Internet and Web marketing should not occur in a vacuum. Market forces suggest that Internet marketing will eventually be the predominant form of marketing, but it will not replace the effectiveness of *combining and integrating* electronic and traditional media.

   Use the right combination of media to most effectively reach your target audience. Print advertising may continue to generate awareness for your company, your products, and your services, and direct mail may continue to generate and qualify leads. Do not abandon these media prematurely, but in every case, *integrate* the Internet into your media plans and *escalate* your use of Internet marketing.

Whenever possible, establish a campaign-specific URL that leads to a Web response area designed to capture and qualify a lead. Ask prospects and customers to provide e-mail addresses, and request permission to communicate with them via e-mail. Use direct mail and advertising to drive people to Web response forms and your Web site. Support your Web activities by leveraging the messaging and offers from other media and making everything work together.

2. *Internet direct marketing is 60 to 65 percent cheaper than traditional direct mail marketing.* The Yankee Group believes Internet direct marketing will account for at least 50 percent of all the advertising dollars spent on the Internet by 2001, and that b-to-b e-commerce will grow at a compound annual growth rate of over 40 percent in the next five years.

Research by The Yankee Group indicates that Internet direct marketing represents a *threefold cost-savings* for direct marketing. Moreover, The Yankee Group says that Internet direct marketing can bring *up to ten times the return* of a traditional direct marketing campaign, when considering original and follow-up campaigns applied to the same product. The areas in which you will achieve the largest savings are likely to be fulfillment, delivery, medium used, and analysis. The economics of Internet marketing make a compelling case for gradually moving promotional dollars from other media to Internet forms of promotion. Cost alone should not drive marketing decisions, but cost-effectiveness and media efficiency are powerful motivators for choosing one medium over another.

Electronic media turns traditional media cost structures upside down. With Internet marketing, there is nothing to print and mail, there are no advertising materials to reproduce, no telemarketing calls to handle. Web sites can reach one, a hundred, a thousand, or a million prospects or customers for about the same cost. With the proper in-house tools, e-mail can be widely distributed without unit cost implications, as with direct mail, and, at least so far, the Internet is a tax-free commerce zone.

The Internet is just as significant a cost-savings medium in product distribution. According to the Organization for Economic Cooperation and Development, it costs $1.00 to distribute an airline ticket electronically versus $8.00 traditionally. It costs just 50 cents to distribute a software product electronically versus $15.00 traditionally.

Use the growth of Internet marketing as a springboard for evaluating your media investments and product marketing and distribution costs on a dollar-for-dollar basis. Compare and contrast the total marketing costs for a direct response advertising, direct mail, or telemarketing campaign versus an Internet-based campaign. If it is feasible, establish head-to-head tests of one medium against the other. Keep audience criteria, the offer, and the basic creative approach the same. Evaluate which medium produces the:

- *highest response rates,*

- *highest quality leads,*

- *best conversion of responses to leads,*

- *best conversion of leads to sales, and*

- *shortest response-to-lead-to-sale time frame.*

3. *Internet direct marketing campaigns can be changed in real time.* One of the Internet's major strategic advantages as a marketing medium is the campaign time to market. Advertising campaigns depend on publication close dates; monthly publications generally require materials 30 to 45 days prior to an issue date. Typical direct mail campaigns take from 6 to 10 weeks to execute. Even telemarketing campaigns may take several weeks to organize and execute.

Time frames associated with Internet marketing are considerably shorter than traditional media time frames. For e-mail, copy can be written and distributed almost instantly, once e-mail addresses are obtained. Web pages can be quickly written, designed, and published to the Web using commonly available tools on almost any computer. Web pages and Web banner ads can literally be changed overnight if need be. Entirely new banner ad campaigns can be created and uploaded within days, making it possible to shift marketing gears quickly based on audience reaction and response.

Electronic media today have no time constraints associated with their availability. Information can be available instantly on the Web or distributed instantly via e-mail, regardless of the audience size. Electronic fulfillment is available for instant unlock or immediate download. "Real-time marketing" becomes a reality under this scenario. While it can be both a blessing and a curse, it can lead to new opportunities for instant evaluation and on-the-spot campaign re-engineering.

4. *The Internet provides "unlimited shelf space" for products.* Amazon.com migrated from millions of books to tens of millions of books, videos, CDs, electronics, household items, and countless other products more rapidly than any "bricks and mortar" operation could ever conceive of doing. Companies who sell on the Internet can challenge convention by making limitless numbers of products available in an electronic store because, if the product is appropriately described and marketed, the buyer does not need to see and touch it.

The vastness of cyberspace is a marketing benefit like no other. Only the Internet can act as a virtual warehouse, extending your inventory and presenting any number of products at any time to customers and prospects anywhere.

5. *The Internet provides worldwide reach for your company.* A company of virtually any size can reach out to the world with its message, products, and services. There are countless stories of tiny organizations, even one-person operations, marketing and selling products and services over the Internet. No other medium provides the low-cost coverage of the Internet, no other form of communication the worldwide penetration of the Web. Small organizations can appear to be large, and, more important, they can gain the same marketing advantage on the Internet as do corporate giants.

With no time zones and no meeting protocol, electronic business can be conducted 24 hours a day, seven days a week, in every corner of the world—and the Internet marketer need never leave his or her office. This factor alone fuels the growth of the Internet as a medium of unlimited potential on a worldwide scale.

6. *The Internet makes one-to-one marketing a reality, if it is executed properly.* One-to-one marketing is, at its heart, the simple notion of building a relationship that extends from one party to another. If the individualization of the Internet is maximized, one-to-one marketing can be a powerful and lasting way of doing business. More than that, Internet marketing could create a one-to-one standard for doing business worldwide, and with that will come the availability of mass market tools that will ensure its continued existence.

As with most information technologies, early products are introduced to the marketplace at premium prices. After competitors enter the market and the product category becomes both accepted and desirable, prices begin to moderate. Often, "light" versions of products enter the market to serve the low end.

Already, we have seen the migration toward lower cost e-mail and Web tools. In many cases, e-mail software and Web browsers are now bundled in free with ISP Internet access services. The same is becoming true of Internet database marketing tools and e-commerce applications. High-end comprehensive solutions will always be available at premium prices, but lower cost products with limited functionality will suffice for a large part of the market. That means that one-to-one marketing, e-commerce, real-time collaboration, and other Internet advances could reach well beyond a small percentage of Internet marketers. In fact, Internet marketers can purchase e-commerce services on a subscription or service bureau basis, avoiding the internal cost of establishing such an operation.

In the final analysis, you will not only need to convey the specific benefits of Internet marketing—you will also need to spread the word throughout your company that it will be *a profitable venture.* There are certainly up-front and continuing costs related to Internet marketing, but a thorough analysis should show that Internet marketing compares very favorably to the use of traditional media and marketing methods.

The Internet Marketing Audit

An audit is a first step in analyzing your existing use of Internet marketing and moving forward with wide-scale implementation. Use the audit checklist shown in Figure 12.3 to help assess your "Internet marketing readiness"—to define and answer questions and determine needs. This will help you as you begin to formulate a comprehensive action plan.

The Internet Marketing Action Plan

By completing the Internet Marketing Audit Checklist, you have taken a first important step in assessing your overall readiness for the transition to Internet marketing. Soon, you will see how to use the checklist to help develop a specific action plan for implementing Internet marketing, but first, we need to address two important factors that will have an impact on your plan.

Developing the Action Plan

Although each Internet Marketing Action Plan will be unique to a marketing organization's specific needs, these are the basic steps to follow in developing your own action plan.

1. *Assess your Internet marketing readiness.* Now is the time to evaluate your organization's Internet marketing capabilities. You need to be ready to transition to Internet-based marketing now. Use the Internet Marketing Audit Checklist to assess your readiness.

    Do not let the assessment process deter you. The fact is that most of the business-to-business marketing world is just beginning to apply Internet marketing in a disciplined, integrated way. The important thing is to understand your current state of readi-

Does your organization currently have, or do you plan to add within 12 months:	YES	NO
A corporate network (LAN and/or WAN)	❏	❏
Communication via e-mail *outside* your organization	❏	❏
A corporate Web site	❏	❏
In-house	❏	❏
Outsourced	❏	❏
An intranet	❏	❏
In-house	❏	❏
Outsourced	❏	❏
An extranet	❏	❏
In-house	❏	❏
Outsourced	❏	❏
A Webmaster, or someone primarily responsible for corporate Internet usage	❏	❏

Do you currently use, or do you plan to use within 12 months:		
Direct mail and other traditional media to drive traffic to your Web site	❏	❏
The Web as a response path in direct marketing campaigns	❏	❏
Campaign-specific URLs to track response by campaign	❏	❏
Web Response Forms to capture leads	❏	❏
Outbound e-mail as a promotional response, fulfillment, follow-up or continuity medium	❏	❏
Links to other Web sites	❏	❏
Online advertising such as banner ads, interstitials, or e-mail newsletter sponsorships as appropriate	❏	❏

Figure 12.3.   Internet marketing audit checklist. (*continued on next page*)

ness and recognize where you are today—and where you will need to be.

2. *Prepare your management for the Internet-dominated future.* The Internet has already captured top-of-mind awareness amongst senior management at many companies. You should have little resistance to the adoption of Internet marketing, but you will need to be an advocate. Make sure your management understands the value of Internet marketing and recognizes its

Do you currently use, or do you plan to use within 12 months:

Online events or seminars	❑	❑
Online informational fulfillment	❑	❑
Online demos and trials, if appropriate	❑	❑
Distribution of live products over the Internet, if appropriate	❑	❑
Participation in Web communities	❑	❑
A Web community of your own	❑	❑
Participation in affiliate programs	❑	❑
An affilitate program of your own	❑	❑

Does your Web site or extranet currently have, or do you plan to add within 12 months:

Web response pages or response forms	❑	❑
An Internet-integrated database component for capturing/tracking visitor data	❑	❑
Web database capability to dynamically generate personalized pages on-the-fly	❑	❑
Automatic e-mail response capability	❑	❑
Cookie technology for visitor tracking	❑	❑
Electronic (online) fulfillment	❑	❑
Electronic solutions center: matching products/services to customer or prospect needs	❑	❑
Internet-enhanced customer marketing: private access customer areas or extranets	❑	❑
Electronic commerce: order entry, processing, tracking	❑	❑
Support of partners via the Internet, if appropriate	❑	❑

Figure 12.3. Internet marketing audit checklist. *(continued from previous page)*

inevitability. Share Internet marketing information from authoritative sources with your management. Make sure they know what their competitors are doing. Use the resources in Appendix A for your research.

If you are in a position to do so, serve on or chair a committee in your organization that is charged with developing a strategic plan for using the Internet as a business, not just a marketing tool. Chances are, management is already on a course to use the Internet strategically as part of the company's overall business plan—so you can take advantage of that business condition to benefit your own marketing program.

With senior management already aware of and planning for the ascension of the Internet, you have a rare opportunity to position Internet marketing and electronic commerce as a logical subset of your organization's entire Internet business plan. By riding the plan's coattails, you can push Internet marketing a lot further, a lot faster. Organizational acceptance and support of Internet marketing will be your ultimate reward.

3. *Develop the action plan.* Some organizations are more technologically ready than others are, and some marketers may be further ahead than you are. Although business-to-business marketers are leading the charge, different companies are in different stages of readiness or implementation. After all, Internet marketing that is measurable is, for many, a new concept.

As with any good marketing plan, your Internet marketing action plan should include:

- *Objectives: general and specific,*

- *Products and services to be promoted,*

- *Competitive environment,*

- *Market opportunities,*

- *Marketing program strategy,*

- *Audience characteristics and selection criteria,*

- *Media usage and integration,*

- *Offer development,*

- *Creative execution,*

- *Lead qualification, lead fulfillment, and response management,*

- *Lead and sales tracking,*

- *Response and results analysis,*

- *Measurement criteria,*

- *Technical requirements for implementation,*

- *Staffing and organizational needs, and*

- *Program budgets and schedules.*

Implementing the Action Plan

The action plan should allow for a transitional stage, a period of time during which you consciously move your marketing programs more and more toward Internet marketing. Recognize that your plan should be flexible and may need to undergo continuous refinement and modification as conditions in your market change.

Refer to the Internet Marketing Audit Checklist and work towards turning the "no" answers into "yes" answers over time. Be sure your company is in a position to support current and future Internet marketing initiatives. If possible, help your company develop criteria for the acquisition of technology that will be required to implement Internet marketing on a broad scale. Lobby for assistance from outside resources and outsourcing of Internet services if needed to support Internet marketing initiatives.

Use the media integration plan outlined earlier to capitalize on the Internet trajectory. Start to integrate the Internet with your use of traditional media if you have not already done so. Test the effectiveness of the Internet as a lead generation and qualification medium. Compare and contrast Internet marketing campaigns with traditional media campaigns. Closely monitor Internet usage and evaluate results.

Increase your reliance on the Internet as time progresses, especially if prospects and customers seem receptive to Internet marketing. Let your audiences drive your use of the Internet—*ask them* how they wish to receive information and if the Internet is the medium they most prefer. Ask them for permission to use e-mail to communicate with them, and determine if they have an interest in having Web pages delivered directly to their desktops. Survey your customers regularly on their acceptance of Internet marketing.

Establish promotional guidelines that require consideration of the Internet in every marketing program. Do not execute any marketing program that does not have an Internet marketing component, and always take the time to spread the news internally (and externally if appropriate) of your Internet marketing successes.

In-House or Outside?

As part of your Internet marketing action plan, you will want to decide whether or not you will be in a position to implement programs in-house or with the assistance of outside resources. To help you make that decision, it is probably a good idea to identify the deliverables and analyze each in relation to your in-house capabilities. Figure 12.4 is just one example of such an analysis. You will note that some deliverables are handled with a combination of in-house and outside resources. It is likely that your situation will change and that at times you may have to outsource only part of the responsibility for some Internet marketing deliverables.

Suppose you decide to run a virtual seminar, for example. If that event includes streaming sound or video, you may want to use an outside resource—a Web hosting service that has the server capacity and capability of handling streaming media. This may be a more desirable solution than burdening your in-house Web server. Also keep in mind that it may take more than one outside resource to meet your needs at any given time. A Web hosting service would be a good resource for the technical implementation of a virtual seminar, but you may also need an outside interactive agency to create and execute the virtual seminar itself.

Staff Requirements for Internet Marketing

Earlier we mentioned the fact that you might have to retrain existing staff or even replace them with interactive marketing specialists. As In-

Plan Deliverable	Handling:	
	In-house	Outside
Technology		
Internet access		X
E-mail capabilities		
Marketing e-mail address for inquiries	X	
Broadcast capabilities for		
e-mail promotions and e-mail newsletters		X
Web Capabilities		
Corporate Web site hosting	X	
Web response areas and forms	X	
Marketing database integration	X	X
E-commerce applications		X
Maintenance and Back-office		
Web site on-going maintenance		X
Electronic response and lead management		X
Marketing database management	X	X
Managing Web site links	X	
Managing e-mail newsletter programs	X	
Managing customer extranet	X	
Managing partner extranets	X	
Creation and Execution		
E-mail	X	
Updating Web site pages	X	X
Web response areas and forms	X	
Banner ad campaigns		X
Virtual events		X
Order generation		X
Electronic fulfillment materials	X	X
Web community activity	X	
Participation in others' affiliate programs	X	
Management of own affiliate program		X

Figure 12.4. Action plan deliverables.

ternet marketing continues to grow in importance for your organization, it would be prudent to analyze marketing staff requirements and make adjustments in the future.

In some cases, you may be better off contracting outside freelance resources or working with interactive agencies on a project or program basis. Very often, outside resources have a level of expertise and a team of skilled professionals already working in a cohesive group. You might not be able to match this expertise with existing in-house staff, and personnel situations or budgets may prevent you from recruiting the necessary personnel.

Whether you are evaluating outside resources or planning to add in-house staff, the following job descriptions might be helpful to you. These are generally the types of positions that should be considered in staffing an Internet marketing function. All of these individuals should have a demonstrated comfort level with Internet technology, and all should at least be familiar with basic e-mail and Web tools.

Internet Marketing Manager

- Manages programs, personnel and budgets

- Motivates, leads, and supports the Internet marketing group

- Is responsible for training of group personnel

- Ensures that policies and procedures are followed

- Assigns responsibilities, tasks, and schedules

- Makes hiring, promotion, and compensation recommendations

- Tailors job descriptions to personal goals of personnel

- Maintains marketing partner relationships

- Interfaces with senior management regarding Internet marketing strategies

Marketologist

- Participates in developing strategic Internet marketing program

- Maintains high level of knowledge of Internet and Web technologies

- Recommends new technologies in collaboration with IT department

- Acts as Marketing liaison with internal IT resources and outside resources

- Manages Internet marketing media plan

- Measures and analyzes Internet marketing program results

- Acts as marketing strategist for creative execution

Internet Marketing Producer

- Facilitates the execution of Internet marketing strategies

- Works in close collaboration with Marketologist, Media, and Creative personnel to build interactive programs

- Develops, applies, and integrates Internet technologies and implements programs

- Publishes and maintains Web pages

Internet Marketing Media Specialist

- Researches Internet media and develops Internet media plans

- Places Internet media

- Evaluates and analyzes results of Internet marketing programs

Internet Marketing Creative Specialist: Copy

- Helps develop Internet marketing creative strategies

- Works in close collaboration with Internet marketing team

- Researches competition

- Writes copy for e-mail, online advertising, and Web forms and pages

Internet Marketing Creative Specialist: Art

- Helps develop Internet marketing creative strategies

- Works in close collaboration with Internet marketing team

- Creates graphics and graphic design for Web pages, response forms, and online advertising

The Internet Will Change Marketing Forever

In the era of Internet direct marketing, leads may come into your marketing pipeline from any source, qualified or unqualified. However, the e-mail and Web response paths may turn out to be the channel through which you acquire your *highest quality leads*. Eventually, it may be the channel of preference for many prospects and customers.

If this is the trend in Internet-based lead generation, it bears careful watching in your company. It implies that it will be more important than ever to utilize the Internet to generate and qualify leads in the first place, *because chances are they will be better quality leads*. Of course, it will be imperative to include a Web response path in your direct marketing promotions as the Web becomes the preferred method for response.

It will be increasingly common for marketers to accept lead generation program responses via campaign-specific URLs leading to Web response forms and pages, or by establishing full-fledged response centers on their Web sites. Prospects will get what they need through electronic fulfillment on Web sites, with the availability of information unlocks or downloads providing marketers with a distinct advantage over competitors. In many cases, customers already purchase products or services online, unlock purchased software or information instantly, or subscribe to services that offer to review, cull, and deliver Internet-based information to them.

One of the strengths of Internet marketing will be its ability to facilitate prospect and customer cultivation. As e-mail becomes an accepted means of marketing communication to reach qualified prospects and customers, you will be able to use it as a promotional vehicle to update key constituents on a periodic basis. The e-mail newsletter is gaining wide acceptance as a format, as both customers and qualified prospects elect to subscribe to such publications.

Areas of Web sites are increasingly dedicated to customers, and extranets have evolved into customer and key prospect information and service centers. Web-based communications, in the form of Web sites that customers and prospects visit or Web pages that are pushed to customer and prospect desktops, are commonplace.

You can see the implications of Internet marketing just by noting how it pervades every step of the lead generation and qualification process. At this point, the Internet components do not replace other media—all media work together in a closely coordinated effort, supporting one another. Prospects need to be able to choose the way they wish to respond and receive information. This is a key concept, because it is will define the future of marketing communications:

> *Prospects and customers will define the way you, the marketer, communicate with them. They will drive the communication process instead of the marketer.*

This fundamentally changes the marketer/prospect relationship forever. With the empowerment of the prospect, the marketer's role will be to deliver what the prospect asks for, when the prospect asks for it, using the delivery channel of the prospect's choice. With the emergence of one-to-one customer relationships, the marketer will need to learn from the customer's interactions with the marketer and use that data to continuously refine the customer-marketing program.

This is only the beginning. At its current rate of adoption, Internet marketing is no longer an option but a necessity. With its true cost saving and timesaving benefits, as well as the growing demand by prospects and customers, the Internet will become the core medium in the entire marketing process.

In many respects, Internet marketing has now come full circle. Marketers who are moving aggressively towards it recognize that it does not work in a vacuum; that to be most effective, marketing programs need to integrate Internet advertising with traditional forms of advertising, and that traditional forms of fulfillment and customer service need to meld with e-business practices.

Forrester Research, in its June 1999 report on "Driving Site Traffic" coined a phrase that could define this emerging intermingling of media: *synchronized advertising*. Forrester says the concept is to link "traditional advertising's branding strength with the Web's power to tailor messages based on a consumer's media consumption and purchase behavior."

Beyond that, says Forrester Research in a February 2000 report, is the next marketing frontier, "presence awareness." Forrester defines presence awareness as "the ability to know a person's availability and status across all communication channels." Forrester sees presence awareness as a kind of "electronic peripheral vision" that Internet-based applications will someday incorporate. This means marketers will have a more in-depth understanding of what customers and prospect want, and when they want it, regardless of how they interact with the company. With the advent of wireless communications, this concept could extend even beyond today's physical boundaries.

These possibilities make the future all the more exciting for b-to-b marketers. The real way to succeed with Internet marketing may well be to view it as the logical extension of the marketing process, integrated seamlessly with traditional marketing in a way that almost disregards the differences and capitalizes on the combined strength of both.

Note

1. Melissa Bane, Director of Internet Market Strategies, The Yankee Group, "Is Successful Web Marketing a Myth?" Sales and Marketing Series: Web Marketing—Myth and Reality, a presentation of the Massachusetts Software Council, Natick, Massachusetts, February 6, 1998.

A Final Word

The Internet is at the center of a fundamental business shift. It has become the core of a new Information Economy, and it is yet to become the core of marketing. The Internet's inevitability, its wide adoption as an interactive communications tool, and its emergence as a system of commerce are converging on direct marketing and the marketing world in general and pressuring them to change, rapidly and dramatically.

Even now, the rules of Internet marketing are being re-written, which is why this book's Web site is an important source of updated information.

Internet marketing has gone beyond its early experimental stage. E-commerce is in its third generation. An October 1999 report released by Forrester Research suggests that "post-Web retailers" will be the ultimate e-commerce winners as the market becomes saturated. These retailers, says Forrester, will concentrate on anticipating shoppers' needs, expanding products and services to meet those needs, and selling through multiple retail channels, not just the Web. This notion is supported by the June 2000 E-tail Economic Study conducted by McKinsey/Salomon Smith Barney. The study suggests that it is those e-tailers who cross the lines between stores, catalogs, and e-commerce who will survive. "Pure plays," or Internet-only retailers, lose money every time they sell anything, according to the study.

Database-driven Internet personalization is now standard practice. One-to-one relationship marketing is fast becoming a necessity in e-business. CRM (Customer Relationship Management) is one of the hottest business sectors. Already, b-to-b marketers large and small are using Internet marketing today to generate and qualify leads, hold successful Internet events, execute instant fulfillment, enhance customer relationships, and generate orders. They are joining Web communities and, in some cases, starting their own portals. They are building affiliate marketing programs and forming new kinds of Internet partnerships.

All kinds of advances will drive the Internet, and Internet marketing, to new heights, some of which today might be unimaginable. Convergence of the Internet and telecommunications, the connections between the Internet and cable television, the onward march of broadband, voice-based Internet access, and the emergence of a truly wireless Internet will do much to drive widespread adoption. Other trends, such as the growth of ASPs (Application Service Providers), will bring sophisticated e-commerce and e-business applications to even the smallest of companies. Backwards integration of the Internet into bricks-and-mortar companies, who will start using the Internet to run their traditional businesses, will have a far-reaching effect. The June 2000 approval of a Federal e-signatures bill will make digital signatures as legal as those executed on paper. Broadening demographic usage of the Internet, from teens to seniors and men to women, will continue to spread its popularity. The reliance on e-mail by every consumer and business person will likely cause it to dominate every other form of communication, even the telephone.

These are vast, fundamental changes we are witnessing now. And we are only at the beginning of the technology curve.

And what of b-to-b marketing? I have worked with b-to-b companies for over two decades. I learned about the awesome power of direct marketing and witnessed firsthand what it could achieve.

As a direct marketer who cut his teeth on direct mail, at first I found the swift move to Internet marketing unnerving. I am a complete convert now.

The adoption of the Internet reminds me of the desktop publishing revolution. I remember when typesetters and paste-up artists were swept away by the flood of computer technology, some doubting it would take hold. Now everything in every design department at every ad agency or publication is done on computer disk. The productivity and quality improvements have been monumental. No one looks back upon the "good old days" of typesetting and manual paste-up with fondness anymore.

Fortunately, it is *marketing* that early on drove the growth of the Internet, and it is marketing that will now be one of its primary beneficiaries. Internet marketing will *become* the new direct marketing because of its inherent direct marketing power. After all, isn't Internet marketing in reality interactive, personalized, one-to-one direct marketing? Even more than that, the Internet is the marketing medium that can *truly complete the selling cycle* by letting prospects not only learn about a product online, but buy it online. If Internet marketing is applied intelligently, it can fulfill the promise of direct marketing in the Age of the e: totally measurable, results-oriented, repeatable and highly efficient.

To survive and thrive, you, as a b-to-b marketer, must embrace Internet marketing at once. You will integrate it into your overall marketing strategy, capitalizing on the combined strength of online and offline media. And if you're to succeed, you will understand that the Internet is destined to become the central core of your marketing strategy.

The demarcation between traditional marketing and Internet marketing is blurring rapidly, and it is not merely in marketing. In fact, the entire business world is adopting the Internet as a business platform. The Disneys of the world are buying into it, and the Procter & Gambles of the world are advertising on it. It is the Ciscos, Dells, and IBMs of the world who are leading the revolution. And it is such Dot Coms as Amazon, eBay, and America Online who are re-shaping business as we know it.

Internet marketing is the new marketing, based on timeless marketing principles, that will drive b-to-b now and in the future. I have personally witnessed this transformation in my own direct marketing business. Our clients now use traditional media to drive prospects and customers to Internet events and Web sites. E-mail, newsletter ads, online advertising and Web sites are becoming the primary marketing media of choice, working in conjunction with traditional direct mail and advertising to *improve the marketing ROI*.

I know for certain that the fundamental principles of direct marketing will not only survive—they will flourish as the basic tenets of Internet marketing. I am enthusiastic and positive about the emergence and the future of Internet marketing, which has so much to offer to so many— with such extraordinarily compelling and proven benefits. In the end, it is all about building better, more productive relationships with prospects and customers...the simplest of notions, but all the more challenging to achieve as marketing becomes more sophisticated and complex. Fulfilling and rewarding marketing relationships will be the norm in the Age of the e.

Appendix A:

Other Resources

Web Sites Mentioned in This Book (in order of appearance, first reference only)

Note: These URLs were active at time of publication, but Web site addresses can change or be abandoned without notice. For the most up-to-date list of URLs, check this book's companion Web site. All of these URLs start with *http://* which most browsers recognize, so it is not listed. URLs are typically not case sensitive, but it is best to enter addresses in all lower case.

Chapter 1: Business-to-Business Direct Marketing—A Crash Course

www.usps.gov
www.postofficeonline.com

Chapter 2: The Age of the "e"

www.statmarket.com
www.inktomi.com
www.idc.com

www.etforecasts.com
www.acnielsen.com
www.jup.com
www.forrester.com
www.yankeegroup.com
www.gartnergroup.com
www.greatdomains.com
www.internetwk.com
www.bluemountain.com
www.mediametrix.com
www.aol.com
www.csi.com
www.prodigy.com
www.the-dma.org
www.ftc.gov
www.fccfbi.gov
www.cyberatlas.internet.com
www.commerce.net
www.webtv.com
www.microsoft.com
www.wgate.com
www.mediaone.com
www.netzero.com
www.altavista.com
www.directechemerge.com
www.amazon.com
www.dell.com
www.gigabuys.com
www.cisco.com
www.intel.com
www.individual.com

Chapter 3: Generating and Qualifying Leads with Your Web Site

www.poynter.org/eyetrack2000/index.htm
www.webtrends.com
www.netgen.com
www.netgen.com/emetrics/
www.position-it.com

www.promotingyoursite.com
www.ups.com
www.gte.com
www.intuit.com
www.netb2b.com
www.monsanto.com
www.colehersee.com
www.deere.com
www.enron.com
www.ml.com
www.baxter.com
www.ibm.com
www.ge.com
www.adp.com
www.eastman.com
www.kpmg.com
www.realnetworks.com
www.att.com
www.fedex.com
www.officemax.com

Chapter 4: Generating and Qualifying Leads with Online Advertising

www.iab.net
www.emarketer.com
www.adrelevance.com
www.unicast.com
www.engage.com
www.cmpnet.com
www.zdnet.com
www.netratings.com
www.doubleclick.net
www.flycast.com
www.adforce.com
www.ad-venture.com
www.b2bworks.net
www.247media.com
www.b2bfreenet.com
www.webconnect.com

www.adnetwork.linkexchange.com
www.smartclicks.com
www.alexa.com
www.enliven.com
www.bluestreak.com
www.wired.com
www.cnet.com
www.juno.com
www.fidelity.com
www.compaq.com
www.promotions.com
www.coolsavings.com
www.valuepage.com
www.freeforum.com
www.clickrewards.com
www.flooz.com
www.mypoints.com
www.cybergold.com
www.thebullseye.com
www.spidertop.com

Chapter 5: Generating and Qualifying Leads with E-mail

www.messagingonline.com
www.imtstrategies.com
www.onelist.com
www.webpromote.com/pmguide
www.21stcm.com
www.directmedia.com
www.amlist.com
www.idglist.com
www.postmasterdirect.com
www.worldata.com
www.yesmail.com
www.lists.com
www.topica.com
www.idg.net
www.clickz.com
www.clickzguide.com

www.flycast.com
www.1to1.com
www.zoomerang.com
www.deja.com
www.messagemedia.com
www.digitalimpact.com
www.responsys.com
www.exactis.com
www.egghead.com
www.e-dialog.com
www.messagemates.com
www.indimi.com
www.mediasynergy.com
www.radicalmail.com
www.zaplet.com
www.egain.com
www.wilsonweb/wmt5/viral-principles.htm
www.wilsonweb/wmt5/viral-deploy.htm

Chapter 6: Using Internet Events for Marketing

www.bn.com
www.notharvard.com
www.real.com
www.activate.com
www.broadcast.com
www.enen.com
www.webcasts.com
www.akamai.com
www.placeware.com
www.presentation.net
www.mshow.com
www.centra.com
www.latitude.com
www.eventshome.com
www.inetevents.com
www.b-there.com
www.iconvention.com
www.allmeetings.com

www.go-events.com
www.eventweb.com
www.meetingevents.com
www.seminarfinder.com
www.seminarinformation.com
www.seminarplanet.com
www.seminarsource.com
www.techweb.com/calendar
www.tscentral.com
www.centranow.com
www.iplanet.com/netforums/
www.oracle.com/seminars
www.placeware.com/seminar
www.webex.com
www.mindspringbiz.com
www.corpu.com
www.cyberstateu.com
www.digitalthink.com
www.smartforce.com
www.smartplanet.com
www.lotus.com

Chapter 7: Executing e-Fulfillment

www.digimarc.com
www.gocode.com
www.mgisoft.com
www.nwfusion.com
www.ecommercial.com
www.entrypoint.com
www.3com.com
www.freei.net
www.marimba.com
www.adobe.com
www.about.com
www.northernlight.com
www.download.com
www.onsale.com
www.mcafee.com/cybermedia

www.wsj.com
www.biztravel.com
www.expedia.com
www.travelocity.com
www.digitrends.net/digitrends/dtonline/features/sections/fulfillment/
www.dhlmasterclass.com
www.marketfirst.com
www.marketsoft.com
www.netquartz.com
www.netship.com
www.submitorder.com

Chapter 8: Building Customer Relationships

www.crmcommunity.com
www.crmdaily.com
www.accelerating.com
www.acuity.com
www.aspect.com
www.beasys.com
www.bowstreet.com
www.brightware.com
www.broadvision.com
www.epage.com
www.epiphany.com
www.eshare.com
www.kana.com
www.liveperson.com
www.neteffect.com
www.netperceptions.com
www.peoplesupport.com
www.servicesoft.com
www.iaexpress.com
www.netbytel.com
www.netcallusa.com
www.landsend.com
www.mathworks.com
www.sun.com
www.atg.com

www.builder.com/Business/Personal
www.personalization.com
www.asponline.com
www.intranets.com

Chapter 9: Using Business Communities and Exchanges

www.netscape.com
www.ask.com
www.directhit.com
www.4anything.com
www.google.com
www.hotbot.com
www.infoseek.com
www.lycos.com
www.yahoo.com
www.geocities.com
www.hypermart.net
www.business1.com
www.thestandard.com
www.adauction.com
www.comparenet.com
www.ebay.com
www.fairmarket.com
www.freemarkets.com
www.priceline.com
www.tradeout.com
www.planetit.com
www.channelweb.com
www.edtn.com
www.earthweb.com
www.dice.com
www.datamation.com
www.developer.com
www.itknowledge.com
www.itworld.com
www.internet.com
www.e2open.com
www.allbusiness.com

www.bcentral.com
www.bizbuyer.com
www.bizprolink.com
www.buyerszone.com
www.commerceinc.com
www.inc.com
www.office.com
www.onvia.com
www.ariba.com
www.industry.net
www.iprocure.com
www.manufacturing.net
www.procurenet.com
www.productnews.com
www.purchasepro.com
www.suppliermarket.com
www.verticalnet.com
www.chemdex.com
www.ventro.com
www.medcast.com
www.sciquest.com
www.enermetrix.com
www.ecitydeals.com
www.gsaauctions.gov
www.midrangeuser.com
www.news400.com
www.myhelpdesk.com
www.webharbor.com
www.espeed.com
www.guru.com
www.newmediary.com
www.sales.com
www.siebel.com
www.deepcanyon.com
www.mysap.com
www.oraclexchange.com
www.321website.com
www.buyerweb.com
www.comercis.com
www.commerceone.com

www.delphi.com
www.prospero.com
www.egroups.com
www.esociety.com
www.excite.com
www.ibelong.com
www.involv.com
www.participate.com
www.peoplepanel.com
www.viewlocity.com

Chapter 10: Developing Internet Partnerships

www.linkshare.com
www.iconomy.com
www.escalate.com
www.b2brover.com
www.associate-it.com
www.refer-it.com
www.befree.com
www.clicktrade.com
www.cj.com
www.kinzan.com
www.nexchange.com
www.affinia.com
www.bidfocus.com
www.buytelco.com
www.ebates.com
www.enews.com
www.isyndicate.com
www.networksolutions.com
www.promisemark.com
www.qspace.com
www.sundial.com
www.verisign.com
www.webtrends.com
www.3com.com/partners/
www.teamplayersprogram.com
www.oracle.com/partners/

www.uu.net
www.grainger.com
www.works.com
www.hotwire.com
www.respond.com

Chapter 11: Selling on the Internet

www.aberdeen.com
www.mysimon.com
www.rusure.com
www.dash.com
www.iship.com
www.estamp.com
www.stamps.com
www.openmarket.com
www.electrom.com
www.cybercash.com
www.instabuy.com
www.americanexpress.com
www.gator.com
www.nextcard.com
www.eocnet.com
www.npd.com
www.supermarkets.com
www.coupons.com
www.insight.com
www.gigabuys.com
www.dell-host.com
www.GE.com
www.marshall.com
www.necx.com
www.nexcdirect.necx.com

Chapter 12: Integrating Online and Offline Marketing

www.chasmgroup.com
www.ceoexpress.com

Web Sites of Interest to the Business-to-Business Marketer

The best way to find sites of interest is to use major Web search engines, entering combinations of appropriate keywords. After you find a site of value to you, be sure to add it to your browser as a "bookmark." I have compiled and categorized a list of sites in an effort to reduce your search time. All of these sites are linked on the book's Companion Web site.

Advertising, Direct Marketing, Marketing and Sales

www.admedia.org	The "Internet Advertising Resource Guide"
www.adsmart.com	Internet advertising data
www.adage.com/interactive	Advertising Age Interactive Daily
www.ad-guide.com	International guide to Internet marketing
www.adresource.com	Ad Resource from Internet.com
www.ana.net	Association of National Advertisers
www.marketing.org	Business Marketing Association
www.builder.com	How to build better Web sites
www.clickz.com	ClickZ Internet Marketing Network
www.digitrends.net	Digitrends Daily
www.the-dma.org	Direct Marketing Association
www.directechemerge.com	Information for business-to-business direct marketers
www.directmag.com	DIRECT magazine
www.directresponse.com	Direct marketing search site
www.dmnetwork.com	Direct marketing search site
www.dmnews.com	DM News
www.dmplaza.com	Direct marketing search site
www.ecommercetimes.com	e-Commerce Times
www.emarketer.com	eMarketer news and statistics
www.freepromote.com	Free Web site promotion
www.iconoclast.com	Iconoclast e-letter
www.idmb.org	Internet Direct Marketing Bureau
www.justsell.com	Sales portal
www.m1to1.com	Peppers and Rogers Group

www.marketingcentral.com	Comprehensive marketing services site
www.marketingclick.com	Marketing news, events, and bulletin boards
www.marketing computers.com	Marketing Computers magazine
www.mediafinder.com	Media information
www.myprospects.com	My Prospects (create lists)
www.netb2b.com	Net Marketing/B-to-B magazine
www.professionalcity.com	Resource center with a Marketing sub-site
www.promoting yoursite.com	Promoting Your Web Site
www.rankthis.com	Your Web site ranked in search engines
www.sales.com	Sales portal sponsored by Siebel
www.shop.org	An association of Internet retailers
www.smei.org	Sales and Marketing Executives International
www.software marketing.com	Software Marketing Journal
www.srds.com	SRDS-list information online
www.targetonline.com	Target Marketing magazine
www.usps.com	U.S. Postal Service, "Internet Branch"
www.wdfm.com	Web Digest for Marketers
www.webpromote.com	WebPromote e-mail marketing information
www.wilsonweb.com	Wilsonweb's Web marketing information

Internet Advertising Networks and Placement Services

www.adauction.com	Ad Auction
www.doubleclick.net	DoubleClick
www.flycast.com	FlyCast
www.ad-venture.com	ad-VENTURE Network
www.b2bworks.net	B2BWorks Network
www.247media.com	24/7 Media

www.webconnect.com	WebConnect
www.adnetwork.link exchange.com	LinkExchange
www.smartclicks.com	SmartClicks

Business Information

www.all-biz.com	The "all business network"
www.bannerstake.com	Keyword competitive research
www.bpubs.com	Business publications search engine
www.business2.com	BUSINESS 2.0 magazine
www.ceoexchange.com	Online topics and discussion for CEOs
www.companysleuth.com	Competitive intelligence
www.dbusiness.com	Local business news
www.fastcompany.com	FAST COMPANY magazine
www.forbes.com	The Forbes "Digital Tool"
www.hoovers.com	Comprehensive source for information on companies of all kinds
www.infousa.com	Information for small business
www.ideacafe.com	A nifty site for small businesses
www.inc.com	Inc. magazine
www.netlibrary.com	Net Library
www.wsj.com	The Wall Street Journal
www.your-nation.com	Compare demographic data from country to country

E-mail List Vendors, Services, and Technologies

www.amlist.com
www.cmgdirect.com
www.e-dialog.com
www.messagemates.com
www.mediasynergy.com
www.postmasterdirect.com
www.radicalmail.com
www.worldata.com

www.yesmail.com
www.21stcm.com

Internet News

www.businesstech.com	The use of Internet technology for business
ebiz.businessweek.com	Business Week's "e.biz"
www.commerce.net	"Industry consortium" for Internet commerce
www.cmpnet.com/netbiz	Internet business site
www.hot100.com	The hottest Internet sites, and more
www.internet.com	All things Internet
www.internetnews.com	The latest news of the Internet
www.thestandard.com	The Industry Standard magazine
www.wired.com	Wired Digital

Internet Research

www.aberdeen.com	Aberdeen Group
www.activmedia.com	ActivMedia
www.computer economics.com	Computer Economics
www.commerce.net/research	Commerce.net and Nielsen Media Research
www.cyberatlas.com	CyberAtlas (Internet.com)
www.cyberdialogue.com	Leading online research company
www.delphigroup.com	The Delphi Group
www.ecommerce.gov	U.S. Dept. Of Commerce electronic commerce site
e-commerce.research.ml.com	Merrill Lynch E-Commerce Reports
www.emarketer.com	Comprehensive site for electronic marketing stats
www.forrester.com	Forrester Research
www.gartner.com	GartnerGroup
www.greenfieldonline.com	Greenfield Online
www.idc.com	IDC

www.jup.com	Jupiter Communications
www.iab.net	Internet Advertising Bureau
www.mediametrix.com	Media Metrix
www.netratings.com	Net Ratings (Nielsen Media Research)
www.npd.com	NPD Group
www.statmarket.com	Daily Internet statistics
www.webcriteria.com	Web Criteria
www.webreference.com	Web Reference site for Webmasters
www.yankeegroup.com	Yankee Group

Launching Pads, Timesavers, and Cool Things

www.555-1212.com	Telephone lookup
www.askjeeves.com	Easy to use, mega-search engine
www.biztravel.com	For all your business travel needs
www.ceoexpress.com	One of the best places to start for information of all kinds
www.corporate information.com	A site with links to information on companies worldwide
digital.daytimer.com	Free personal calendar
www.dictionary.com	Word definitions
www.efax.com	Free fax and voicemail at your e-mail address
www.eletter.com	Do direct mail using the Internet
www.hightechgateway.com	Launching pad for high tech sponsored by industry consultant PRTM
www.hotofftheweb.com	Web page capture
www.industry.net	Super site for access to industries
www.IT-radar.com	IT marketplace
www.iship.com	Consolidated shipping information
www.jumbo.com	Free and shared software downloads
www.learn2.com	Learn about anything
www.mapquest.com	The Internet's premier mapping service
www.messageblaster.com	An all-inclusive Web messaging service
www.productnews.com	Super site for access to thousands of industrial products
www.smartship.com	Consolidated shipping information

www.stpt.com	"Starting Point," a launching pad to a variety of information
www.supporthelp.com	An online search resource for the technology industry
www.technewsworld.com	Technology news from around the world in real-time
www.verticalnet.com	Super site for access to selected vertical industries
www.whowhere.com/ Business	Find people and companies

Leading Information Technology News Super Sites

www.earthweb.com
www.idg.net and www.itworld.com
www.itknowledge.com
www.techrepublic.com
www.news.com (www.cnet.com)
techweb.cmp.com
www.zdnet.com

Web Portals and Search Engines

www.about.com
www.allonesearch.com
www.altavista.com
www.go.com
www.excite.com
www.hotbot.com
www.google.com
www.infoseek.com
www.lycos.com
www.msn.com
www.netscape.com
www.northernlight.com
www.snap.com
www.webcrawler.com
www.yahoo.com

Barry's Favorite E-mail Newsletters About Marketing
(Subscribe free at the sites listed below)

www.clickz.com	*ClickZ Today*
www.channelseven.com	*Channel Seven*
www.cyberatlas. *internet.com*	*CyberAtlas*
www.digitrends.net	*Digitrends and eBiz Daily*
www.ecommercetimes.com	*E-Commerce Times*
www.emarketer.com	*eMarketer*
www.eventweb.com	*EventWeb Newsletter*
www.iconoclast.com	*Iconoclast*
www.1to1.com	*INSIDE 1to1 – Peppers + Rogers* *Group*
www.wdfm.com	*Web Digest For Marketers*
www.webpromote.com	*Web Promote Weekly*
www.wilsonweb.com	*Web Marketing Today*

Books of Special Relevance to the Business-to-Business Marketer

Most of these books can be purchased at a discount through this book's companion Web site or through any online bookseller.

Cliff Allen, Deborah Kania, and Beth Yaeckel, *The Internet World Guide to One-to-One Web Marketing.*
> A comprehensive guide to one-to-one marketing on the Web with lots of examples, tips, and techniques.

Rick Bruner, *Net Results: Web Marketing that Works.*
> Textbook-style but with lots of useful advice on brand building, direct marketing, and more.

Bob Donath, Carolyn K. Dixon, Richard A. Crocker, and James Obermayer, *Managing Sales Leads: How to Turn Every Prospect into a Customer.*
> This book, written by inquiry handling pros, is one of the few to cover the entire process, authoritatively and comprehensively. It is

both readable and practical, loaded with facts and advice for exactly how to manage your entire sales lead process.

Seth Godin, *Permission Marketing*.
Destined to become an e-marketing classic, this book by an Internet visionary gets to the heart of a key Internet marketing issue: Prospects will ultimately call the shots by giving marketers permission to send them marketing messages.

John Hagel, Arthur G. Armstrong, *Net Gain*, also *Net Worth*.
Pronouncements about market expansion using virtual communities.

Denny Hatch, Don Jackson, and Donald R. Jackson, *2,439 Tested Secrets for Direct Marketing Success*.
A compendium of advice from the pros. Kind of an encyclopedia of what to do (and what not to) with pearls of wisdom from all corners of the direct marketing world. If getting through all of them does not exhaust you, the tips are very valuable.

Christina Ford Haylock, *Net Success: 24 Leaders in Web Commerce Show You How to Put the Web to Work for Your Business*.
An inside look at leaders in e-business.

Shel Holtz, *Public Relations on the Net*.
How to use the Internet for PR.

Shannon Kinnard, *Marketing with E-mail*.
A comprehensive resource for e-mail marketers.

Jim Kobs, *Profitable Direct Marketing*.
A classic in direct marketing from a knowledgeable pro. His list of "99 proven offers" is as good as any ever published.

Jesus Mena, *Data Mining Your Website*.
How to use data mining to profile customers and created personalized e-commerce programs.

Geoffrey A. Moore, *Crossing the Chasm* and *Inside the Tornado*.
Moore studied Silicon Valley companies and wrote *Crossing the Chasm*, which became a marketing classic. In this book, he explores

the technology product life cycle and shows what companies go through to achieve marketing success. This and the previous volume are must-reads for IT marketers.

Edward L. Nash, *Direct Marketing: Strategy, Planning, Execution*, Third Edition.
> One of the most comprehensive overviews of direct marketing. Includes details of database marketing, infomercials, interactive marketing. Also information on planning, mailing lists, print media, and more.

Don Peppers, Martha Rogers, *The One to One Enterprise: Competing in the Interactive Age*.
> Peppers and Rogers bring their industry-leading one-to-one thinking to the Interactive Age.

Don Peppers, Martha Rogers, *The One to One Fieldbook*.
> A step-by-step guide to putting one-to-one marketing into practice.

Don Peppers, Martha Rogers, *The One to One Manager*.
> Why not apply the one-to-one concept to people who've done it well?

Jerry I. Reitman, Editor, *Beyond 2000: The Future of Direct Marketing*.
> What better way to get a true perspective on the future of direct marketing than from some of the world's leading direct marketing experts. Each shares a unique viewpoint in this provocative and useful compendium of opinion and insight.

Ernan Roman, *Integrated Direct Marketing*.
> Roman was writing about integration long before it reached its current "hot topic" status. He intelligently describes how to put together mail and telemarketing to squeeze the most out of your direct marketing investment, and cites successful case histories.

Patricia B. Seybold, *Customers.com*.
> This forward-thinking work by the founder of a technology consulting firm quickly became a best seller, and rightly so. It shares strategies for orienting your company to customers, including in-depth examples of companies who use the Internet to do it right.

Dick Shaver, *The Next Step in Database Marketing: Consumer Guided Marketing.*
Largely a book for consumer marketers, the concept of consumer guided marketing bears consideration by all direct marketers—because it is really about efficiency, one-to-one database marketing, and respecting an individual's privacy.

Thomas M. Siebel, *Cyber Rules.*
Strategies for excelling at e-business by the founder of Siebel Systems.

Barry Silverstein, *Internet Marketing for Information Technology Companies.*
By the author of *Business-to-Business Internet Marketing*, this is the first book to cover proven online techniques that increase sales and profits for hardware, software, and networking companies.

Joseph Sugarman, *Marketing Secrets of a Mail Order Maverick.*
One of the true direct marketing visionaries, Joe Sugarman has done it all and is more than willing to share his war stories and strategies for success with readers. Both entertaining and educational.

Bob Stone, *Successful Direct Marketing Methods,* Sixth Edition.
If you're going to buy just one direct marketing book, this is it. It is the most authoritative text on the business, covering every aspect in plenty of detail.

Susan Sweeney, *101 Ways to Promote Your Web Site.*
Details numerous ways to advertising, promote, and generate public relations for any organization's Web site.

Joan Throckmorton, *Winning Direct Response Advertising: From Print Through Interactive Media.*
Another living legend in the direct marketing business, Joan Throckmorton takes you through the whole gamut of direct marketing—advertising, mail, and interactive.

Lester Wunderman, *Being Direct: Making Advertising Pay.*
Authored by one of the greats of the direct marketing business. Combines autobiography with advice and wisdom—and shares

Wunderman's vision of where direct marketing is headed. Entertaining and insightful.

Robin Lee Zeff, Brad Aronson, *Advertising on the Internet, Second Edition*.
Covers Internet advertising in depth.

Jan Zimmerman, *Marketing on the Internet, Fourth Edition*.
Updated fourth edition is a comprehensive guide to marketing on the Internet. Includes the ABCs of Internet marketing, how to create and distribute info-tools, how to create a Web site, multimedia, e-commerce basics, and more.

Appendix B:

Glossary

The following glossary of direct and Internet marketing terms was compiled especially for business-to-business marketers.

80/20 Rule Also known as "Pareto's Principle." States a comparison of relative weight in marketing terms, such as "20 percent of the customer base generates 80 percent of the company's sales."

Affiliate, Associate Affiliate marketing is a form of partnering that has been popularized on the Internet. Basically, a Web marketer offers affiliates the opportunity to share in revenue by getting referral fees or sales commissions on goods and services sold via the affiliate's Web site. The affiliate, or associate, is an organization/firm that participates in an affiliate marketing program.

AIDA A direct marketing concept that represents the way a respondent is engaged: Awareness, Interest, Desire, Action.

Audience Typically, the individuals you are trying to reach with a direct marketing campaign. In business-to-business marketing, a commonly held theory is that there is no single large audience, but rather audience segments (see *Segmentation*).

Banner, banner ad A small advertising area on a Web site.

Benefit What an individual derives from a product or service; what a product or service really does for the prospect or customer.

Bingo cards, bingo leads Cards or leads that are returned with little or no information to enable the market to qualify the leads; "raw" responses.

Bookmark A Web site or page saved via the Web browser for future reference.

BRC Business Reply Card.

Broadband A very high speed means of transmitting data now being used by cable and telephone companies to provide Internet access.

Browser The software that allows viewing of HTML documents or Web pages. The two leadng browsers are Netscape (Navigator or Communicator) and Microsoft Internet Explorer.

Business reply Mail that carries a business reply permit so that it can be returned at the marketer's cost.

B2B; B2C "B2B" or B-to-B refers to business-to-business, which means businesses who market directly to other businesses; "B2C" is business-to-consumer, or businesses who market directly to consumers.

Cable modem A modem that facilitates Internet access via television cable (See *Broadband*).

CGI Common Gateway Interface. Programming used most often to enable interactive forms and counters.

Channel marketing Marketing done to or through other channels, such as retailers, distributors, and resellers.

Chat Generally refers to online dialogue, typically conducted via e-mail, or in a "chat room," or via instant messaging.

Click, click-through The advertising version of a "hit"—when the viewer of a banner ad clicks on it; or clicking on an area of a Web page to open a link.

Closed loop system Generally refers to a lead generation and fulfillment process in which the lead goes from an inbound response through qualification, fulfillment, follow-up, and conversion to sale, with tracking and feedback mechanisms established along the way.

Community A Web site, newsgroup, or discussion group that shares common characteristics. Web-based communities share information and provide services to community members.

Compiled list A list that is composed of names and addresses, telephone numbers, and/or e-mail addresses from non-response sources, such as directories or phone books.

Cookie A piece of data sent by a Web server to the visitor's computer to identify that visitor's computer when it connects again with the Web page.

CPM Cost per thousand. Applies to purchasing media, usually print advertising, mailing lists, and broadcast, also for banner ads.

Cross-functional direct marketing Marketing to multiple individuals or decision-makers in different functional areas within a company.

Customer An individual who does business with a company; typical classifications are former, dormant, active, or current. Customers can also be ranked based on purchase criteria (see *RFM*).

Cyberspace The imaginary location of the Internet.

Database, database marketing A computerized file of information about individuals, which includes basic contact information, response and/or purchase history, and other historic, transactional sales, and marketing data. Database marketing is the practice of using databases to improve the marketing process.

DHTML Dynamic HTML; provides additional interactive capabilities beyond HTML.

Dimensional Any mailing that is odd-sized or three-dimensional in nature, such as a tube or box.

Direct marketing, direct response The discipline of results-driven, response-oriented marketing. Direct marketing includes any medium used responsively, including direct response advertising, direct mail, telemarketing, direct response television, direct response radio, and interactive media.

Domain name A name assigned to a Web site or area on the Internet.

Download The process of copying one or more files from one place to another, usually from a Web server to a computer.

DSL (Digital Subscriber Line) A technology that uses basic telephone lines to provide Internet access at very high speed.

E-business The general term, popularized by IBM, for conducting business electronically.

ECML (Electronic Commerce Modeling Language) A new emerging standard for universal acceptance of online payments.

E-commerce The general term for selling online.

E-mail Any electronic message sent over a network.

E-mail newsletter A periodic news publication, sent in the form of an e-mail.

Exposures See *Impressions*.

Extranet An Internet-enabled network designed primarily for a company's internal use, but that allows select outsiders, such as customers, partners, and suppliers, in **E-zine** An electronic magazine or e-newsletter.

FAQs Frequently Asked Questions.

Feature What a product does; a product attribute or quality, unrelated to how it benefits an individual.

Flame A negative response to unsolicited e-mail.

FSIs Free Standing Inserts; advertising inserted into or with publications.

Fulfillment Generally refers to materials sent in response to an inquiry, or to the process of sending those materials.

GIF Graphical Interchange Format; an electronic image file format.

Guestbook Typically, a registration area on a Web site.

Hit An interaction or request made to a Web server. A page can be "hit" numerous times by one visitor, and therefore hits are not a measure of the number of visitors.

Hits The number of clicks to a Web page.

Home page The primary page of a Web site.

Hosting The process of setting up a Web server and administering a Web site.

House list, house file A mailing list or database of prospects and/or customers that belongs to a company; can be maintained in-house or by an outside firm.

HTML The HyperText Markup Language used so that browsers can view words on Web pages.

HTTP HyperText Transfer Protocol, the protocol used to transport Web-based information.

Hybrid list Typically a compiled list that has been enhanced with response data or additional marketing information.

Hyperlink A link to a Web page.

Icon A graphic, picture, or small graphic element.

Impressions The number of times a banner ad appears in an established period of time, typically a month.

Interactive media Usually refers to the Internet, World Wide Web, and CD-ROMs; also means any medium that encourages interaction.

Internet A computer network of networks; the world's largest network allows computers to connect with one another.

Internet address Any location on the Internet.

Internet Explorer Microsoft's Web browser.

Interstitial Web advertising that appears or "pops up" between Web pages.

Intranet An Internet-enabled network used internally by a company or organization.

IP The Internet Protocol, the protocol used for Internet transmission.

ISP Internet Service Provider, an organization that provides access and other Internet-related services

Java; JavaScript; Java applets A language developed by Sun that has become the basis for many Internet applications; scripting or applications driven by Java.

JPEG Joint Photographic Experts Group; refers to a compressed graphic image format.

Keycode A code assigned to a list to identify it as part of a mailing. The code could also represent other criteria, such as geography, company size, industry type, job title, etc.

Lead Generally a prospect that has not yet been qualified.

Lead processing The process of qualifying, fulfilling, distributing, and tracking leads.

Mailbot An automatic e-mail responder or response program.

Marketing database See *Database*.

Marketing Pyramid A tool that can be used to break audiences into identifiable segments.

Match code A code used to identify a specific name and address record. Usually the match code is made up of some combination of pieces of data from the name and address and other identifiable data.

Microsegmentation The process of dividing an audience into very small, identifiable segments based on defined criteria or combinations or criteria.

MSA Metropolitan Statistical Area; a geographical area encompassing a city.

Netiquette Good manners on the Internet; i.e., not sending spam, respecting others' privacy, etc.

Netscape The company that pioneered the Web browser, first with Netscape Navigator.

NCOA National Change of Address processing or program.

Nixie Mail returned with a bad address.

OEM Original Equipment Manufacturer.

Offer The "underlying" offer is the company, its products and services, and the perception of those things by a particular audience. The "direct marketing" or "promotional" offer is the incentive offered by the advertiser/marketer to elicit a response.

Online Usually refers to being on the Internet or on the Web; connected to a network.

Package Generally refers to a direct mail package, which typically includes an outer envelope, letter, brochure and/or other inserts, and a reply device.

Page See *Web page.*

PDF (Portable Document Format) A form of publishing that retains the original document's characteristics; created by Adobe.

Permission e-mail, permission marketing The concept of sending email or marketing only to individuals who give their permission to receive the marketing messages.

Personalize Direct mail that utilizes the individual's name or other unique data that is referenced in the copy.

Plug-in Software that "plugs in" to a Web browser to enable added functionality, such as the receipt of sound or multimedia.

POP Point of Presence; the physical place of connection from a computer to the Internet.

Portal A destination site on the Web; can be an outgrowth of a search engine, or a specialized destination, such as a business-to-business portal.

Premium An offer or incentive for responding.

Prospect An individual with the potential to purchase a product or service.

Pull Generally, interactive media that "pulls" the user to it, such as a Web site.

Push Generally, interactive media "pushed" to the user, such as outbound e-mail or Web pages delivered to a user's computer.

Qualification process The process of qualifying a prospect to determine likelihood of purchase.

Qualification questions A set of questions designed to qualify and prioritize prospects prior to advertising.

Reader service number Numbers assigned by publications to handle inquiries to print advertising.

Relationship direct marketing Direct marketing that is intended to build an ongoing relationship through periodic contact over time.

Reply device A reply card, reply form, or any other response piece that the respondent returns to the marketer.

Response list A list made up of individuals with a propensity to respond, based on the fact that they responded to something already; typically, a list of subscribers, members, buyers, donors, etc.

Response management The process of managing responses or leads from the time they are received through conversion to sale.

Response path Any method established to facilitate a response, such as a BRC, inbound fax, inbound telephone, e-mail, or a Web URL.

RFM Recency/Frequency/Monetary data, which helps determine the value of a customer. Recency refers to when the customer last purchased, frequency to how often, and monetary to how much.

Rich media The term generally applied to online advertising that incorporates multimedia, sound, motion, interactivity, or e-commerce.

Rollover Moving the cursor over a specific area of a Web page.

Screen, screening In direct marketing, typically refers to the administrative, mailroom, or receptionist screening process of mail or phone calls in a larger company

Search engine A program that accesses information via a process of matching keywords; there are numerous search engines on the Web.

Segmentation The process of dividing an audience into identifiable segments based on defined criteria or combinations or criteria.

Selection criteria Refers to the available data used to select segments of mailing lists, such as geography, size of company, industry, job function, job title, etc. Selection criteria typically add to the CPM of a rental list.

Self-mailer A mailing piece that is self-contained.

SET Secure Electronic Transaction protocol for e-commerce payment transactions.

SIC Standard Industrial Classification code, a common list selection criterion.

SOHO Small Office Home Office, a rapidly growing business segment.

Source code A code that identifies the original source of a name.

Spam Unsolicited or unwanted e-mail.

Sticky sites Web sites that use techniques to get visitors to "stick" or stay on the site and return to the site; these techniques may include free e-mail and incentive offers.

Surfing Reviewing Web sites or moving through Web pages.

Suspect A potential prospect.

Targeting The most common direct marketing practice; the practice of identifying an audience or audience segment, developing an offer for that audience, and promoting it through audience-appropriate creative.

Telemarketing, telesales Telemarketing refers to inbound or outbound prospect or customer contact via telephone with the objective of promotion or qualification. Telesales is the same process but with the objective of selling a product or service.

Universe The total number of individuals who could conceivably be reached with a specific direct marketing campaign.

Upload The process of sending one or more files from a computer to a server or another computer.

URL Uniform Resource Locator; an Internet location or a Web address**Usenet** An Internet-related network that includes e-mail and newsgroups.

VAR Value-Added Reseller.

Variable Usually refers to a field on a database in which information changes based on the individual record. The variable can then be used in direct mail copy or a telemarketing script to build a relationship with the individual. An example might be the amount of money a customer spends with a company in a year, which would vary from customer to customer.

Versioning Using variables to create versions of direct mail copy to personalize and appeal to specific characteristics. In business-to-business direct mail, versioning by industry or job function has been generally shown to increase response rates.

Viral marketing Marketing that spreads rapidly via e-mail or other Internet communications.

Virtual event, online event, Web event An event that occurs online, via the Web.

Visit One user accessing one Web site at any given time.

Webmaster Typically, an individual in an organization responsible for the organization's Web site and, sometimes, for Internet usage.

Web page An individual document on a Web site or on the Web. A Web page can be heavily graphical and include sound, photography, multimedia, and interactivity, depending on the technologies used to create it.

Web response form A form designed to capture visitor contact and often qualification information.

Web site A site or collection of pages on the World Wide Web.

WWW, World Wide Web The area of the Internet that contains HTML.

XML (Extensible Markup Language) A language that rivals HTML and is gaining in popularity.

Index

Reader Feedback Sheet

Your comments and suggestions are very important in shaping future publications. Please email us at *moreinfo@maxpress.com* or photocopy this page, jot down your thoughts, and fax it to (850) 934-9981 or mail it to:

Maximum Press

Attn: Jim Hoskins

605 Silverthorn Road

Gulf Breeze, FL 32561

_____

_____

_____

_____

_____

_____

_____

_____

_____

_____

_____

_____

_____

_____

_____

_____

_____

_____

_____

_____

*101 Ways to Promote
Your Web Site
Second Edition*
by Susan Sweeney, C.A.
552 pages
$29.95
ISBN: 1-885068-45-X

*Marketing
With E-Mail
Second Edition*
by Shannon Kinnard
352 pages
$29.95
ISBN: 1-885068-51-4

*Business-to-Business
Internet Marketing,
Third Edition*
by Barry Silverstein
528 pages
$29.95
ISBN: 1-885068-50-6

*Marketing on
the Internet,
Fifth Edition*
by Jan Zimmerman
480 pages
$34.95
ISBN: 1-885068-49-2

*Internet Marketing
for Information
Technology
Companies*
by Barry Silverstein
464 pages
$39.95
ISBN: 1-885068-46-8

*Internet Marketing
for Your Tourism
Business*
by Susan Sweeney, C.A.
592 pages
$39.95
ISBN: 1-885068-47-6

*Building Intranets
with Lotus Notes &
Domino, 5.0,
Third Edition*
by Steve Krantz
320 pages
$39.95
ISBN: 1-885068-41-7

*Internet Marketing for
Less Than $500/Year*
by Marcia Yudkin
334 pages
$29.95
ISBN: 1-885068-52-2

To purchase a Maximum Press book, visit your local bookstore
or call 1-800-989-6733 (US) or 1-850-934-4583 (International)
online ordering available at *www.maxpress.com*